MANSLAUGHTER, MARKETS, AND MORAL ECONOMY

China's remarkable economic expansion in the eighteenth century – propelled by large-scale changes in agriculture, demographics, land use, and property rights – had far-reaching social consequences. One important result of the growing population and deepening commercialization of the rural economy was a relative scarcity of land. Just as this problem increased, the new complexity of property rights in land outgrew the customary law, challenging long-held traditions and the shared ideology that governed economic exchange and land ownership in rural China.

In this book, Thomas Buoye reconstructs and analyzes the everyday struggles of the common people to cope with changing concepts and laws regarding property rights in this shifting social landscape. Drawing on a large body of documented homicide cases originating in property disputes during the Qianlong reign (1736–1795), he vividly reveals the competing visions of social justice and economic self-interest that existed in rural society at this time. This unique window onto Chinese society allows new insight into China's protracted struggle, beginning in the late Ming and continuing through the Qing dynasty, to come to grips with the increasing privatization of land and to refine and enforce property rights accordingly.

Buoye's historical analysis challenges the "markets" and the "moral economy" theories of economic behavior. Applying the theories of Douglass North for the first time to this subject, the author uses an institutional framework to explain seemingly irrational economic choices. He examines demographic and technological factors, ideology, and political and economic institutions in rural China to understand the link between economic change and social conflict.

Thomas M. Buoye is Associate Professor of History at the University of Tulsa. He is the author of *A Study Guide to the Chinese: Adapting the Past, Facing the Future* (University of Michigan Center for Chinese Studies Publication, 1991). His articles have appeared in *Late Imperial China* and *Peasant Studies.*

Cambridge Studies in Chinese History, Literature and Institutions

General Editor, Denis Twitchett

MANSLAUGHTER, MARKETS, AND MORAL ECONOMY

Other books in the series

Victor H. Mair Tunhuang Popular Narratives
Ira E. Kasoff The Thought of Chang Tsai
Chih-P'ing Chou Yüan Hung-tao and the Kung-an School
Arthur Waldron The Great Wall of China: From History to Myth
Hugh R. Clark Community, Trade, and Networks: Southern Fujian Province from the Third to the Thirteenth Centuries
Denis Twitchett The Writing of Official History Under the T'ang
J. D. Schmidt Stone Lake: The Poetry of Fang Chengda
Brian E. McKnight Law and Order in Sung China
Jo-Shui Chen Liu Tsung-yüan and Intellectual Change in T'ang China, 773–819
David Pong Shen Pao-chen and China's Modernization in the Nineteenth Century
J. D. Schmidt Within the Human Realm: The Poetry of Huang Zunxian, 1848–1905
Arthur Waldron From War to Nationalism: China's Turning Point, 1924–1925
Chin-Shing Huang Philosophy, Philology, and Politics in Eighteenth-Century China: Li Fu and the Lu-Wang School under the Ch'ing
Glen Dudbridge Religious Experience and Lay Society in T'ang China: A Reading of Tai Fu's "Kuang-i chi"
Eva Shan Chou Reconsidering Tu Fu: Literary Greatness and Cultural Context
Frederic Wakeman, Jr. The Shanghai Badlands: Wartime Terrorism and Urban Crime, 1937–1941
Sarah A. Queen From Chronicle to Canon: The Hermeneutics of the Spring and Autumn Annals According to Tung Chung-shu
J. Y. Wong Deadly Dreams: Opium, Imperialism, and the *Arrow* War (1856–1860) in China
Norman Kutcher Mourning in Late Imperial China: Filial Piety and the State

Manslaughter, Markets, and Moral Economy

Violent Disputes over Property Rights in Eighteenth-century China

Thomas M. Buoye

University of Tulsa

CAMBRIDGE UNIVERSITY PRESS

CAMBRIDGE UNIVERSITY PRESS
Cambridge, New York, Melbourne, Madrid, Cape Town, Singapore, São Paulo

Cambridge University Press
The Edinburgh Building, Cambridge CB2 2RU, UK

Published in the United States of America by Cambridge University Press, New York

www.cambridge.org
Information on this title: www.cambridge.org/9780521640459

First published 2000
This digitally printed first paperback version 2006

A catalogue record for this publication is available from the British Library

Library of Congress Cataloguing in Publication data

Buoye, Thomas M.
Manslaughter, markets, and moral economy: violent disputes over property rights in
eighteenth-century China / Thomas M. Buoye.
p. cm. – (Cambridge studies in Chinese history, literature, and institutions)
ISBN 0-521-64045-8 (hardbound)
1. Violence – China – History – 18th century. 2. Social conflict – China –
History – 18th century. 3. Right of property – China – History – 18th century.
I. Title. II. Series.
HN740.Z9V53 2000
303.6′0951′09033 – dc21 99-16949
CIP

ISBN-13 978-0-521-64045-9 hardback
ISBN-10 0-521-64045-8 hardback

ISBN-13 978-0-521-02781-6 paperback
ISBN-10 0-521-02781-0 paperback

Contents

Maps, Figures, and Tables

Qing Dynasty Emperors' Reign Dates

Reign Title	**Dates**
Shunzhi	1644–61
Kangxi	1662–1722
Yongzheng	1723–35
Qianlong	1736–95
Jiaqing	1796–1820
Daoguang	1821–50
Xianfeng	1851–61
Tongzhi	1862–74
Guangxu	1875–1907
Xuantong	1908–11

Weights and Measures

Area

1 *mu*	= approximately 1/6 of an acre
100 *mu*	= 1 *qing*

Volume

1 *shi*	= approximately 1 bushel
1 *shi*	= 10 *dou*
1 *dou*	= 10 *sheng*

Money

1 *liang*	= 1 ounce of silver
1 *liang*	= 10 *qian*
1 *qian*	= 10 *fen*
1 *wen*	= 1 copper cash
1 *liang*	= 1,000 copper cash
1 *tael*	= 1 silver *liang*

Acknowledgments

I have accumulated many intellectual, personal, and institutional debts in the course of writing this book. Because this book began as a dissertation thesis, I must thank, first and foremost, my teachers at the University of Michigan – Albert Feuerwerker, Charles Tilly, and Ernest Young – who together taught me all that I know about historical research. I will be eternally grateful to them for their generous, ongoing support and encouragement. Needless to say, if I have failed to apply their lessons well, the fault is entirely my own. I have benefited enormously from their guidance on my earlier work as well as their comments on this manuscript. Special thanks are also due to Douglass North and R. Bin Wong, both of whom did me the honor of reading and commenting on an earlier version of the entire manuscript. Their advice and suggestions were invaluable. The suggestions and criticisms of Denis Twitchett, the series editor, and an anonymous reader also enriched and improved the manuscript. Other scholars critiqued parts of the manuscript, and I thank each of them: Lynda Bell, Patrick Blessing, David Feeny, James Feinerman, Harold Kahn, Noriko Kamachi, Robert Marks, Ramon Myers, David Ownby, William T. Rowe, and Barbara Sands.

Most of the research for this book was done at the Number One Historical Archives in Beijing. I am beholden to the staff of the Number One for their assistance, patience, and guidance. In particular, I must thank Ju Deyuan and Zhu Shuyuan for their help during my visits to Beijing. Without their help, this project would never have been completed. The Qing History Research Center at Renmin University, which sponsored me as a research student and later as a visiting scholar, must also be thanked. As a graduate student, my advisors, Wei Qingyuan and Li Hua, provided guidance and advice and hospitality. Similarly, Dai Yi, Luo Ming, Cheng Chongde, and Guo Chengkang have been both inestimable colleagues and teachers. The library of Qing History Research Center was also a precious resource for hard-to-find journals and reference works. During research trips to Guangdong, I was aided by Ye Xianen and Chen Chunsheng. In the United States, I must acknowledge Wan Weiying, Head of the Asian Library at the University of Michigan, an enormously kind man and extraordinary librarian.

A fringe benefit of working at the Number One Historical Archives has been getting to know other American colleagues who study the Qing dynasty. Fortunately, my visits to the Number One overlapped with those of Beatrice Bartlett, Philip Kuhn, and James Lee. Personally introducing me to key staff members at the Number One Archives and the Qing History Research Center at Renmin University, Philip Kuhn used his own stature and well-deserved respect among Chinese scholars to facilitate my research. Beatrice Bartlett shared her unique and legendary knowledge of Qing documents, saving me time and frustration. Likewise, James Lee was most generous in sharing his knowledge and experience in the Number One Archives. Other scholars who shared their thoughts and insights along with the trials and tribulations of archival research while working at the Number One were Robert Antony, Adrian Davis, Helen Dunstan, Mark Elliot, Andreas Kemper, Bob Marks, and Jack Wills.

Financially, the Committee of Scholarly Communications with China (in its earlier incarnation as CSCPRC) with funding from the Department of Education supported my initial research in Beijing. I am also indebted to the Research Office at the University of Tulsa for several Faculty Development Grants and the Oklahoma Foundation for the Humanities, which also supplied several summer grants that underwrote research and writing. I also appreciate the timely assistance of Robert Lawless, President of the University of Tulsa, whose office provided a subvention for this book.

I appreciate everyone who contributed to this book's production. In particular, I thank Mary Child, who shepherded my manuscript from the review process to final production, and Christine A. T. Dunn, a superb copy editor who saved me from making several errors.

Personally, I must also thank my family and friends for their support over the many years. My sisters and brother, their children and spouses, helped in ways too varied and numerous to be recounted. Without their love and encouragement I would not have completed this work. I must thank my brother-in-law, John, individually because he actually read the entire manuscript, correcting many infelicities. I have also been blessed with many good friends and classmates, many of whom provided a warm bed, cold beer, and a comfortable place to stay during sojourns in Beijing, Ann Arbor, and Hong Kong. I must thank Emma and Max, Greg and Selina, Trish and John, Ingrid and David, Pi-p'ing and Bill, Priscilla and Sam, Scott and Carrie, and Sophie and Max.

Introduction

Reconstructing and analyzing the everyday struggles of the common people within the context of the large-scale changes in the structure of the eighteenth-century Chinese economy and society is the central task of this book. More specifically, I seek to explain how the demand for changes in economic institutions and property rights, which was induced by demographic and commercial expansion, violently impinged on the lives of rural Chinese. By any measure, the economic expansion of the Chinese economy during the eighteenth century was astounding. One need look no further than China's population, which surpassed 300 million by the end of the Qianlong reign (1736–95), to understand the magnitude of the economic expansion of the eighteenth century. Intensification of cultivation, deepening commercialization of the rural economy and specialization in cash crops, introduction of new-world crops, government support for land reclamation, large-scale internal migration, and refinements and innovations in property rights and economic institutions all contributed to the economic development of the eighteenth century. Without any major improvements in technology, the eighteenth-century economy demonstrated a remarkable capacity to absorb a more than twofold increase in population. At the macroeconomic level, China's economy was more prosperous and productive by the close of the eighteenth century and evidence suggests that many peasant households adjusted to the demands of expanding markets and population growth and improved their standard of living.[1]

Despite the impressive achievements of the Chinese economy during the eighteenth century, many historians, applying the yardstick of the Industrial Revolution in the West and mindful of the subsequent decline

1 See Fang Xing, "Qingdai Jiangnan nongmin di xiaofei" (Consumption of Jiangnan peasants in the Qing dynasty). *Zhongguo jingjishi yanjiu* 1996, 3: 91–8.

of the Qing dynasty after the eighteenth century, have debated the historical significance of this remarkable period of intensive economic growth. As a result, efforts to characterize late imperial economic growth have given us some colorful rhetoric from the poetic "sprouts of capitalism" to the more scientific-sounding "high level equilibrium trap." Most recently, R. Bin Wong has employed the term *Smithian dynamics*, likening "the increase in cash-cropping, handicrafts and trade that marked Chinese economic growth between the sixteenth and nineteenth centuries" to the preindustrial economic growth of Europe described in Adam Smith's *Wealth of Nations*.[2] The term *Smithian dynamics* has the advantage of acknowledging the vibrancy of the late imperial economy without implying how it should have or could have developed further. In a similar vein, this study will draw on a theory of structure and change in economic history based on experiences in the West to explain social conflict and economic change in China, but also to elaborate and enrich our broader understanding of economic behavior in preindustrial societies.

While the debate over the nature of China's preindustrial growth will continue, for the purposes of this study it is sufficient to note that the unprecedented demographic and economic expansion of the eighteenth century was more than adequate to induce demand for changes in economic institutions and property rights that were essential to the operation of China's increasingly complex commercial economy. Since the Chinese economy remained primarily agrarian, the focus of this book is property rights in land. As Yang Guozhen's research on Chinese land contracts has demonstrated, the struggle to refine and enforce property rights in land was a protracted process that began during the late Ming dynasty (1368–1644) and continued into the early Qing dynasty (1644–1911).[3] It was marked by the increasing privatization of land, the rise of "commoner" landlords, the erosion of extra-economic controls over tenant farmers, the appearance of permanent tenancy rights, the division of topsoil and subsoil (the development of "one field, two lords" [*yitian liangzhu*] property rights in land), and the increasing reliance on written contractual agreements. Yang's painstaking research provides empirical evidence of the gradual and diverse transformation of property rights in land and economic institutions that attended and furthered economic development during the late Ming and early Qing. As Yang's work illustrates, regardless of how we characterize economic

2 R. Bin Wong, *China Transformed*, p. 17 (Ithaca, NY: Cornell University Press, 1997).

3 See Yang Guozhen, Chapter 1, *Ming Qing tudi qiyue wenshu yanjiu* (Research on Ming-Qing period land contracts), (Beijing: Renmin Chubanshe, 1988).

change in late imperial China, it is impossible to ignore its multiform impact on rural society in the eighteenth century.

The transformation of China's rural economy during the eighteenth century also entailed some unfortunate and tragic consequences – homicides related to violent disputes over property rights. Violent disputes over property rights were a widespread problem during the Qianlong reign. Each of the incidents recounted in the following text was obtained from a homicide report contained in a routine memorial to the Ministry of Justice (*xingke tiben*). These violent vignettes of rural society are the foundation for this study of economic change and social conflict. The nature of the data provides an intimate look at social conflict while the size of the sample and its historical and geographic scope allows for a broad investigation of the connection between social conflict and economic change in eighteenth-century China. The three killings briefly recounted as follows are but a small sample of the fatal beatings, bludgeonings, and even shootings related to property-rights disputes, but they serve to illustrate the types of disputes contained in this study.

In 1785, Chen Wenyou of Dongguan county in Guangdong province lost his lease on the land that he had cultivated for thirty years when Huang Guiji offered the landlord, He Jiewan, a higher rent. Later Chen Wenyou argued and fought with Huang Guiji. After Chen struck him with a bamboo pole, Huang fled, threatening to report the assault to the county magistrate. Chen returned home and told his wife, Ms. Zhu,[4] about the altercation. Anxious and fearing further trouble, Ms. Zhu upbraided her husband for his incompetence. Distraught over losing his land and rankled by the scolding his wife had given him, Chen decided to kill his wife and implicate Huang Guiji in the hope of blackmailing him into returning the land. Chen went into the kitchen and got a cleaver. Chasing his wife around their home, Chen hacked her twice on the left side of the skull and landed repeated blows on the top of her head. Carrying her body to Huang's front gate, Chen began shouting that Huang had attacked his wife. Overwhelmed with anger, Huang rose to confront Chen, but his elderly mother, Ms. Yu, grabbed at his clothing to prevent him from leaving the house. Huang was moving forward with such force that his clothing tore and his mother fell to the floor and sustained a fatal injury. Chen Wenyou's

4 Married women are usually referred to either by their husband's surname followed by the character *shi* and their own family surname. Sometimes the husband's name is omitted. For convenience sake, I have dropped the husband's surname and use Ms. and the woman's own family surname.

wife died later that afternoon. Huang's mother died in the morning of the next day.[5]

In another case in 1749, Wang Chen of Wenshang county in Shandong province leased 24 *mu* from Guo Jingyuan. Guo Jingyuan lived some distance from the field so he entrusted Cheng Zhao with the management of the land. One morning, after it had rained, Wang Chen decided it was time to plant soybeans. He went to see Cheng Zhao to request the seeds. Cheng not only refused to provide the seeds, he criticized Wang for being lazy and demanded that he return the land. Wang Chen suggested that they wait until after autumn harvest. Cheng spurned his request and accused Wang of dishonesty. Wang desperately replied: "If you demand that I return this land now is it not the same as killing my family?" At that, Wang lowered his head and attempted to butt Cheng. Cheng punched him in the left temple. Wang tried again to butt him with his head, but Cheng sidestepped him. Wang fell to the ground, injuring his left ear and the left side of his head. He died of his wounds two days later.[6]

In Cangxi county in Sichuan, Liu Shiwei had adopted his cousin's son, Liu Huihai, when he was orphaned at the age of five in 1724. While still a child, Liu Huihai inherited some land from an uncle. Twenty-three years later, in 1747, Liu Shiwei wanted to sell the land to a tobacco grower from Hunan for 140 ounces (*liang*) of silver, but he needed Liu Huihai's signature on the sale contract. Despite Liu Shiwei's repeated urgings, Liu Huihai refused to approve the sale. Eventually, Liu Huihai fled to another county to escape Liu Shiwei's incessant pressure. In the spring of 1748, Liu Shiwei sent his sons, Liu Zichao and Liu Zifang, and two others to fetch Liu Huihai. When they found Liu Huihai, they bound him and forced him to return. Liu Shiwei again urged Liu Huihai to approve the sale. He reminded Huihai that he had raised him from infancy and cared for him until he had married. At last Liu Shiwei lost his temper and cursed him vehemently. Huihai responded that selling his adopted son's land demonstrated that Shiwei "had no conscience." Shiwei ordered his son to tie Huihai to a tree. Shiwei began beating Huihai with a wooden pole, but Huihai stubbornly refused to approve the sale, "even if Liu Shiwei beat him to death." Furious, Shiwei picked up a rock and struck Huihai at the base of the throat, killing him.[7]

5 Xingke tiben (Routine Memorials to the Ministry of Justice, hereafter XKTB) 3564, QL 51.5.5. Dates are given in reign year, month, and day, according to the lunar calendar. QL 51.5.5 = fifth day of the fifth lunar month in the fifty-first year of the reign of the emperor Qianlong (1786).

6 XKTB 0714, QL 15.4.17.

7 XKTB 0761, QL 16.5.20.

Taken individually, the homicides recounted above might simply be considered regrettable acts of violence with little significance beyond the tragedy of the families involved. But these violent disputes, and hundreds of similar ones, take on greater significance when examined in the broader social and economic context of the extraordinary demographic expansion and the growing commercialization of the Chinese economy during the eighteenth century. Briefly stated, my argument is that the economic changes of the eighteenth century, most importantly deepening commercialization and an unprecedented level of population growth, caused a shift in the relative value of two key factors of production, land and labor, and provided incentives to define and enforce property rights in land more strictly. These conditions exacerbated disputes over long-standing property-rights issues such as boundary and water rights, and heightened tensions over issues that were closely related to changing economic conditions in the eighteenth century such as rent defaults, redemptions of conditional land sales, and evictions.

This shift in the relative value of land and labor altered the balance of economic power between tenants and landlords, whose basic relationships had already begun undergoing a profound transformation during the Ming dynasty (1368–1644). During the early Qing dynasty (1644–1911), landlords lost most of their extraeconomic controls over tenants. The extent of these changes was reflected in a concomitant series of government policies that abolished the residue of servile tenancy and revised the system of taxation, effectively abolishing the poll tax and thereby placing the primary tax burden on land. Population growth during the eighteenth century, however, once again shifted the balance of economic power in rural society in favor of landowners. The increasing value of land induced demand for changes in property rights and economic institutions and triggered violent conflicts. Disputes over property rights in land were so sufficiently serious and widespread that they prompted the central government to revise the Qing law code, predominantly in favor of landowners. For example, under certain conditions defaulting on rent became a criminal offense and restrictions were placed on the right to redeem conditional land sales. Nevertheless, despite government efforts to clarify property rights in land, at the grassroots level private efforts to protect existing property rights or to define new property rights continued, and these efforts created the *potential* for violent disputes.

Evidence from homicides related to property-rights disputes show that over the course of the eighteenth century, refinements of property rights benefited landowners and insulated them from violent disputes. Similarly, violence abated as innovations in property rights gained wider acceptance and were incorporated into written contracts. As property rights were defined more clearly and violent disputes declined, the focus of disputes shifted. For example, as the relative value of labor decreased, peasants were increasingly forced to compete amongst themselves for a limited supply of land and disputes between competing tenants were more common. As we shall see when we compare disputes within Guangdong, and among Guangdong, Sichuan, and Shandong provinces, violent disputes exhibited significant regional and temporal variation. Most, but not all, of the temporal and geographic variation in the patterns of violent disputes can be traced to the variable effects of commercialization and population growth across space and over time. Although the patterns of violence related to property rights varied widely in Guangdong, Sichuan, and Shandong, over time homicides related to disputes over property rights declined as a percentage of all homicides related to land debt disputes in all three provinces. The variations in temporal and spatial distributions of disputes were important indicators of the complicated social ramifications of the eighteenth-century demographic and commercial expansion.

At the outset, it should also be noted that resorting to violence to settle property-rights disputes was not the norm in rural China during the eighteenth century, nor was it an effective method for resolving competing claims over property rights. Private mediation or official adjudication were the socially acceptable venues for the resolution of disputes. However, as an examination of violent disputes preceded by efforts at official adjudication will reveal, the effectiveness of these peaceful remedies was dependent on the disputants' shared ethical norms and the mutual acceptance of the legitimacy of evolving property rights and economic institutions. For example, a recurring source of tension was the persistence and resiliency of the concept of land as inviolable patrimony that was often at odds with the newly emerging concept of land as an alienable commodity. Until the concept of land as an alienable commodity was more widely incorporated into private contracts and more clearly specified in the Qing legal code, conflict was inevitable and mediation was difficult. Thus, understanding competing beliefs and expectations about how the economy and society should work is important because it affected individual reactions to economic change. In fact, in response to demands for change in the existing structure of property rights and economic institutions, peasants, landlords, and government officials frequently voiced ideological and moral concerns, often in defense of the status quo. But, as the analysis of violent disputes shows, these appeals could not staunch the demand for changes in property rights and economic institutions that economic self-interest had induced. Competing visions of the legitimacy of economic institutions and property rights, and frustration on the part of those who perceived "injustice" in the newly emerging structure of property rights and economic institutions in the eighteenth century were often at the heart of violent disputes.

The title of this book, *Manslaughter, Markets, and Moral Economy*, points to three major components of the study. *Manslaughter* simply refers to the primary source materials and indicates the gravity of these disputes. Information on violent disputes has been obtained from routine memorials to the Ministry of Justice that were part of a collection of homicide reports related to disputes over land and debt (*tudi zhaiwu*). Most of these homicides were the outgrowth of unpremeditated, small-scale altercations between individuals who did not have a long-standing grudge or a prior intent to kill, and every dispute involved the loss of at least one life.[8] Given that the focus of this study is social conflict and economic change, homicide reports are singularly valuable source materials that dramatically illustrate the property-rights issues that often incited lethal violence. The provenance of these documents and their value as sources for the study of social conflict and economic change are discussed in detail in the Appendix. Here it is worth noting briefly that because the overwhelming majority of capital crimes were reviewed at every level of administration, homicide reports provide a large body of documents systematically compiled according to strict administrative requirements, which were consistent throughout the period under consideration.

Scholars have noted the value of homicide reports to historical studies. As one historian has stated, it is "the one crime for which evidence is most reliable."[9] Another advantage of homicide reports, as one expert on violent crime has noted, is that "when dealing with data on homicide . . . we can be more confident that trends reflect real changes in social behavior." Victimization studies have found that homicide is the "most accurately recorded violent crime." In this way the "slippage" between the crime and court records is "probably less for homicide than other crimes against persons."[10] Unfortunately for this study, the docu-

8 Approximately 5% of the cases used in this study were classified as premeditated or intentional homicide. There were also a few cases in which individuals were driven to suicide.

9 Lawrence Stone, p. 22, "Interpersonal Violence in English Society," *Past and Present* (1983) 101: 22–33.

10 Ted Robert Gurr, pp. 297–9, "Historical Trends in Violent Crime: A Critical Review of the Evidence." pp. 295–353 in *Crime and Justice: An Annual Review of Research*, M. Torny and N. Morris, eds., Vol. 3 (Chicago: University of Chicago Press, 1981).

ments limit the focus to only the most extreme examples of violent disputes. Thus, although homicides related to disputes over property rights declined over time, we cannot automatically assume that disputes in general, not to mention violent disputes that did not result in homicide, also declined. However, given that most of these homicides were unpremeditated crimes of passion and that "homicides usually are the result of particularly successful (or unlucky) assaults,"[11] it is unlikely that the rate of homicide would increase or decrease without a parallel shift in the rate of serious assaults. Given the fact that the overwhelming majority of homicides were the outgrowth of unpremeditated assaults, it does not seem unreasonable to assume that a decline in homicides related to disputes over property rights reflected an overall decline in serious assaults and violence related to disputes over property rights.

Reconstructing violent disputes related to property rights provides an opportunity to evaluate theories of economic behavior in preindustrial rural society. *Markets* and *moral economy* refer to two different aspects of economic behavior, both of which are important to understanding the connection between economic change and social conflict. Here I do not mean to conjure up a tired debate about the economic behavior of peasants.[12] Instead, I use the terms as shorthand for two larger sets of concerns that go beyond the historical study of agrarian economies. Markets represent neoclassical economics that have been useful to historical research, particularly the assumption of scarcity and competition, and the importance of market forces. Neoclassical economics has proven to be a powerful tool for explaining market economies in developed countries, but its assumptions of zero transaction costs and that change occurs in frictionless markets via changes in relative prices has limited its usefulness for historians studying preindustrial economies. This is not to say that neoclassical principles have not been helpful in understanding the direction of macroeconomic change in late imperial China and elsewhere. For example, in the eighteenth century many individuals acting in their economic self-interest responded to the increase in the relative value of land, population growth, and increasing commercialization exactly in ways that neoclassical economic principles would

11 Ibid., p. 300.

12 See James C. Scott, *The Moral Economy of the Peasant: Rebellion and Subsistence in Southeast Asia* (New Haven: Yale University Press, 1976), and Samuel Popkin, *The Rational Peasant: The Political Economy of Rural Society in Vietnam* (Berkeley: University of California Press). For a discussion of these two works that demonstrates that many of the difference are more apparent than real, see Daniel Little, Chapter 2, *Understanding Peasant China* (New Haven: Yale University Press, 1990).

predict. Among other things, they intensified cultivation, reclaimed wasteland, and enforced property rights in land more strictly. At the same time, others resisted the prevailing economic trends. They objected to the curtailment or abridgment of customary rights and invoked ethical arguments in the face of the advance of market forces in ways consistent with the assumptions of the moral economy argument.

Moral economy is shorthand for what has also been called substantive economics, which stresses informal institutions, conventions, customs, and moral beliefs that are other important components of economic behavior. The moral economy argument, which can be traced to the work of Karl Polanyi,[13] an early and persuasive critic of neoclassical economics, offers a cogent challenge to neoclassical analysis of economic change in preindustrial societies. Proponents of the moral economy have argued that the assumptions of neoclassical economics did not apply until the advent of capitalism transformed the economies of the West and subsequently the world. According to Polanyi, capitalism destroyed the cultural foundations of both the English laboring class in the early nineteenth century and "native tribes in Africa." Discussing colonial Africa, Polanyi stated that the "catastrophe of the native community is a direct result of the rapid and violent disruption of the basic institutions of the victim."[14] Referring to the Western exploitation of Africa, Polanyi argued that the transformation of labor and land into commodities, which had been the prerequisite for the development of capitalism in Europe, was "only a short formula for the liquidation of every and any cultural institution in an organic society." Another classic statement of the moral economy argument can be found in E. P. Thompson's influential article on food riots in eighteenth-century England. Thompson described the violent consequences resulting from the undermining of "paternalist market regulations" that were the institutional expressions of the moral economy in eighteenth-century England.[15] Shifting the focus eastward, James Scott made a similar argument when he identified incorporation into the world market economy as the force that undermined the

13 Karl Polanyi, *The Great Transformation* (Boston: Beacon Press, 1957). Polanyi argued persuasively that the predominance of the self-regulating, impersonal market historically was a nineteenth-century phenomenon and not a natural component of human behavior. Writing in the mid-twentieth century, Polanyi attempted to show how fascism, socialism, and the New Deal were all responses to the inevitable self-destructiveness of impersonal market forces.

14 Ibid., p. 159.

15 E. P. Thompson, "The Moral Economy of the English Crowd in the Eighteenth Century," *Past and Present* (February 1971) 50: 76–136.

moral economy in Southeast Asia. According to Scott, reciprocity, forced generosity, communal land, and work sharing were hallmarks of the moral economy of Southeast Asia until colonialism transformed the region.[16]

As I will demonstrate in my analysis of violent disputes, the values and institutions that substantivist economics emphasize were also an integral part of the economic calculus of peasant farmers, tenants, and landlords in China. The economic changes that rippled through China's agrarian economy during the eighteenth century placed severe pressure on long-held values and conventions that had legitimized and supported property rights. The response of rural inhabitants to the shift in the balance of economic power between land and labor was complicated, but many individuals resisted economic change on ethical grounds in ways that were consistent with moral economy arguments. Violent disputes over property rights can partly be explained in terms of the erosion of these shared beliefs that were incompatible with the newly emerging structure of property rights and economic institutions in the eighteenth century. My objection to the moral economy argument is on historical grounds. As noted, these individuals were locked in struggles with others who did respond to market forces in a manner consistent with assumptions of neoclassical economics, and these struggles occurred in the highly commercialized, preindustrial society of eighteenth-century China, before the nineteenth-century advent of the militant commercial powers of the West.

To understand violent disputes over property in their broader economic context requires a more comprehensive understanding of structure and change in economic history. For this I have relied on the work of Douglass North. Over the past two decades North has elaborated a theory of structure and change in economic history that emphasizes the central place of economic institutions.[17] According to North, the key determinants of historical economic growth include demography, technology, the ideology of a society, and political and economic institutions. The emphasis on institutions and property rights permits North to reconcile the apparent contradictions between neoclassical economic and

16 James C. Scott, 1976.

17 North has published numerous articles and books over the years. For instance, *The Rise of the Western World* (Cambridge, UK: Cambridge University Press, 1973), coauthored with Paul Thomas; *Structure and Change in Economic History* (New York: W. W. Norton, 1981); and *Institutions, Institutional Change and Economic Performance* (New York: Cambridge University Press, 1990).

substantivist approaches to economic history. In an article addressing the work of Karl Polanyi, North supported the contention that the price-making market as the dominant "transactional mode" was primarily a nineteenth-century phenomenon and not a deep-rooted historical form of human behavior, but he disagreed with the claim that resource allocation historically has not been based on economizing behavior.[18] North rebutted this argument using transaction cost analysis to illustrate how various modes of economic exchange described by Polanyi reduced transaction costs and, therefore, were actually examples of economizing behavior.

Transaction costs are the costs of specifying and enforcing contracts. These costs vary with the difficulty of measuring goods and services; enforcing property rights; the scope of the exchange process; and the strength of the society's underlying ideological beliefs. As an economy grows and becomes more complex, there is a greater need for well-defined and enforceable property rights. Transaction cost analysis allows North to expose the weaknesses of both the substantivist and neoclassical economists and to devise a more compelling theory of structure and change in history. Since neoclassical analysis does not account for these costs, its application to historical studies has limited usefulness. It is not my intention to use eighteenth-century China as a test case to "prove" North's theory. Rather, I rely on his insights as a guide to understanding structure and change in economic history and the connection between social conflict and economic change.

Reconstructing violent disputes over property rights and their temporal and geographic distribution within the context of the large-scale economic and social changes of the eighteenth century sets the stage for the central task of this book – establishing the link between social conflict and economic change in eighteenth-century China. In addition to elucidating an important aspect of the social and economic history of late imperial Chinese history, the analysis of violent disputes over property rights also offers valuable insights into the nature of structure and change in economic history and the social consequences of economic change. These insights can enrich our understanding of the importance of economic institutions and ideology as determinants of economic development.

18 Douglass North, p. 707, "Markets and Other Allocation Systems in History: The Challenge of Karl Polanyi," *Journal of European Economic History* (Fall 1977), 2: 703–16. Polanyi used the term *transactional mode* to describe different forms of economic exchange. For example, reciprocity, householding, price-making markets, etc. were all transactional modes according to Polanyi.

Chapter 1 presents a review of the relevant literature on economic change and the social structural factors of economic development in late imperial China, and it argues for the usefulness of adopting a new theoretical framework based on the work of Douglass North. Relying on primary and secondary sources on population, migration, land reclamation, commercialization, price fluctuations, and government economic policies, Chapter 2 provides the broader context for understanding the large-scale demographic and economic trends in which violent disputes occurred. Chapters 3 and 4 present a detailed qualitative analysis of change over time in the major issues, participants, and official disposition of 385 disputes that occurred in Guangdong province. For heuristic purposes, the issues that caused disputes have been divided into two broad categories, contractual and noncontractual disputes, based on the relationships between the disputants. Noncontractual disputes, the subject of Chapter 3, involved disputes over water rights and boundaries. While these disputes did not necessarily entail newly emerging property-rights or enforcement mechanisms, it is clear that they were often related to the population growth and commercialization of the eighteenth century. For example, the fragmentation of land into smaller plots, which was a by-product of the commoditization of land, complicated access to irrigation networks essential for rice cultivation and thereby increased the potential for disputes over water rights. Similarly, the division of land into smaller plots as well as the reclamation of wasteland required the demarcation of new boundaries that sometimes led to disputes. Contractual disputes, the subject of Chapter 4, included rent defaults, redemptions of conditional sales, and evictions. For the most part, contractual disputes involved reactions to refinements and alterations to property rights and economic institutions that were newly emerging in the eighteenth century. For example, as land was bought and sold with greater frequency, efforts to curtail and circumscribe rights of redemption caused many disputes. A qualitative analysis of the issues that caused disputes reveals that the gradual changes in property rights and economic institutions that continued throughout the eighteenth century clearly influenced the tenor and focus of disputes. Although the basic issues were the same, a rent default that occurred during the early Qianlong period prior to the widespread use of rent deposits was quite different from a rent default dispute that occurred in the later Qianlong period when competition among tenants was keen and rent deposits insulated landlords from direct involvement in violence.

Several striking features of the temporal and geographic distributions of violent disputes in Guangdong are presented and analyzed in Chapter

5. One unambiguous feature of the geographic distribution is that homicides related to disputes over property rights did not simply mimic a general pattern of homicide in Guangdong province. There were significant differences at both the county and prefectural levels in the geographic distribution of homicides related to property-rights disputes as compared to other homicides related to land and debt. Two additional features of the geographic and temporal patterns, the lack of violent disputes in the economic core and periphery of the province and the general decline over time in violent disputes also leads me to argue strongly for a relationship between the temporal and geographic patterns of violent disputes over property rights and the variable impact of population growth and commercialization across time and space.

As we shall see in Chapter 5, violent disputes over property rights were most likely to occur in a zone between the core and the periphery at a time when rice prices were most volatile. As Robert Marks's groundbreaking environmental and economic history of South China has shown, agriculture in the Pearl River Delta region had already become highly commercialized in the late seventeenth century. For example, in the Pearl River Delta area the "landlord gentry class" provided the capital to peasant families to convert rice paddies to fish ponds with mulberry trees planted on the embankments in response to the foreign demand for silk in the late seventeenth century.[19] As a result, peasant households became dependent on the market to purchase rice and the impact of commercialization was felt early and profoundly in this region. Apparently, the demand for changes in property rights and economic institutions was also felt earlier. In his work on land contracts, Yang Guozhen found that violent disputes over property rights were a recurrent problem in the Pearl River Delta during the late Ming and early Qing. It would appear that issues that caused violence in other parts of Guangdong during the Qianlong reign (1736–95) had already been confronted in the Pearl River Delta earlier, and that many of the innovations and refinements in property rights that mitigated violent disputes elsewhere in Guangdong during the eighteenth century had already been incorporated into land contracts in the Pearl River Delta in the late Ming and early Qing.[20]

The spatial pattern of disputes also suggests a connection to the long-term trends in the economic core of the province. As many scholars have

19 Robert B. Marks, Chapter 5, *Tigers, Rice, Silk, and Silt* (New York: Cambridge University Press, 1997).
20 See Yang Guozhen, Chapter 7.

noted, with more land devoted to the cultivation of cash crops, the Pearl River Delta became a rice-deficit region. By the middle of the eighteenth century, the demand for rice in this core region led to the development of a well-integrated market for rice centered on the provincial capital, Guangzhou.[21] Given the importance of location and transportation costs as determinants of both land use and land values, it would be reasonable to assume that the development of a well-integrated market for rice centered on Guangzhou would influence the pattern of land use and would affect land values throughout the province. As I will also argue in Chapter 5, the prevalence of violence in counties bordering on the economic core where land values would have been most sensitive to price fluctuations in the regional rice market was another strong indication that violent disputes over property rights were closely tied to the ongoing impact of commercialization during the eighteenth century. It was no fluke that the decline in violent disputes also coincided with the development of a well-integrated market and the stabilization of rice prices in the 1760s.

Chapter 6 compares violent disputes in Guangdong, Shandong, and Sichuan provinces. Extending the scope of the study to two additional provinces is crucial to understanding the complex nexus of social conflict and economic change. Each of these provinces exhibited significant differences in violence related to property-rights disputes. However, one consistent pattern in all three provinces was the decline over time in homicides related to disputes over property rights. Interestingly, the overall level of violence among the three provinces varied notably. For example, in Shandong province violent disputes over property rights were very rare. A qualitative analysis of disputes in Shandong reveals that the disputes occurred mostly among competing peasants who appear to have been much poorer than their counterparts in Sichuan and Guangdong, and that landowners in Shandong exercised greater control over their tenants and hired laborers. Based on the findings for Guangdong, that violent disputes were more likely to occur during periods when innovations in economic institutions and property rights were newly emerging, the fact that landowners in Shandong enjoyed greater control over tenants and laborers may have been an indication that the balance of economic power between land and labor had shifted earlier and more sharply in Shandong. In Sichuan province, a large portion of the population was recent migrants who, therefore, did not have long-

21 See Robert Marks, "Rice Prices, Food Supply, and Market Structure in Eighteenth-Century China," *Late Imperial China* (December 1991) 12.2: 64–116.

standing personal ties to their land. This information provides a useful and revealing counterpoint to both Guangdong and Shandong.

Chapter 7 addresses the use of violence to settle property-rights disputes. As noted earlier, violence was neither a wise nor an effective response to disputes over property rights. In fact, nearly two-thirds of the individuals who initiated violence ended up as homicide victims and those who killed in violent disputes almost always were sentenced to death. The futility of violence leads to a major question that this study seeks to answer. Why did individuals resort to violence? The shortcomings of the legal system would appear to be one answer. Yet, an examination of deadly disputes that were preceded by official intervention reveals that the courts were accessible and that county magistrates were normally competent, thorough, and fair when adjudicating disputes. The fact that these disputes nonetheless ended in violence was not an indication of a failure on the part of the magistrate or the civil courts. In fact, magistrates were flexible and innovative in their decision making, relying on the legal code as well as custom and culture to settle disputes. Unfortunately, the economic changes that generated property-rights disputes also undermined the shared ethical norms of rural communities that, given the limited resources at the disposal of county magistrates, were critical to enforcing official decisions. With limited means to coerce compliance with their decisions, no matter how skilled the magistrate might have been, violence was difficult to avoid, and disputants were less likely to seek mediation when the parties to a dispute viewed changes in economic institutions as unjust. Until economic institutions were adjusted to reflect changing realities and until these economic institutions were widely accepted as fair, violent disputes, some of which ended in homicide, were inevitable. Based on my reading of hundreds of homicide reports, I have concluded that in many cases the reason for the resort to violence lies in the frustration and anger of those who found it difficult to accept the changing economic and social order that the eighteenth-century commercial and demographic expansion had wrought.

In Chapter 8, I explore the implications of this study for our understanding of the social and economic history of late imperial China. Homicide reports related to disputes over property rights provide a rich resource to study social conflict and economic change, and offer a unique view of the ways in which individuals experienced the large-scale economic changes that transformed eighteenth-century China. As the tragic events recorded in Qing homicide reports graphically demonstrate, economic development often entails dire social consequences that should not be ignored. Limiting economic history to the study of production and distribution of costs and benefits is not sufficient. Institutions and ideology are critical to the understanding of historical change.

1
Economic Change, Social Conflict, and Property Rights

Since the normalization of diplomatic relations between China and the United States in the 1980s, American scholars have gradually gained access to a wide range of primary source materials that have enriched the quality and extended the scope of historical research on China. Throughout the 1950s and 1960s, the limited access to primary sources stifled the field of Chinese social and economic history in the United States. Except for the works of several Chinese-born scholars, such as Ho Ping-ti, who produced the classic work on demographic history;[1] Chang Chung-li, whose work on the gentry class remains standard reading;[2] and Hsiao Kung-ch'uan, who wrote a comprehensive guide to rural society,[3] most of the research done in English focused on foreign trade, the treaty ports, or early efforts at industrialization. Conceptually, models derived from European economic history weighed heavily on the scholarship of this period and this produced some rather odd attempts to cast Chinese history in terms of the supposed normative stages of Western development.[4] Generally, the economic stagnation of pre–Opium War China was taken for granted, and comparisons of Western development with Eastern stagnation were frequent. Ironically, the Marxist approach of Chinese and Japanese scholars prevalent at that time, although meant to challenge mainstream Western scholarship, also contributed to estab-

1 Ho Ping-ti, *Studies in the Population of China, 1368–1953* (Cambridge, MA: Harvard University Press, 1959).

2 Chang Chung-li, *The Chinese Gentry: Studies on Their Role in Nineteenth Century Chinese Society* (Seattle: University of Washington Press, 1955).

3 Hsiao Kung-ch'uan, *Rural China: Imperial China in the Nineteenth Century* (Seattle: University of Washington Press, 1967).

4 For example, see John K. Fairbank, Alexander Eckstein, and L. S. Yang, "Economic Change in Early Modern China: An Analytic Framework," *Economic Development and Cultural Change* (October 1960) 9.1: 1–26. According to Fairbank, et al., p. 3, "the best known agent of change in the nineteenth century" was the "growth of Western trade at Canton." Elsewhere, there is a comparison of the Confucian versus the Protestant ethic.

lishing the paradigm of Western progress, the Industrial Revolution, as the yardstick for measuring historical development.

After the establishment of the People's Republic of China in 1949, historical research in China was entirely recast in terms of the normative stages of Marxist historical development. Two popular topics in post-1949 Chinese historiography were studies of peasant uprisings and the identification of the "sprouts of capitalism." This research produced a wealth of information on the economic history of late imperial China. Unfortunately, political constraints often weighed heavily on Chinese scholars, and Western historians quickly criticized the stilted ideological platitudes that suffused the arguments and conclusions of post-1949 historical writings. In Japan, the Marxist influence on studies of Chinese history was reflected in the emphasis on class-based struggle and an ongoing debate over the timing of the transition from "feudalism" to "capitalism." The history of the development of modern landlordism and the process of class differentiation have been among major research topics in Japanese scholarship. Ideological considerations aside, until recent times Japanese and Chinese historians preceded their American counterparts in more actively investigating the social and economic history of late imperial China. Furthermore, the Marxist approach did produce some interesting social and economic histories that eventually forced Western scholars to reconsider the economic history of pre–Opium War China.[5]

A turning point in Western studies of China's economic history came in 1973, when Mark Elvin's pioneering work, *The Pattern of the Chinese Past*, was published. Elvin's wide-ranging thesis drew heavily on Japanese scholarship and stimulated an extensive reexamination of

5 For an assessment of Chinese historical studies prior to the Cultural Revolution, see Albert Feuerwerker, "China's History in Marxian Dress," pp. 14–44 in *History in Communist China*, edited by Albert Feuerwerker (Cambridge, MA: M.I.T. Press, 1968). Feuerwerker, p. 20, was highly critical of the efforts to reinterpret Chinese history according to the normative stage of Marxist historical development, but he did acknowledge that it revealed an extent of commercialization and advanced development of handicraft production that Western historians previously had overlooked. For an assessment of the immediate post–Cultural Revolution period, see Kwang-Ching Liu, "World View and Peasant Rebellion: Reflections on Post-Mao Historiography," *Journal of Asian Studies* (1981) 60.2: 295–326. Foon Ming Liew, "Debates on the Birth of Capitalism in China During the Past Three Decades," *Ming Studies* (Fall 1988) 26: 61–75, provides a handy bibliography of major Chinese articles.

For Japanese scholarship, see Linda Grove and Joseph Esherick, "From Feudalism to Capitalism: Japanese Scholarship on the Transformation of Chinese Rural Society," *Modern China* (October 1980) 6.4: 397–438. For more recent work, see Joshua A. Fogel, *Recent Japanese Studies of Modern Chinese History* (Armonk, NY: M. E. Sharpe, 1984) and *Recent Japanese Studies of Modern Chinese History (II)* (Armonk, NY: M. E. Sharpe, 1989).

Chinese history from the Song dynasty (960–1280) onward. Most relevant to the research in this book was his focus on changing economic institutions during the late imperial period. According to Elvin, absentee landlords were more common during the sixteenth century and relations between tenants and landlords moved toward a more contractual basis, "unsoftened and unstrengthened by personal contacts."[6] Elvin introduced the "high-level equilibrium trap," the idea that China was on the verge of economic crisis because historically the country had achieved population growth, transportation efficiency, agricultural productivity, and economic commercialization unprecedented in preindustrial societies without the benefit of technological breakthroughs that led to an industrial revolution in the West. Under these conditions, the amount of surplus product above what was needed for subsistence steadily shrank, while the cost of labor was so cheap that there was little incentive to adopt labor-saving technologies. Presuming the existence of the high-level equilibrium trap, Elvin maintained that it was the "historic contribution of the modern West to ease and then break the high-level equilibrium trap in China."[7] For a time the high-level equilibrium trap proved to be an appealing model for many Western scholars. It explained Chinese economic history in the familiar terms of neoclassical economic theory and it allowed for a positive evaluation of the Western intrusion into China. While it remains a controversial construct that some have construed as an apology for imperialism, the "trap" model did mark a new stage in the development in Chinese economic history.

Over the past two decades, other economic historians also began to explore macrolevel changes in the structure of the late imperial economy. Growth of markets, influence of government policies, and a leveling of class barriers were frequently cited as contributing to economic development. For example, Thomas Metzger narrowed his focus to 1500–1800, a period of impressive quantitative economic growth. According to Metzger, organizational changes, such as more land being exchanged in markets transactions and an erosion of class distinctions that weakened the privileged sector of the economy, fostered this growth.[8] Evelyn Rawski's early work examined commercialization of agriculture in South China largely from a neoclassical economic

6 See Mark Elvin, Chapter 15, *The Pattern of the Chinese Past* (Stanford: Stanford University Press, 1973).

7 Ibid., p. 315.

8 Thomas A. Metzger, "On the Historical Roots of Economic Modernization in China," pp. 3–14 in *Modern Chinese Economic History*, C. Hou and T. Yu, eds. (Taipei: Academia Sinica, Institute of Economics, 1979).

perspective and concluded that the premodern Chinese economy "was capable of a dynamic response to changing economic conditions."[9] In a more recent summary of economic change during the late imperial period she has cited the influx of silver bullion and the monetization of the economy; development of markets; relaxation of government control; and greater economic freedom and exposure to risk for peasants as important features of the economy of late imperial China. Rawski credits the increase in agricultural productivity and improvements in the rights of tenants, relative to landlords, to the developing markets and increased commercialization that began in the late Ming. According to Rawski, the spread of contractual arrangements between tenants and landlords was a sign of a long-term trend toward the triumph of the market economy.[10] While I agree entirely with Rawski's conclusions, my own work seeks to shed light on the social consequences of these important economic developments.

In a more ambitious work covering two thousand years of history, Kang Chao rejects Marxist and other "Western-centric" interpretations and argues for the uniqueness of China's historical experience.[11] Like Metzger and Rawski, Chao also relies heavily on neoclassical economic concepts of market forces to build his argument. According to Chao, an "atomistic market economy," within which the household was the most important economic unit, had existed in China since ancient times. Family values, which were peculiar to the Chinese, shaped important economic decisions. Chao argued that Chinese families placed such an extraordinarily high value on producing male heirs that even in the face of economic hardships neither nuptiality nor fertility were delayed. Consequently, China's population continued to expand, depressing wages and creating conditions more favorable to household production in industry and tenancy in agriculture. Some have criticized Chao's Malthusian reinterpretation of Chinese economic history because he lacks the necessary demographic data to support his broad arguments.[12] However, although he may overemphasize population growth as well as China's cultural uniqueness, his work does provide important evidence of "a severe state of land fragmentation" in the late Ming and early Qing

9 Evelyn Rawski, p. 162, *Agricultural Change and the Peasant Economy of South China* (Cambridge, MA: Harvard University Press, 1972).

10 See Evelyn Rawski, "Economic and Social Foundation of Late Imperial Culture," pp. 3–33 in *Popular Culture in Late Imperial China*, D. Johnson, A. J. Nathan, and E. S. Rawski, eds. (Berkeley: University of California Press, 1985).

11 Kang Chao, *Man and Land in Chinese History* (Stanford: Stanford University Press, 1986).

12 See Ramon H. Myers, "Review Article: Land and Labor in China," *Economic Development and Cultural Change* (July 1988) 36.4: 797–806.

that is relevant to this study.[13] Chao makes a persuasive argument that population pressure contributed to the fragmentation of land holdings and that commercialization and the "back flow" of commercial capital into the rural land market prevented a high concentration of land ownership in "traditional" China.[14]

Questions of interpretation aside, the studies mentioned share a broad temporal framework that permits analysis of large-scale economic change over several centuries of Chinese history from the late Ming to the twentieth century. Similarly, each of these historians presented a dynamic picture of economic change in late imperial China in which it was assumed that individuals responded rationally to market forces. While most of these economic historians made some effort to address the social impact of economic change, that was not their major intention and it would be unfair to criticize them on those grounds. Nevertheless, from the point of view of someone interested in the relationship between economic change and social conflict, the fact that neoclassical economic analysis ignores institutional settings and positive transaction costs is a serious omission and leads to a more general criticism of this type of analysis. In an insightful critique of neoclassical economic theory, Ronald Coase lamented the separation of theory from subject matter in economics that he termed "blackboard economics."[15] Noting the level of abstraction that economics could sometimes reach, Coase complained that "the consumer is not a human being but a consistent set of preferences" and "exchange takes place without any specification of its institutional setting."[16] Thus while economic historians such as Rawski and Chao made a clear contribution to the field that forced other scholars to reconsider the historical development of China's economy, their type of analysis cannot account for those individuals who resisted economic changes and the social costs of that resistance.

In contrast to Rawski and Chao, Robert Marks's work on Haifeng county in eastern Guangdong from the late Ming to the 1930s focuses

13 Chao, p. 100–1. 14 Ibid., p. 107.

15 Ronald Coase, p. 19, *The Firm the Market and the Law* (Chicago: University of Chicago Press, 1988). A recognition of the importance of the institutional setting and positive transaction costs lead Coase to analyze the firm, the market, and the law – the major components of the institutional structure.

16 Ibid., p. 3. Coase demonstrates his point with a delightful and informative essay on the history of the administration of lighthouses in Britain. Economists, from Mill to Samuelson, have cited the example of the supposed unprofitability of privately owned lighthouses as evidence to justify economic intervention by government to provide necessary services that the private sector has no incentive to supply. On the contrary, Coase's essay shows that there was a period when private individuals profited handsomely from administrating lighthouses.

on the social consequences of long-term economic change on peasant society. Marks identifies three successive phases of class conflict. Initially, the class struggles between peasant and landlord of the late Ming destroyed the large, landed estates and freed peasants from their servile status, paving the way for the small landholding economy of the Qing dynasty. During the first two centuries of Qing rule, regional or lineage-based social conflict, which cut across class lines, was more prevalent. Marks argues that when China was integrated into a world capitalist market during the second half of the nineteenth century, the ameliorating influences of the moral economy of the peasant were undermined and class conflict reemerged.[17] While Marks highlights some important social consequences of economic change, my own research suggests that he exaggerates both the degree of class solidarity among the peasantry and the stability of the moral economy of traditional society. As violent disputes over property rights during the Qianlong reign abundantly demonstrate, the struggle over property rights produced intraclass as well as interclass violence prior to China's integration into a world capitalist market.

Philip Huang's work presents a more stimulating and controversial examination of long-term economic change and peasant revolution. Tracing the economic and social developments of the late imperial and the Republican period in Hebei and Shandong provinces, Huang offers a more nuanced interpretation of Chinese peasants and agrarian change from the Qing dynasty through the Communist Revolution that stresses the multidimensional characteristics of peasant households and the rural economy. Huang delineates various strata of peasant society to illustrate the complex impact of economic change and the different social and political consequences of these changes for each stratum of peasant society. Huang demonstrates, for example, that the appearance of wage laborers, which many Marxist historians had cited as evidence of burgeoning rural capitalism, was actually an indication of the depressed economic conditions of rural China. According to Huang, the "twin pressures of involution and social stratification without the relief of dynamic economic growth" created the socioeconomic background of the Communist Revolution.[18] In a more recent study of the Yangzi Delta from 1350–1988, Huang again maintains that conceptions of rural development based on Western experience do not apply to

17 Robert B. Marks, pp. 282–9, *Rural Revolution in South China* (Madison: University of Wisconsin Press, 1984).

18 Philip C. C. Huang, pp. 306–9, *The Peasant Economy and Social Change in North China* (Stanford: Stanford University Press, 1985).

China.[19] Huang argues that growth without development, which he labels "involutionary growth," distinguished the commercialization of the Chinese economy. Huang's work has drawn criticism from a number of scholars.[20] Recent work on Jiangnan by Li Bozhong, in particular, convincingly refutes the notion of involutionary growth for the period prior to 1850.[21] Still, Huang's effort to reexamine Chinese economic history was a significant departure from previous studies and certainly has sparked a lively debate that can only benefit the field. Conceptually, his approach – which acknowledges the multistranded relationships of peasant society, the variable impact of economic change, and the limited usefulness of Western models of development – places the historical development of China's peasant economy in a new light.

Despite differences of method and interpretation, taken as a whole the works discussed earlier at least put to rest the notion that premodern China's economy and society were stagnant or stationary and undercut the argument that cultural differences can greatly explain the divergent paths followed by China and the West.[22] Still, the historical experience of the West overshadows scholarly efforts to understand Chinese economic history. Recently, economic historians have attempted to free the field from the conceptual grip of the Industrial Revolution.[23] In *Growth Recurring*, Eric Jones distinguished intensive economic growth, which he defined as long-term per capita growth, from its most recent variant, modern economic growth based on industrialization.[24] According to Jones, although the Industrial Revolution represented a profound shift in the course of economic history, it was not the first time intensive

19 Philip C. C. Huang, *The Peasant Family and Rural Development in the Yangzi Delta, 1350–1988* (Stanford: Stanford University Press, 1990).

20 See Loren Brandt's review of Philip C. C. Huang's *The Peasant Economy and Social Change in North China*, in *Economic Development and Cultural Change* (April 1987), 35.3: 670–81; Ramon Myers's "How Did the Modern Chinese Economy Develop? A Review Article," *Journal of Asian Studies* (August 1991) 50.3: 604–28; and R. Bin Wong, "Chinese Economic History and Development: A Note on the Myers-Huang Exchange," *Journal of Asian Studies* (August 1992) 51.3: 600–11.

21 See Li Bozhong, *Agricultural Development in Jiangnan, 1620–1850* (New York: St. Martin's Press, 1998).

22 See Mark Elvin, "Why China Failed to Create an Endogenous Industrial Capitalism: A Critique of Max Weber's Explanation," *Theory and Society* (1984) 13: 372–92. Interestingly, with the notable exception of R. Bin Wong's recent book (cited in Note 20) few scholars have explored the similarities between China and the West that might explain the comparable levels of economic development prior to 1500.

23 Recent literature on the Industrial Revolution in England has found that the transition to industrialism was more gradual than previously thought. For a succinct summary of recent research, see Joel Mokyr, "The Industrial Revolution and the New Economic History," in *The Economics of the Industrial Revolution*, J. Mokyr, ed. (Lanham, MD: Rowman and Littlefield, 1985).

24 Eric L. Jones, Chapter 1, *Growth Recurring* (New York: Oxford University Press, 1988).

economic growth managed to "bubble up through the stately rising dough of extensive growth."[25] Taking economic growth as "a basic and restless trait" of human beings, Jones convincingly argued that the structure of political and economic institutions was largely responsible for obstructing the underlying tendency for economic growth.[26] Abandoning the Industrial Revolution as the yardstick for measuring economic development frees scholars to examine preindustrial intensive economic growth in China and elsewhere on its own terms. Li Bozhong's work on Jiangnan offers excellent examples of the benefits of this approach.[27]

As noted previously, in a broader effort to "dislodge European state making and capitalism from their privileged position as universalizing themes," R. Bin Wong undertakes a fresh approach to comparing the economic and political changes of China with Europe, not only to establish differences but as part of a "larger program of identifying similarities and connections."[28] Wong's work identifies the long-term trajectories of economic change in late imperial China and finds that the increased cash cropping, handicrafts, and trade in the Chinese economy from the sixteenth to the nineteenth century displayed Smithian dynamics, which need not necessarily lead to sustained increases in per capita incomes. In this way the vibrancy and significance of the late imperial Chinese economy can be acknowledged without labeling it a failure because it did not produce an industrial revolution.

With mixed results, social historians have explored the economic roots of social unrest and economic historians have addressed the social consequences of economic development. If nothing else, recent scholarship demonstrates that placing social conflict and economic

25 See Jones, Chapter 2. Among other examples of preindustrial intensive economic growth, Jones cited the impressive levels of economic growth in Song Dynasty China. See Mark Elvin, 1984, Chapter 14, and Robert M. Hartwell, "Demographic, Political, and Social Transformations of China, 750–1550," *Harvard Journal of Asiatic Studies* (1982) 365–442. Why did China fail to sustain and deepen the economic growth of the Song? According to Jones, the "derivative effects" of the Mongol conquest produced "the rigid values and defensive institutions" that were rational responses to the events of the twelfth and thirteenth centuries. These values and institutions were more conducive to rent-seeking rulers who appropriated economic surpluses to satisfy their own luxury demands. See Jones, Chapter 7. According to Charles Hucker, p. 3, *The Ming Dynasty* (Ann Arbor: University of Michigan, Center for Chinese Studies, 1978), the "capriciously absolutist pattern" of government of the Ming dynasty (1368–1644), which replaced the Mongol Yuan dynasty (1260–1368), perpetuated this institutional structure. For an insightful account of how the Confucian elite wittingly and unwittingly assisted in the furtherance of "Ming despotism," see John Dardess, *Confucianism and Autocracy* (Berkeley: University of California Press, 1983).

26 Jones, Chapter 1. 27 See Li Bozhong, Chapter 9.

28 R. Bin Wong, 1997, pp. 1–2.

change at the heart of a study of late imperial China is a difficult task. Furthering our understanding of social conflict and economic change in Chinese history requires a significant body of data on social conflict and a theoretical model of structure and change in economic history that can incorporate the insights from both market and moral economy models. Reports of homicides related to disputes over land provide a systematic body of data for the study of social conflict. Combining this data with a theory of structure and change in economic history provides the basis to elucidate the relationship between social conflict and economic change in eighteenth-century China.

Economic Change and Property Rights: A Theoretical Framework

As noted, over the past two decades Douglass North has elaborated a theory of structure and change in economic history that emphasizes the central place of political and economic institutions. According to North, to understand historical economic change we must examine a wide range of economic and political institutions. "Institutions are a set of rules; compliance procedures; and moral and ethical behavioral norms; designed to constrain the behavior of individuals."[29] Constitutional rules comprise the fundamental laws that "specify the basic structure of property rights and control of the state." Operating rules, which include property rights and institutional arrangements, "specify terms of exchange within the framework of constitutional rules."[30] The normative behavioral rules, which include ideology broadly defined, are "codes of behavior aimed at legitimating the constitutional and operating rules." Because they constituted the operational level economic institutions of the eighteenth-century rural economy, this book will primarily examine changes in property rights and the normative behavioral rules that governed land transactions and the use of land.

While neoclassical economic theory has been a powerful tool to explain economic performance as well as a wide range of human behavior, North identified two problems of the neoclassical world: There are no organizations or institutions except the market; and economic change occurs in an impersonal market via a shift in relative prices without regard to transaction costs.[31] Building upon the earlier work of

29 Douglass North, 1981, pp. 201–2.
30 Ibid., Chapter 15.
31 See North, Introduction, for the full rebuttal to the application of neoclassical theory to historical studies.

Ronald Coase,[32] North points out that effective price-making markets require readily enforceable and well-defined property rights for the goods and services being exchanged, a condition that has never been obtained historically. For this reason, structure and change in economic history cannot be explained without reference to political and economic institutions and the historical forces that shaped them. Restating the traditional production relationship, North maintains that the total cost of production consists of the resource inputs of land, labor, and capital involved in transacting – "defining, protecting and enforcing the property rights to goods" – as well as the inputs involved in transforming the physical attributes of a good.[33]

Transaction Costs

Transaction costs vary with the costs of measuring goods and services and enforcing property rights; the scope of the exchange process; and ideological attitudes. The larger the scale of trade, the more complex it becomes and the greater the need to specify and enforce property rights. Based on the complexity of exchange, North distinguishes three general forms of exchange: personalized exchange; impersonal exchange; and impersonal exchange with third-party enforcement.[34] It is important to note that North identifies forms of exchange, each of which has its own set of costs and benefits. Some forms of exchange preceded others, but these forms of exchange do not represent historical stages of development. Although technological advances have made more complex and efficient forms of economic exchange possible, older forms of exchange retain certain advantages and may continue to exist side by side with more recent ones. Consequently, it is possible for a particular economy to exhibit a variety of forms exchange.

Historically, personalized exchange characterized by small-scale production and local trade was most common. Personalized exchange entails very low transaction costs because the size of the market is small, there are many repeat dealings, and parties to the exchange possess intimate knowledge of each other. The "dense network of social interactions" lowers transaction costs. However, reliance on personal exchange limits the extent of the market, raises transformation costs, and reduces

32 See Coase, Chapter 2, for an illustration of how higher transaction costs increase the likelihood of nonmarket allocation systems.

33 Douglass North, 1990, p. 28.

34 Ibid., pp. 34–5.

potential productivity.[35] Increases in the size and scope of markets has usually led to more complex forms of impersonal exchange. According to North, the early development of long-distance and cross-cultural trade, and the fairs of medieval Europe were forms of impersonal exchange in which "parties were constrained by kinship ties, bonding, exchanging hostages or merchant codes of conduct."[36] Impersonal exchange with third-party enforcement has been a more recent phenomenon. It enables higher levels of productivity, but due to the high degree of specialization and interdependence the cost of transacting increases and the need for well-defined and enforceable property rights emerges.[37] Consequently, we find that the economic role of the state as the third-party enforcer of property rights has expanded as the complexity of economic interaction has increased.[38]

As North points out convincingly, even under the best circumstances enforcement and definition of property rights are imperfect and entail costs that limit the range of market transactions. Since neoclassical analysis does not account for these costs, its application to historical studies has limited usefulness. North also criticized substantivist interpretations of economic history, such as that of Karl Polanyi.[39] In an article addressing the work of Polanyi, North supports the contention that the dominance of the price-making market as a "transactional mode" was primarily a nineteenth-century phenomenon, but he rejected Polanyi's claim that resource allocation has not been based on economizing behavior.[40] Polanyi maintained that the dominant transactional modes prior to the nineteenth century were reciprocity; obligatory gift giving between kin and friends; and redistribution – obligatory payments to central political or religious authorities. While market systems were oriented toward wealth maximizing, reciprocity and redistribution were grounded in kinship and status, and political or religious affiliation, respectively.[41] Contrary to the substantivist's arguments, North concluded that nonprice or nonmarket allocation of goods and services can

35 See Douglass North, "Institutions, Transaction Costs and Economic Growth," *Economic Inquiry* (July 1987) 25: 419–28.

36 North, 1990, p. 34. 37 North, 1987, pp. 420–21.

38 For example, in the United States, the government's share of GNP increased from 2.3% in the nineteenth century to 24% in the twentieth century. See Douglass North, "Government and the Cost of Exchange in History," *Journal of Economic History* (June 1984) 44.2: 255–64.

39 Polanyi.

40 Douglass North, "Markets and Other Allocation Systems in History: The Challenge of Karl Polanyi," *Journal of European Economic History* (Fall 1977) 2: 709. Polanyi coined the term *transactional mode* to describe different forms of exchange. For example, reciprocity, householding, price-making markets, etc. are all transactional modes.

41 Ibid., p. 707.

be considered economically rational responses to high transaction costs. To a lesser extent, North's theory also addresses a major inconsistency in Marxist interpretations that is particularly relevant to this study. North's objection to Marxist analysis was directed at the assumption that individuals will forgo self-interest for the sake of class interests.[42] Indeed, as evidence of property right disputes presented in the following paragraphs will amply demonstrate, depending on the issue, location, and time period, intraclass conflict was as likely to occur as interclass conflict. Transaction cost analysis allows North to expose the weaknesses of Marxist, substantivist, and neoclassical economists and to devise a more compelling theory of structure and change in history.

Historical Determinants of Economic Growth

As mentioned earlier in this book, according to North, the key determinants of historical economic growth include demography, technology, the ideology of a society, and political and economic institutions. The effects of demographic and technological shifts have generally been the most easily observable and well-understood components of historical economic growth. Technologically, there were no major innovations in Chinese agriculture during the eighteenth century.[43] Increased production was largely due to added inputs of labor, improved planting techniques, and specialization.[44] Population growth, on the other hand, was perhaps the most important factor creating pressure for economic change and will be discussed separately in Chapter 2. In broaching the question of the role of ideology, North raised an issue often skirted in

42 See North, 1981, pp. 60–1. North was, however, quick to note that the strength of Marxist analysis can be found in its inclusion of institutions, property rights, the state, and ideology into economic theory and its focus on the tension between the production potential of a society and the structure of property rights as the source of structural change. According to North, among major economic theorists only Karl Marx incorporated political and economic institutions into economic analysis.

43 A notable exception was the introduction of the deep-tilling plow that was recorded in 1747. See Ye Xianen, p. 37, "Luelun Yong Qian shiqi shehui jingji di jiegouxing bianqian ji qi lishi diwei (A brief discussion of changes in the structure of the social economy of the Yongzheng and Qianlong periods and its historical position). *Zhongguo jingjishi yanjiu* (1991) 4: 33–45. While Ye cites the introduction of this plow, he stresses the importance of improved seed selection and new crops as reasons for increased output.

44 Fang Xing, p. 32, "Qingdai nongmin jingji kuoda zaishengchan di xingshi" (The form of "extended reproduction" in the Qing peasant economy), *Zhongguo jingjishi yanjiu* (1996) 1: 32–46. Li Bozhong, on the other hand, considers these types of improved techniques technological changes. He draws a contrast between "skill-oriented" technologies common in East Asia and "mechanical" technologies common in the West. See Li Bozhong, p. 168.

economic history, and his most recent work has focused more intently on this relatively unexplored and complex factor in economic behavior.[45] Ideology, broadly defined, explains how people view the world and make moral and ethical judgments. This is critical to the efficiency of any economic organization because there is no economic system or political entity powerful enough to monitor and enforce property rights everywhere and at all times. While a state by definition has a comparative advantage in coercive power, all states must rely to some degree on ideology to maintain power. It is crucial for the maintenance of social stability that a substantial majority of the population believe that existing economic institutions are fair. The extent to which Chinese rulers relied on Confucianism to weld together the ruling class of scholar bureaucrats is well known, but in the Chinese countryside at the grassroots level, ideology, broadly defined, was also an important underpinning to the rural economy. As the disputes over property rights featured in this book will illustrate, different perceptions of the mutual obligations of tenant and landlord, and ethical judgments regarding new concepts of land ownership and other economic institutions were at the heart of many altercations.

Western studies of the late imperial Chinese economy have already addressed some of the key determinants of economic development identified by North. Focusing on property rights and ethical norms, Mi Chu Wiens has explored the changing concepts of tenant and landlord in eighteenth-century China. Wiens contrasts the moralistic codes that governed relations between landowners and bond servants in the sixteenth century with the system of private land ownership or contractually oriented tenancy based on contractual agreements of the nineteenth century.[46] Wiens found that in the period from 1500–1800 there was a growing alienation and antagonism between tenant and landlord as contractually oriented tenancy became more prevalent. The growing importance of land over labor was also reflected in the proliferation of contractual agreements, which were indicative of the ongoing efforts to refine and elaborate property rights in land. Contemporaneous with the refinement of property rights in land was the wilting away of bonded servitude that can be considered a form of property rights in human beings.

Wiens's insightful work delineates the extreme boundaries of the continuum of economic institutions, from bonded servitude in the Ming

45 See North, 1990.

46 See Wiens, Mi Chu, "Lord and Peasant in China: The Sixteenth to the Eighteenth Centuries," *Modern China* (January 1980) 6: 3–39.

to rent bursaries in the nineteenth century, that I have used to orient my study of property-rights disputes. As the temporal and geographic pattern of disputes over property rights indicates, changes in economic institutions varied over time and across regions, reflecting the variable effects of the economic forces that induced demand for change in institutions. Broadly speaking, and with due regard for temporal and regional variations, the eighteenth century was arguably the period when economic institutions were in the midst of this important transformation. According to Wiens, the deterioration of tenant-landlord relations also meant a growing role for the state as mediator between tenant and landlord. As we shall see, local magistrates in the eighteenth century shouldered the heavy burden of dealing with disputes over property rights addressing local interests; contractual agreements; and the refinements of property rights and regulations on land transactions that had been codified in the Qing legal code. Balancing these competing claims often proved to be a daunting task for local officials, as we will see in Chapter 7.

Also, the evolving role of political institutions as a determinant of economic change has not been ignored. In an excellent study of the economic role of the state in China, Peter Perdue examined government contributions to the promotion and maintenance of the agricultural economy of Hunan Province from 1500–1850.[47] Distinguishing three stages of state involvement in the economy, Perdue noted that government intervention in the economy, while variable and limited, was by no means inconsequential. During the early Qing, the government carried out an aggressive policy designed to restore the foundations of agriculture after the devastation of the Ming-Qing interregnum. In the eighteenth century, when economic recovery was well under way, the local officials were drawn into land disputes, which arose as commercialization undermined property rights grounded in customary law. According to Perdue, officials in Hunan sometimes issued regulations to clarify ambiguities in customary practices related to land sales, but local officials often resorted to invoking "ideals of cooperation for mutual benefit," when regulations did not settle the question.[48] (Evidence from violent disputes reveals similar practices in Shandong, Sichuan, and Guangdong.) In the nineteenth century, population pressure and commercialization increased unabated and created additional tensions between the state and local interests. Perdue presented convincing

47 Peter Perdue, *Exhausting the Earth: State and Peasant in Hunan, 1500–1850* (Cambridge, MA: Harvard University, Council on East Asian Studies, 1987).

48 Ibid., p. 163.

evidence of the state's ability to take an economic leadership role. Although the economic role of the state in China was more extensive than most historians have previously thought, Perdue maintained that it was still far short of what he terms "the thoroughgoing rationalization of property rights that occurred in Europe."[49]

Applying North's Theory to China

Geographically, North's work deals almost exclusively with the Western world. Still he has influenced some historians of China, such as Chen Fu-mei and Ramon Myers.[50] Chen and Myers provided solid empirical evidence, in the form of written contracts based on customary law, to illustrate the importance of property rights for economic development in late imperial China.[51] According to Chen and Myers, the network of customary law, the inhibited role of the state, and ordinary market mechanisms "constituted the organizational foundations" of economic and demographic growth after the seventeenth century. More recently, Myers also has emphasized the positive role of the state in supporting and enforcing customary law.[52] Chen and Myers focus on the role of customary law, which partly accounted for the economic growth of the late imperial period, and they supply some useful empirical evidence in the form of private contracts to illustrate their points.[53] Unlike Chen and Myers, who examine the smooth workings of the property rights system, my study focuses on the struggle to define and enforce property rights at the grassroots level as a source of social conflict during a period of economic change.

A sophisticated application of a theory of property rights to Asia can be found in David Feeny's work on Southeast Asia. Feeny uses the

49 Ibid., p. 150.

50 Tai-shuenn Yang's "Property Rights and Constitutional Order in Imperial China," unpublished Ph.D. diss., Indiana University, 1987, represents a misguided attempt to apply North's theory to China. Perhaps the most disappointing aspect of this work was its thoroughly ahistorical method. Secure in the assumption that nothing about China changed for over 2,000 years, Yang plucks examples from across the broad span of Chinese history with little regard for their historical context.

51 Fu-mei Chen and Ramon Myers, "Customary Law and the Economic Growth of China during the Ch'ing Period," *Ch'ing Shih wen-ti* (1976) 3.5: 1–32.

52 Ramon Myers, p. 275, "Customary Law, Markets, and Resource Transactions in Later Imperial China," in *Explorations in the New Economic History: Essays in Honor of Douglass C. North*, R. L. Ransom, R. Sutch, and G. M. Walton, eds., pp. 273–98 (New York: Academic Press, 1982).

53 North acknowledges that voluntary organizations are capable of establishing and enforcing property rights but they are not as efficient as the state that has the power to tax. See Douglass North and Paul Thomas, pp. 7–8.

decline of property rights in human beings, corvée, and slavery over the course of the nineteenth century to illustrate the dynamics of economic change in Thailand.[54] Rising land values and increasing commercialization, including international trade, "obviated the need for human-property rights" and created the incentive for institutional change.[55] Politically, Thai rulers were willing to abolish these forms of servitude because they mostly benefited their political rivals in the nobility. In another article, Feeny has compared the development of property rights in land in Thailand, Burma, India, and the Philippines in the nineteenth and twentieth centuries.[56] Using the ratio of the export price of land-intensive agricultural products to the import price of manufactured goods as a proxy for land rents, Feeny found that rising land value increased interest in acquiring land and utilizing the system of property rights.[57] Not surprisingly, greater utilization of the system of property rights exposed the system's weaknesses and led to an increase in property disputes.[58] Although Thailand differed significantly in the amount of untapped land available and the extent of Western domination of its economy, the general pattern of the development of property rights in Thailand resembled the late imperial Chinese experience in two important ways. As land values rose and agriculture became more commercialized, both countries experienced a decline in property rights in human beings and a refinement of property rights in land. Feeny's work supplies insightful theoretical refinements and a useful point for comparison for China.

Linking small-scale social conflicts to the large-scale economic changes of the eighteenth century requires a theory of structure and change in economic history that takes into account political institutions, property rights, and ideology. For the purposes of this study, property rights are defined as the sanctioned behavioral relationships among individuals that govern their interactions around and their use of resources. These rights may be formal or informal, expressed or implied, written or unwritten, and they find their expression in the laws, customs, and mores of a society. In eighteenth-century China, property rights were usually expressed in written contracts grounded in local custom. Situated in the personal, day-to-day realm of economic activity, property

54 See David Feeny, "The Decline of Property Rights in Man in Thailand, 1800–1913," *Journal of Economic History* (June 1989) 49.2: 285–96.

55 Ibid., pp. 285–6.

56 See David Feeny, "The Development of Property Rights in Land: A Comparative Study," in *Toward a Political Economy of Development*, R. H. Bates, ed. (Berkeley: University of California Press, 1988).

57 Ibid., p. 294. 58 Ibid., pp. 283, 294.

rights were the most malleable and mutable component of the institutional structure of the economy. Consequently, property rights are also more likely to produce disputes. Historically, the impetus to define and enforce new property rights has emerged under one or more of the following conditions: shifts in the relative value of the factors of production; major technological innovations; or an increase in the size of the market. In eighteenth-century China, commercialization and a steady increase in population produced incentives for altering existing property rights. According to neoclassical economic theory, the market will determine these adjustments; but in the real-world context of institutions and positive transaction costs, adjustments do not take place so smoothly. Alternatively, according to the moral economy model, social networks and ethical norms should ameliorate the consequences of economic change. This may often be the case, but when an economy is undergoing change on the scale experienced in eighteenth-century China, these ideological props of the economy may no longer suit the times. In fact, as I will demonstrate, the process of defining and enforcing new property rights was protracted, arduous, and often quite bloody.

2

"Population Increases Daily": Economic Change during the Eighteenth Century

Before examining violent disputes over property rights in detail, it is necessary to delineate their political, social, and economic contexts. In 1644, Manchu troops, with the collaboration of Chinese armies of the crippled Ming dynasty (1368–1644), entered Beijing and established the Qing dynasty. Fighting between rebel peasant armies and government troops had left large areas of China devastated in the closing years of the Ming dynasty and it took the Manchu rulers four decades to consolidate their control. During that time the Qing armies successively quelled persistent peasant uprisings; eradicated the last remnants of Ming loyalist forces in southern China; and suppressed the Sanfan Rebellion, a challenge from their erstwhile Chinese collaborators. When the fighting ended in 1683, a period of recovery ensued and created the foundation for over a century of political stability. Historians have eloquently described the grand achievements of this unprecedented era of peace and sustained economic and territorial expansion known as the "High Qing."[1] Beneath the surface, in the realm of the "little tradition," however, the broad economic changes of the eighteenth

1 See Albert Feuerwerker, *State and Society in Eighteenth-Century China*, Michigan Papers in Chinese Studies, No. 27 (Ann Arbor: University of Michigan, Center for Chinese Studies, 1976), and Frederic Wakeman, Jr., "High Ch'ing: 1683–1839," pp. 1–28 in *Modern East Asia: Essays in Interpretation*, J. B. Crowley, ed. (New York: Harcourt, Brace, and World, 1970). Also see Susan Naquin and Evelyn Rawski, *Chinese Society in the Eighteenth Century* (New Haven: Yale University Press, 1987).

century were engendering tensions that sometimes erupted into violent disputes.

Politically, the Manchu conquerors implemented several important institutional innovations designed to safeguard the power of the alien minority. For example, the Banner Military System supplied a reliable and loyal armed force. The Court of Colonial Affairs (*Lifan Yuan*) handled diplomatic relations between the court and non-Han peoples on the northwestern frontiers. The Grand Council consolidated several central-government agencies under the emperor's direct control, checking the power of the overwhelming Han Chinese bureaucracy. Finally, the Imperial Household Department, the emperor's personal treasury, provided the imperial clan with a direct source of revenue outside the control of the regular government administration. The daily administration of the Chinese portion of the Manchu empire, however, remained largely in the hands of about 40,000 Han Chinese bureaucrats recruited through the civil-service examination system. Sharing a common class and ideological background, these bureaucrats faced the challenging task of administering an ever-growing population and increasingly complex economy. Over time, the task became more burdensome because, notwithstanding the economic and demographic expansion of the eighteenth century, the size of the imperial bureaucracy remained fixed. Despite these enormous challenges most officials served the dynasty well, as evidenced in their handling of disputes over property rights.

Socially, the peasant household was the most important unit of production and consumption, and economic decisions were made accordingly. For the most part, these households shared a culture that valued the accumulation of land and the expansion of their lineages. The absence of primogeniture meant that land holdings remained modest, though in Guangdong some powerful lineages were able to accumulate large, corporately held estates. For the most part, contractual agreements based on customary law governed economic relationships between households. The effectiveness of customary law was dependent on the shared values and perceived fairness that the economic changes of the eighteenth century seriously eroded. As the examination of violent disputes will reveal, the erosion of existing economic institutions and the shared ethical norms that buttressed them were frequently at the heart of many violent disputes. Before addressing political and social institutions further it will be necessary to outline the important economic changes of the early Qing. Because two-thirds of the disputes examined in this study occurred in Guangdong, special attention will be given to that province.

Commercialization

Although agriculture continued to dominate the Chinese economy throughout the eighteenth century, it would be a serious error to overlook the changes in economic institutions that distinguished this period. The eighteenth century witnessed an increased specialization and commercialization of agriculture; rising prices for grain; innovations in fiscal policies; an extension of the area under cultivation and an intensification of agriculture on existing land; large-scale migrations; and unprecedented levels of population growth. In recent years, among historians the consensus view has been that China's rural economy was increasingly commercialized during the eighteenth century and that this commercialization had a broad impact on the forms of land tenure and patterns of landholding.[2] While a wide variety of descriptive evidence has been marshalled to support this contention, which I believe is correct, no one has yet devised an adequate method to quantify the degree of commercialization or its rate of change over time. Instead, the evidence must be pieced together from a variety of official and unofficial sources.

Using data on the establishment of customhouses and customs revenues, Fan I-chun has argued that the expansion of the customs system from 1400–1850 "indicates that the socio-economic development in traditional China had reached a new stage."[3] The Qing government upgraded more and more local customhouses during the Yongzheng (1723–35) and Qianlong (1736–95) reigns to tax the burgeoning interregional trade. Furthermore, the geographic scope of interregional trade also expanded. Whereas Ming customhouses were concentrated in areas along the Grand Canal and the lower Yangzi River, the Qing extended customhouses to the middle and upper Yangzi and opened new coastal customhouses from Guangdong to Manchuria and deeper into the interior.[4] As for revenues, Fan provides statistics that show a sharp upsurge in custom revenues from 1686 to 1788 and, reflecting the new scope of interregional trade, a relative decline in revenue collected along the Grand Canal from over 90% of all revenues in the late

2 See Kang Chao, 1986, Chapter 6; Susan Naquin and Evelyn Rawski, pp. 101, 221; and Peter Perdue, Chapter 5.

3 Fan I-Chun, p. 71 in "Long-distance Trade and Market Integration in the Ming-Ch'ing Period, 1400–1850," Ph.D. diss., Stanford University, 1992.

4 Ibid., p. 93.

Ming to 36% in 1788.[5] Evidence from custom revenues indicates that both Sichuan and Guangdong, as well as other inland and southern provinces, were deeply enmeshed in this expanding regional trade by the eighteenth century.[6] Addressing G. William Skinner's model of macroregions, Fan concludes that there was "a large closely integrated market area covering several of the regions designated by Skinner."[7] This included most of North China, the Upper and Middle Yangzi Valley, and the Southeast Coast.

The significance of foreign trade in the development of the late imperial economy was apparent as early as the sixteenth century, particularly in southeast China, where the capitals of both Guangzhou and Chaozhou prefectures were important international ports.[8] An inflow of silver bullion from both Japan and the Spanish colonies of the New World furthered the monetization of the rural economy during the sixteenth century. The sharp increase in the silver revenue that Chinese government vaults registered from 1571 onward coincided with the establishment of Manila as a major base for Spanish traders, a relaxation in trade restrictions by the Ming government, and the rise of Nagasaki as the center for Sino-Japanese trade.[9] Foreign silver was so important that William Atwell has speculated that the decline of imports in the 1630s, after Spanish officials tightened control over the movement of bullion, may have contributed to undermining the political stability of the Ming dynasty (1368–1644). Richard von Glahn, on the other hand, agrees that the influx of foreign silver had a substantial impact on the Ming economy, but presents evidence that silver imports did not decline during the late Ming. Furthermore, he blames seventeenth-century monetary problems on a greater demand for silver and money in general, rather than a shortage of silver.[10] Guo Chengkang has made a similar argument for price inflation that occurred during the Qianlong reign.[11]

Foreign trade, which had been suppressed during the early Qing dynasty, recovered in 1684 after the Kangxi emperor lifted the coastal pacification policy that had been instituted to deny Ming loyalist forces

5 Ibid., p. 120. 6 Ibid., p. 200 (Sichuan), p. 238 (Guangdong). 7 Ibid., p. 296.

8 Li Hua, p. 40, "Qing chao qianqi Guangdong di shangye yu shangren" (Guangdong commerce and merchants in the early Qing dynasty), *Xueshu yanjiu* (1983) 2: 39–44.

9 William Atwell, pp. 80–1, "International Bullion Flows and the Chinese Economy 1530–1650," *Past and Present* (May 1982) 95: 68–90.

10 See Richard von Glahn, "Myth and Reality of China's Seventeenth-Century Monetary Crisis," *Journal of Economic History* (June 1996) 56.2: 429–54.

11 See Guo Chengkang, "Shiba shiji Zhongguo wujia wenti he zhengfu duice" (The problem of eighteenth-century Chinese price inflation and government countermeasures), *Qingshi yanjiu* (1996) 1: 8–19.

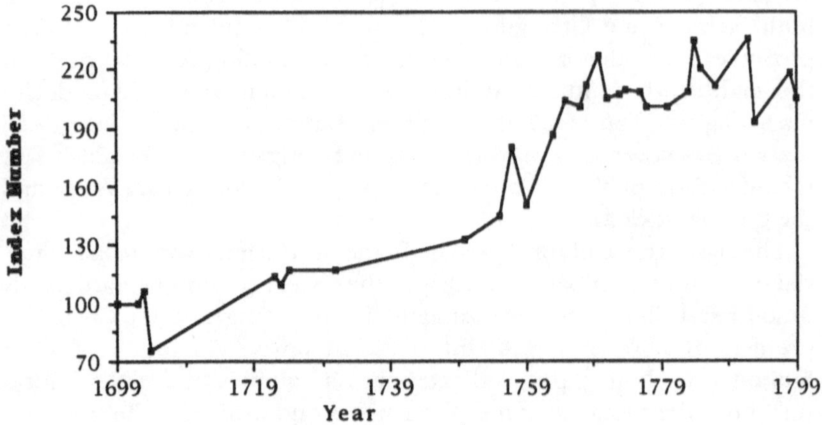

Figure 2–1 Index Number of Raw Silk Prices in Guangzhou, 1699–1799

based in Taiwan access to the mainland. Speaking of Guangdong province, one historian has stated that "the explosive growth of Chinese coastal and foreign trade" after 1684 stimulated commercialization of agriculture in Guangdong.[12] In fact, Guangdong provided the largest share of customs revenues in the coastal trade from 1735 to 1812 in large part due to the transshipment of foreign goods.[13] From the first quarter of the eighteenth century to 1800, foreign trade into the provincial capital of Guangzhou, as measured in thousands of tons, grew eightfold.[14] The specialization and commercialization of agriculture in Guangdong was further fueled in 1759 when the provincial capital, Guangzhou, became the only legal port of entry for foreign trade. While we can only estimate the full dimensions and effects of foreign trade on Guangdong, as the graph in Figure 2–1 indicates, the price of silk,[15] an important export commodity, rose steadily throughout the eighteenth century, thereby increasing the amount of silver circulating in the Guangdong economy. As Robert Marks points out, the impact of foreign demand for Chinese silk greatly contributed to the transformation of agriculture in the Pearl River Delta, where farmers switched from rice cultivation and the fish pond and fruit tree system of farming to the

12 Robert B. Marks, 1997, p. 193.
13 Fan I-Chun, p. 241. 14 Based on figures cited in Naquin and Rawski, p. 103.
15 Yeh-chien Wang, pp. 364–5, "The Secular Trend of Prices during the Ch'ing Period (1644–1911)," *Journal of the Institute of Chinese Studies of the Chinese University of Hong Kong* (December 1972) 5.2: 347–68.

mulberry embankment and fish pond system in order to increase the supply of mulberry leaves, silkworms, cocoons, and silk.[16] It is important to note that throughout most of the eighteenth century China enjoyed a favorable balance of trade with the West. Chinese merchants and possibly silk producers benefited from foreign trade during this period. The deleterious effects of foreign competition on some handicraft industries and the rise in opium imports were not acutely felt until the nineteenth century.[17] For the most part, foreign trade had a positive and transformative impact on the Chinese economy during the eighteenth century.[18]

While the expansion of the network of customhouses and the upsurge in customs revenues were unambiguous evidence of the macrolevel economic development of the eighteenth century throughout most of China, this evidence only hints at the variable spatial and temporal impact of commercialization. Fortunately, Chinese historians have provided some in-depth studies that shed light on this regional variation. For example, Fang Xing compared densely populated and economically advanced Jiangnan with strife-torn and renascent Sichuan to reveal how the effects of commercialization and population growth varied over time and across regions. According to Fang, peasant households in Jiangnan responded to market forces during the late Ming and early Qing in part by shifting resources to more-profitable sidelines. For example, many households increased the amount of land used to raise mulberry for silk production. Based on Fang's rough estimates, peasant households planted 70% of their land in grain and 30% in mulberry, consequently increasing their incomes by one-third.[19] From the mid-Ming to the early

16 Robert B. Marks, 1997, p. 129.

17 On handicrafts, see Albert Feuerwerker, pp. 123–63, *Studies in the Economic History of Late Imperial China: Handicraft, Modern Industry, and the State* (Ann Arbor: University of Michigan, Center for Chinese Studies, 1995). According to Feuerwerker, the impact of imported textiles, which was not significant until after the Opium War, was mixed. While imports clearly hurt some native producers, in some areas the availability of cheap yarn boosted the development of local weaving.

18 Although the Chinese government was still capable of controlling and regulating foreign trade during the eighteenth century, tensions between local Chinese and foreign traders were apparent. According to evidence from a homicide report, in 1785 a Chinese agent escorted a British trader on a trip upriver to purchase supplies. While the Chinese agent was purchasing vegetables, the British trader went into a nearby temple and "toyed" with some statues. Two locals rebuked him, and fighting ensued. The result was one dead British trader. Unfortunately, the document contained no details on the trial or sentencing. See SS 3612, QL 50.11, Vol. 6 (day unknown).

19 Fang Xing, 1996b, pp. 33–5.

Qing, the amount of land planted in cotton also increased. Jiangnan households combined grain and cotton farming with weaving, which utilized the labor of old and young, male and female members of the household. Sichuan, on the other hand, became a major rice-producing area by the Yongzheng reign (1723–35) after it had been repopulated with migrants from southeast China who brought with them better farming techniques and new crops. The Chengdu plateau, where a double crop of rice and beans could be grown, was particularly productive thanks in part to an influx of migrants from Guangdong and Fujian.[20] According to Fang, in Sichuan – where farms were larger, taxes lower, and rents cheaper – farmers concentrated on rice production to meet the growing demand in Jiangnan and other regions where households grew more cash crops. Peasants in Sichuan, who were largely self-sufficient in grain, benefited from the more than threefold increase in the price of rice in Chongqing from 1735 to 1826. While Jiangnan households shifted labor and land away from grain, Sichuan households purchased more land and concentrated on grain production. Fang's research neatly captures one aspect of the significant regional diversity and interdependency of the eighteenth-century economy.

For Guangdong province, Ye Xian'en has used local gazetteers to trace the relationship between population density and commercialization in the Pearl River Delta during the late Ming and early Qing. According to Ye, population pressure spurred the intensification, specialization, and commercialization of agriculture. Commercialization created employment opportunities in transportation, services, and handicrafts industries, which absorbed surplus labor and increased the number of people dependent on the market for grain and other daily necessities.[21] Although Ye's examples are compelling, it is difficult to gauge precisely the rate of change over time because the data he used were taken from gazetteers that local scholars compiled at irregular intervals during the eighteenth century. Thus, these sources do not supply uniform coverage for each county or prefecture.

Regardless of the actual degree of commercialization, one thing is certain: Local markets clearly proliferated throughout China during the eighteenth century. Culling information from local gazetteers, Hayashi Kazuo found that the number of markets and their geographic density in Guangdong increased steadily from the Ming to the twentieth

20 Ibid., pp. 38–9.
21 Ye Xian'en, 1984, p. 88.

century. According to Hayashi, the largest increase occurred in the seventeenth and eighteenth centuries, and the Pearl River Delta experienced the highest concentration of markets.[22] In another study, also based on local gazetteers, Li Hua concluded that the influence of markets had penetrated all the way down to the village level in Guangdong during the early Qing.[23] Turning to China as a whole, research by Xu Tan demonstrates that beginning in the middle of the Kangxi reign (1662–1722) the proliferation of rural markets was common in economically developed areas of China, including Guangdong, Sichuan, and Shandong. According to Xu, rural markets that had been increasing steadily since the mid-Ming declined in number during the Ming-Qing transition but recovered and exceeded the Ming level of development during the eighteenth century.[24] The evidence from national and provincial level data clearly demonstrate the widespread impact of commercialization on the rural economy.

How did the commercialization of the Chinese economy affect local society? Fortunately, homicide reports related to disputes over debts provide rich anecdotal evidence of commercial activities at the grassroots level.[25] Lineage organizations and wealthy gentry (*shishen fuhu*) frequently organized and maintained markets at the village level, and these local markets sometimes became objects of violent competition.[26] For example, in Hetian village (*xiang*), Dongguan county, Guangzhou, two branches of the Fang lineage organized complementary periodic markets (*xuchang*) in 1785.[27] As the market organizers, the Fangs collected 3 or 4 copper cash (*wen*) from each peddler and stall owner. Presumably, these revenues were not insubstantial, since a dispute between the two branches of the lineage over their collection ended in homi-

22 Hayashi Kazuo, pp. 84–6, "Min-Shin jidai, Kanto no kyo to shi: Dentoeki ichiba no keitai to kino ni kan suru ichi kosatsu" (A survey of the structure and function of traditional markets: Fairs and market towns of Guangdong province during the Ming and Qing periods), *Shirin* (1980) 63: 69–105. Because Kazuo relies on gazetteers, the geographic and temporal coverage of his study are not always consistent.

23 See Li Hua.

24 Xu Tan, pp. 13–14, "Ming Qing shiqi nongcun jishi di fazhan" (Development of rural markets during the Ming and Qing), *Jingji shi* (1997) 5: 13–33.

25 As mentioned in the introduction, the document collection from which the property-rights disputes were drawn also contained cases related to debts (*zhaiwu*). See Appendix A.

26 Xianen Ye, 1984, p. 85.

27 When referring to locations, I will give the county name followed by the name of the prefecture in which it was located. In cases where the prefectural capital reported homicides directly, I have maintained the convention, for example, Jiaying county, Jiaying.

cide.[28] In another dispute in 1765, the Yan lineage lost a lawsuit over control of a local market to the He lineage. Shortly afterwards, a member of the Yan lineage killed a member of the He lineage in revenge.[29] Albeit extreme, these homicides provide examples of the intensity and violent potential of economic competition during the eighteenth century.

These cases involved struggles within and between lineages for control over local markets. Additional evidence from homicide reports also demonstrates that many individuals and households actively engaged in commerce. Homicides related to disputes over debts arising from small-scale commercial transactions occurred in Guangdong, Shandong, and Sichuan. Many of these disputes were between residents of the same village or county and involved no more than a few hundred copper cash for goods bought on credit. Examples of larger-scale and longer-range commerce, from interprefectural to interprovincial, also are readily available. For instance, in 1791 merchants from Dianbai county, Gaozhou, traveled to Maoming county, Gaozhou, to purchase two water buffaloes for 11,700 in copper cash.[30] In 1755, a merchant from Guishan county, Huizhou, traveled to Boluo county, Huizhou, to purchase tobacco on consignment.[31] In 1744, Li Junyi, a merchant from Nanhai county, Guangzhou, traded in miscellaneous goods (*zahuo*) in Lingshan county, Lianzhoufu. After earning 6,200 copper cash, which he temporarily deposited locally, Li set out for the prefectural capital to purchase more goods. Tragically, Yang Chengxing, who lived next door to the home where Li was staying in Lingshan county, ambushed Li and shot him dead in the course of a bungled robbery.[32] In another example of interprefectural trading, Wang Siman and Chen Yunzou of Xingning county, Jiaying prefecture, made their livings transporting bamboo and selling it in Longchuan county in the neighboring prefecture of Huizhou.[33] Turning to interprovincial trade, in 1780 an entrepreneur from Xingguo county, Jiangxi province, opened a tobacco store in Lianzhou county, Guangdong.[34] In 1771, two members of the Hakka minority from neighboring Fujian province arrived in Jiaying prefecture, to buy pigs.[35] Evidence from disputes in Sichuan also reveals long-range

28 Neige Xingke shishu (hereafter SS), 3590, QL 50.7, Vol. 5; QL 50.7.20.
29 SS 2595, QL 30.9, Vol. 4; QL 30.9.29.
30 XKTB 3716, QL 56 (month and day unknown).
31 XKTB 1053, QL 20 (month and day unknown).
32 SS 1565, QL 10.7, Vol. 1; QL 10.7.29.
33 SS 3585, QL 50.6, Vol. 7; QL 50.6.27.
34 XKTB 3226, QL 45 (month and day unknown).
35 XKTB 2398, QL 36 (month and day unknown).

interprovincial trade. In 1751, Yi Huai from Wuling county in Hunan came to Baozhou county in Sichuan to sell sugar.[36] Also in 1751, Zhou Bikui from Sanyuan county, Shaanxi province, established a salt shop in Yongming county, Sichuan.[37] The accounts of these transactions have survived only because they were related to a homicide. Presumably, most commercial transactions were nonviolent, and, while it would be risky to generalize based only on these examples, the frequency of these petty disputes indicates that rural inhabitants were active participants in market exchange.

Examples of specialization in agriculture and handicrafts from counties throughout Guangdong, Shandong, and Sichuan were illustrative of the growing influence of commercialization in agriculture and handicrafts. For example, in Sichuan tobacco was an important crop in Fuzhou county and cotton was grown in Guanganzhou, Changshou, and Renshou counties. Migrants to Sichuan from Guangdong and Fujian also brought such cash crops as sugar cane and tobacco to Sichuan.[38] As early as the late Ming dynasty, the Pearl River Delta was renowned for its combination of agriculture, silk reeling, and pisciculture on reclaimed silt deposits. The proliferation of pisciculture combined with mulberry cultivation and silk weaving in the Pearl River Delta also meant less land devoted to grain.[39] In Guangdong, over three-quarters of the arable land in Shunde county was devoted to fruits. Similarly, Nanhai and Panyu counties were important producers of fruits such as lichees and "dragon eyes" (*longyan*). Dongguan county was famous for its jasmine and sugar cane. Zengcheng county, as well as Yingde county; Xuwen county; and Denghai county were also important centers for sugar cane cultivation in Guangdong. Also in Guangdong, Heshan county produced tobacco, while Sihui and Xinxing counties were known for their Mandarin oranges. Even the remote prefecture of Qiongzhou, present-day Hainan province, shipped betel nuts and coconuts throughout the province.[40]

36 XKTB 0755, QL 16 (month and day unknown).

37 XKTB 0803, QL 16 (month and day unknown).

38 Liu Zhenggang, p. 75, "Qingdai Sichuan Man Yue yimin de nongye shengchan" (The agricultural production of Fujian and Guangdong immigrants to Sichuan in the Qing)," *Zhongguo jingjishi yanjiu* (1996) 4: 71–9.

39 Gao Wangling, pp. 106–7, "Chuantong moshi di tupo Qingdai Guangdong nongye de jueqi" (Breaking the traditional mold: The rise of Qing-era Guangdong's agriculture), *Qingshi yanjiu* (1993) 3: 105–13.

40 Tang Sen and Li Longqian, pp. 9–10, "Ming Qing Guangdong Jingji zuowu di zhongzhi ji qi yiyi" (The cultivation of economic crops in Guangdong and its significance during the Ming and Qing), pp. 1–21 in *Ming Qing Guangdong shehui jingji xingtai yanjiu* (Research on the economic formation of society in Guangdong during the Ming and Qing), Guangdong History Institute, ed. (Guangdong: Renmin Chubanshe, 1985).

In Shandong, cotton cultivation, which had been common in the northern and western areas of Dongchang, Linqing, and Wuding prefectures, spread south and east in the Yellow River basin to Qidong, Zhangqiu, and Zouping counties; Gaofan and Boxing counties; and Putai and Lijin counties. Peanuts, soybeans, and tobacco were also important cash crops in Shandong.[41] The extension of the area under cultivation of cash crops meant that in many areas the amount of land planted in grains was shrinking and more peasants were dependent on the market for grain. For example, a clear indication of the growing demand for grain and the intensification of agriculture in Guangdong came in 1764, when local officials began reporting winter wheat harvests in addition to the early and late rice crops in Guangdong. Triple cropping was widespread in Guangdong, where approximately two-thirds of all counties reported winter harvests after 1764. Double cropping of rice and beans or wheat on the Chengdu plain in Sichuan was also common, and some farmers also planted triple crops of wheat, rice, and beans. Double cropping was also practiced in parts of Jiangsu, Anhui, Zhejiang, Hubei, and Hunan provinces.[42]

Rice Prices

According to Ramon Myers, after 1700 most prices rose "slowly and inexorably" throughout China.[43] Wang Yeh-chien has assembled an impressive array of grain price data that indicates that there were "few exceptions to the long inflationary trend in the eighteenth century."[44] Rice price information for Guangdong is particularly plentiful. As the graph in Figure 2–2 illustrates, over the course of the Qianlong reign (1736–95) the price of rice rose steadily in Guangdong.[45] The increase during the early years of the Qianlong reign actually was a con-

41 Ye Xian'en, 1991, p. 41.

42 Guo Songyi, pp. 24–5, "Qingqianqi nanfang dao zuo qu di liangshi shengchan" (Grain production of Southern paddy rice areas in the early Qing), *Zhongguo jingjishi yanjiu* (1994) 1: 1–31.

43 Ramon Myers, pp. 71–2, *The Chinese Economy: Past and Present* (Belmont, CA: Wadsworth Press, 1980).

44 Wang Yeh-chien, p. 51, "Secular Trends of Rice Prices in the Yangzi Delta, 1638–1935," pp. 35–68 in *Chinese History in Economic Perspective*, T. Rawski and L. Li, eds. (Berkeley: University of California Press, 1992).

45 Chen Chunsheng, Chapter 4, Table 4.1, "Qingdai Qianlong nianjian Guangdong di mi jia he miliang maoyi" (Rice prices and trade in Guangdong during the Qianlong years), unpublished M.A. thesis, Zhongshan University, Department of History, 1984.

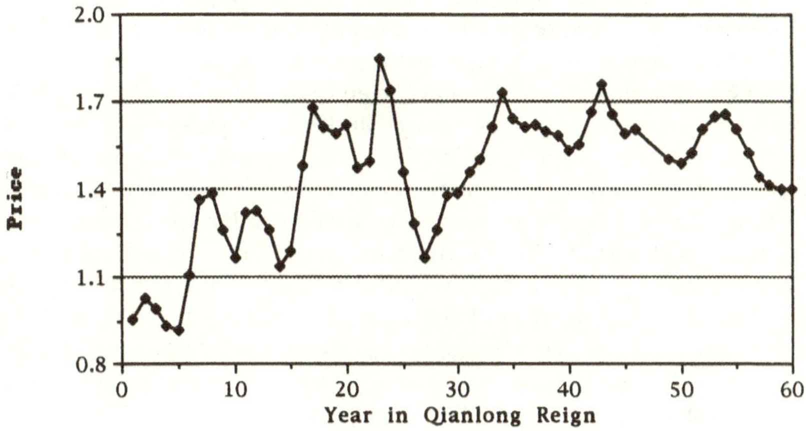

Figure 2–2 Average Price[a] of Rice in Guangdong
[a]Price in ounces of silver per *shi* of grain.

tinuation of a rise that began several years earlier. Price data for the Yongzheng reign (1723–35) indicate that prices were significantly lower. For example, in 1730, the eighth year of the Yongzheng reign, the average price of rice in Guangdong was .56 *taels* per *shi.*[46] Eleven years later, in 1741, the sixth year of the Qianlong reign, the price had doubled to 1.1 *tael.* The overall trend in rice was clearly upward, but here were significant fluctuations in prices and regional variation, which the broader trends based on average prices conceals.

Based on their extensive research on rice prices in Guangdong, Robert Marks and Chen Chunsheng have divided the eighteenth century into three periods: 1) 1707–31, 2) 1731–58, and 3) 1762–1800.[47] During the first period, prices were "virtually trendless" and were characterized by sharp fluctuations that were due to bad weather. A linear increase of 1.2% per annum occurred during the second period and aroused the concern of provincial officials. The third period witnessed a slow, steady increase after a sharp drop-off from the 1758 peak.

46 Chuan Han-sheng and Richard Kraus, p. 57, *Mid-Ch'ing Rice Markets and Trade* (Cambridge, MA: Harvard University, East Asian Research Center, 1975). Chuan and Kraus, as well as Myers, 1980, also noted that although prices were lower during the Yongzheng reign, they tended to fluctuate more sharply.

47 Robert B. Marks and Chen Chunsheng, "Price Inflation and Its Social, Economic and Climatic Context in Guangdong, 1707–1800," *T'oung pao* (1995) 81.1: 109–52.

This trend continued until the late 1770s when prices declined gradually. Overall prices were much more stable in the third period.[48] Marks and Chen analyzed the long-term trends of rice prices based on five factors: 1) population growth and the amount of cultivated land; 2) the monetary system; 3) climatic change and harvest yields; 4) state intervention in food supply and markets via the state-managed granary system; and 5) the development of an integrated market for rice as factors to explain price behavior. To briefly summarize some findings relevant to this study, Marks and Chen state that the annual rate of increase in rice prices was less than the rate of population growth despite the fact that cultivated land increased by only 10 to 20%, and the amount of land devoted to commercial cash increased steadily.[49] Not surprisingly, climatic change and harvest yields were important factors explaining rice price trends. Most importantly, Marks and Chen found that the price stability from 1762–1800 was coincident with an increase in the money supply and the development of an integrated market for rice centered on Guangzhou.[50] All evidence points to an increasingly sophisticated and stable marketing structure in Guangdong. This analysis of long-term trends in rice prices and the development of an integrated market for rice also has important implications for understanding the temporal and geographic pattern of violent disputes over property rights in Guangdong that I will address in Chapter 5.

Inflation in rice prices was troubling to officials at all levels of government, and various measures were taken to remedy the situation. In an effort to ensure supply, exports of rice from Guangdong were banned outright as early as the Kangxi reign (1661–1722). Siam (now Thailand) and Annam (now Vietnam) became important sources of rice imports during the Qianlong reign (1736–95) and the government provided incentives to increase imports.[51] For example, in 1741 Chinese merchants who imported large quantities of rice from Siam, where rice sold for .35 to .4 *taels* per *shi* in 1743, were exempted from taxation.[52] Another statute granted minor degrees (*jiansheng*) to merchants who imported 2,000 *shi* or more of grain from Siam. For example, in 1763 a merchant named Huang Mingxun received a degree for importing

48 Ibid., pp. 111–12. 49 Ibid., pp. 114–18. 50 Ibid., p. 150.

51 See Chen Chunsheng, 1984, pp. 19–21. According to Chen, Jiangxi, Hunan, and Fujian provinces also exported grain to Guangdong, but the Guangxi trade, which was organized by merchants from Guangdong, was by far the most important source.

52 Li Pengnian, pp. 85–6, "Luelun Qianlong nianjian cong Xianluo yun mi jinkou" (A brief account of the importation of rice from Siam in the reign of the Qing emperor Qianlong), *Lishi dangan* (1985) 3: 83–90.

2,869.8 *shi* of grain from Siam, after local officials assured the emperor that Huang had not engaged in hoarding or profiteering.[53] In Guangdong, as well as other provinces, the establishment of "ever-normal" granaries was another measure aimed in part at stabilizing grain prices. The history of the granary system throughout China has been well documented.[54] Research for Guangdong province reveals that by the 1760s officials in Guangdong kept silver on hand, relying on the market to purchase grain when needed, rather than storing large amounts of rice.[55]

Concerned with the steady increase in rice prices, which occurred even during years of bumper harvests, the Qianlong emperor ordered provincial officials to determine the reasons for rising rice prices. Noting the physical limitations of agricultural expansion, the governor of Hunan expressed the widely held belief that the steady rise in the price of rice was an "inevitable" consequence of a "rapidly increasing population."[56] Undoubtedly, burgeoning populations in general and larger nonagricultural populations dependent on the market for grain pushed prices up, but that was only part of the answer. The commercialization of agriculture was another factor placing upward pressure on rice prices. As previously noted, in many areas of Guangdong it was much more profitable to plant cash crops. In fact, according to estimates made by Chen Chunsheng, a major reason that Guangdong had become a grain-deficit region prior to experiencing the full effects of the demographic expansion of the eighteenth century was because one-third to one-half of all arable land was being planted in specialty or commercial crops.[57] Despite the shift in cropping patterns, however, provincial officials often associated rising prices with growing population pressure on land.

Population Growth during the Eighteenth Century

Population grew steadily after the consolidation of Qing rule in the late seventeenth century. According to Ho Ping-ti's classic study, China's

53 Huke Tiben nongye lei (hereafter HKTB), 0046, QL 29.2.18.

54 See Pierre-Etienne Will and R. Bin Wong, Chapter 1, *Nourish the People: The State Civilian Granary System in China, 1650–1850* (Ann Arbor: University of Michigan, Center for Chinese Studies, 1992).

55 Robert B. Marks, 1998, p. 248.

56 Ho Ping-ti, p. 268.

57 Chen Chunsheng, 1984, p. 15.

total population had reached 313 million in 1794.[58] Unfortunately, national or provincial level estimates of population data for the eighteenth century have limited usefulness for this study since the unit of analysis for property-rights disputes is the county (*xian*). Conceivably one might attempt to estimate county-level population, but provincial officials compiled county-level population figures using household registration (*baojia*) records, most of which have not survived. Although a recent reexamination of Qing population history suggests that limitations on the government's capability to compile accurate population data during the late Ming may have exaggerated the dramatic shifts during the transition from Ming to Qing,[59] most historians would agree that nationwide, population had roughly doubled by the end of the eighteenth century. Data problems notwithstanding, it is clear that the Chinese population had reached unprecedented levels during the Qianlong reign.

The demographic recovery of the eighteenth century has usually been attributed to peace and political stability. In his study of government administration and population growth in Imperial China from the third century B.C. to the Qing dynasty, Linong Zhou found a "close correlation" between population growth and improved government administration of relief and welfare, which the Qing government handled with "sophistication."[60] Other historians have cited stable agricultural output due to global warming from 1680–1820, and evidence of early marriages and thus increased fertility as contributing factors.[61] While China was nowhere near a Malthusian crisis (a point I will address further), by the late eighteenth century contemporary observers – such as Hong Liangji,[62] an official and insightful commentator on social and political matters – expressed their growing concerns about the unprecedented population growth. Hong noted that the potential consequences of an unlimited increase in population included a reduction

58 Ping-ti Ho, p. 281. Dwight Perkins estimates the total population at 100–150 million in 1650, 200–250 million in 1750, and 410 million (+/–25 million) in 1850. See Dwight Perkins, p. 216, *Agricultural Development in China (1368–1968)* (Chicago: Aldine Publishing Co., 1969).

59 William Lavely and R. Bin Wong, pp. 738–9, "Revising the Malthusian Narrative: The Comparative Study of Population Dynamics in Late Imperial China," *Journal of Asian Studies* (August 1998) 57.3: 714–48.

60 Linong Zhou, p. 228, "Effects of Government Intervention on Population Growth in Imperial China," *Journal of Family History* (1993) 18.3: 213–30.

61 See Xianen Ye, 1991, p. 35, for global warming, and Zhou Zuoshao, p. 62, "Qingdai qianqi renkou wenti yanjiu lunlue" (Brief discussion of research on population question in the early Qing period), *Ming Qing shi* (1997) 2: 59–64, for early marriages.

62 Despite the fact that Hong Liangqi's writings (1746–1809) predated those of Thomas Malthus (1766–1824) by several years, he has been known as the "Chinese Malthus."

in per capita income; an unequal distribution of wealth; and rising prices. Hong maintained that the government could alleviate the hardships of a burgeoning population by opening virgin land and facilitating migration; lowering taxes; exhorting the people to utilize their energy and cultivate their lands to the fullest; prohibiting luxurious living; and equalizing the acquisition of wealth.[63]

Based on my reading of Ministry of Revenue routine memorials from provincial officials, many officials shared Hong's views regarding the potential effects of population growth. However, despite statements by Qing officials, which advocated the equalization of wealth, I have found no evidence of efforts to redistribute land or other property. As for taxes, the Kangxi emperor had frozen the land tax decades earlier and there were no further reductions in the land tax during the eighteenth century. In fact, Kangxi's tax policy may have encouraged population growth. According to Dai Yi, the elimination of the poll tax and the shifting of the tax base to land in 1723 removed any tax penalty on having children.[64] For what it was worth, there was no shortage of official exhortation for people to work harder. Ultimately, government initiatives to promote land reclamation and to facilitate migration were the most significant and far-reaching responses to population growth during the eighteenth century. In fact, such initiatives were not new, in one form or another they had been a central component of Qing policy since the dynasty had been established.

Land Reclamation during the Early Qing, 1644–99

In the waning years of the Ming dynasty, peasant uprisings engulfed large areas of the empire. Many people lost their lives, and still more were left homeless and bereft of the means to resume farming. According to one estimate, only 30% of the land under cultivation during the reign of the Ming emperor Wanli (1573–1619) was being tilled in 1651 during the Shunzhi emperor's reign (1644–61).[65] The Qing government acted promptly and initiated a series of measures designed to alleviate economic distress and restore the government's fiscal base.

63 See C. F. Lung, "A Note on Hung Liang-chi the Chinese Malthus," *Tien Hsia Monthly* (October 1935) pp. 248–50.

64 Dai Yi, p. 2, "Jindai Zhongguo renkou di zengzhang he qianxi" (Increase and migration of modern China's population), *Qing shi yanjiu* (1996) 1: 1–8.

65 Jiang Taixin and Duan Xueyu, p. 47, "Lun Qingdai qianqi tudi kentuo dui shehui jingji fazhan di yingxiang" (Discussion of the influence of land reclamation on socioeconomic development in the early Qing period), *Zhongguo jingjishi yanjiu* (1996) 1: 47–62.

Abandoned land, which fell into two categories – "abandoned lands without owners" (*wuzhu huangdi*) and "abandoned lands with owners" (*youzhu huangdi*) – was a critical problem. For example, a survey of nine prefectures in Shaanxi Province revealed that 80% of the land was abandoned.[66] In 1644, the Shunzhi emperor issued an edict that allowed dislocated peasants to till "ownerless" land, and provided material assistance and tax breaks to landlords to encourage them to find new tenants. In 1649, another edict allowed dislocated peasants to take permanent possession of ownerless land and to be enrolled in the local *baojia* register.[67]

Warfare continued through most of the Shunzhi reign. Consequently, efforts to stimulate land reclamation, while extensive, were uneven, and policy changed quickly in response to fiscal exigencies. In 1650, land reclamation became a criterion for evaluating the performance of bureaucrats at the provincial level and below. Honors, rewards, and promotions were granted to officials based on the amount of land reopened in their jurisdictions. In 1653, a brief effort was made to use the military to till abandoned fields. While this practice had a long history in border regions, it proved ineffective elsewhere and was abandoned after only three years. In 1656, the government provided funds for seeds, tools, and draught animals to peasants and landlords as an incentive to open more land. In 1657, the government adopted an expanded system of rewards, which included grants of official rank, for landlords who restored large amounts of land to cultivation.[68] Given the uncertainty surrounding government policy, particularly in the case of tax breaks and remissions, many peasants and landlords remained cautious in their efforts to reclaim land during the early years of the Qing.

Historically, tax remission was a form of disaster relief, but during the Qing dynasty tax remissions were also used to stimulate economic recovery. Some historians have argued that in addition to economic considerations, Qing emperors also saw tax remissions as a means to alleviate class and ethnic tensions. According to this argument, the Manchu Qing rulers employed tax remissions to win the support of the Han Chinese landlord classes. The same historians have maintained that the Kangxi emperor's 1710 edict, which ordered that rents should be reduced in

66 Peng Yuxin, p. 6, *Qingdai tudi kaiken shi* (The history of land reclamation in the Qing era), (Beijing: Nongye Chubanshe, 1990).
67 Guo Songyi, 1980, p. 116.
68 Ibid., pp. 115–33.

accord with tax concessions, indicated that the government was also concerned with reducing class tensions between tenants and landlords. These historians concluded that tax remissions were beneficial because they reduced class and ethnic tensions and, to the extent that they left more capital in the hands of agricultural producers, they also represented a form of investment in the productive power of the traditional economy.[69] Whatever interpretation one prefers, tax remission policies clearly had political as well as economic motivations.

After the subjugation of Taiwan in 1683, the Kangxi emperor (1662–1722) effectively completed the establishment of Qing rule over China. Under these conditions, efforts to revive agriculture were more consistent. With the economy more stable and fewer demands on the imperial treasury, the Kangxi emperor extended tax concessions on newly reopened land to three, six, or ten years depending on the region and quality of the land. Kangxi also supplied more funds for seeds, tools, and the repair of irrigation systems. These efforts apparently succeeded. By 1716, provincial officials no longer emphasized dislocated peasants and abandoned lands as serious problems. Although the Kangxi emperor's policies on land reclamation were effective, they had an unforeseen consequence. Tax concessions created opportunities for tax evasion and the Kangxi emperor, whose reputation for benevolence arose in part from his generous grants of tax remissions, was unwilling to deal sternly with officials who failed to meet tax quotas. Rejecting a system of strict rewards and punishments, the Kangxi emperor opted for "gentle persuasion" and limited his actions to moral exhortations.[70] His successor, the Yongzheng emperor (1723–35), however, came to power determined to address the problem more forcefully.

Hidden Land

As the agrarian economy recovered, a new issue attracted the attention of the Chinese government. The problem of "hidden land" (*yindi*), which referred to reclaimed lands that were not reported to the central government for taxation, was apparent as early as 1712. Hidden lands included both small plots of land that peasants had reclaimed but had

69 Hu Chunfan, Hua Yu, Huang Shiqing, and Wen Ji, pp. 155–65, "Shilun Qing qianqi di juanmian zhengze" (Preliminary discussion of tax remission policy in the early Qing), in *Qingshi yanjiu ji* 3: 150–65, Chinese People's University, Qing History Research Center, ed. (Chengdu: Sichuan Renmin Chubanshe, 1984). Hu concluded that this policy also strengthened the "feudal economy," creating a greater obstacle to the development of capitalism.

70 Ibid., p. 24.

not reported to local officials, and land that had been reported to local officials but had not been reported to the central government by the local officials. In the latter case, local officials collected taxes and pocketed the receipts. Apparently, this problem was widespread. Some high-level officials complained that despite seventy years of Qing rule, tax collections were only 10% of those collected in the Ming.[71] These same officials called for harsh penalties and thorough investigations. Although the Kangxi emperor had ignored such pleas, when the Yongzheng emperor succeeded to the throne in 1723 fiscal reform was a top priority.

Yongzheng attacked corruption, took decisive steps to halt tax arrears, and attempted to rationalize fiscal administration.[72] In 1727, the emperor ordered the Ministry of Revenue to undertake a thorough investigation to determine the total amount of untaxed land under cultivation; to ascertain the amount of unused land available in the empire; and to update the tax rolls. Provincial officials carried out the investigations with some difficulty. The original edict of 1727 set a one-year deadline for the completion of this survey, but this proved unrealistic. In Guangdong alone, the emperor granted five separate one-year extensions.[73] To justify the extensions, provincial officials offered a variety of excuses, ranging from embezzlement by local officials to the stupidity of the people. In 1728, the Governor of Guangdong described four abuses in land reclamation and offered five suggestions for improvements. According to the Governor, the wealthy and powerful "local bullies" (*haoqiang*)[74] wrongly appropriated new lands; county clerks were corrupt; there was insufficient capital (*gongben*); and the quality of available land was too poor to support high tax rates. As a remedy, the governor suggested clarifying boundaries; halting harsh exactions; loaning seed to peasants; reducing tax rates; and offering further unspecified economic inducements to encourage reclamation.[75] As we shall see in an in-depth examination of land reclamation policy in Guangdong province, which will be the primary focus of my analysis of violent disputes, official concerns shifted throughout the Qianlong reign, but a perceived shortage of quality arable land remained the underlying concern.

71 Madeline Zelin, p. 23, *The Magistrate's Tael* (Berkeley: University of California Press, 1984).

72 Ibid., Chapter 3. 73 HKTB 69, QL 2.13.2.

74 The phrase most often used was *haoqiang*, a shortened form of *tuhao lieqiang*, which usually is translated as "local bullies."

75 *Qingshi gao jiaozhu* (Draft history of the Qing dynasty), Vol. 5, Sec. 127, p. 3,456 (Taipei: China Central Library, 1987).

Efforts to encourage land reclamation in Guangdong during the Qianlong reign can be traced through routine memorials to the Ministry of Revenue (*huke tiben*) and direct memorials to the emperor (*zhupi zouzhe*). Several overarching concerns of the officials were discernible in these documents. Tension between the need to open more land and ecological concerns; government concern for poor, land-hungry peasants; admonitions against the dominance of powerful and wealthy local bullies; and complaints about inept and corrupt officials at the local level permeated these reports. Based on the major concerns of government policy, four phases in the development of official policy toward land reclamation in Guangdong can be discerned.

Land Policy in Guangdong

Phase One: Taxation, 1727–41

In the second year of Qianlong's reign, 1738, the provincial governor of Guangdong reported the findings of a province-wide land survey to the Ministry of Revenue. According to this report, based on a survey completed in 1732, the twelfth year of the Yongzheng reign, there was a total of 685,092.8 *mu* of land in Guangdong that could be "readily reclaimed" (*keken*). All of this land had been included in the Ming land tax quota for the province, but it had fallen into disuse, or at least had "fallen" from the tax rolls, during the dynastic transition. In addition, there was also 2,268,187.2 *mu* of land that was "difficult to reclaim" (*nanken*). Apparently, this was land not included in the Ming tax quota because it had not previously been cultivated.[76] From 1732 through 1735, residents of Guangdong reclaimed 456,216.1 *mu* of land, which was part of the original tax quota for the province, but only 215,640.4 *mu* of difficult-to-reclaim land entered the tax rolls. At this point, land was still available, but it was inferior in quality. Tax evasion was the more serious problem during the early years of the Qianlong reign.

Concern about the recovery of taxes and frequent references to "hidden land" dominated Ministry of Revenue memorials.[77] With regard to taxation, land was frequently discussed in terms of whether or not it was within the original tax quota (*yuan'e*), which was based on a Ming dynasty land survey conducted in 1600.[78] With reference to the Ming tax rolls, land was broadly classified as "outside the original tax quota"

76 HKTB, 97, QL 3 (month and day unknown). 77 HKTB 69, QL 2.13.2.

78 Yeh-chien Wang, p. 22, *Land Taxation in Imperial China, 1750–1911* (Cambridge, MA: Harvard University Press, 1973).

(*e'wai*) or "within the original tax quota" (*e'nei*). Four types of land were distinguished: "quota land," military land (*tuntian*), difficult-to-reclaim land (*nanken*), and coastal and riverine silt deposits (*shatan*).[79] Quota land referred to all land that had been rated for taxation during the Ming but was currently untaxed (except for lands turned over to military control during the Kangxi reign). Quota land was higher-quality arable land that had been abandoned during the dynastic transition or in some way had slipped from the tax rolls. This land was distinguished from the other types because it had been cultivated and rated for taxation in the past, and could be returned to cultivation easily without much investment. Apparently, in the case of quota land the real problem was tax evasion, not reclamation. Tax evaders were granted amnesty if they voluntarily reported "hidden" land. But since the quality of quota land was high, no special tax incentives were recommended for farmers who brought quota land under cultivation.

For military land, difficult-to-reclaim land, and coastal and riverine silt deposits, officials did suggest some forms of tax relief. For example, tax abatements were recommended for military land, which was coastal land that had been evacuated as part of the Kangxi emperor's coastal pacification policy from 1661–68.[80] After this policy was rescinded, civilians began to reoccupy these areas. Tax abatement was necessary because these lands required substantial investment, particularly to refurbish dikes.[81] Difficult-to-reclaim land included hilly, sandy, and salty lands that had never before been cultivated. A lower tax rate was recommended for this type of land. Finally, *shatan*, coastal and riverine silt deposits or bottom land, was another important category of land that had been outside the original tax quota. *Shatan* was not eligible for lower tax rates; but in recognition of the labor required to bring *shatan* under cultivation, there was an extended grace period before taxation began. This type of land was most prevalent in the six counties – Nanhai, Panyu, Xiangshan, Dongguan, Shunde, and Xinhui – located in the Pearl River Delta.

Although provincial officials made other desultory comments on

79 In modern times, this type of land is referred to as *shatian*, literally "sand field." In eighteenth-century documents, however, this type of land is referred to as *shatan*, literally "sand embankment."

80 HKTB, 97, QL 3.4.7.

81 Under the coastal pacification policy, residents were forced to evacuate their land to eliminate support for pirates and Ming loyalists based in Taiwan. Ye Xianen and Tan Dihua, p. 51, "Lun Zhujiang sanjiaozhou di zutian" (On clan land in the Pearl River Delta), pp. 22–64 in *Ming Qing Guangdong shehui jingji xingtai yanjiu* (Research on the economic formation of society in Guangdong during the Ming and Qing), Guangdong History Institute, ed. (Guangdong: Guangdong Renmin Chubanshe, 1985).

a variety of issues, such as competing claims to land and local corruption, the overriding concern expressed in reports of this period was taxation and fiscal accounting. The emphasis was clearly on improving administration. The warning signs of a burgeoning population such as the upward spiral of rice prices that was just beginning in the early 1740s, were not serious enough to turn official attention away from taxation.

Phase Two: Encouragement of Reclamation, 1742–73

As early as 1728, some provincial officials had expressed concern about Guangdong's expanding population. Contemporary observers also noted the unequal distribution of Guangdong's population. In 1728, the Governor of Guangdong suggested that residents of eastern Guangdong's Huizhou and Chaozhou prefectures should be urged to reclaim land in the western prefectures of Zhaoqing, Gaozhou, Lianzhoufu, and Leizhou. Furthermore, because land in these areas was difficult to reclaim, he thought the government should supply financial support and tax breaks.[82] Approximately ten years later, the Secretary of the Ministry of Revenue Hai Wang, citing the overcrowding in Huizhou and Chaozhou prefectures, requested funds to sponsor land reclamation in Gaozhou, Leizhou, and Lianzhoufu.[83] Nevertheless, it took several more years before the need to encourage reclamation took priority over tax collection.

The agrarian economy of Guangdong had reached an important turning point early in the Qianlong reign. In 1742, the governor of Guangdong, Wang Anguo, memorialized to request a tax exemption for all "miscellaneous" (*lingxing*) small plots of land on hillsides and in sandy soil.[84] Governor Wang reported that population was "increasing daily" and that there was a need to assist poor people. The proposed exemption was only to apply to poor-quality land that was difficult to till. Governor Wang pointed out that this type of land was not suitable for growing grain, but could be used for potatoes, tobacco, sugar cane, and other crops. The output would not amount to much, but it would mean a little more income for the "common people" (*baixing*). According to the report, the quality of the land was so poor that taxation would be an unfair burden and a disincentive to reclamation. The rationale for the request was to provide relief to poor people, and the exemption was

82 *Qingshi gao jiaozhu*, p. 3,456.

83 HKTB, 67, QL 2.4.12. 84 HKTB, 56, QL 6.7.17.

only to apply to poor-quality land. Governor Wang's arguments proved persuasive, and the emperor approved the tax exemption.[85]

Easily accessible, arable land was clearly in short supply in Guangdong by this time, and the provincial government was concerned. The policy of tax exemption was further extended during this period in an effort to open new lands and encourage migration. In 1752, the Governor General of Guangdong and Guangxi, Chen Dashou, informed the emperor that there was a lot of unused land of poorer quality in Gaozhou, Leizhou, and Lianzhoufu prefectures.[86] The Governor General reported that residents of Huizhou, Chaozhou, and Jiaying, the more populous prefectures of eastern Guangdong, had been invited to resettle there.[87] According to a survey conducted in 1749, there were 75,782 *mu* available in the western prefectures. In a subsequent memorial, Governor General Chen reported that 67,988 *mu* had been reclaimed. In 1760, then Governor General Li Shiyao reported tax exemptions for land reclaimed in Nanxiong and Shaozhou prefectures in northern Guangdong. According to Governor General Li, this poorer quality land was suitable only for potatoes, paulownia, and tea.[88]

Tax exemptions were not the only incentives used to encourage land reclamation. In 1758, the Governor General of Guangdong, Yang Yingju, reported on the situation in Qinzhou county in Lianzhoufu. In 1756, there were 3,151.5 *mu* of land available in Qinzhou. However, local residents did not have the means to reclaim it. According to Governor General Yang, a local official personally raised funds and the local peasants supplied the necessary strength to reclaim the land. The local government collected rent at a rate of .7 *shi* per *mu* of land, for a total return of 2,206 *shi* annually. Similar arrangements were in place in Shicheng and Huazhou counties in Gaozhou prefecture.[89]

Phase Three: Prohibition on Shatan, 1774–85

Shatan, land formed from silt deposits that collected in coastal areas at the mouths of rivers or along riverbanks, was the most important source of new land in Guangdong throughout the Qianlong period. Contemporary accounts indicate that *shatan* was difficult to reclaim, and com-

85 HKTB 56, QL 6.7.17.

86 Guangdong has two prefectures that in pinyin are rendered *Lianzhou.* In order to distinguish them in English, I will refer to the far western prefecture as Lianzhoufu.

87 ZPZZ 19, QL 16.2.15.

88 ZPZZ 33, QL 24.3.28.

89 ZPZZ 24, QL 22.7.17.

peting claims to newly formed *shatan* frequently led to lawsuits.[90] According to regulations on setting boundaries, when the outlines of the *shatan* first "appeared," the boundaries should be delineated by markers. After the water receded from the land and dikes were constructed, the claimant was required to report the claim to the local officials and to put up an announcement stating the name of the area and the size of the plot. After a month, the local magistrate would personally measure the land and inform the local constable (*dibao*) and owners of adjacent land. If the claim was legitimate and did not encroach upon neighboring fields, then the magistrate would set the boundaries and register the owner's name, amount of land, and tax liability. The new owner received a deed (*shouzhi*), and the land became his permanent property. Anyone who made a counterclaim after land was registered would be severely punished.[91]

Policy toward *shatan* also serves to illustrate the government's social concerns. As early as 1739, officials complained that wealthy families (*haojia*) and great clans (*dazu*) were monopolizing control of *shatan*. The Secretary of the Ministry of Revenue recommended limiting wealthy families and great clans to 1,000 *mu* of *shatan*. "Little people" (*xiaomin*) would be allowed to take up to 500 *mu* of "child" fields adjacent to the fields of wealthy families.[92] (Child fields were silt deposits that accumulated along the embankments of enclosed *shatan*.) According to Fu Tongqin, tenant seizures of child fields were common.[93] Although there is no evidence that officials successfully enforced these limitations, concern over the unequal distribution of *shatan* was a recurrent theme in official communications.

Surprisingly, given the fact that provincial officials often complained about the number of lawsuits that disputes over *shatan* caused, this type of land accounted for only four homicides related to disputes over property rights in Guangdong. The fact that the *shatan* was "virgin" land to which no one had any prior claims might explain the lack of violence. Or it may have been due to the fact that the government instituted elab-

90 Yang Guozhen, Chapter 7, *Ming Qing tudi qiyue wenshu yanjiu* (Research on Ming-Qing period land contracts), (Beijing: Renmin Chubanshe, 1988). Many of the contracts that Yang compiled for Guangdong were for *shatan* that were the subject of legal disputes.

91 HKTB 0097, QL 3.4.7. 92 Ibid.

93 Fu Tongqin, pp. 69–71, "Ming Qing shiqi di Guangdong shatian" (Bottom land [shatian] in Guangdong during the Ming and Qing periods), pp. 65–74 in *Ming Qing Guangdong shehui jingji xingtai yanjiu* (Research on the economic formation of society in Guangdong during the Ming and Qing), Guangdong History Institute, ed. (Guangdong: Renmin Chubanshe, 1985).

Table 2–1. *Homicides Involving* Shatan *in Guangdong*

Year	Location
1745	Xinhui, Guangzhou[a]
1750	Guishan, Huizhou[b]
1750	Changle, Jiaying[c]
1786	Qingyuan, Guangzhou[d]

[a]XKTB 0476, QL 10.2.2.
[b]XKTB 0717, QL 15.2.12.
[c]XKTB 0736, QL 15.1.24.
[d]XKTB 3540, QL 51.5.12.

orate procedures for establishing a claim to this type of land. Alternatively, the "sand offices" that large lineages established to organize reclamation efforts, collect rents, and protect claims may have served to limit small-scale disputes, though they did provide the potential for larger-scale mobilization for defensive and offensive purposes in the nineteenth century.[94] In fact, there were only four homicides related to disputes over *shatan* in this sample, and in the Pearl River Delta, where *shatan* were most common, there were very few homicides related to disputes over land. By comparison, disputes over reclaimed land other than *shatan* accounted for fourteen disputes in Guangdong. Regardless of the type of land, however, only eighteen cases, less than 5% of all disputes in Guangdong province, involved recently reclaimed land of any type. (See Table 2–1.)

Despite the earlier enthusiasm for reclamation of *shatan*, by 1774 government officials were expressing ecological concerns. In Guangdong and other provinces, the construction of embankments necessary to reclaim *shatan* sometimes interfered with the natural drainage of rivers.[95] The problem became so severe that Li Shiyao, Governor General of Guangdong, prohibited the construction of *shatan* that blocked waterways. This prohibition remained in effect for twelve years. Judging from

94 Frederic Wakeman, Jr., p. 159, *Strangers at the Gate* (Berkeley: University of California Press, 1966).

95 Peter Perdue, pp. 219–32. According to Perdue, excessive dike building in Hunan during the mid-eighteenth century led to official action to destroy illegal dikes.

the comments in subsequent memorials, overzealous bureaucrats took this prohibition to heart and refused to issue permits for any *shatan*, regardless of its location. It was not long, however, before the ban was rescinded in response to revived official concern for the shortage of arable land and the social consequences of population pressure.

Phase Four: Return to Promotion of Reclamation, 1786

In 1786, the Governor of Guangdong, Sun Shiyi, requested that the ban on reclaiming *shatan* be lifted. Sun began his argument by noting Guangdong's dependence on Guangxi for grain and the lack of arable land, which comprised only 30% of the total area of the province. Surveys that Sun ordered revealed that *shatan* in the six counties of Nanhai, Panyu, Xiangshan, Dongguan, Shunde, and Xinhui did not block waterways or obstruct drainage. The evils traceable to the ban on reclaiming *shatan*, however, were quite serious. According to Sun, good people naturally feared the law and refrained from constructing *shatan*, but the powerful (*haoqiang*) monopolized the land and resorted to violence to make their claims. Officials had failed to explain the ban adequately, and this caused confusion. Some merchants conspired with salt workers to open *shatan* using the pretext that they were building salt flats. Lower-level officials were corrupt and received bribes. Governor Sun feared that if the ban were not lifted, people would abandon the land, creating a haven for bandits. Some good people might even resort to banditry themselves. If, however, the poor were allowed to obtain the benefits of opening the land, it would destroy the breeding grounds for bandits and deter pirates.[96] By raising the issue of banditry, Sun heightened the sense of urgency and added a new twist to the old argument in support of protecting the "little people."

According to one historian, reports of new land dropped off dramatically once the Ming quotas were reached because local officials did not wish to incur the ill will of their constituents by raising their tax burden, and the exemption of miscellaneous lands provided a convenient cover for not reporting new lands.[97] New land was reported in Guangdong throughout the Qianlong period, though most of this land was either poor in quality or *shatan*, which required a great deal of investment of capital and labor before it could be made cultivable and was located in a handful of counties along the coast or near river deltas. In the latter half of the eighteenth century, quality arable land in Guangdong province was at a premium. The figure of 685,092.8 *mu* cited in the

96 ZPZZ 101, QL 50.8.18. 97 Yeh-chien Wang, p. 22, 1973.

land survey completed in 1732 was land that had been tilled in the past but had subsequently fallen into disuse during the Ming-Qing transition. By 1735, 456,216.1 *mu* of this land were back on the tax rolls, and most of the remainder was reclaimed by 1742.[98] Once the Ming-level tax quotas were reached, the urgency expressed over reporting hidden lands abated and there was relatively little new high-quality land reported after 1751. There simply were no new sources of high-quality arable land left in the province. Land reclamation alone could not solve the problems of China's burgeoning population, and by 1793 the Qianlong emperor was again expressing concern over population pressure on the land.[99]

The situation in Sichuan and Shandong was similar to that of Guangdong in one important respect: The reclamation of high-quality arable land virtually ended by the early Qianlong reign. Sichuan province was arguably among the most devastated provinces during the Ming-Qing transition in large part due to the late-Ming peasant uprising led by Zhang Xianzhong, which contributed to toppling the Ming in the early seventeenth century. The Qing rulers actively promoted, and financially and materially supported, the resettlement of Sichuan. This resettlement will be discussed in detail in Chapter 6. For now it is sufficient to note that the resettlement of Sichuan was so successful that by the early Qianlong reign the governor of Sichuan requested a halt to government efforts to encourage migration to Sichuan because there was no longer land available for reclamation.[100] Similarly, in Shandong over 2,000,078 *mu* were reclaimed from the Kangxi (1661–1722) to the Jiaqing reign (1796–1820), but fully 1,600,606 *mu* (80% of the total) were reported prior to the Qianlong reign.[101] Evidence from Guangdong, Sichuan, and Shandong provinces reveals that the ongoing efforts by the Qing government to promote land reclamation had succeeded. By the end of the eighteenth century, there were no new sources of high-quality arable land left to exploit.

Malthusian Crisis?

During the eighteenth century, most of China witnessed a slow but steady increase in population, and new sources of high-quality arable

98 HKTB 56, QL 6.7.17.

99 Xing Long, p. 53, "Renkou yali yu Qing zhongye shehui maodun" (Population pressure and social contradictions in the mid-Qing), *Zhongguo shi yanjiu* (1992) 4: 51–8.

100 Peng Yuxin, p. 389, *Qingdai tudi kaiken shi ziliao huibian* (Compilation of materials on the history of land reclamation in the Qing era), (Wuhan: Wuhan Daxue Chubanshe, 1992).

101 Ibid., pp. 300–1.

land were in short supply by the end of the century. Arable land per capita was undoubtedly falling, but at what rate? Given the difficulty of calculating data on population and arable land, it is not surprising that estimates of land per capita vary among historians. According to Fan Shuzhi, per capita arable land was 5.98 *mu* in 1675, 3.75 in 1766, and 1.78 in 1859.[102] Other historians give figures of 4 *mu* per capita for 1753 and 2.6 for 1784;[103] 3.53 *mu* per capita for 1766 and 2.09 for 1820;[104] and 4.82 *mu* per capita for 1724 and 3.42 for 1784.[105] The decline seems steep, and it is possible that increased productivity offset smaller plot sizes during the eighteenth century,[106] but these estimates indicate that the trend in land per capita was steadily decreasing from the eighteenth century to the nineteenth century.

Were land values affected? Systematic data on land prices do not exist, but several scholars have attempted to reconstruct them. Li Wenzhi has estimated that land values were ten times higher in the Qianlong reign (1736–95) compared to the Kangxi reign (1661–1722) due to population increases and improved productivity of land.[107] Rents were also on the rise, but, according to Li, land prices were increasing faster than rents due to a "craze" to "chase land" by officials and wealthy merchants who stored their wealth in the traditional safe haven, land. Based on records of land purchases by lineages, Kang Chao has found that land prices in Zhejiang and Jiangxi were relatively stable until 1750, when prices began rising.[108] Also, as noted in Chapter 1, Chao found evidence of greater fragmentation of land holdings, as land owners were only willing to sell small portions of their increasingly precious resource. Based on data for Jiangsu province, Fang Xing found land prices increasing nearly tenfold from the Kangxi reign (1662–1722) to Jiaqing reign (1796–1821) in Zhejiang.[109] All the available qualitative data point to rising land values during the eighteenth century.

Although population continued to grow while new sources of high-quality arable land were increasingly hard to find throughout the eigh-

102 Fan Shuzhi, p. 133.
103 Xing Long, p. 53. 104 Zhou Zuoshao, p. 61.
105 Ye Xian'en, 1991, p. 35.
106 According to Li Bozhong, this was the case for Jiangnan in the eighteenth century. See Li Bozhong, Chapter 7.
107 Li Wenzhi, p. 1, Lun Qingdai Yapianzhan qian dijia he goumai nian" (Discussion of land prices and amortization in the Qing era prior to the Opium War), *Zhongguo shehui jingji shi yanjiu* (1989) 2: 1–12.
108 Kang Chao, p. 730, "New Data on Land Ownership Patterns in Ming-Ch'ing China – A Research Note," *Journal of Asian Studies* (August 1981) 40.4: 719–34.
109 Xing Fang, 1996b, p. 44.

teenth century, it would be a serious mistake to suggest that China was on the verge of a Malthusian crisis in the eighteenth century. Recent research by William Lavely and R. Bin Wong has found "scant evidence that Chinese mortality rates in the late eighteenth and early nineteenth century exceeded those of agrarian Europe before the Industrial Revolution," and nutrition and living standards were not significantly lower nor were they declining in the early nineteenth century.[110] Commercialization and intensification of agriculture, and a government-sponsored program of land reclamation and migration, supported the economic prosperity and the unprecedented demographic expansion of the eighteenth century. All available evidence suggests that at the macro-level China enjoyed intensive economic growth during the eighteenth century. At the same time, this steady rise in population and growing commercial complexity also induced a demand for change in economic institutions and property rights. Rising prices for land, a burgeoning population, and the potential gains to be made from participation in a vibrant market economy provided potent incentives to refine and improve property rights in land. Indeed, the commercialization of the eighteenth century would not have been possible without changes in property rights and improvements in contracts that reduced transaction costs and facilitated exchange in an increasingly complex market economy.

At this point, it is important to place the commercialization of the eighteenth century in historical perspective. The commercialization of the Chinese economy was both a dynamic and transformative process. Depending on the historical circumstances, commercialization will affect various segments of society differently. As with all large-scale economic change, the social and private costs and benefits will not be distributed equally. As in the case of China, those segments of society that were hurt by the newly emerging structure of property rights, which commercialization generated in the eighteenth century, may have been beneficiaries of earlier periods of market expansion. To state the point simply, history matters. Thus, in order to understand the social consequences of economic change in the eighteenth century, we must briefly examine structure and change in the seventeenth-century economy.

Decline of Bonded Servitude in Agriculture

An important historical trend from the sixteenth to the eighteenth century was the gradual demise of bonded servitude in agriculture. For

110 Lavely, William, and R. Bin Wong, p. 738. They also argue that female infanticide was used to restrain fertility in response to economic conditions.

a number of reasons, commercialization has often been cited as a factor that encouraged landlords to abandon bonded servitude in favor of tenancy. During the Ming dynasty, bond servants, agricultural laborers, and tenant farmers who entered into a servile relationship with their masters, usually via a written bond or contract, comprised an important part of the agricultural workforce, which also included free tenants and long-term hired laborers.[111] Legally, bond servants were considered "base people" (*jianmin*) inferior to commoners (*liangmin*) and were punished more severely than commoners. Conversely, if a landlord beat a bond servant to death he was not subject to capital punishment.[112] During the sixteenth and seventeenth centuries, all tenants and hired laborers were subjected to varying degrees of extra-economic control. Bond servants may merely have represented the most extreme form of servile labor.

While bond servants clearly were socially and legally inferior to their master, in the late Ming a paternalistic moral code and the concept of "mutual assistance and support," which implied a reciprocal relationship, governed the relationship between master and bond servant.[113] Legally, only individuals of noble rank or members of the imperial family were allowed to keep bond servants. As early as 1387, the Ming legal code outlawed the use of servile labor by commoners.[114] Nevertheless, wealthy commoners, including large landowners and merchants, frequently "possessed" bond servants. One practice often employed to bypass legal restrictions was the adoption of "sons" and "sons-in-law" or the conversion of slaves to "hereditary servants."[115] In this way, bond

111 The extent of bonded servitude in the Ming remains an open question. For a succinct summary of the diverse opinions regarding bondservants, see Joseph P. McDermott, "Bondservants in the T'ai-hu Basin During the Late Ming: A Case of Mistaken Identities," *Journal of Asian Studies* (August 1981) 40.4: 675–718. McDermott discusses several important works in Chinese, Japanese, and English, including Fu Yiling's and Xie Guozhen's early work.

112 Li Wenzhi, p. 15, "Cong dichuan xingshi di bianhua kan Ming Qing shidai dizhuzhi jingji di fazhan" (A look at the development of the Ming-Qing era landlord controlled economy, from changes in the form of land rights), *Zhongguo shehui jingji shi yanjiu* (1991) 1: 12–22.

113 Mi Chu Wiens, pp. 304–5, "The Origins of Modern Chinese Landlordism," pp. 285–344 in *Festschrift in Honor of the Eightieth Birthday of Professor Shen Kang-pao* (Taipei: Lianjing shuju, 1976).

114 Mi Chu Wiens, 1980, p. 5.

115 Kang Chao, 1986, pp. 138–9. In some ways, this concept of family was similar to the Roman and Greek idea of the family of a household that included common descendants as well as all property and servants. See Moses I. Finley, pp. 17–19, *The Ancient Economy* (Berkeley: University of California Press, 1985).

servant status was often transmitted from father to son. There was a clear bifurcation of bond servants between those who served as managers, who sometimes amassed great wealth, and field workers, who, except for their servile status, resembled tenants.[116]

Extraeconomic control over bond servants was sometimes quite broad. Although bond servants paid rent, their service could be sold with land or separately. Tied to the land they tilled, bond servants also owed labor services, such as serving at weddings or funerals, and their marriages could be arranged by their masters.[117] While debts or economic hardship frequently forced free peasants into servitude, others became bond servants voluntarily in order to avoid taxation or in return for a bride.[118] Whatever historical significance one chooses to assign to bonded servitude, however, due to a variety of economic, social, and political factors discussed in the following text, the fact remains that bonded servitude in agriculture, a form of property rights in human beings, had almost completely disappeared by the eighteenth century.

The decline of bonded servitude over the course of the seventeenth century has been attributed to a variety of economic and demographic trends, Qing government policies, and the violent actions of bond servants. Improvements in the status of agricultural laborers during the late sixteenth and early seventeenth centuries in China arose from demographic conditions similar to those that occurred in Europe during the fourteenth century. In Europe, the Black Death, the effects of which were made more severe due to widespread malnutrition that resulted from a decline of agriculture, led to a sharp decline in population. This triggered a crisis in the feudal economy that, in some areas of western Europe, created a labor scarcity that forced landowners to make concessions to peasants.[119] Late Ming China also experienced several widespread and deadly epidemics of uncertain dimensions.[120] In terms of loss

116 Tanaka Masatoshi, pp. 192–3, "Popular Uprisings, Rent Resistance and Bondservant Rebellions in the Late Ming," pp. 165–214 in *State and Society in China*, Linda Grove and Christian Daniels, eds. (Tokyo: University of Tokyo Press, 1984). This distinction would seem to bolster the contention that the bondservant can best be understood as a legal status rather than an economic class. See also McDermott, p. 677.

117 Han Hengyu, pp. 90–4, "Luelun Qingdai qianqi di dianpu zhi" (An observation on servile tenancy in the early Qing), pp. 89–110 in *Qingshi luncong* (Symposium on Qing history) 2, Chinese Academy of Social Sciences, History Research Institute, ed. (Beijing: Zhonghua shuju, 1980).

118 McDermott, pp. 681–5.

119 Maurice Dobb, pp. 48–51, *Studies in the Development of Capitalism* (New York: International Publishers, 1963). See also North and Thomas, p. 73.

120 See Helen Dunstan, "The Late Ming Epidemics: A Preliminary Survey," *Ch'ing shih wen-t'i* (1975) 3.3: 1–59, and Mark Elvin, 1973, pp. 308–9.

of life, this period has been compared to the devastation of the Taiping Rebellion in the nineteenth century. Estimates of the decline in population in affected areas range from 30 to 40% for the epidemics of 1588 and 1641, respectively.[121] According to one estimate, China's population did not recover to the Ming peak of 150 million in 1600 until at least 1700.[122] These natural disasters, coupled with the casualties of the peasant uprisings and warfare during the dynastic transition, clearly had a devastating impact.

Commercialization has often been cited as another factor that encouraged landlords to abandon bonded servitude in favor of tenancy. The influx of New World silver during the Ming facilitated the monetization of the economy and paved the way for the Single Whip fiscal reforms. The Single Whip reforms commuted labor services to a poll tax paid in silver. The elimination of corvée levies meant that government officials needed to purchase labor services. This, in effect, created a market for labor services that provided new opportunities for individuals who formerly may have entered bonded servitude. In this way, labor had also become a commodity.

Another result of commercialization was the exodus of many landowners from the countryside to the cities, drawn by the amenities and economic opportunities of urban life. Farming with bond servants, which was usually based on share rents, required a high degree of supervision. The movement of landowners to the city made direct supervision of agriculture difficult and more costly. As a result, many landlords were willing to relinquish their direct control over production in return for fixed rents. Tenants were willing to accept, and sometimes even demanded, fixed rents, because it meant they could more easily capture the gains from future improvements and intensification of agriculture.[123] Consequently, sociomoral relationships between landlords and tenants were gradually replaced by a contractually based commercial relationship characterized by increasing autonomy for peasants.[124]

The disappearance of bond servants, however, was not merely a result of catastrophe and commercialization. Peasant uprisings in the late Ming also hastened the elimination of property rights in human beings. In south and southeast China, "rampant uprisings" demanded improve-

121 Wiens, 1980, p. 10. 122 Ho, pp. 265–6.

123 Liu Yongcheng, 1979b, p. 55, "Qingdai qianqi diannong kangzu douzheng di xin fazhan" (The new development of tenant rent resistance struggles in the early Qing period), pp. 54–77 in *Qingshi luncong* (Symposium on Qing history) 1, Chinese Academy of Social Sciences, History Research Institute, ed. (Beijing: Zhonghua shuju, 1979).

124 Wiens, 1980, p. 9.

ments in peasant welfare and reform of tenancy arrangements.[125] Peasants systematically refused to pay rent, demanded rent reductions, called on officials to institute uniform weights and measures (landlords were known to cheat tenants by using oversized measure to collect rents), and insisted on the abolition of extra labor services to landlords. According to Tanaka Masatoshi, official reports used terms such as *stubborn* and *crafty* to describe these rebellious peasants, which indicated that their actions were willful resistance and not due to famine or economic hardship.[126] Peasants were obviously willing and ready to exploit their improved bargaining position vis-à-vis landlords during the early Qing. Consequently, peasants gained more economic and personal freedom, and landlords lost many of their privileges and extraeconomic controls over peasants during the late Ming and early Qing.[127]

Developments in Guangdong province during the sixteenth and seventeenth centuries generally mirrored nationwide changes. Violent bond servant uprisings occurred in a number of counties in Guangdong during the Ming-Qing interregnum. For example in Qingyuan county, Guangzhou, in 1647, three years after the founding of the Qing dynasty, rebellious "tenant servants" (*dianpu*) killed their landlords and occupied their fields. Thirteen landlords, three of whom were imperial degree holders, were killed, and the reporting official personally supervised the troops who arrested the rebels.[128] Other uprisings were reported during the early Qing in Heping county, Huizhou; Pingyuan county, Jiaying; various areas of Nanxiong prefecture; Raoping, Denghai, and Chaoyang counties in Chaozhou; Qingyuan, Xinhui, Shunde, Xiangshan counties in Guangzhou; and Gaoyao and Kaiping counties in Zhaoqing.[129] Peasant uprisings in the late Ming severely weakened the ability of landlords to exert extraeconomic controls over their tenants throughout China.

125 Ibid., p. 28. 126 Tanaka, p. 206.

127 Jiang Taixin, pp. 133, 136, "Qingdai qianqi yazuzhi di fazhan" (Development of the rent deposit system in the early Qing period), *Lishi yanjiu* (1980) 3: pp. 133–49.

128 *Kang, Yong, Qian shiqi cheng xiang renmin fankang douzheng ziliao* (Materials on urban and rural peoples' struggles in the Kangxi, Yongzheng, and Qianlong periods), People's University, Qing History Research Center, ed., pp. 124–5 (Beijing: Zhonghua shuju, 1979) (hereafter, KYQ).

129 For Qingyuan, Xinhui, and Gaoyao, see Han, p. 101. For Kaiping, see Elvin, 1973, p. 246. For Chaoyang, Shunde, and Xiangshan, see Wei Qingyuan, Wu Qiyan, and Lu Su, p. 34 "Qing dai nubi zhidu" (The bond servant system of the Qing dynasty), pp. 1–55, in *Qingshi luncong* (Symposium on Qing history) 2, Chinese Academy of Social Sciences, History Research Institute, ed. (Beijing: Zhonghua shuju, 1980). For Raoping, Heping, Nanxiong, and Denghai, see Xie Guozhen, Appendix, *Mingdai nongmin qiyi shiliao xuanbian* (Selected historical materials on peasant uprisings in the Ming dynasty), (Fuzhou: Fujian Renmin Chubanshe, 1981).

Property Rights in Land

In addition to the disappearance of bonded servitude, significant developments in property rights in land had also begun to appear in more economically advanced regions of China. Fixed rents, rent deposits, absentee landlordism, permanent tenancy, the division of topsoil and subsoil rights, and the increasing use of contracts were all indications of these institutional changes that reduced transaction costs and clarified property rights. Many of these changes came about gradually over the course of the late Ming. According to Yang Guozhen, initially most landlords opposed the practice of tenants subletting land, but as early as the Ming Emperor Wanli's reign (1573–1619) their tacit acquiescence to tenants who sublet eventually led to the appearance of subsoil and topsoil rights in contracts. By the Qing dynasty, it had become a widely accepted custom throughout China.[130] Fang Xing has characterized this period of economic history, which was marked by a decline in the special privileges and extraeconomic controls that landlords had exercised over tenants, as a shift from a seigneurial landlord (*lingzhu*) to a commoner landlord (*dizhu*) economy.[131] Other historians have used the terms *official-gentry* (*guanshen*) or *aristocratic* (*guizu*) *landlords* to describe this vanishing breed of landlord. While economic and social forces impelled institutional change, the policy of the Qing founders also facilitated the emergence of a commoner landlord economy.

The Qing founders were undoubtedly aware that the concentration of economic power in the hands of seigneurial landlords and their exploitation of the peasantry through such means as bonded servitude had contributed to the social unrest and political instability of the late Ming. Early Qing land policies designed to revive agriculture and to check the power of the seigneurial landlords also hastened the formation of a commoner landlord economy. The Qing conquerors granted control of large portions of the Ming royal estates to the tenants who tilled the land and also limited the size and scope of their own land grants to "meritorious officials" to avoid the excesses of the previous dynasty.[132] There were military colonies (*tuntian*), imperial estates, and banner lands under state control during the early Qing, but these lands were gradually "privatized" under the "lash" of commercialization and the differentiation of the peasantry.[133] According to one estimate,

130 Yang, 1988, p. 100.
131 See Fang Xing, 1983, 2: 88–99.
132 Li, 1991, p. 14. 133 Ibid.

nationally 70 to 80% of land was in private hands by the early Qing.[134] Unlike the forceful seizures of land that had occurred during the late Ming, this "privatization" occurred as more and more of these lands were bought, sold, mortgaged, or leased on long-term contracts to private citizens. For the most part, the Qing government acquiesced in this process, though an additional tax, which fell on the tenant, was placed on state-owned lands that had been set aside to supply tribute grain (*caoyun tuntian*).[135]

To further limit the influence of official-gentry landlords, the new dynasty limited their tax exemptions and more forcefully collected tax arrears. For example, the Shunzhi emperor limited everyone from first-degree officials to first-degree licentiates (*shengyuan*) and clerks to an individual, rather than household, exemption from the corvée tax. Furthermore, when the Kangxi emperor needed revenue to fund military expenses, he ordered a 30% tax increase on "official-gentry households" (*guanshen hu*).[136] The curtailment of gentry tax privileges limited their ability to acquire land through commendation (*touxian*) from peasant households, a common means for extraeconomic land accumulation in the Ming, and diminished their capacity to build large estates. In addition to weakening the economic power of official-gentry households, the abridgment of their tax privileges meant that purchase became the primary method for accumulating land.

As Yang Guozhen's study of contracts has demonstrated, legal restrictions on the land sales eased significantly during the late Ming and early Qing.[137] Official permission to sell land was no longer necessary, and the long-standing custom of obtaining written approval from relatives and neighbors prior to a land sale gradually disappeared, weakening private interference in land sales. Some contracts still mentioned perfunctorily that neighbors and relatives had been consulted prior to land sales, but even this type of statement was omitted from some contracts. According to Yang, this type of change reflected both a major attack on traditional common-property relationships and an unstoppable historical trend.[138] This was another indication that the concept of land as an alienable commodity was supplanting the historical concept of land as inviolable patrimony.

Land sales became more frequent and also more complex. As noted previously, Li Wenzhi has found that a "craze" for purchasing land by officials and landlords drove up land prices faster than rents. In 1740, the Qianlong emperor expressed concern that wealthy merchants were

134 Yang, 1988, p. 18. 135 Li, 1991, p. 13. 136 Ibid., p. 16.
137 Yang, 1988, Chapter 1. 138 Ibid., p. 31.

taking advantage of a drought in the mid-Yangzi River valley to accumulate land at bargain prices.[139] Li cites several examples of merchants buying thousands of *mu* of land in the Qianlong and Jiaqing (1796–1820) reigns. Sales were also common between individual peasants and some wealthy peasants obtained enough land to become landlords.[140] Qualitative evidence also suggests that the frequency of sales of individual plots was also increasing. For example, in Suzhou during the Qianlong reign, it was reported that ownership of land changed several times within a ten-year period and that the turnover of land sales was ten times faster than it had been in the Kangxi reign.[141] The rapid turnover of land in market weakened personal connections to land and obviated property right claims based on historic family ownership.

As land sales became more frequent, the Qing government was concerned about lawsuits and loss of revenue. In 1750, the Qianlong emperor required that all provinces adopt a uniform document (*shuiqi*) to register land sales to simplify paperwork, avoid corruption, and eliminate tax evasion and lawsuits.[142] A variety of forms of conditional sales and the division of topsoil and subsoil rights, the "one land, two owner" system, reflected both the growing complexity, and the refinement and sophistication of property rights in lands.

By the early eighteenth century, Qing China was on the verge of an extended and unprecedented period of economic and demographic growth. With state support, vast areas of war-ravaged territory had been restored and improved. Qing officials were careful to nurture and support the revival of the rural economy to ensure domestic tranquility. Simultaneously, customs revenues that indicated the growth and health of the market economy augmented Qing coffers. By the early Qing, the final vestiges of servile tenancy had disappeared, and tenants enjoyed greater personal and economic freedom. Landlord control, which had extended over economic as well as personal matters, was severely curtailed, and contractual agreements supplanted the moralistic tenant-landlord relationships of an earlier time. As population grew steadily after the consolidation of Qing rule in the late seventeenth century, the owners of land watched the value of their capital increase. Overall, the economy experienced an impressive period of intensive economic growth during which both land and labor became frequently traded commodities. Intensive economic growth did not occur without revisions to the customary laws and the shared ideology that governed economic exchange in rural China. But as the relative scarcity of land

139 Li, 1989, p. 10. 140 Ibid. 141 Xing, p. 56.
142 Yang, 1988, p. 78.

increased and the complexity of the market grew, the pressure to refine and enforce property rights in land increased and with it the *potential* for disputes that sometimes became violent. Just as violence attended the decline of bonded servitude, revisions to property rights in land, erosion of shared ethical norms, and adjustments to customary law also entailed human costs. It was in the competing visions of social justice and economic self-interest that we can find the source of violent disputes over property rights. Perhaps because changes in economic institutions rose incrementally from the grassroots level, the struggle over property rights in land was protracted and small scale.

3

"As Before Each Manage Their Own Property": Boundary and Water-rights Disputes

By the early eighteenth century, establishing property rights in land had replaced maintaining property rights in human beings, bonded servitude, as a serious locus of social conflict. Violence on the order and magnitude of the bond servant uprisings and large-scale peasant uprisings of the Ming-Qing transition would not reappear in China until the close of the eighteenth century. As property rights in land became the focus of contention, social conflict became more personalized, communal, and small scale compared to the unrest of the seventeenth century. Struggles over property rights in land in the eighteenth century were comparatively less dramatic, but they were still significant. Although each violent dispute over property rights recounted in the following text possessed its own distinct set of circumstances and any individual dispute taken in isolation would be open to a variety of interpretations, an examination of disputes in Guangdong over a sixty-year period reveals a vivid picture of economic change and social conflict in rural society. From this picture, it is possible to discern the link between the individual struggles of common people and the broader economic trends of the eighteenth century.

As land increased in value and the economy became more commercialized, the potential for disputes and violence was twofold. On the one hand, population pressure and rising land values intensified and aggravated mundane disputes over land and strained the existing structure of property rights in land. Even the simplest dispute over land took on greater urgency as the relative scarcity of land increased. On the other hand, rising land values and market forces provided incentives to both tenants and landlords to extend or refine their property rights, which, in turn, raised new issues and heightened social tensions. For purposes of exposition and comparison, I have divided the major issues that led to disputes into two general categories, contractual and noncontractual, based on the relationship between the participants in the disputes. The categorization of disputes according to major issues is unavoidably a subjective process. While many violent disputes were straightforward and unambiguous, others were complex and convoluted. Disputes over land sales, evictions, and rent defaults could be particularly nettlesome and sometimes arose from erroneous or fraudulent claims. In categorizing each case, I based my decision on the proximate cause of the dispute. The groupings are necessarily broad, but careful analysis of individual disputes will reveal the diversity of issues within the larger categories.

Noncontractual disputes reveal the strains on the existing structure of property rights, as opposed to contractual disputes that illustrate efforts to create new economic institutions or to eliminate existing rights. Since noncontractual issues such as disputes over water rights and boundaries, were issues that arose within the existing property-rights structure, explaining these disputes within the broader historical context of the eighteenth century may appear to be stretching a point. These were not issues that inspired novel innovations in property rights. When addressing the causes of the boundary and water-rights disputes, county magistrates frequently responded with the rather bland phrase "as before each manage their own property." While I am willing to concede that conflicts over water rights and boundaries were familiar sources of disputes, I would also maintain that even these seemingly mundane issues were frequently related to the large-scale structural changes in the economy described in Chapter 2. For example, as land was bought and sold with greater frequency, holdings became more fragmented. The division of land into smaller plots required the redrawing of boundaries and also complicated access to irrigation systems, thus creating the potential for more water-rights and boundary disputes. Finally, it is important to remember that this study only includes disputes that ended in homicide, which presumably represent only a fraction of the total number of disputes, whether violent or nonviolent.

Boundary Disputes (64 Cases)

Measurement of a good or service is an essential feature of any system of property rights. In the case of land, this includes the delineation of the physical boundaries of a plot of land. The most frequent causes of boundary disputes included the reduction of the area occupied by boundary markers (e.g., trees, raised footpaths, embankments, or other structures that defined boundaries between fields) in order to maximize the amount of land under cultivation; overplanting boundaries or harvesting crops from adjacent fields; disagreements over the boundaries of newly reclaimed land; and encroachment or violation of land reserved for graves. Flooding or changes in the course of waterways, the removal of dirt or clay from neighboring fields in order to repair embankments, and division of property among heirs also accounted for some disputes. Several examples will serve to illustrate the variety of boundary disputes.[1]

The desire of land-hungry peasants to garner the greatest return from their land was apparent in boundary disputes that arose when peasants attempted to maximize the amount of land under cultivation. For example, Feng Deng and Zhang Wanxiang had neighboring fields in Qingshan county, Qiongzhou. A bamboo wattle separated the two fields. On QL 24.7.26 (1742), Feng Deng cut down the wattle and planted some "coarse grains" (*zaliang*) between the two fields. Zhang suspected that Feng had encroached on his land and went to stop him. Feng and Zhang argued and Zhang shoved Feng. Feng struck back, injuring Zhang's ribs and knocking him to the ground. Liao Junyi, a bystander, arrived too late to stop them. "Unexpectedly," the injury was serious and Zhang died a short while later.[2] In this case, the magistrate blandly noted, as many other magistrates did in similar cases, that the boundaries should be observed as they had been in the past. This type of boundary dispute was quite common. Twenty similar cases involving the destruction or removal of trees or alterations in the embankments or raised footpaths, which served as boundary markers, occurred in various counties throughout Guangdong over the course of the Qianlong reign. While this garden variety boundary dispute was undoubtedly not uncommon in eighteenth-century Guangdong, that such simple disputes should escalate to homicidal violence this often was indicative of the times.

1 As in previous chapters, I have not translated homicide reports verbatim. In general, most reports were very terse, though some portions of the report such as the descriptions of the violence were written in excruciating detail. Consequently, in recounting the disputes, I have chosen to refrain from direct quotations unless it is necessary to convey the judgments or nuances of the reporter.

2 XKTB 1450, QL 25.7.7. The use of the term *unexpectedly* was commonly used when a victim died some time after the violent incident. This was a "marker" for the higher-level officials who reviewed the report and indicated that the seriousness of the injury was not readily apparent at the time of the assault. For an analysis of the representation of homicide in official reports, see Thomas Buoye, "Suddenly Murderous Intent Arose: Bureaucratization and Benevolence in Eighteenth-Century Qing Homicide Reports," *Late Imperial China* (December 1995) 16.2: 95–130.

As noted earlier, during the eighteenth century the imperial government promoted land reclamation as one solution to alleviate the pressure of China's burgeoning population. Despite the fact that the Ministry of Revenue had promulgated detailed regulations for processing claims to wasteland, competing claims still gave rise to violent disputes. For example, in Deqingzhou county, Zhaoqing, Mi Yixiang and his brother inherited land that their uncle had purchased from the Liang family. Erroneously assuming that another piece of wasteland recently reclaimed by the Liangs belonged to the plot that he had inherited, Mi Yixiang sued the Liangs. The case was heard, and the presiding magistrate ruled that the land should be surveyed after the harvest. On QL 19.5.28 (1740), Mi Yixiang and his brother, Mi Wenxiang, attempted to stop Liang Dade, his wife, Ms. Deng,[3] and Liang's father from harvesting their crop. In the ensuing fracas, Ms. Deng went to the defense of her husband. She attacked Mi Wenxiang by seizing him by the testicles. Mi Yixiang came to his brother's aid and struck Ms. Deng twice with a wooden pole. Ms. Deng was seriously wounded and died seventeen days later.[4]

In this case, the Mis may have genuinely believed that the land in question was part of their inheritance. Their contempt for the official decision to postpone the survey until after the harvest and their willingness to confront the Liangs, however, may have been indicative of the weakness of their claim or their lack of confidence in the court. (Homicides preceded by official adjudication will be examined in detail in Chapter 7.) Whatever the actual circumstances may have been, the magistrate, Chang Zhenji, was clearly sympathetic to the Liangs and ruled that the land in question was indeed their property. As for the criminal matters, because Ms. Deng's death was the result of a subsequent infection, Mi Yixiang, who had assaulted her, was not sentenced to death. Instead, he was ordered to pay 20 *liang* of silver to Ms. Deng's family, flogged, and banished 1,000 *li* for "doing what should not be done" (*buying zhong*).[5] His brother, Mi Wenxiang, also was flogged for interfering with the Liang's harvest.

3 Married women were often referred to only by their maiden names.

4 XKTB 1068, QL 20.6.13.

5 See Derek Bodde and Clarence Morris, p. 159, *Law in Imperial China* (Cambridge, MA: Harvard University Press, 1967). According to Bodde and Morris, *buying zhong* is an abbreviated reference to a "common catch-all statute." Apparently, the "doing what should not be done" law was frequently used to punish any objectionable behavior not covered under a specific statute. I have encountered numerous cases in which this statute was invoked. For example, a landlord who leased his field to a new tenant simply to obtain a higher rent was punished under this statute for creating the situation that led to a lethal confrontation between the previous and current tenant.

Competing claims to newly opened land were responsible for eighteen disputes in this sample. Perhaps the clearly articulated regulations for the opening and reporting of *shatan* (see Chapter 2), the highly valued riverine and coastal bottom lands, reduced the likelihood of violence. Alternatively, the bulk of the available *shatan* may have already been brought under cultivation prior to the Qianlong reign. (According to Yang Guozhen, the reclamation of *shatan* was well under way in the Ming dynasty.[6]) In the eighteen disputes over reclaimed land, only four were fought over *shatan*. The remaining disputes were over marginal land, hill land, and land abutting graves. In one case that took place in 1744, Li Rusong and others attempted to reclaim land that had been the site of a village reservoir. Despite a lawsuit to block his efforts, Li proceeded until a violent confrontation with a fellow villager halted his plans.[7] The fact that Li Rusong would disregard the protest of his fellow villagers and reclaim land that had been a village reservoir was a clear indication that arable land was in short supply and that common land, like this village reservoir, were also in danger of being privatized.

With land in short supply, both the dead and the living competed for its use. An additional eight disputes burst into violence over accusations that existing graves had been violated or that newly constructed graves encroached on cultivated land. For example, in Haifeng county, Huizhou prefecture, Chen Ruizhang and Chen Qizhang had a plot of land on which they grew potatoes. The land abutted Lin Daihou's ancestral graves. On his way to visit the graves, Lin noticed that the potatoes were planted too close to the graves. Violence began after Lin tore up the potatoes.[8] The cultural and social importance of proper burial and maintenance of graves in Chinese society need not be recounted here. As this case and others reveal, the demand for land was sufficiently great that some peasants even were willing to risk violating graves. As we shall see in Chapter 6, when we examine a different set of disputes, some individuals went so far as to exhume the graves of their own ancestors.

Purloining produce from an adjacent field during a harvest, whether intentional or accidental, was another source of boundary disputes. For example, Huang Shouguan and Liu Shiquan lived in the same village in Xinhui county, Guangzhou. Huang Shouguan had been a hereditary servant (*shipu*) in Chen Maozhuo's household. Huang's land was located near a plot of land that Liu Shiquan tilled. They both planted sweet potatoes. On QL 8.8.8 (1743) in the afternoon, Liu Shiquan was returning

6 Yang, 1988, p. 362. 7 SS 1574, QL 10.11.13, Vol. 3.
8 XKTB 3198, QL 45.7.9.

home from the market. From the road, Liu thought he saw Huang Shouguan stealing sweet potatoes from his field. Huang Shouguan rebuked him for making wild allegations. Liu ridiculed Huang for having been the hereditary servant of the Chen family. Huang was "displeased" and threatened to ask the local constable (*dibao*) to measure the plots in question to the "inch."

Liu lost his temper and pinned Huang's hand behind his back with one hand and began to throttle him with his other hand. Huang became "agitated" (*jingji*) and punched Liu in the head. Huang's father, Huang Jingyou, saw that Liu would not release his son. Fearing that his son would be injured, Huang Jingyou began to pound on Liu's back, but Liu only squeezed Huang's throat tighter. Huang Shouguan was in unbearable pain. Freeing his hand, Huang struck Liu in the chest and pushed him away. Quickly, Huang punched Liu in the stomach, knocking him to the ground. At that moment Liu Shiquan's brother, Liu Liangshao, having heard the altercation, came to the scene, but was too late to stop the fighting. They carried Liu Shiquan to Huang Jingyou's home, where he died the same night.[9]

Seven other comparable boundary disputes began when one peasant accused a neighbor of harvesting the crop from his field. In the case recounted in the previous paragraph, the magistrate ruled that the sweet potatoes in question did not belong to Liu, though the issue hardly seemed important after the homicide. It is also worth noting that the threat to involve the local constable incited Liu Shiquan to violence. Although magistrates usually adjudicated disputes fairly and competently when given the chance, enforcement was often problematic; and when yamen underlings became involved in coercing compliance, they often precipitated violence. This is an issue I will return to in Chapter 7. Another interesting feature of this dispute was the effect of Huang Shouguan's social status as a former hereditary servant, which Liu used to taunt him. Although the Yongzheng emperor abolished the inferior legal status of bonded and hereditary servants a decade earlier, Huang was sentenced under the law governing killings of commoners by servile laborers (*nupu*).[10] Consequently, Huang was sentenced to the more severe punishment of beheading. Uncertainty over changes in

9 *Qingdai dizu boxiao xingtai* (Forms of rent exploitation in the Qing period), pp. 751–2, Number One Historical Archives of China and Institute of Historical Research of the Chinese Academy of Social Sciences, eds. (Beijing: Zhonghua shuju, 1982) (hereafter, QDB).

10 No explanation was provided as to why Huang still bore the stigma of his former status. One can only speculate that perhaps Yongzheng's decision only applied to future generations.

legal status and suspicion or fear of yamen underlings exacerbated disputes over land.

Most boundary disputes were usually small scale and spontaneous, but occasionally they could be quite large and exceedingly violent. One of the most brutal killings took place in Changle county, Jiaying. Indicative of the extent to which land holdings could be fragmented, Wu Fachang possessed fourteen separate parcels of enclosed land that totaled 30 *shi*. Wu also had two sons, Wu Huancheng and Wu Bacheng. Because of Wu Bacheng's "perverse nature,"[11] Wu Fachang only allotted Wu Bacheng 4 *shi* to till and to establish a separate household. Wu Fachang and his eldest son, Wu Huancheng, tilled and managed the remaining land and an additional mountain plot. According to the report, Wu Bacheng's hatred for his elder brother began at this time.

On QL 40.7.27 (1775), Wu Bacheng took an iron harrow and went to the mountain plot to remove some stones. When he arrived, his brother Wu Huancheng was already there. Huancheng informed him that he had no claim on the mountain plot. Huancheng seized Bacheng's harrow and threw it on the ground. Bacheng tried to pick it up, but Huancheng pushed him to the ground. As Bacheng got up, Huancheng raised a stone-cutting ax to hit Bacheng. Bacheng deflected the blow with his harrow. He struck Huancheng in the back with the harrow and knocked him to the ground. According to the magistrate's report, at this point Wu Bacheng's accumulated anger for his brother overwhelmed him. In a fit of sudden rage, he grabbed the ax and repeatedly struck his brother on the skull, neck, and shoulders. Wu Ronghao, who had been working in a neighboring field, saw what happened but was too late to stop it. Often violence ended when a third party arrived on the scene or when a victim was obviously incapacitated, but this incident was different.

Wu Bacheng dropped the ax and fled. He arrived at Shuangtou market, where he saw Wu Huancheng's son Wu Guisheng watching an outdoor play. Bacheng's anger was still not "extinguished," so he decided to kill Wu Guisheng. Returning home, he got a vegetable knife that he used to attack Wu Guisheng. Guisheng fled and Bacheng pursued him, stabbing him in the hand. Bacheng eventually caught him and pulled him to the ground. As Guisheng called for help, Bacheng stabbed him in the head twice. Guisheng died on the spot.[12]

11 Although nearly every document used the stock phrases to refer to the killer as violent by nature and ignorant of the law (see Note 9, Chapter 2), this was the only homicide in which the killer was labeled "perverse." As this incident indicates, the term was probably justified.

12 XKTB 2746, QL 40.10.14.

Gruesome violence of the type perpetrated by Wu Bacheng was unusual, though not unique. In this particular case, the gravity of the crime was compounded because the killings were deemed intentional, the victims were two males of the same family, and one victim was the elder brother of the killer. For his lurid crimes, Wu Bacheng received the most severe form of capital punishment under Qing law, lingering death (*lingchi chusi*). Twenty-four slices were administered to the limbs before the condemned was beheaded.

Guangdong was well known for strong lineages that served economic as well as social and religious functions. As noted in Chapter 2, lineages played an important role in creating *shatan* in the Pearl River Delta. The fact that lineages and villages corporately owned land also created the potential for large-scale boundary disputes in Guangdong. In fact, the third-largest dispute examined in this sample, which involved twenty-four active participants, was a boundary dispute that occurred in Chaoyang county, Chaozhou, on QL 59.5.23 (1794). The dispute arose when Lin Shenglin noticed that Zheng Zhaoxiong had taken dirt from the area surrounding his ancestral graves. A shouting match between Lin and Zheng drew the attention of clansmen (*zuren*) on both sides. Eventually, a battle ensued between fourteen individuals surnamed Lin and ten individuals surnamed Zheng.

While pointing out that the Zhengs were at fault for violating the Lins' graves, the investigating magistrate punished the Lins severely for their violent deeds. Suspiciously, all six victims in this battle were Zhengs, but according to the magistrate's report the fighting was not premeditated.[13] No weapons were used other than ordinary, though potentially lethal, farm implements, such as scythes. Still, one suspects that the Lins may have set an ambush for the Zhengs, although the magistrate clearly stated that the incident was unplanned. Regardless of what the true circumstances of the violence might have been, it serves to illustrate how even a seemingly minor dispute could erupt into a frenzy of violence.

Another large-scale boundary dispute pitted the residents of Huanggang village in Dongguan county, Guangzhou, against the residents of Shangliao village in Guishan county, Huizhou. In this episode, the dispute was over the harvesting of reeds that grew on Daluping Mountain, which separated the two villages. The trouble began on QL 50.8.18 (1785) when Yi Xuetai and Huang Bida from Huanggang were cutting reeds and drying them in the sun. Ceng Yugui, Ceng Yuchang, and Zhang Yesan of Shangliao saw this and went to stop them. An alterca-

13 XKTB 4061, QL 60.3.14.

tion ensued and the Shangliao residents routed the Huanggang residents and confiscated their reeds.

The next day, Ceng Yugui, Zhang Yasan, and Xie Wanyou were on their way to Qingxi market in Guishan. On the road, Ceng Yucheng, who was carrying a scythe because he was on his way to cut reeds, joined them. As they passed Huanggang village, Huang Bida and Yi Chaowang stopped them and demanded compensation for the reeds they had confiscated the previous day. Chen Shijin of Huanggang also came to support his fellow villagers at that time. Still, the Shangliao residents refused and an argument began. Ceng Yucheng cursed Chen Shijin and used his scythe to hack at him. Chen tried to block the blow with his hand. Three fingers on his left hand were cut and his right thumb was severed. Yi Chaowang removed the carrying pole from his baskets and hit Ceng Yucheng over the head. Zhang Yasan tried to protect Ceng Yucheng by using his carrying pole as a weapon, while Huang Bida beat him on the arms and legs with his own pole.

Xie Wanyou saw that Ceng and Zhang were injured, and he joined in the battle. Xie hit Yi Chaowang with his pole and chased him away. While Xie pursued Yi Chaowang, he met Yi Tingwang, who was returning to the village. Yi Tingwang cut Xie with his scythe. Xie then went after Yi Tingwang. Yi Xuetai, who was also returning to Huanggang after cutting reeds, blocked Xie's path. Xie lifted his pole to strike Yi Xuetai, but Yi struck him first and broke his arm. At this point, Yi Decan and Chen Guxian arrived and broke up the fighting. Both villages reported the incident to their respective magistrates. Xie Wanyou died on QL 50.10.2 (1785).[14] Once again, the investigating magistrate explicitly stated that violence was unpremeditated. Whatever the case may have been, this melee indicates that violent disputes were not entirely limited to small-scale incidents. It also demonstrates that intense competition over land during the eighteenth century also threatened customary rights to glean common land like the reed stands of Daluping Mountain.

Common Characteristics of Boundary Disputes

Although there was considerable variety in the proximate causes, scale, and tenor of boundary disputes, there were also several similarities. Geographically, except for the fact that there were relatively more boundary disputes in Shaozhou prefecture, the overall pattern for boundary dis-

14 Although the death came more than thirty days after the assault, the normal time limit for homicide was extended to fifty days because Xie had a broken bone (see Appendix A).

Map 3–1 Guangdong Province Boundary Disputes[a]

[a] Fourteen locations unknown.

putes was similar to the general pattern for all disputes. The fact that eastern Guangdong, which provincial officials often complained was overcrowded, had relatively more disputes, and the far western prefectures, which provincial officials had identified as outlets for excess population, were the most peaceful areas suggests some relationship with population pressure. (See Map 3–1.)

Table 3–1. *Total Participants and Duration for Boundary Disputes*

Number of Participants	Number of Disputes
Two	26
Three	13
Four	9
Five–nine	16
Ten or more	1[a]
Total	65
Duration	
One day or less	41
One day–one month	5
Estimated within one month	6
One month–one year	9
More than one year	4
Total	65

[a]Twenty-four participants.

As Table 3–1 illustrates, most boundary disputes were small-scale, sudden acts of violence. The average number of participants in a boundary dispute was 3.92, and 73% of the disputes involved only two to four participants. Only thirteen disputes grew out of long-standing disagreements of one month or more. Boundary disputes were usually straightforward, and apparently Chinese peasants responded quickly to perceived encroachments on their land. Forty-one disputes (63%) began and ended within a single day. Prior efforts at mediation were rare in violent boundary disputes. The fact that lawsuits preceded only six disputes in this sample might indicate that official adjudication of boundaries may have been effective. In fact, as I will argue in Chapter 7, based on evidence from homicides in which official adjudication preceded the violent dispute, magistrates were usually fair and competent.

There was a monthly pattern to homicides related to property disputes that seemed to follow the seasonal rhythms of agriculture. Using disputes from all sources for which the precise date of the homicide was

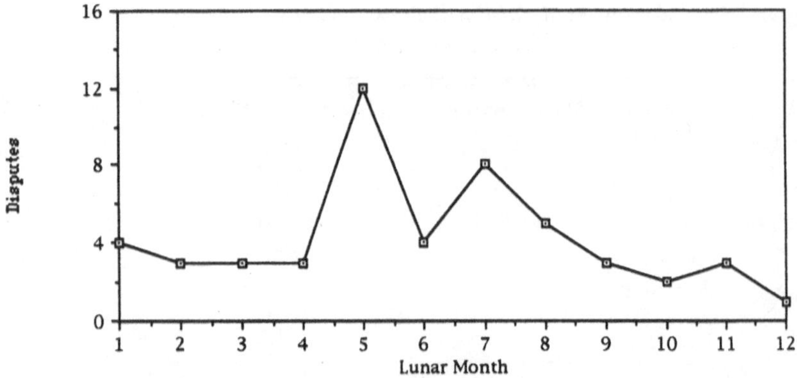

Figure 3–1 Boundary Disputes by Month[a]

[a]Excluding fourteen disputes for which the precise date was unknown.

known, the seasonal pattern of boundary disputes, however, is perhaps the most difficult to explain (see Figure 3–1). Boundary disputes occurred more evenly throughout the year, with the exception of a sharp upswing in the fifth month, shortly before the end of the first growing season. Not surprisingly, many boundary disputes occurred near harvest time. However, if the violence was related to the harvest, logically we would expect a similar upswing during the second growing season, but there was none.

Disputes over Water Rights (108 Cases)

Even under the best conditions, defining property rights in water presents an array of nettlesome issues. Referring to the problems of defining property rights in water on the Great Plains of the United States, Anderson and Hill have noted that the special properties of water, which "moves freely over many different pieces of real estate and can change course over time,"[15] complicate the development of property rights and ownership of water. Given the fundamental importance of water for the irrigated rice-paddy agriculture of Guangdong province and the fact that water is inherently difficult to manage, it is not surprising to find that among all the issues examined in this sample, competition for control of irrigation systems or access to water was a major cause of

15 Terry L. Anderson and P. J. Hill, p. 176, "The Evolution of Property Rights: A Study of the American West," *Journal of Law and Economics* (April 1973) 18.1: 163–79.

violent disputes.[16] Based on the water-rights disputes in this sample, the variability of rainfall, and the engineering expertise and social co-operation required for water management influenced the timing and scale of many disputes.

Seasonal fluctuations of supply notwithstanding, the physical properties of water present additional problems. Irrigation systems in Guangdong were complex and extensive.[17] A single water source might supply many different farmers, and the management of water was frequently vested in lineage or village-organized associations. Compounding the problem was the fragmentation of holdings that was a by-product of the commercialization of land. As land was divided into smaller parcels, irrigation networks had to be extended to reach plots that were not adjacent to existing channels; and to ensure the flow of water, greater cooperation was required among neighbors. In fields without direct access to the irrigation channel, a farmer was totally dependent on the cooperation of his neighbor for access to water. Maintaining irrigation systems also required funding and management. Evidence from homicide reports indicates that the going rate for maintenance on irrigation systems in the latter part of the Qianlong reign was 3 *sheng* of grain per *mu* of land for a lineage-managed system in Renhua county, Shaozhou, and also for a communal-based system in Boluo county, Huizhou.[18] From the perspective of violent disputes, the high degree of interdependence within a single irrigation system meant that there generally was a greater potential for disputes over water. The tendency for individuals to form associations to reduce the costs of maintaining irrigation systems also meant that when a dispute gave way to confrontation there was a potential for large-scale violence.

Most water-rights disputes in this sample occurred when someone drained water from a neighboring field, released excess water into a neighboring field, or obstructed or diverted the usual flow of water within an existing irrigation system. The accounts of the circumstances leading up to the disputes were quite similar over time and across the

16 If we consider disputes from all sources, both archival and published, rent defaults (106 disputes) were a close second to water rights. However, if we exclude documents from the Grand Secretariat Registry and published documents, which heavily favored rent defaults, water rights outnumbered rent defaults by a considerable margin, eighty-six to fifty-three.

17 See Akira Morita, *Shindai suirishi kenkyu* (Research on irrigation in the Qing dynasty), (Tokyo: Aki Shobo, 1974) for the definitive work on irrigation during the Qing dynasty.

18 For Boluo county, see XKTB 2733, QL 40.1.1. For Renhua county, see XKTB 3261, QL 45.6.5. In the former case, the person in charge of the maintenance organized the users to administer a beating to a member who refused to pay his dues.

province. Violence often struck with lightning speed, and, although water-rights disputes were more likely than other types of disputes to produce large-scale donnybrooks, most disputes were small in terms of numbers of participants. Typically, an individual acted immediately after catching a neighbor in the act of illegally diverting or obstructing the normal flow or customary allocation of water. One might be tempted to speculate about the existence of perdurable animosities, but almost every document contained the routine statement that no prior grudge existed between the disputants. Furthermore, whatever the past relationship between the parties to the disputes may have been, it was clear from the homicide reports that retaliation against discovery of a transgression was usually swift and decisive.

A dispute that occurred in Chaoyang county, Chaozhou prefecture, on QL 9.8.10 (1744), was similar in most respects to many water-rights disputes. Cao Aying and Zhang Boxin used the same irrigation channel. Cao's field was upstream from Zhang's field. When Zhang found that Cao had blocked the flow of water to his field, he used a hoe to remove the obstruction. Cao's cousin, Cao Atai, saw Zhang and began to argue with him vociferously. Chen Xingxin, a passerby, came forward and broke up the argument. Cao Atai returned home and informed Cao Aying of Zhang's actions. Cao Aying became angry and proceeded to the field to confront Zhang. When Cao arrived, Zhang used his hoe to repel him. With Zhang in pursuit, Cao fled to a shed near an adjacent field. Cao emerged from the shed wielding a night protection (*fangye*) spear[19] and charged Zhang, landing a blow on his chin. Zhang fought back with his hoe. Finally, Cao became incensed and again charged Zhang with his spear, piercing Zhang's left lung. Zhang fell to the ground and after a while died.[20]

In the case described, the dispute arose when water was withheld. In Haiyang county, Chaozhou, the opposite situation occurred. Chen You and Su Xiumeng had adjacent fields that received water from the same irrigation system. Su's field was upstream from Chen's. After a heavy rain on QL 59.8.8 (1794), Su opened a hole in his dike and drained the excess water into Chen's field. Chen feared damage to his crop and went

19 Since commoners were not permitted to possess weapons, local magistrates felt compelled to explain the existence of any items, other than ordinary farm implements, which were used as homicide weapons. Thus, officials frequently described items, which obviously were exclusively used as weapons, as "night protection" devices. Apparently, this subterfuge placated their superiors since, with the exception of one case in which a magistrate tried to pass off a firearm as a night protection device, higher-level officials did not question this practice.

20 XKTB 0434, QL 10.3.11.

to rebuke Su. Su became angry, and an argument began. While they were arguing, three of Chen's clansmen (*zuren*) – Chen Tingxian, Chen Ana, and Cheng Wenyu, returning home carrying bundles of straw – interceded and urged them to stop. Su cursed them and used the handle of his hoe to hit Chen Wenyu in the forehead. Chen Wenyu jabbed Su in the left leg and arm with an "iron-mouth" (*tiezui*) staff. Su then turned on Chen Wenyu. Meanwhile, Chen You took a "night protection" spear from his shed and stabbed Su in the back. Su turned and struck Chen You in the eye. Chen You then stabbed Su in the stomach. Su, having received several serious wounds, fell to the ground. At that moment, Su's elder brother, Su Mu, who was returning home with some firewood, saw that his brother was in trouble and went to help. Chen Tingxian struck him on the arm with a pole. Su Mu struck back, hitting Chen Tingxian in the chest and knocking him to the ground. Zheng Chengying and Zhang Jin were passing by at the time, but they arrived too late to stop the fighting. Both Su Xiumeng and Chen Tingxian died from their wounds.

The incidents recounted were representative of the majority of the water-rights disputes in this study. Quite often farmers did not have direct access to irrigation channels and water flowed through one field to the next. As landowners sold off portions of their land and holdings became more fragmented, the opportunity for disputes was enhanced because neighbors had to cooperate to maintain the flow of water. More than any other issue, however, water-rights disputes sometimes erupted into great brawls. The following case, which took place in Jieyang county, Chaozhou, on QL 4.8.18 (1739), illustrates the manner in which the interdependence of numerous peasants could enmesh them in violent struggle. It also shows the limited effectiveness of taking a dispute to court when enforcement mechanisms were weak.

Land belonging to individuals surnamed Xie was upstream from land owned by individuals surnamed Yang. In preparation for the planting season, Xie Mingxuan, a landlord and a minor-degree holder (*jiansheng*), blocked the irrigation channel and created a reservoir next to his field. Rains had been deficient that year, and Xie's reservoir reduced the amount of water reaching the Yangs' fields. The Yangs sued, and the previous magistrate ordered Xie Mingxuan to release the water. Xie complained that this would damage his embankments, and he "repeatedly" blocked the Yangs whenever they tried to open a channel from his reservoir. Apparently, the magistrate was unable to compel compliance with his decision.

On QL 3.8.19 (1738), Yang Zixiang and his clansmen (*zuren*) Yang Baicai, Yang Azi, and Yang Aliang went to release water from Xie's reservoir. Xie's tenants Xiong Aling and Xie Hengfa saw them and stopped them. Afterwards, Xie Hengfa went to inform Xie Mingxuan, but Xie Mingxuan had already gone to the county seat to pay taxes. Instead, Xie Hengfa informed Xie Mingxuan's mother. After eating breakfast, Xie Hengfa and Xiong Aling returned to work in the field. Xie Ada, Xie Azhe, and Xie Ashang were also at work in their fields. They all received water from the reservoir created by Xie Mingxuan. In the afternoon, Yang Zixiang, Yang Baicai, Yang Azi, and Yang Ahai, each carrying a hoe, returned to the scene to release water from the reservoir. Xie Hengfa and Xie Azhe happened to be carrying scythes, and Xie Afeng was holding a spade. According to the official account, the Xies "unreasonably"[21] blocked the Yangs.

Yang Zixiang argued with Xie Hengfa. Hearing this disturbance, Xie Ashang and Xie Aling took bamboo spears from their shed and went to the scene. Fighting began. Yang Baicai used the handle of his hoe to strike Xie Hengfa. Xie Hengfa attacked him with his scythe and wounded him in the ribs. Carrying a bamboo spear, Xia Azhang went after Yang Azi, who defended himself with his hoe. Xie Kechang stabbed Yang in the ribs with a spear. Eventually, everyone became embroiled in the fighting. Yang Aliang used the handle of his hoe to strike Xie Azhe. In retaliation, Xie wounded Yang Aliang in the shoulder with his scythe. Yang Zixiang lifted his hoe and struck Xie Afeng. Xie Afeng ran away, and Yang pursued him.

Meanwhile, Xie Mingxuan had returned home from paying taxes. He heard the news about the Yangs going to the field that morning and went to investigate. When he arrived, he saw Yang Zixiang chasing Xie Afeng. Xie Mingxuan took a piece of firewood from Xiong Aling's shed and went to stop him. Yang Zixiang defended himself from Xie Mingxuan with his hoe and at the same time swung the hoe at Xie Afeng. Xie Afeng dodged him and struck him with his spade. Yang was wounded in the leg and fell to the ground. Huang Guishen, who had been working in a distant field, arrived, but was too late to stop the fighting. Yang Zixiang was seriously injured and soon died. Yang's son, Yang Awan, reported the incident to a "local authority" (*liancong*), Yang Wen.[22]

Unfortunately, a large portion of this report, including the details on the sentencing, did not survive. We do know that Xie Mingxuan was stripped of his degree after the local authority complained that he was

21 Throughout the official account of this incident, the actions of the Xies were consistently described as either "unreasonable" or "unjustified." Apparently, this was done since there had been an official judgment authorizing the Yangs to access the water supply.

22 XKTB, 0165, QL 5 (month and day unknown).

"relying on his credentials to avoid testifying to the facts." Interestingly, it appears Xie Xingxuan temporarily relied on his status as a degree holder to defy the court order that allowed the Yangs access to the water. However, Xie's status did not protect him from punishment once violence and homicide occurred. Another interesting feature of this case is the involvement of the *liancong*. The homicide report provides no details regarding the role of the *liancong*, leaving open the possibility that this may have been a position in an unofficial local militia. If this were true, it may be that the origin of local militia was related to the need for a reliable local institution to enforce the property rights in land.

The two largest disputes in my sample, in terms of total participants and loss of life, were also over water rights. Interestingly, both disputes occurred in Jieyang county, Chaozhou. On QL 55.8.14 (1790), a total of thirty-one persons, fifteen surnamed Cai and sixteen surnamed Xie, clashed, and ten people died.[23] (Unfortunately, there is no way to tell if this was the same group of Xies involved in the incident mentioned earlier, which occurred in the same county roughly fifty years earlier.) Jieyang county was also the scene on QL 30.3.10 (1765), when sixteen persons surnamed Wu clashed with eleven persons, most of whom were surnamed Jiang. A protracted melee, which left six people dead, began when the Wus attempted to remove a dam that the Jiangs had constructed in the channel of a shared irrigation system.[24] In both cases, the investigating magistrates were careful to explain that these conflicts were not premeditated or organized. As I have argued elsewhere, Qing magistrates normally downplayed evidence of premeditation and erred on the side of leniency when reporting homicides.[25] Organized violence or feuding was a particularly sensitive issue that could lead to censure of the local magistrate.

Common Characteristics of Water-rights Disputes

Geographically, water-rights disputes were comparatively widespread, but the dominance of violence-prone Chaozhou prefecture, particularly Chaoyang and Jieyang counties, was most striking for water-rights disputes (see Map 3–2). The amount and timing of rainfall were very important for rice cultivation. Judging from some reports on agriculture in Guangdong, the eastern areas of the province were most susceptible to the vagaries of weather. For example, in 1741 a combination of insuf-

23 XKTB 3781 QL 56 (month and day unknown). 24 XKTB 1748, QL 30.11.28.
25 See Buoye, 1995.

Guangzhou
01 Nanhai
02 Panyu
03 Shunde
04 Dongguan
05 Conghua
06 Longmen
07 Zengcheng
08 Xinhui
09 Xiangshan
10 Sanshui
11 Xinning
12 Qingyuan
13 Xinan
14 Huaxian

Shaozhou
15 Qujiang
16 Lechang
17 Renhua
18 Ruyuan
19 Wengyuan
20 Yingde

Nanxiong
21 Baochang
22 Shixing
23 Nanxiong

Huizhou
24 Guishan
25 Boluo
26 Changning
27 Yongan
28 Haifeng
29 Lufeng
30 Longchuan
31 Lianping
32 Heyuan
33 Heping

Chaozhou
34 Haiyang
35 Fengshun
36 Chaoyang
37 Jieyang
38 Raoping
39 Huilai
40 Dapu
41 Chenghai
42 Puning

Zhaoqing
43 Gaoyao
44 Sihui
45 Xinxing
46 Yangchun
47 Yangjiang
48 Gaoming
49 Enping
50 Guangning
51 Kaiping
52 Heshan
53 Deqingzhou
54 Fengchuan
55 Kaijian

Gaozhou
56 Maoming
57 Dianbai
58 Xinyi
59 Huazhou
60 Wuchuan
61 Shicheng

Lianzhoufu
62 Hepu
63 Qinzhou
64 Lingshan

Leizhou
65 Haikang
66 Suixi
67 Xuwen

Qiongzhou
68 Qingshan
69 Dengmai
70 Dingan
71 Wenchang
72 Huitong
73 Lehui
74 Lingao
75 Danzhou
76 Changhua
77 Wanzhou
78 Lingshui
79 Yazhou
80 Ganen

Luodingzhou
81 Dongan
82 Xining
83 Luoding

Lianzhou
84 Yangshan
85 Lianshan
86 Lianzhou

Jiayingzhou
87 Changle
88 Pingyuan
89 Zhenping
90 Jiaying
91 Xingning

Map 3–2 Guangdong Province Water-rights Disputes[a]
[a] Twenty locations unknown.

ficient rainfall after the early harvest (which hampered transplantation of rice seedlings) and heavy rains just prior to harvest time had a disastrous impact on crop yields across the entire province.[26] A year later, in eastern Guangdong, insufficient rainfall prevented the transplanting

26 HKTB 54, QL 6.11.16.

of seedlings in nine counties in Chaozhou and Jiaying prefectures.[27] Another report on drought conditions in 1745 reported that within a single county, crop damage varied significantly based on the access to irrigation systems. In Chaoyang county, Chaozhou, in areas with access to irrigation, the harvest, including sweet potatoes and sugar cane, was good and a tenth of the area had surpluses. In areas at higher elevations, where irrigation systems were not as effective or extensive, estimates of the negative impact of the drought varied from 50 to 60% to 80 to 100% reductions in the crop.[28] Still, it is important to note that although adverse weather and environmental features may have increased the likelihood of disputes over water in some areas, it does not explain why such disputes turned violent.

In general, disputes over water rights, like boundary disputes, were abrupt, volatile, and rarely preceded by mediation. In fact, no other issue burst into bloody violence as quickly as water-rights disputes. Only two disputes were outstanding for over a month, while most degenerated into vehement bickering and brawling seemingly without a moment's notice (see Table 3–2). In terms of scale, disputes over water rights averaged 4.5 persons per dispute, slightly larger than other types of disputes, but differences over water rights engendered a significantly greater share of large-scale disputes. Of the eighteen disputes with ten or more participants in this sample, half were water-rights disputes. Undoubtedly, this tendency was partly due to the fact that when an irrigation system was large any changes in the distribution of water could potentially affect a great number of peasants. Similarly, lineages or village organizations "corporately" owned and maintained the larger irrigation systems. When a serious threat to their common interest arose, these organizations apparently were able to mobilize their clientele to defend their rights.

Turning to the monthly distribution of water-rights disputes, we find three peak periods for water-rights disputes in the third, sixth, and eighth lunar months. Virtually no disputes occurred from the tenth to the second lunar months (see Figure 3–2). The monthly pattern seems to have been related to the fluctuations in the demand for water during the growing seasons and the seasonality of rainfall. This pattern also underscores the suddenness and spontaneity of water-rights disputes. Apparently, the water requirements of paddy rice were such that peasant cultivators could not long tolerate disruptions in the normal distribution of water. Not surprisingly, under these conditions disputes over water were usually dealt with swiftly and decisively.

27 HKTB 0081, QL 7.9.17. 28 ZPZZ 0012, QL 15.10.11.

Table 3–2. *Total Participants and Duration for Water-rights Disputes*

Number of Participants	Number of Disputes
Two	41
Three	21
Four	17
Five–nine	20
Ten or more	9[a]
Total	108
Duration	
One day or less	85
One day–one month	8
Estimated within one month	13
One month–one year	2
More than one year	0
Total	108

[a]Includes the two largest incidents, involving 27 and 31 individuals.

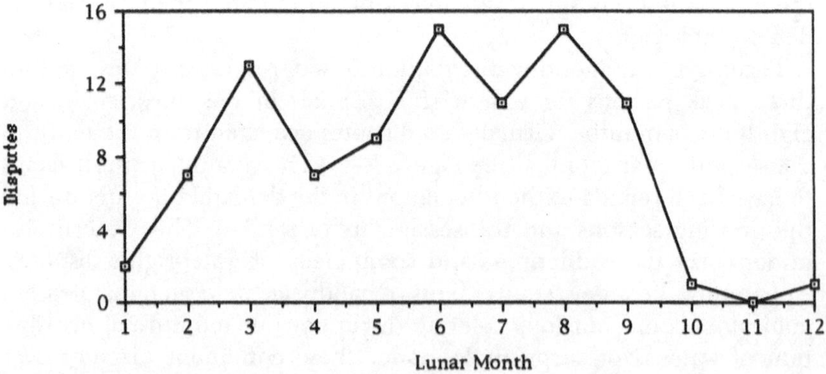

Figure 3–2 Water-rights Disputes by Month[a]

[a]Excluding sixteen disputes for which the precise date was unknown.

Although noncontractual disputes usually reveal less about the evolution of property rights during the eighteenth century, these disputes were indicative of the rising tensions in rural society that the tightening of control over land had spawned. On a case-by-case basis, the connection between these disputes and the larger changes in the economy may not always be apparent. However, when viewed in their entirety over a sixty-year period on a province-wide basis, the connection becomes somewhat clearer. In Chapter 5, I will present a further analysis of the overall temporal and geographic distribution of all types of disputes to illustrate this point, but first I will present a detailed examination of contractual disputes.

4
"Crafty and Obdurate Tenants": Redemption, Rent Defaults, and Evictions

Contractual disputes include three major issues: redemption of conditional sales, rent defaults, and evictions. Unlike water rights and boundary disputes, in which the issues were clear-cut and the juxtaposition of plots of land determined the proximate cause of the disputes between neighbors, contractual disputes were rooted in violations of written or oral agreements between individuals who may not have known each other personally. Boundary and water-rights disputes were age-old issues, but contractual disputes reveal the dynamics of the broader changes taking place in the rural economy during the eighteenth century. Contractual disputes were more closely related to the increasing competition to define and enforce property rights in land that characterized the eighteenth century. Furthermore, these were issues that had aroused the concern and drawn the attention of provincial-level officials who commented on them in their communications to the central government. In the case of redemptions of conditional sales and rent defaults, these also were issues that prompted several amendments of substatutes to the Qing law code, leading to the criminalization of rent defaults under some circumstances and restrictions on the right of redemption.

Redemption and Other Disputes over Land Sales (56 Cases)[1]

The overwhelming majority of the disputes in this category were related to redemptions (*huishu*) of conditional sales (*dianmai*).[2] Redemption

1 In addition to redemption disputes (49 cases), disputes over sales or transfers of ownership or transfers of control of land (7 disputes) are also included in this category.
2 The processes of redemption and conditional sales will be explained more fully.

refers to the right of the original owner of a plot of land to buy it back at the original sale price. Conditional sales were usually made for less than the full market value of the land, and the seller often remained on the land and paid rent to the buyer. Sometimes the purchaser tilled the land himself or leased it to a tenant. In any case, the income that the purchaser derived from the land can be considered a form of interest paid on the amount that the purchaser had advanced. Over time, conditional sales were more clearly distinguished in contracts. Prior to the Qianlong reign, if the land had belonged to a particular family for several generations and was considered part of the family's patrimony, the right of redemption was generally presumed. If a particular parcel of land had been bought and sold numerous times, and had in essence become a commodity, the right of redemption could not be presumed, unless it was specifically stipulated in the terms of the sale. Contracts that clearly specified the terms under which redemption was possible became more common over the course of the eighteenth century. Customarily, redemption was only allowed after a predetermined period of time had elapsed, but in practice some individuals claimed redemption rights on sales that had been consummated decades earlier. As explained in the following text, the practice of redemption had existed for centuries, but, as the need to revise the Qing code and the violent incidents described as follows indicate, disputes over redemption had become a serious problem in the eighteenth century.

The right to redeem land was an accepted custom in China that predated the Qing dynasty. H. F. Schurmann refers to this type of sale, as practiced in the Song and Yuan dynasties (960–1368), as "limited tenure." According to Schurmann, if the seller could not repurchase the land within the designated time period, full title to the land accrued to the buyer.[3] The practice of conditional sales has generally been associated with the deep personal bond that peasants felt for their land. According to Henry McAleavy, most peasant proprietors were loathe to part with their land, and conditional sales usually took place when a peasant needed cash for a funeral or marriage and was "forced" to part with some of his land. According to Yang Guozhen, conditional sales

The *dian* has also been translated as *mortgage, pawn, pledge,* as well as *conditional sale.* The term *dang,* usually translated as *pledge* or *pawn,* was also sometimes used in Guangdong. While *dang* and *dian* were sometimes indistinguishable in practice, *dang* was usually used when the land was put up as security for a loan. With regard to the disputes, I have chosen to designate this particular issue *redemption disputes* since the cause of the dispute was usually over the conditions under which the land could be repurchased.

3 H. F. Schurmann, p. 513, "Traditional Property Concepts in China," *Far Eastern Quarterly* (1956) 15.4: 507–16.

Table 4–1. *Guangdong Counties Where Landowners Left Their Villages to Engage in Trade or Business*

Year	Location
1742	Jieyang, Chaozhou[a]
1743	Wengyuan, Shaozhou[b]
1750	Raoping, Chaozhou[c]
1755	Panyu, Guangzhou[d]
1771	Haiyang, Chaozhou[e]
1775	Chaoyang, Chaozhou[f]
1790	Shicheng, Gaozhou[g]

[a]QDB, pp. 497–500.
[b]QDB, pp. 607–8.
[c]XKTB 0706, QL 15.9.4.
[d]XKTB 1051, QL 20.3.15.
[e]XKTB 2321, QL 36.12.4.
[f]XKTB 2732, QL 40.4.24.
[g]XKTB 3792, QL 55.8.20.

were very common in the Ming and "flourished" in the Qing.[4] The price was usually 60–80% of the price that could be obtained in an outright sale. The original seller could redeem the land after a mutually agreed upon time period, but the seller could not be compelled to redeem the land before the minimum time period had expired.[5] The conditional sale was subject to regional variations; but prior to the eighteenth century, the custom normally favored the original owner of the land and reflected the general acceptance of the belief that individuals had inalienable rights to land that had been in their families for generations. This is what I mean when I refer to the concept of land as patrimony.

Redemption disputes afford some intriguing glimpses into the relationship between land and commerce, which contradict the conventional view that peasants only sold land to meet extraordinary expenses such as funerals or weddings. Reflecting the growing commercialization

4 Yang, 1988, p. 42.
5 Henry McAleavy, p. 406, "*Dien* in China and Vietnam," *Journal of Asian Studies* (May 1958) 17.3: 403–15.

of the eighteenth century, redemption disputes from Guangdong reveal that some conditional sales were transacted to raise cash to invest in trade or business (see Table 4–1). In seven disputes over conditional sales, landowners who sold their land conditionally immediately left their villages to engage in business or trade (*waichu shengli* or *waichu maoyi*). Five cases specifically mentioned that the funds obtained through the conditional sales of land were invested in a business. For example, Wu Aman of Chaoyang county, Chaozhou, turned over control of his 1.4 *mu* plot of land to his brother Wu Rongchuang when he left the village to do business (*waichu shengli*) in Qiongzhou prefecture. Later, Wu Rongchuang sold the land conditionally and went to join his brother.[6] In another case, in Haiyang county, Chaozhou, three branches (*fang*) of the Yang lineage rotated management of a corporately owned field (*changtian*). (Income from the field was meant to defray the costs of lineage-sponsored rituals.) In 1768, the head of one lineage conditionally sold his right to manage the field for 8,000 copper cash (*wen*) and went to Qiongzhou prefecture to enter into business.[7]

Unfortunately, the homicide reports contained no information on the size or nature of the trade or businesses. Nevertheless, these cases do show that it was possible for landowners to use either the equity or the income from their land to obtain capital and enter into commerce or trade. Thus, selling land was not necessarily the desperate act of downwardly mobile peasants. While the sample is admittedly small, using land as a springboard to enter trade or business appears to have been an economic alternative available to some peasant farmers. Since it was likely that most individuals who sold land conditionally to invest in trade or commerce were not involved in a homicide, the practice was probably not uncommon.

With the growing commercialization of the rural economy in the eighteenth century, land was bought and sold more freely and the practice of redemption became a regular point of contention. Whatever the motivation for conditional sales, abuses of the practice were sufficiently serious to draw the attention of high officials. For example, a report from the Governor General of Guangdong, Emida, in 1735 described the range of problems that abuses of redemption could cause. Among the evil customs the Governor General enumerated were grandsons making claims on land sold by their grandfathers; threats to commit suicide to implicate individuals who refused to grant redemptions, the commendation of land to powerful families who would better able to press claims; and demands for supplemental payments to compensate

6 XKTB 2732, QL 40.4.24. 7 XKTB 2321, QL 36.12.4.

for the increased value of the land since the conditional sale had occurred. He also complained of "evil tenants" (peasants who sold land conditionally and continued to till the land as tenants) who often refused to pay rent. "They curse their landlords and threaten them with violence."[8] The Governor General concluded his memorial with a call to clarify the terms of land sales.

In response to disputes arising from conditional sales, the Qing law code was revised twice during the Qianlong reign to distinguish between "live" sales (*huomai*), which could be redeemed, and "outright" sales (*juemai*), which were final.[9] In 1740, a new substatute provided that if the contract governing the sale of land clearly stated an outright sale and there no was clear statement regarding supplemental payments (*zhaotie*), then redemption should not be allowed. The new substatute further stated that, when a contract does not specify an outright sale or clearly fix a time limit for redemption, middleman should be allowed to estimate a one-time supplemental payment and then have the parties sign a contract as an outright sale. If the buyer of the land is unwilling to pay the supplement, the original owner may buy his land back at the original price. If the outright sale is clearly stated in the contract and kin or neighbors of the original owner try to force a redemption at a lower price, they should be punished.[10] Strange as it may seem, it was not uncommon for the original landowner to demand supplemental payments to compensate for increases in the value of the land since the time of the conditional sale, and, as we shall see in the following text, in some cases the original owners did receive multiple supplemental payments before a violent dispute ensued.

In 1756, another new substatute held that contracts for conditional sales must include the phrase *huishu*. In the case of outright sales, contracts must also clearly state that there is no future possibility of redemption (*juemai yong bu huishu*). Sales made prior to this regulation, which had not specified a time limit, could not be redeemed after thirty years. If there was no mention of outright sale, the redemption should be decided according to the terms of the contract. When the time period for redemption was unclear and there was no mention of outright sale,

8 KYQ, p. 126.

9 See Yang Guozhen, 1984, 1: 101–18. George Jamieson, et al., p. 154, "Tenure of Land in China and the Condition of the Rural Population," *Journal of the North China Branch of the Royal Asiatic Society* (1888) 23: 59–174.

10 Ma Jianshi and Yang Yutang, eds., p. 436, *Daqing luli tongkao jiazhu* (Compendium of revisions to the Qing law code), (Beijing: Zhongguo Zhengfa Daxue Chubanshe, 1992).

the sale would be considered outright if the land was not redeemed within thirty years. The law also stated that those who cause disorder and struggle should be punished. In both cases, punishment would be administered according to the "doing what should not be done" (*buyingzhong*) law, a catchall law used to punish any actions that a magistrate deemed improper.

Whether it was entrepreneurial peasants attempting to take advantage of commercial opportunities or land-hungry or impoverished sons or grandsons of individuals who had sold land before the eighteenth century seeking land to till or attempting to garner the increased value of the land, many individuals were using, and sometimes abusing, the right to redeem land sales during the Qianlong reign. With the right to redeem becoming a source of contention, the central government was forced to take action simply to safeguard public order. Whatever the reasons for engaging in a conditional land sale, problems related to the practice were sufficiently widespread and frequent to compel the central government to add two new statutes to the law code. The fact that both laws were added to the code during the first two decades of the Qianlong reign, when rice prices (see Chapter 5) and, presumably, land values were rising sharply, also indicates that disputes over conditional sales was related to economic changes. Interestingly, in addition to clarifying the practice of conditional sale, both laws also made it a crime to abuse the right to redeem conditional sales. As the cases described in the following paragraphs illustrate, such legislation was not entirely effective in limiting violence or disputes.

Among the proximate causes of redemption disputes were flat refusals to allow original owners to redeem land sales; violations of time restrictions on redemptions; demands for supplemental payments by the original owner or his relatives; resale of land before the original seller had an opportunity to redeem; and fraudulent conditional sales or "double" conditional sales of the same parcel of land. At the heart of all these disputes was the tension between the concept of land as an alienable commodity and land as an inviolable patrimony. An examination of redemption disputes reveals quite clearly the violent potential created when the pressure of economic change induced demands to alter the customs and norms of rural society.

Redemption disputes were perhaps the most complex of all property-rights issues. In some cases, the disputes spanned several generations and embroiled several different families. For instance, a dispute among the Liu, Wang, and Huang families, which occurred in Heyuan county, Huizhou, on QL 12.9.22 (1747), could be traced back to a land sale that took place sixty-one years earlier. In 1686, Liu Chengyou's grandfather received 5.8 ounces (*liang*) of silver to relinquish his tenancy rights to a plot of land that he had sold conditionally to Wang Weikang's grandfather Wang Guoyu.[11] A year after this payment, Wang Guoyu conditionally sold the land to Huang Maohua's father, Huang Tiaojie. According to the terms of this sale, the land could be redeemed in ten years. After that time period had expired, Huang Tiaojie sold the land to Huang Yasi's father, Huang Xiaozhong, for 9 ounces of silver. This time, the deed did not contain a clause regarding redemption.

In QL 12.6 (1747), Liu Chengyou's elder brother Liu Chengzhang had managed to raise the original sale price of 5.8 ounces of silver that his grandfather had received in 1686. Liu asked two village elders (*xianglao*), Liao Tingzhang and Zhong Liuzhang, to arrange the redemption of the land from Wang Guoyu. Wang Guoyu kept .8 ounce for himself and accompanied Liu Chengzhang to see Huang Maohua. Initially, Huang Maohua was unwilling to redeem the land. Zhang Dejie (apparently Huang's friend) urged him to accept the money and acquiesce in the transfer of the land. Huang Maohua accepted the money and gave his "deed" to Liu Chengzhang. Because it was the sixth month and the seedlings had already been transplanted, it was decided to split the crop at the season's end. Thereupon, Liu Chengzhang and the others dispersed.

Subsequently, Huang Maohua and Zhang Dejie went to see the "current owner," Huang Xiaozhong, to request a redemption. Producing his deed, which stated a sale price of 9 ounces of silver and which did not include a provision for redemption, Huang Xiaozhong refused the request to redeem the land. Huang Maohua and Zhang Dejie kept the money they had earlier received from Liu and left. They divided the money between themselves but did not inform Liu Chengzhang about what had transpired. This set the stage for a fatal confrontation.

On QL 12.9.22 (1747), Liu heard that Huang Yasi and his brother Huang Shiyong were at the field harvesting the crop. Assuming that the

11 While it was never explicitly stated in the document, it appears that Liu Chengyou's grandfather had previously sold his "ownership" rights on this land to Wang Guoyou. The literature on land rights in China often refers to the distinction between "surface" rights, the ownership of the topsoil of the land, and also the tenancy rights and "bottom rights," the rights to the subsoil and the tax obligation for the land. The division of land ownership in this way has frequently been attributed to the growing commercialization of agriculture and the desire of peasants to retain some tie to their land. A peasant could sell his land but retain the right to till it. References to this practice are quite common in the secondary English- and Chinese-language sources, but those actual phrases were never used in any of the 630 documents that I read for this study. Therefore, I have avoided the use of these terms even in circumstances where the context seems to suggest that they might be appropriate.

field had been redeemed, Liu Chengzhang and his brother Liu Chengyou went to the field to receive their share of the harvest. An argument ensued. Liu Chengyou hit Huang Yasi with a wooden staff. Huang Shiyang and Huang Yasi immediately fled, but Liu Chengyou pursued them. Enraged, Huang Yasi entered his shed, which was located on a nearby embankment, and got a fowling piece to "frighten" Liu Chengyou. Unintimidated, Liu lowered his head and began climbing the embankment to attack Huang. According to Huang's later testimony, the gun was old and faulty, his hand was shaking, and the gun accidentally went off. Huang claimed that he did not know that one or two small stones were packed in the barrel along with the gunpowder. The gun discharged and fatally wounded Liu in the head.[12]

The magistrate who investigated the homicide ordered that the 5.8 ounces of silver should be returned to the Liu family. Under the "doing what should not be done" law, the magistrate also sentenced Wang Guoyu, Huang Maohua, and Zhang Dejie to be flogged for cheating the Liu family. The land in question remained under the control of Huang Xiaozhong since the right to redeem had expired. Surprisingly, because shootings were almost always treated as intentional killings, the magistrate accepted Huang Yasi's excuse that the shooting was accidental. Thus, Huang Yasi avoided decapitation and instead was sentenced to strangulation.

Similar cases, in which individuals sought to redeem land that their grandfathers had sold, were not uncommon. For example, in a case that occurred on QL 12.9.28 (1747, location unknown), Lan Qing attempted to redeem land that his grandfather had sold to Liao Xianhui. Liao Xianhui, however, had already resold the land to Liao Dingwan. Violence erupted when Lan Qing and a friend, Ceng Zaoxiu, attempted to harvest the contested field. Sadly, both men were killed in the ensuing affray, but the magistrate did rule that the Lan family could redeem the land since the original sale to Liao Xianhui had included a redemption clause.[13]

Including the incident described, there were eight disputes in this sample in which individuals attempted to redeem land that their grandfathers had sold decades earlier. In six disputes for which we have some record of the magistrate's decision regarding the land, only once did a magistrate uphold a claim for redemption that had not been explicitly stated in the original terms of the sale. This suggests that legislation enacted through imperial edicts did have some effect at the local level.

12 XKTB 0733 QL 15.2.4. See also QDB, pp. 512–14.
13 SS 1573, QL 10.11, Vol. 4; QL 10.9.28.

At the very least, these laws provided some guidance for county magistrates who adjudicated disputes. All eight cases mentioned earlier occurred prior to the Qianlong emperor's 1756 edict that stated that if the period for redemption was not explicit in the terms of sale, a sale would be considered final when the land was not redeemed within thirty years. In fact, evidence from disputes that were preceded by lawsuits shows that the local magistrates consistently followed the provisions of the Qing code (see Chapter 7).

While disputes over redemption continued throughout the Qianlong reign, the proximate causes of disputes shifted away from unstipulated, ambiguous, cross-generational claims toward disagreements over the interpretation of expressed terms of sale. For example, a dispute over compensation for improvements made to land between the Lai and Chen families occurred in Jiaying county, Jiaying, on QL 40.2.5 (1775). Lai Jiankang had purchased two plots of land from Chen Fubai for 15.6 ounces of silver in 1765. The terms of the sale stated clearly that the land could be redeemed in nine years and that at the time of the redemption the original seller would provide compensation for the costs of improvements and the addition of any adjacent wasteland. Lai subsequently enclosed the original field and brought an additional 1 *mu* of adjacent wasteland under cultivation. When this case went to court (this lawsuit will be examined in detail in Chapter 7), it centered exclusively on the amount of compensation for the 1 *mu* of added land.

Reasonable disagreements over the terms of sales or tenuous claims based on custom engendered many disputes, but sometimes fraud and deceit were at work. If the seller of the land could not afford to redeem the sale after the time limit for redemption had elapsed, he might accept a supplemental payment and the sale would then be permanent. Legally, accepting a supplemental payment made the sale final, but that did not prevent sellers from requesting multiple payments. Based on cases examined in this sample, up to three payments were not uncommon. (Yang Guozhen has found evidence of five or more demands in his study of contracts.)[14] In Puning county, Chaozhou, Hong Naijing conditionally sold 3 *mu* to his clansman, Hong Shimei, for 64 ounces of silver. Hong Naijing retained the right to buy the land back in six years. His son Hong Akui remained on the land as a tenant. Less then a year later, Hong Naijing was poor and asked for a supplemental payment. He received 15,000 copper cash. Two months later, Hong's second request for money was turned down.

14 Yang, 1988, p. 36.

At this point, Hong Naijing attempted to sell the land to another clansman, Hong Kerong. This was blatantly illegal, and Hong Kerong, knowing that Hong Naijing did not have clear title to the land, turned him down. Apparently, the word of Hong Naijing's attempted fraud got around. Later, at the Lihu market, Hong Zhiming (the brother of Hong Shimei) confronted Hong Alian (the tenant and son of Hong Naijing) over his father's duplicity. Hong Alian vehemently denied it. A struggle ensued, and Hong Alian's uncle, Hong Akui, came to his nephew's defense. Cursing Hong Akui for joining the fray, Hong Zhiming yanked Hong Alian's queue and refused to let go. Hong Alian became "excited" and brandished a small hatchet to "scare" Hong Zhiming. Wielding his ax, Hong Alian opened a gash in Hong Zhiming's chest. In pain, Hong Zhiming released Hong Alian and fell to the ground. The wound was deep, and Hong Zhiming died later that evening.[15] The magistrate who investigated the homicide ruled that Hong Shimei could retain the use of the land for six years, as stated in the original agreement, and only then could Hong Naijing redeem the land.

In China, kin and neighbors customarily had first claim to land transactions and interference by family and neighbors sometimes complicated otherwise routine land transactions. As noted, this custom had been substantially eroded by the Qing, but it had not completely disappeared. For example, in Panyu county, Guangzhou, the Tai brothers, Tai Shizhang, Tai Shiming, and Tai Shijing, conditionally sold land that they had inherited from their father to a clansman (*zuren*). Later, Tai Shiming redeemed the land without incident. By the time the land was redeemed, its value had risen substantially. Trouble arose when Tai Shizhang, who was destitute, demanded that Tai Shiming pay him the cash equivalent to his share of the increased value. The incident ended tragically when Tai Shizhang killed his elder brother, a serious crime for which he was sentenced to beheading.[16] A similar case occurred in Dongan county, Luoding, when cousins Liu Bi, Liu Run, Liu Zhi, and Liu Dai redeemed land that their fathers had sold during the Kangxi reign (1662–1722). Liu Run held the deed to the land. Later, Liu Run claimed the land was entirely his own and sold it to Chen Changming. A subsequent lawsuit declared the sale illegal. Violence erupted later when Liu Bi caught Liu Run stealing grain from the field.[17] As these cases indicate, whether the motivation was need or greed the increasing commercialization of land led to the erosion and abuse of the custom that kin and neighbors had the first claim to land.

15 XKTB 1747, QL 30.11.6. 16 XKTB 0423, QL 10.6.3.
17 XKTB 0706, QL 15.4.9.

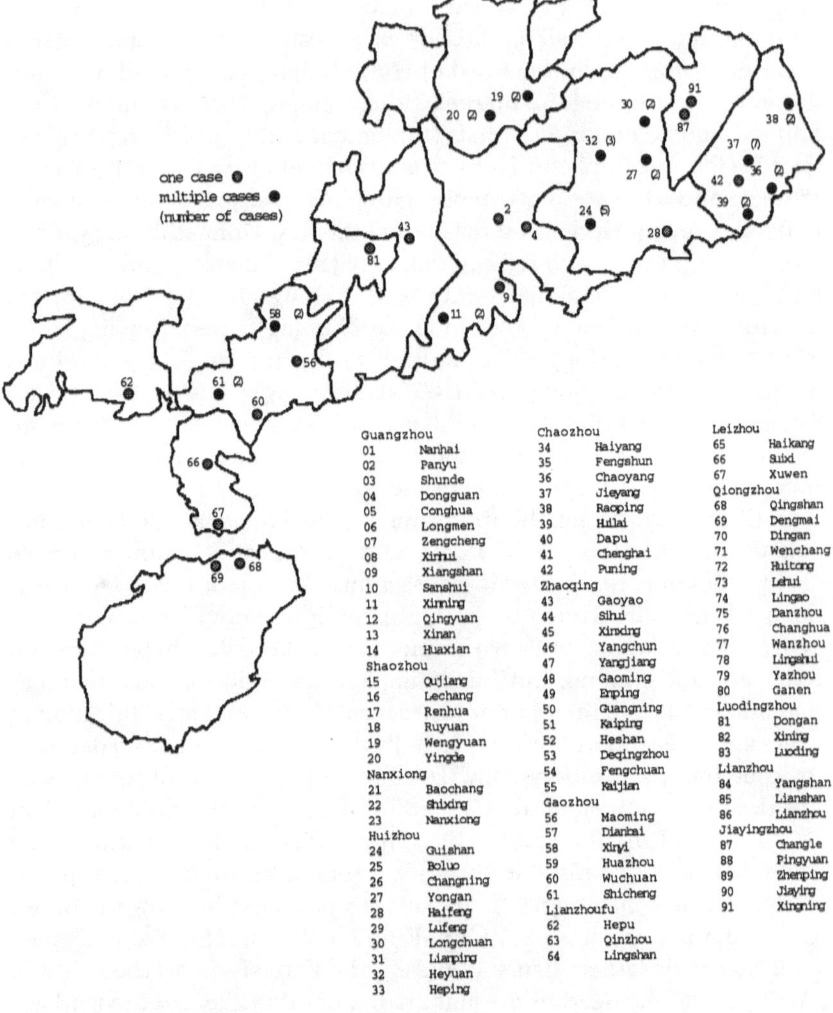

Map 4–1 Guangdong Province Redemption Disputes[a]

[a]Eight locations unknown.

Common Features of Redemption Disputes

Geographically, the distribution of redemption disputes was similar in most respects to other types of disputes, with Chaozhou prefecture first in violence, though Huizhou prefecture was a very close second. The only notable deviation from the usual geographic pattern was the rela-

Table 4–2. *Total Participants and Duration for Redemption Disputes*

Participants per Dispute	Number of Disputes
Two	18
Three	7
Four	9
Five–nine	18
Ten or more	3
Total	55
Duration	
One day or less	12
One day–one month	21
One month–one year	17
More than one year	5
Total	55

tively small number of disputes in Guangzhou prefecture (see Map 4–1). With 4.5 individuals per dispute, redemption disputes were slightly larger than the average for all disputes, perhaps because these disputes were more complex and frequently involved disputes between families rather than individuals. Redemption disputes were also somewhat more protracted than noncontractual disputes, as were other contractual disputes (see Table 4–2). More than a third of all redemption disputes (42%) were outstanding for more than one month. Prior mediation was most common in redemption disputes, perhaps because parties to the dispute often had written contracts or deeds that a magistrate could review. Sorting out the claims and counterclaims, which sometimes spanned generations, may also explain why lawsuits preceded roughly a fifth (21%) of all redemption disputes in this sample.

The monthly distribution of redemption disputes (see Figure 4–1) indicates that there was a certain degree of opportunism in the timing of redemption disputes. The monthly pattern reveals two peaks in the fifth and ninth lunar months, the two months that preceded the early and late harvests. As stated, individuals who sold land conditionally had the right to redeem the land after a certain time period elapsed, but the

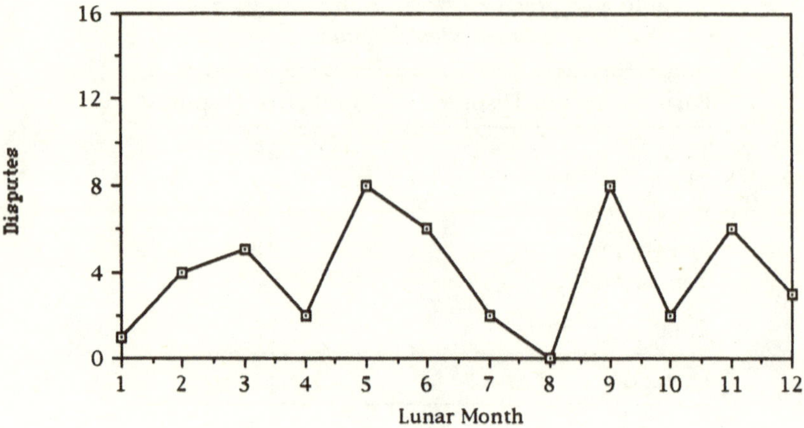

Figure 4–1 Redemption Disputes by Month[a]

[a]Excluding eight disputes for which the precise date was unknown.

precise date often was not specified. Redemptions occurring in the fifth or ninth month entailed the prospect of losing or gaining an entire harvest. Under these circumstances, the stakes were higher, because there were both immediate and long-term consequences to the redemption. Thus, the monthly pattern may not have been coincidental, and there may have been some connection between the timing of the redemption and the use of violence.

Rent Defaults and Other Disputes over Rent (109 Cases)[18]

It should be noted at the outset that nearly half of the disputes examined in this category were obtained from published sources. Since one purpose for publishing these documents was to illustrate rent resistance (*kangzu*) or the "structure of rent exploitation" (*dizu boxiao xingtai*), this is not surprising. Published sources invariably favored contractual disputes that exemplified class conflict but virtually ignored what I have designated as noncontractual disputes, which were more likely to occur between competing peasants. While forty-five of the one hundred and nine rent defaults examined in this sample were obtained from pub-

18 This category includes primarily rent defaults (ninety-nine cases), in addition to other disputes related to the payment of rent (ten cases).

lished sources, only one of the one hundred and eight water-rights disputes was obtained from published sources. Consequently, if one relied solely on the published sources to analyze property-rights disputes, intraclass conflict would be seriously underrepresented. On the other hand, the fact that Chinese researchers examined the entire collection of over 56,000 homicide reports related to land and debt proved to be extremely useful for understanding the temporal pattern of disputes (see Chapter 5).

At first glance, the rent default might seem to be an age-old, mundane issue. Rent defaults were not uncommon in earlier periods of Chinese history. Evidence obtained from the accounts of one wealthy family, which spanned several decades of the late Ming dynasty, reveals that many tenants failed to pay their rent in full at one time or another, and one-third were delinquent in ten or more years over the several decades covered by the sources.[19] Uncertainties like the vagaries of weather or unforeseen personal hardship might easily cause a peasant to default on his rent. Rent-default disputes, however, were not always quite that simple. In fact, in this sample of 109 rent-default disputes, there were only twelve disputes in which tenants pleaded for relief because they had had a poor harvest; a family member was stricken with illness; or they were just too poor to pay. Rent defaults were not simply the result of misfortune or bad luck. In fact, when defaulting on rent was criminalized in 1727, the law specifically applied to "crafty and obdurate" tenants who *refused* to pay rent. Chinese scholars refer to this phenomenon as "rent resistance" (*kangzu*) to distinguish it from defaults arising from circumstances beyond the control of the tenant. Thus, while rent defaults could have occurred for any number of reasons, the fact that the Qing government criminalized willful rent defaults in 1727 clearly indicates that defaulting on rent had become a more complex and serious problem by the early eighteenth century. A careful examination of rent-default disputes during the Qianlong reign exposes the simmering class and social tensions that were part of the increasingly aggressive efforts to define property rights in land during the eighteenth century.

The proximate cause of each rent-default dispute was the same, failure to pay rent, but the reasons for failing to pay the rent and the manner in which the disputes unfolded clearly changed over time. Furthermore, these disputes must be viewed within the larger context of "rent

19 Kang Chao, 1981, p. 733. Chao's evidence comes from a single source in the Jiangnan region.

resistance" that can be traced back to the late Ming dynasty. Tanaka Masatoshi has found that large-scale rent resistance had been common in the late Ming in Jiangsu, Fujian, Huguang, and Henan provinces. Some tenants organized leagues that drew members from several villages and bargained with landlords to reduce rents. According to Tanaka, rent resistance, which was not due to famine or natural disasters, became part of daily life by the seventeenth century. As markets expanded, some tenants profited from selling grain that should have been used for rent. Other tenants paid their rent in poor-quality rice and threatened landlords with violence when they objected.[20] As Tanaka's research demonstrates, the connection between rent resistance and commercialization can be traced to the late seventeenth century.

The problem of rent resistance continued after the founding of the Qing in 1644. According to Liu Yongcheng, an upsurge in rent resistance, and demands for rent reduction and permanent tenancy began during the Kangxi reign (1662–1722) and crested in the Qianlong reign. Liu maintains that rent resistance was related to the shift from share rents to fixed rents, the increased personal and economic freedom that peasants had won during the Ming-Qing transition, and increased commercialization of the economy.[21] Share rents, which were common during the Ming dynasty, had distributed the risk of poor harvest and the benefits of greater productivity more evenly between landlord and tenant, but the spread of fixed rents in kind, which became prevalent by the Qianlong reign, placed the risks and benefits almost exclusively on the tenant.[22] Before the demographic upswing began in the Qianlong reign, fixed rents largely benefited tenants.

20 Tanaka Masatoshi, pp. 205–9.

21 Liu Yongcheng, 1979b, pp. 55–7.

22 Liu Yongcheng, 1980, p. 57, "Qingdai qianqi di nongye zudian guanxi" (Agricultural tenancy relations in the early Qing period), pp. 56–88 in Chinese Academy of Social Sciences, History Research Institute, ed., *Qingshi luncong* (Symposium on Qing history) 2 (Beijing: Zhonghua shuju). See also Xiuyuan Song, p. 568, "Qingdai qianqi dizu xingtai di fazhan bianhua" (The development and change in forms of rent in the early Qing period), pp. 568–76 in *Ming Qing dangan lunwen xuanbian* (Selected essays on Ming Qing documents), Zhu Jinfu, ed. (Beijing: Archives Publishing House, 1985). Song supports the assertion that fixed rents in kind had supplanted share rents by the Qianlong reign. Based on an examination of 853 documents related to rent in Qianlong, only 97 referred to share rents. In 110 cases out of 385 used in this sample for Guangdong in which the type of rent was known, including all disputes regardless of issue, 7 were share rents and 103 were fixed rents, of which 93 were fixed in kind and 10 were fixed in cash.

With greater economic freedom and access to markets, peasants became more productive. Landlords also sought to capture a greater share of the increased productivity, but this was difficult to the extent that fixed rents had become the norm. Liu Yongcheng depicts rent resistance and demands for permanent tenancy as a response to the struggle between tenants and landlords to capture a larger share of the rising agricultural productivity.[23] A report from Qingyuan county, Guangzhou, in 1732 on efforts to standardize weights and measures indicated that this struggle took many forms.[24] According to this report, a local official attempted to standardize the market *dou*, a dry measure for grain purchases, which was not the same size as the rental *dou*, a dry measure for rent payments made in grain. Apparently, the size of the rental *dou*, which was determined by the fertility of the land, could be 10–50% larger or smaller than the newly decreed standard market *dou*. Ostensibly, this standardization of the market *dou* had no relation to the rental *dou*, but both landlords and tenants attempted to exploit the difference for their individual benefit. The memorial ordered that if the market *dou* was used for rent payments, the payment should be adjusted to avoid discrepancies in the amount of rent.

The report went on to comment on other aspects of the agrarian economy that suggest that the balance of economic power in rural society had yet to shift in favor of landlords at the start of the Qianlong reign. It noted that rents in Guangdong were generally very light, in some cases not exceeding 30% of the output of the land. Furthermore, when tenants opened new land belonging to landlords, they sometimes retained all the additional output. The report concluded with a call for severe punishments if such swindling and cheating continued. Apparently, as Guangdong entered the eighteenth century, tenants enjoyed a superior bargaining position vis-à-vis landowners and defiance of landlords was not uncommon. One local gazetteer referred to "evil tenants who look upon avoiding rent as a given" in the early eighteenth century.[25] It would seem that peasants had exploited their greater economic freedom effectively during the early years of the Qianlong reign. But over the course of the Qianlong reign, rising population and a growing shortage of quality arable land clearly favored landlords and led

23 On this point, Tanaka would also agree. He also argues that productivity increased after tenants gained more economic freedom. But tenants faced increasing demands from "usurious merchants" and landlords who sought to capture a share of this greater productivity. See Tanaka, p. 209.

24 KYQ, pp. 124–5. 25 Ibid., p. 126.

to an important innovation in economic institutions: the use of the cash rent deposit.

Rent Deposits

Fan Shuzhi has argued that as population increased and with it the relative scarcity of land, landlords gained the upper hand over tenants and were able to extract deposits from the peasants, which afforded them some protection against rent defaults.[26] Some historians have interpreted the rent deposits as a defensive response taken by landlords to counteract tenant rent resistance.[27] For landlords, particularly for absentee landlords, the rent deposit clearly provided a measure of financial security against defaults. Deposits were paid in cash and could equal up to three years worth of rent. In addition to serving as a guarantee for rental income, the deposit also served as a ready source of capital that could be loaned to generate income from interest payments. Under these circumstances, landlords often accepted lower rents in exchange for cash deposits and still increased their income because the interest earned from loaning the deposit was greater than the income lost by reducing rents.[28]

While some Chinese historians have argued that deposits were a form of exploitation, to the extent that the deposit provided more-secure tenure, tenants also benefited. Local customs varied, but payment of the rent deposit usually entitled the tenant to some long-term rights such as the right to transfer the tenancy to a third party and the right to "permanent" tenancy.[29] Ostensibly, the payment of a deposit gave the tenant the right to sublet or sell the right to tenancy.[30] This has led some historians to draw a link between the rent deposit and the division of topsoil and subsoil rights in China, but, as disputes discussed in the following text reveal, this link was tenuous. Another historian, Fang Erkang, straddled the issue by claiming that although the payment of deposit meant a lower rent, the deposit also robbed tenants of badly needed capital for investment.[31]

Initially, rent deposits and fixed rents seem to have favored tenants

26 Fan Shuzhi, p. 134, Many of Fan's examples are from Hunan province.

27 Feng Erkang, p. 61, "Qingdai di yazuzhi yu zutian guanxi dijubu bianhua" (Rent deposits in the Qing period and changing tenancy relations), *Nankai Xuebao* (1980) 1: 61–7.

28 Jiang Taixin, p. 147.

29 See Song 1985a, p. 825. Also see Fan Shuzhi, p. 130, and Liu, 1980, pp. 72–3.

30 See Song, 1985a, pp. 825–6.

31 Feng Erkang, p. 67.

and peasants because they permitted greater economic freedom and allowed tenants to benefit from the increased commercialization of the agrarian economy.[32] The fact that rent deposits and fixed rents were widespread in the Qing suggests that initially both landlords and tenants perceived them as beneficial. For landlords, rent deposits and fixed rents represented a guaranteed income. For tenants, they represented more-secure tenure and greater freedom to manage land. Most historians also agree that the rent deposit probably contributed to increased productivity because it provided long-term tenure and tenants were more willing to invest in improvements. Similarly, fixed rents also contributed to increased productivity. When rents were fixed, tenants had greater incentives to increase output because they alone benefited from such increases.

The shift to a contractually based tenancy had other consequences. Some historians have argued that the erosion of the paternalistic moral codes that in earlier times had governed the interactions between tenants or bond servants and landlords and the shift toward contractual arrangements "unsoftened and unstrengthened by personal contacts" exposed peasants to greater hardships in bad economic times.[33] Although it has been assumed that tenants who paid deposits strengthened their claim to the land, the payment of rent deposits did not necessarily mean that the right of "permanent" tenancy was automatic or inviolable. Homicide reports reveal numerous cases in which landlords deducted rent arrears from the deposits of tenants who had defaulted and then summarily released their fields to other peasants. In some cases, when a field was sold or ownership was otherwise transferred, the new owner might ignore the rights of a tenant who had paid a deposit to the previous owner.[34] For example, in Chaoyang county, Chaozhou, the Lin lineage rented land set aside to pay for ancestor worship (*jitian*) to Lu Jihai, who in turn sublet the land to Guo Qianxiang. Guo had paid a deposit of 17 ounces in silver for the right to till the land. When the Lin lineage rotated management of the field to another lineage member, a common custom with lineage-owned land, the new manager's son, Lin Ajun, wanted to till the land himself, but he refused to return Guo Qianxiang's deposit. A bloody confrontation followed in which Guo killed Lin.[35]

32 For a discussion of the ways in which these changes favored tenants and small peasants see Fang Xing, 1983.

33 Elvin, 1973, Chapter 15, and Wiens, 1980, p. 4.

34 In Guangdong, there were numerous cases of new owners refusing to refund deposits or to recognize the rights of former tenants. In their articles cited earlier, both Feng Erkang and Jiang Taixin supply similar examples from other provinces.

35 XKTB 0475, QL 10.2.19.

Theoretically, rent deposits and fixed rent in kind were positive developments because they meant greater freedom for peasants. As the previously mentioned case of Guo Qianxiang clearly shows, however, the rent deposit itself was not sufficient to ensure the security of tenure as some scholars have claimed. Guo Qianxiang stood up for his rights, but landlords undoubtedly cowed less-stalwart tenants. In fact, it has been argued that the cash rent deposit could be used as a "hostage" against tenants. Fearing that landlords might refuse to refund their deposits, tenants might continue to till a particular plot of land on terms that they felt to be undesirable rather than risk a confrontation with a recalcitrant landlord.[36]

At the very least, the appearance of rent deposits was an indication that land tenure and ownership were becoming more sophisticated during the eighteenth century. Whatever impact the institution of the rent deposit might have had on individual tenants and landlords, the use of deposits was widespread by the Qianlong and Jiaqing (1796–1820) reigns.[37] According to Song Xiuyuan, rent deposits were a nationwide practice in the Qing.[38] Whether we consider the rent deposit a landlord concession or a new form of exploitation of tenants may depend on a case-by-case analysis. Nevertheless, the rent deposit clearly represented a step toward a more contractually based system of land tenure in which personal ties between landlords and tenants were less significant and economic competition became much sharper. Based on the evidence in homicide cases, the rent deposit appears to have been important as a guarantee of landlord income and less effective as a guarantee of tenant rights.

Rent Resistance

As noted, rent resistance can be traced to the late Ming. Depending on the individual researcher, the term *rent resistance* encompasses a variety of disputes both large and small, violent and nonviolent. Clearly, some rent defaults involved tenants who willfully resisted rent. These were the "crafty" or "obdurate" tenants that the Yongzheng emperor branded as criminals in his 1727 edict. The adjectives *crafty* and *obdurate* were not merely pejoratives, but were used to distinguish tenants who resisted or avoided rent purposefully from those who could not pay their rent

36 Jiang Taixin, 1980, p. 149. 37 Ibid., p. 135.
38 Song Xiuyuan, 1985a, p. 821.

because of economic hardships. The Governor General of Guangdong at the start of the Qianlong reign, Emida, also condemned the pernicious practice: "evil" tenants who refused to pay their complete rent. According to his report, some tenants used the excuse that they had invested in improvements to the land as an excuse to retain control of land even when in arrears. Another type of evil tenant was adept at cheating absentee landlords who were unfamiliar with their property. These tenants altered the shape of fields and sold off portions of the land before returning it to the landlord. The Governor General complained of endless lawsuits and violence that sometimes resulted in homicide.[39]

Improvements in the relative economic power of landlords was discernible in the changes over time in rent disputes. In many of the disputes during the early part of the Qianlong reign, when the balance of economic power favored tenants, landlords often intervened personally to collect back rent or to demand the return of their fields for their personal use. Why would a landlord place himself in a demonstrably dangerous situation? Based on the comments of magistrates who investigated homicides, if a landlord evicted a delinquent tenant the landlord lost his claim to the rent arrears. It seems that magistrates considered the tenant's loss of the use of the land sufficiently severe hardship to negate the debt of unpaid rent. If he had not collected a rent deposit, the landlord had few choices. He could risk a confrontation and dun his tenant, hoping to recoup the arrears, or he could cut his losses and find a new tenant. Perhaps reflecting the delayed impact of population pressure on labor or the resiliency of the mutual respect for tenancy rights among the peasantry, new tenants were either not readily available or were unwilling to replace defaulting tenants during the early years of the Qianlong reign. In the later years of the Qianlong reign, population pressure tilted the balance of economic power in favor of landlords and heightened competition among peasant cultivators for a limited supply of arable land. Consequently, intraclass violence between competing tenants was more common in the closing decades of Qianlong's reign, and bitter moral denunciations directed at replacement tenants often marked these disputes.

Change over time in the participants, and the locus of rent defaults illustrate the relationship between the shifting balance of economic power between tenants and landlords, and the nature and

39 KYQ, pp. 124–5.

content of social conflict over the course of the Qianlong reign. A careful scrutiny of homicides related to rent defaults demonstrates the complexity of the long-term impact of population growth and commercialization on economic institutions and property rights as well as the content and form of violent disputes. The case described in the following text is representative of rent defaults that occurred during the early part of the Qianlong reign. It is similar to thirty-six other cases in which landlords personally took part in the effort to recover rent arrears.

Some landlords attempted to take direct control over their land when a tenant defaulted. For example, Cai Wenshui had purchased 2.7 *mu* of land from Xia Lizhang. Xia continued to till the land and pay rent to Cai. On QL 10.3.22 (1745), Xia owed a total of 8 *shi* of grain. Cai dunned Xia numerous times, but to no avail. Wanting to till the land himself, Cai Wenshui hired his "clansmen" – Cai Lirui (*tangdi*), Cai Yuantang (*zudi*), Cai Wenyuan – and Cai Wentong, and went to plow the field. Xia Lizhang stopped them. Cai Wenshui tried to discuss the situation with Xia, but Xia struck Cai in the leg with a bamboo stick. Cai shoved Xia and knocked him to the ground, injuring his left arm and leg.

While Xia remained on the ground, Huang Mazao and Li Suyuan saw what had happened and came to help Xia up. Cai had already resumed plowing the field when Xia again attempted to stop him. Cai dodged Xia and kicked him in the back and ribs, knocking him down. Xia's son, Xia Shihuan, arrived and cursed Cai and his clansmen. Cai Lirui hit Xia Shihuan in the leg with his hoe. At this point, the fighting ended and the Cais left the scene. Xia Lizhang was carried home, where he died of his injuries two days later.[40] Interestingly, the magistrate in this case sentenced Cai Wenshui to death, but also ruled that Xia's son should be given an opportunity to redeem the land. Clearly, the fact that the Xias had once owned the land was an important consideration for the magistrate, who obviously supported the traditional view of land as patrimony.

Faced with rent arrears, another tactic that landlords frequently employed was to seize animals or to harvest standing grain in lieu of back rent. The following case, which took place in Xinhui county, Guangzhou, was very similar to fifteen other rent default disputes. In QL 3.1 (1738), Huang Jiaren had assumed control of a field that his lineage corporately owned (*changtian*). Huang leased the land to Tan Renhe for an annual rent of 9 *shi*. That year Tan only paid 4 *shi*. (Huang

40 SS 1571, QL 10.11, Vol. 1; QL 10.9.15.

calculated that the 5 *shi* was worth 1,000 *wen*.) On QL 4.8.5, (1739), Huang again dunned Tan, but Tan had no money or grain. Huang took Tan's cow as compensation. Unbeknownst to Huang, Tan later took the cow back.

The next day Huang returned to Tan's home to demand payment. On the road he "happened" to meet his clansman (*zudi*), Huang Jiazu, who accompanied him. At Tan's home an argument broke out between the Huangs and Tan. Seeing that Tan had taken his cow back, Huang again tried to lead it away. Tan tried to stop him, but Huang Jiazu blocked him. Tan twisted Huang's shirt front in his fist and butted him with his head. Huang punched Tan in the ribs. Tan grabbed Huang by the testicles and pulled upward. Huang hit Tan again in the left ear, but Tan would not release him. Huang Jiazu was in great pain and called out for help. Huang Jiaren released the cow and returned to help, but he could not separate Tan and Huang Jiazu. Huang Jiaren struck Tan in the back at the base of the ribs. Tan finally let go and fell to the ground.

At that moment, Tan Zouxiang, Tan Renhe's son, and Huang Jiahe saw what had happened and went to stop them. It was already too late. Huang Jiaren was frightened and fled. Tan Zuoxiang reported the incident to Tan Xiantu, the local constable (*baozhang*), and together they carried Tan's father home. Tan was seriously injured and died that evening. Following the usual practice, the magistrate ruled that Tan's arrears should be forgiven, since he had lost his life. Although Huang Jiaren was responsible for Tan's death, he was not sentenced to death. Under a practice known as *liuyang*, the magistrate commuted Huang's death sentence so that Huang, an only son, could care for his elderly mother, who was over seventy.[41]

As these two cases illustrate, confronting defaulting tenants was a risky proposition. One assumes that the landlords probably only wanted to intimidate their tenants into paying their arrears, but violence was unpredictable. Homicide could occur with unexpected suddenness, and the survivors of the confrontation faced criminal prosecution, which usually meant the death penalty. Not surprisingly, some landlords avoided personal contact with defaulting tenants. There were fourteen disputes in which landlords sent hired workers or younger male relatives, usually a son or nephew, to collect rents. Less often, some landlords relied on "professional" rent collectors and yamen runners to collect delinquent rent. (The role of the yamen underlings in enforcing official decisions will be discussed further in Chapter 7.) In fact, these

41 XKTB 0204, QL 5.7.4.

practices became more common throughout all of China in response to the risks entailed in collecting rents.[42]

While landlords appear to have consciously limited their direct involvement in rent-default disputes, economic and demographic trends eventually contributed to lowering their risk and exposure to violence. Although class conflict was more common in rent defaults, there were twenty-two intraclass disputes between competing peasants. In eight of these disputes, seven of which occurred in the latter third of the Qianlong reign (1775–95), the former tenant accused the succeeding tenant of "seizing" or "stealing" (*duo*)[43] his field or tenancy. From the context of the document it was clear that the "losing" tenant meant to imply that the action was unfair and morally wrong. It would seem that heightened competition among tenants had also eroded the traditional respect for the "moral" claims of fellow peasants. Perhaps because such struggles struck at the foundations of rural society, the accounts of these disputes reveal a deep bitterness and rage on the part of tenants who lost their land and livelihood. The following two examples illustrate the point.

For many years, Li Zixiang of Xinning county, Guangzhou, had leased land from Mei Ruihong, a *shengyuan* degree holder. In QL 38.2 (1773), Mei Ruihong leased the land to Huang Yarong because Li had defaulted on his rent. On QL 39.02.25 (1774), Huang was at the field plowing. Li passed by and saw Huang at work. Li began to criticize him for "seizing" the field that Li had tilled for so long. The two men began to fight. Li clobbered Huang with a pole and Huang fled. Li pursued Huang, hitting him with the pole from behind as he chased him. Huang turned and tried to grab the pole, while Li continued whacking him. Finally, Huang struck Li in the side and knocked him down. Li's younger brother, Li Zishi, and Zhu Tongye witnessed the violence, but were too late to stop it. Li Zishi took his brother home and reported the incident to the local authorities. The magistrate ordered Huang to provide medical treatment (*baogu*) for Li. Li's wounds were serious, and five days later he died. In this case, the landlord was not involved or even aware that a violent dispute had occurred until after the fact.

A similar dispute, which occurred in Lianping county, Huizhou, also demonstrates the advantages that the rent deposit afforded landlords. In 1778, He Yunwei leased a field that was owned by He Weixiu (same

42 See Introduction, p. 7, to *Qingdai tudi zhanyou guanxi yu diannong kangzu douzheng* (Qing dynasty land ownership relations and tenant rent resistance struggles), Number One Historical Archives of China and Institute of Historical Research of the Chinese Academy of Social Sciences, eds. (Beijing: Zhonghua shuju, 1988).

43 The term *dou* can also mean *to take by superior force or skill, to wrest or carry off.*

surname but unrelated). The rent was 4.8 *shi* per year. After several years of partial defaults, He Yunwei owed 8.2 *shi*. On QL 51.2.20 (1786), He Weixiu told He Yunwei to come to his house because he wanted to deduct the back rent from his deposit. He Yunwei was willing to give up the deposit, but he pleaded to be allowed to continue farming. He Weixiu adamantly refused. On the QL 51.3.2 (1786), He Yunwei was on his way to the mountain to gather firewood when he passed the field and saw the new tenant, Liu Wenyou, turning the soil. Because Liu had "seized" his right to tenancy, He Yunwei went to stop Liu. Liu struck He Yunwei over the head with a pole. He Yunwei retaliated by punching Liu. Liu dropped the pole and came towards He Yunwei. He Yunwei ran away with Liu hot on his heels. Enraged, He Yunwei stopped, picked up a rock, and threw it at Liu. The rock felled Liu, striking him in the left temple. Liu died soon afterward.[44]

Here again we find the shifting undercurrent of violence in the Qianlong reign. In both this case and the one described earlier, the delinquent tenants were clearly at fault and without legal recourse, but their moral outrage would not permit them to accept their fate meekly. In both cases their anger was directed at their would-be replacements not their former landlords, who were safely removed from the locus of violence. Except in cases of exceptionally bad harvests, landlords usually enjoyed official support when they evicted a defaulting tenant. Despite their tendency to uphold ethical norms, local magistrates evinced scant sympathy for defaulting tenants who asserted that their tenancy had been unfairly appropriated. In five of the seven disputes for which information on the official disposition of the property-right issues was available, the magistrate flatly rejected claims by delinquent tenants that the new tenants had unjustly "seized" their rights. In all five of these disputes, the magistrate ruled that the landlord was justified in seeking a new tenant when his previous tenant defaulted.

Finally, while intraclass disputes were not unheard of during the early part of the Qianlong reign, there was a noticeable difference between the tenant-tenant violence of the earlier and later periods. For example, in 1736 Li Mingxian of Dianbai county, Gaozhou, rented two plots of land from Huang Shenghuan for 20.5 *shi* of grain. After Li had been in arrears for several years, Huang decided to lease one of the plots to Long Yunyong. On QL 4.11.6 (1739), Li Mingxian went to plow the field as usual. Long Yunyong saw him and went to stop him. Li denied that he owed any rent and refused to leave the field because the landlord had not personally informed him of any changes. Long said nothing and

44 QDB, pp. 473–4.

went home. After reaching home, Long informed his brother Long Yuntian. Long Yuntian became angry. He took a staff and went to confront Li. When Long Yuntian arrived on the scene, Li Mingxian was using a hoe to release water into the field. Long Yuntian hit him across the shoulder with his staff. Li struck back with his hoe, hitting Long in the head at the base of the ear. Long fell to the ground. Li was frightened and ran home. Long Yuntian's cousin (*tangxiong*) passed by and saw that Long Yuntian was injured. He summoned Long Yunyong to help him. Together they carried Long Yuntian to Li Mingxian's home and ordered him to treat the wounds. Apparently, the injuries were extensive for on the 19th day Long died.[45]

Compared to the two tenant-tenant disputes mentioned earlier that occurred in 1774 and 1786 respectively, some important differences were apparent in this dispute that took place in 1739. Despite the fact that Li Mingxian was in arrears on both plots of land, his landlord only relet one of the fields. Furthermore, the landlord avoided a direct confrontation with Li Mingxian when he did not notify Li that the land in question had been leased to a new tenant. The initial reaction of the replacement tenant, Long Yunyong, was also telling. Rather than confront Li Mingxian, Long backed off almost immediately. Even more interesting was the official reaction to this incident. Huang Shenghuan, the landlord, was punished for creating a dangerous situation by not informing Huang that he had leased the field to Long. Huang was punished under the "doing what you should not do" law. Because he was a minor-degree holder (*jiansheng*), however, he received a fine rather than a flogging.

In a very similar case, which occurred on QL 19.11.28 (1754) in Zengcheng county, Guangzhou, He Tingqiu assumed control of a field after his uncle died. Because his uncle owed back rent, the owners of the land, Wang Jingze and Wang Zuoyi, leased the field to Deng Deguang, but did not inform He Tingqiu. Predictably, violence ensued when Deng heard that He Tingqiu was plowing the field. In this case, the presiding magistrate also found that the landlords were culpable for causing the dispute because they had not informed He Tingqiu and, since they were not degree holders, the flogging was carried out.[46] This case and the one described earlier were also telling because they highlight the delicate balance that magistrates sought to maintain between competing economic interests and enforcing property rights on the one hand while maintaining the appearance of fairness and upholding ethical norms on the other hand.

45 XKTB 0207, QL 5.7.3. 46 XKTB 1085, QL 20.7.16.

Common Features of Rent Defaults

Violence in rent-default disputes was almost always small scale, unpremeditated, and took place between neighbors or persons known to each other. At 3.9 persons per dispute, the average number of active participants in rent defaults was just slightly below the overall average of 4.2 for all disputes. Other than an anomalous concentration of rent defaults in relatively peaceful Luoding prefecture, the geographic distribution of rent-default disputes mirrored the overall concentration of disputes in the eastern half of the province (see Map 4–2). Generally, rent defaults had longer gestation periods, with 44% of rent-default disputes simmering for over a month (see Table 4–3). This was probably due to the fact that double-cropping was common in all counties of Guangdong and landlords appeared to have been willing to wait until the following harvest was in before forcefully pressing their claims for arrears.

Compared to other types of contractual disputes, there were relatively few efforts at mediation or lawsuits for the rent defaults in this sample. On the one hand, the longer lag time between the appearance of a dispute and the outbreak of a violent confrontation meant that there was ample time for the parties to a dispute to seek mediation or initiate a lawsuit if they felt that it would be effective. Alternatively, official intervention in rent defaults might have been effective and might have prevented violence. Given the nature of the sources it is impossible to judge the general effectiveness of the courts, but my reading of the sources for all types of disputes leads me to believe that the enforcement of official decisions was less than rigorous and sometimes counterproductive, a point that will be addressed further in Chapter 7. Local magistrates were adept at deciding disputes; but given the difficulty entailed in enforcing officials' decisions and the time and expense of a lawsuit, many individuals appear to have taken matters into their own hands. Furthermore, in the case of rent defaults, the appearance of privately organized rent bursaries during the nineteenth century would also suggest that from the landlords' perspective private initiatives to protect their rights were more efficient and efficacious.[47]

47 Rent bursaries were private organizations that landlords or groups of landlords established to collect rent and manage their properties. This was an example of private individuals designing an institution to enforce property rights in land. According to Yuji Muramatsu, the government eventually lent its support to such organizations in the Jiangnan region. See Yuji Muramatsu, "A Documentary Study of Chinese Landlordism in Late Qing and Early Republican Kiangnan," *Bulletin of the School of Oriental and African Studies* (1966) 29.3: 566–99.

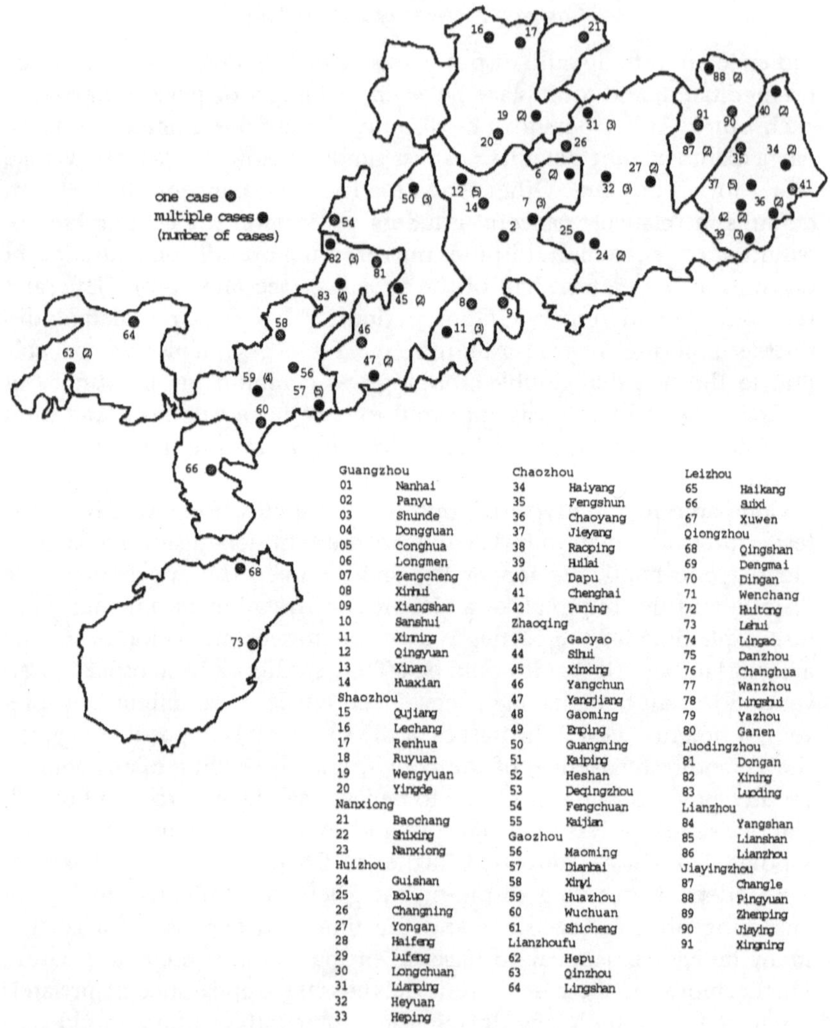

Map 4–2 Guangdong Province Rent-default Disputes[a]

[a] Twelve locations unknown.

The monthly pattern of rent defaults (see Figure 4–2) might explain why a high percentage of rent defaults were drawn-out affairs. The third and sixth lunar months were popular times for rent-default disputes. Rent defaults, like encroachments on boundaries or diversions of water, were blatant and obvious transgressions, but a landlord facing a rent

Table 4–3. *Total Participants and Duration for Rent-default Disputes*

Participants per Dispute	Number of Disputes
Two	31
Three	20
Four	28
Five–nine	27
Ten or more	3
Total	109
Duration	
One day or less	24
One day–one month	34
One month–one year	43
More than one year	8
Total	109

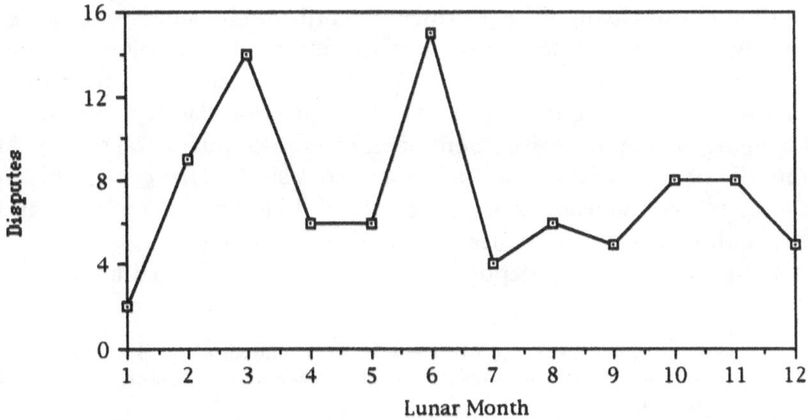

Figure 4–2 Rent-default Disputes by Month[a]

[a] Excluding eighteen disputes for which the precise date was unknown.

default may have been willing to wait until the next harvest before strenuously pressing their claims for back rent. There was always the hope that matters would be settled satisfactorily after the next harvest. On the other hand, some landlords were more impatient. Thus, what we might be seeing are less tolerant landlords pressing their claims at the start of the first growing season in the third lunar month. More-tolerant landlords may have been persuaded to await the first harvest of a new year, which usually occurred in the sixth month, before pressing their claims.

Eviction Disputes (48 Cases)

Included in the category of eviction disputes are all cases in which the attempt to remove a tenant for any reason other than a rent default caused a violent dispute. Most frequently, changes in land ownership – and in the cases of lineage-owned land, changes in management – were the proximate cause of the eviction. In fifteen cases when land had been purchased, the new owner himself, or one of his relatives, attempted to evict the existing tenant. In six other cases, disputes arose when the management of lineage-owned land set aside to pay for the expenses of ancestor worship[48] rotated and the new manager wanted to evict the tenant. In another five disputes, after the landowner died his family tried to evict the tenant. All these cases reflect the highly personalized nature of eighteenth-century rental agreements. Eviction disputes also demonstrate that when new owners took over land they were sometimes reluctant to honor preexisting commitments. This type of dispute was not limited to Guangdong province. Records of civil suits from Baxian county indicate that similar issues caused numerous nonviolent disputes in mid-Qing Sichuan.[49] Eviction disputes provide valuable information on the precarious rights of tenants and the growing class tensions in the changing economic environment of eighteenth-century rural society. At the root of many of these disputes, we once again find the clash between the more economically "rational" concept of land as a commodity and the traditional, "moral" concept of land as patrimony.

Even the use of rent deposits, which supposedly entitled a tenant to

48 The terms *jitian* and *jichan* were also used to designate lineage-owned land, the income from which was set aside to defray the costs of lineage rituals, but *changtian* was used most frequently.

49 Madeline Zelin, p. 513, "The Rights of Tenants in Mid-Qing Sichuan: A Study of Land-Related Lawsuits in the Baxian Archives," *Journal of Asian Studies* (1986) 49.3: 499–526. In forty-three lawsuits, the most common reason for an eviction was a rent default (fourteen). The second most common reason was a change in ownership.

permanent tenure, did not protect some tenants from eviction. Fourteen eviction disputes arose when a landlord attempted to repossess land for personal use. Interestingly, as in the case of rent defaults, there was more direct landlord intervention during the earlier years of the Qianlong reign. Ten disputes that involved direct landlord intervention took place during the first three decades of the Qianlong reign. Often the owner had recently purchased the land. One such dispute took place in Lufeng county, Huizhou, in 1735.[50] Hong Bogao and his brother Hong Botai purchased a plot of land, which was rented to Yang Xinhua. Hong Botai demanded the return of the land from Yang because he planned to till it himself. Yang Xinhua had already planted a crop of sugarcane and wanted to wait until winter, when the sugarcane would be harvested, to return the land. Hong Botai would not consent to this. Later, Hong Bogao went to the field carrying a scythe and began to destroy the sugarcane. Yang Xinhua tried to stop him, and Hong Bogao punched Yang Xinhua. Yang Xinhua became "excited" and took the scythe and repeatedly struck Hong Bogao. The next day, Hong Bogao died.[51] Unfortunately, no information on the magistrate's ruling was available for this case. In other cases, however, when there was no rent default, magistrates did not always support a landlord's claim to repossess.

Sometimes tenants were willing to relinquish land without protest if they received compensation for improvements or had their deposit returned. In four cases, tenants merely asked to have their deposits refunded. For instance, in Boluo county, Huizhou, before he would consent to leave his land, Hong Baizhang demanded a refund of the deposit that his grandfather had paid 46 years earlier when the land was originally sublet. In this case, the magistrate ordered the repayment of the deposit and punished the landlord for precipitating the violence by attempting to seize control of the field.

Unfortunately, the sources do not provide enough background to permit a reliable assessment of claims for compensation for improvements to the land. Undoubtedly, some claims were valid, but some tenants, who were reluctant to give up land, exploited this angle. In fact, the problem was so widespread that it drew high-level government attention. According to a 1735 edict of Emida, the Governor General of Guangdong, these demands could be "unreasonable" or outright fraudulent. For example, some tenants claimed that they should receive long-

50 Due to the time needed for investigation and trials at the various levels of the bureaucracy, this case was not ultimately decided until early in the first year of the Qianlong reign.

51 KYQ, p. 126.

term compensation because the manure that they had applied would benefit the soil for many years to come.[52] The governor general's observations notwithstanding, there were four disputes in which tenant demands seemed quite reasonable.

In Panyu county, Guangzhou, in the heart of Guangdong province, Lan Linqiu tilled land that the Zhong family owned. On this land, Lan had built a "manure pond" (*fenchi*). When the Zhongs sold the land to Wen Yachao, Wen leased the land to his wife's nephew, Zhang Xinggui, to till. Apparently, Lan did not object to the eviction, but he demanded 3 ounces of silver for the manure pond. Zhang refused to pay him.

On QL 9.2.12 (1744), Zhang Xinggui and Wen Yachao went to the field to work. They decided to fill in the manure pond because they did not plan to use it. Lan saw them and went to stop them. An argument started, and Lan cuffed Zhang. Zhang returned the blow, striking Lan in the ribs. Lan picked up a pole, intending to beat Zhang, but Zhang seized the pole before he could strike. At that moment, Wen urged them to stop fighting. Lan suspected that Wen had come to help Zhang, so he cursed him. Wen was insulted and punched Lan repeatedly in the ribs. Zhang then used the pole to push Lan to the ground. Lan fell and injured both his back and his eye. Despite his injuries, Lan got to his feet and the fighting briefly resumed, but Lan was seriously wounded and could not continue. A short while later Lan died.[53]

Although the local government was not reluctant to lend its support to landlord claims, to the extent that the documents provide information on the official disposition of eviction disputes, the state's position was fairly evenhanded. The direct role of the state and also the difficulties inherent in buying and selling land were readily apparent in a dispute from Deqingzhou county, Zhaoqing. Deng Shengxue and his clansmen divided land that included 18 *mu* that Deng Shengxue's grandfather had originally leased several decades earlier. In 1782, the grandson of the original landowner of the 18 *mu* sold it to Fan Yuanhui. From the outset Fan was wary of the Dengs and feared that over the years the Dengs might have altered the boundaries and secretly added some of the leased land to the fields they owned outright. Fan wanted to evict the Dengs and lease the land to Li Huagong, but the Dengs refused to yield their tenancy rights.

In 1783, the early harvest passed without a confrontation. At the late harvest, Fan Yuanhui feared that the Dengs would again "steal" the harvest, so he requested that the local yamen send runners to assist him

52 Ibid., p. 127. 53 XKTB 0453, QL 10.3.23.

in harvesting the field. Deng Shengxue and his clansmen were aware of Fan's plan. They began to harvest the field and store the grain outside the village. This went on for two days. On the third day, Fan arrived with the runners, some hired laborers and his would-be tenant, Li Huagong. None of the male Dengs were around except for Deng Shengxue. He ordered the women, mothers and wives of the Dengs, to harass Fan and his group. The women attacked the group, cursing them and tearing their clothing. Fan went to report this incident to a local official.

Meanwhile, during the fracas, some members of Fan's party discovered and confiscated the grain that the Dengs had harvested and hidden. Deng Shengxue became enraged at this news and berated his sister-in-law, Ms. He, who had been responsible for guarding the grain. Ms. He cursed Deng and attacked him. Deng turned on her with a stick and beat her until she fell, struck her head, and died. Deng then attempted to frame Fan and his group for the murder of Ms. He.

This dispute was unusual in several respects. Behavior as exceedingly reprehensible as Deng Shengxue's was uncommon. Similarly, the extensive involvement of female family members in a violent dispute was also unusual, though there were more than thirty female homicide victims. More importantly, in terms of the rising social tensions associated with economic change, was the use of government runners to assert a claim. There were only a few disputes in my sample, evictions or otherwise, in which a landlord received direct assistance from the local authorities when enforcing a claim, and most occurred later in the Qianlong reign.

Generally, local officials supported evictions if the landlord had purchased the land outright and compensated the tenant if there was a rent deposit. If we consider land as patrimony and land as commodity as the two extremes on a spectrum, the official position was tilted slightly toward patrimony. Compensation for improvements tenants had made were usually not required unless the tenant's family had once owned the land in question. In four disputes in which landlords refused to refund the deposits of evicted tenants, the landlord was held culpable for creating a dangerous situation. The somewhat more "moralistic" attitude of officialdom was also revealed in two cases in which a landlord wanted to evict because another potential tenant offered more rent.

One such dispute occurred in Jiaying, the prefectural seat of Jiaying prefecture on QL 44.2.15 (1779). Fu Zhiheng had leased a field for 6.6 *shi* per annum from Sheng Zheng, the chief monk of Lingguan temple.[54] Fu had leased the land for several years without defaulting. In QL 44.1 (1779), Gu Zhenlue and Gu Zhenjun offered to pay an additional two Mexican silver dollars in rent. According to his deposition, Sheng Deng "greedily" accepted the offer without informing Fu Zhiheng. When Fu and his mother, Ms. Su, tried to stop the Gu brothers from tilling the field, Ms. Su was beaten with a hoe and died nine days later.[55] Regarding Sheng Deng's actions, the magistrates decision in this case was unequivocal. Sheng was defrocked and flogged for creating a dangerous situation. According to the magistrate, evicting a tenant who was not in arrears simply to obtain more rent was wrong.

Common Features of Eviction Disputes

Compared to other types of disputes, the geographic configuration of eviction disputes was skewed more heavily toward the eastern prefectures, but within the eastern prefectures there was a more even distribution among the counties (see Map 4–3). The average number of participants per eviction dispute was 4.3, which is roughly equivalent to the average of 4.2 for all disputes. In terms of duration, eviction disputes, with 43% of all disputes having continued for at least one month, resembled rent defaults very closely, but only ten cases contain evidence of prior efforts at peaceful resolution of the dispute (see Table 4–4). Once again this raises the question of the efficacy of official adjudication and private mediation, which I will defer until Chapter 7.

Given the importance of changes in ownership or management as proximate causes in eviction disputes, one reason for the comparatively longer duration was probably related to the timing of land sales, which usually took place after the late harvest. Even though a tenant may have been informed of his eviction, the reality of the eviction might not be realized until the spring planting began. Lastly, one feature common to many eviction disputes should be noted. In redemptions and rent defaults, the disputants usually had had a long-standing relationship, but in eviction disputes it was often the advent of a new owner or manager that precipitated the dispute. The potentially ameliorating influences of long-standing personal ties between tenant and landlord were absent from eviction disputes. Personal relationships or obligations did not constrain the new landowner. In this way, eviction disputes were representative of the more economically "rational" and impersonal approach to

54 Coincidentally, there was a total of three disputes in which the landlord was a monk, and all three disputes were evictions.

55 QDB, pp. 186–7.

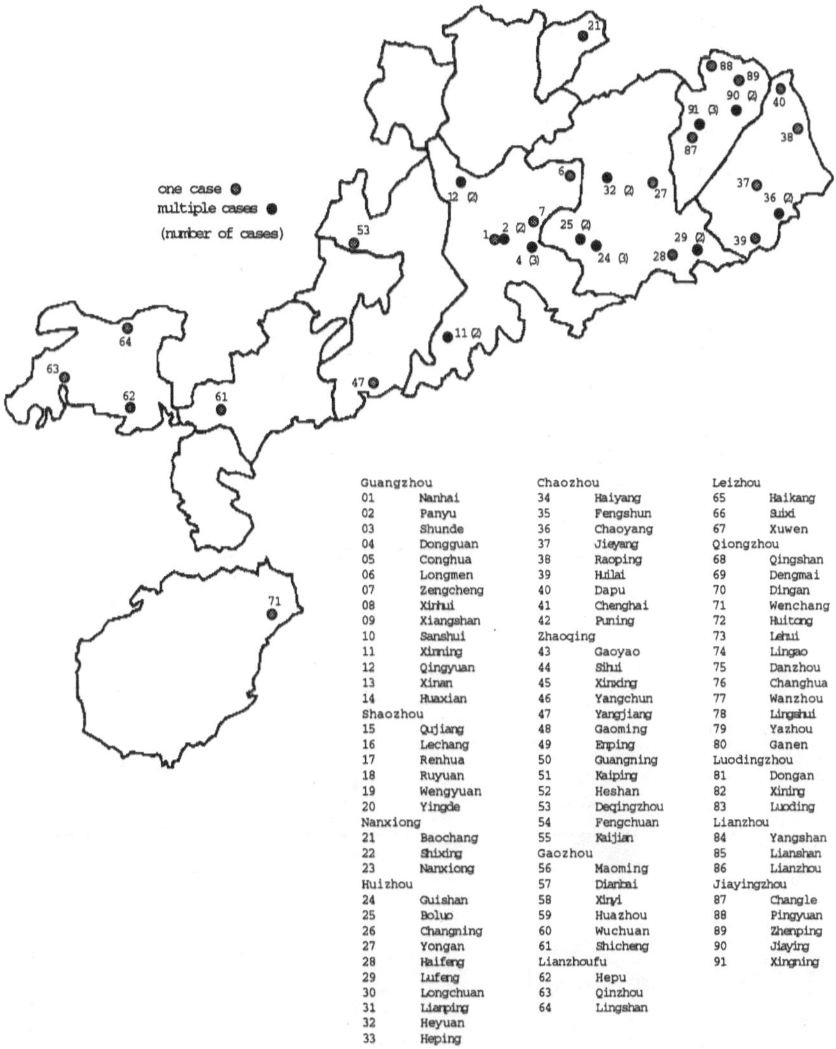

Map 4–3 Guangdong Province Eviction Disputes[a]

[a] Three locations unknown.

land ownership that was becoming common during the eighteenth century.

Nowhere else was the monthly distribution of disputes so unambiguous as in the case of eviction disputes (see Figure 4–3). The third lunar

Table 4–4. *Total Participants and Duration for Eviction Disputes*

Participants per Dispute	Number of Disputes
Two	8
Three	12
Four	13
Five–nine	13
Ten or more	2
Total	48
Duration	
One day or less	9
One day–one month	18
One month–one year	15
More than one year	6
Total	48

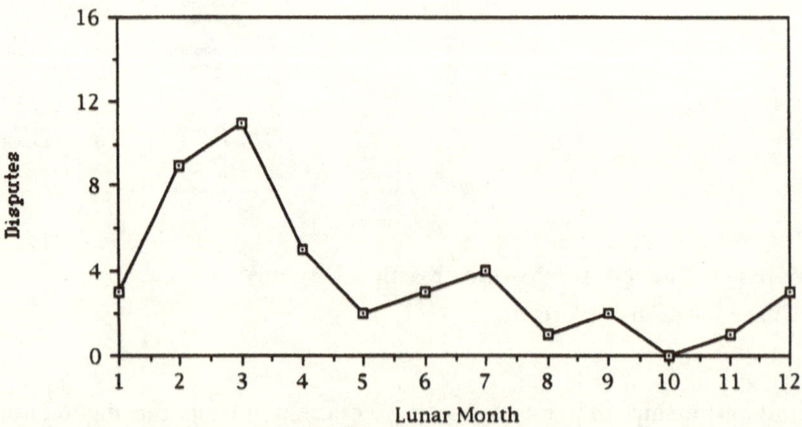

Figure 4–3 Eviction Disputes by Month[a]

[a] Excluding three disputes for which the precise date was unknown.

month, the beginning of the first planting season, was the peak time for eviction disputes. This makes sense when we consider that evictions were closely related to changes in ownership, which usually took place during the winter slack season. This fact set the stage for a confrontation at the start of the new planting season, when new owners frequently attempted evictions. In some cases, tenants were uninformed of the changes and attempted to till the land. In other cases, new owners or managers informed the existing tenant that his rights were suspended, but the tenant still attempted to plant the field. Either way, the most likely time for confrontation was at the start of the new planting season.

The description and analysis of disputes according to major issues has revealed how the nature of some forms of social conflict changed over the course of the eighteenth century, depending on the type of issue involved. The analysis of noncontractual issues revealed how the increase in the relative scarcity of land heightened economic competition and contributed to creating the potential for violence over seemingly straightforward issues like boundaries and water rights. The analysis of contractual disputes provided greater insight into the development of new economic institutions, such as rent deposits, and the refinement and development of property rights during the eighteenth century. These are topics that I will return to again, but first I will examine the overall geographic and temporal distribution of property-rights disputes in Guangdong. While each type of dispute, whether contractual or noncontractual, displayed interesting idiosyncrasies, an analysis of the geographic and temporal distribution of disputes suggests some interesting connections to the broader economic trends of the Qianlong period.

5
Temporal and Geographic Distributions of Property-rights Disputes in Guangdong

As stated in the introduction, an underlying assumption of this study is that population growth and commercialization increased the relative value of land and induced demand to extend or refine property rights, thereby creating the potential for violent disputes. In this chapter, I will examine the temporal and geographic distribution disputes in Guangdong province in order to draw a link between violent disputes and the broader economic changes of the eighteenth century. Unfortunately, the data are not available to measure precisely or systematically the impact of population growth or commercialization over time at the county level, where homicides occurred. Consequently, it is not possible to employ statistical methods to demonstrate a relationship between violent disputes and population growth and commercialization. Instead, I will present the spatial and geographic distributions of violent disputes and argue that these distributions were significant and suggest a plausible link between social conflict and the economic changes of the eighteenth century. If the underlying assumption regarding the connection between economic change and social conflict has merit, we would expect that the distribution of violent disputes over property rights would reflect the variable impact of population growth and commercialization over time and across space in Guangdong province. This assumption seems sound, but the introduction of violence into the argument complicates the matter. Whatever the connection between economic change and social conflict, we must acknowledge that violent behavior has its own complex dynamics that the limitations of the sources prevent us from fully understanding.[1] Nevertheless, by comparing the spatial and temporal pattern of homicides related to disputes over property rights with other types of homicides, I believe that I can make a plausible argument that connects social conflict and economic change.

Accounting for the diverse factors that might have contributed to the location and timing of each violent dispute is beyond the scope of this research. Obviously, the determinants of violent behavior were not exclusively economic. Presumably, personal, psychological, ethnic, and ecological factors also may have influenced the timing and location of these homicides. Thus, any discernible patterns of homicides related to violent disputes over property rights might simply have been indicative of regions or time periods that were particularly prone to violence for any number of reasons (see Table 5–1). The first task, a relatively simple one, will be to show that the geographic distribution of homicides related to property rights was not merely a reflection of a general pattern of violence in Guangdong.

Fortunately, the homicides related to property-rights disputes examined in this study were drawn from a broader collection of homicide reports related to disputes over land and debt. This allows a comparison between homicides related to property-rights disputes and other homicides related to land or debt.[2] Using only those cases directly sampled from archival sources at roughly five-year intervals from the category of land and debt homicides yielded a total of 958 homicides for Guangdong province (see Table 5–1), of which 251 were related to the property-rights issues as defined in Chapters 3 and 4. The other 707 homicides were related to disputes over debts or other land-related issues. Table 5–1 provides a further breakdown of these homicides by

1 Social psychologists have offered two general explanations for aggression: the frustration-aggression theory and learned behavior. See Leonard Berkowitz, pp. 696–8, "Whatever Happened to the Frustration-Aggression Hypothesis?, *American Behavioral Scientist* (May/June 1978) 21.5: 691–708. Other findings of social psychology: that alcohol use diminishes restraints on aggressive behavior, ambient temperature has a curvilinear relationship to aggression, and that averse stimuli will sometimes trigger violent reactions (violence begets violence) seem obvious, though untestable for eighteenth-century China.

2 Land and debt was only one of three major categories. As explained in Appendix A, Chinese archivists divided the collection of homicide reports into four major categories: blows and affrays, land and debt, marriage and illicit sex, and "other." I have only drawn data from the land and debt category. A cursory glance at the listing for other categories indicated that blows and affrays and marriage and illicit sex together probably contained as many, if not more, reports as land and debts.

Table 5–1. *Total Extant Homicide Reports Related to Land and Debts in Guangdong for Sampled Years by Issue*

Issue	Number of Homicides
Property rights in land	251
Debts	253
Other land	176
Loans	157
Wages	50
Others	71
Total	958

issues that I have defined. Briefly, "loans" mainly refers to loans in cash or kind, but also includes a few cases of loans of goods or tools. "Debts" refers primarily to money owed for goods purchased on credit, but does include several homicides related to other types of cash debts. "Other land" covers a potpourri of issues not directly related to property-rights issues, such as alleged violations of principles of geomancy (*fengshui*) and numerous incidents of stray animals feeding on neighboring fields. "Wages" covers unpaid wages for both short- and long-term employment. "Others" includes those cases too disparate to categorize easily.

Table 5–1 includes only those homicide reports that I directly sampled at roughly five-year intervals from the category of land and debt in the routine memorial collection at the Number One Historical Archive in Beijing. First of all, this comparison shows that property-rights issues were only responsible for roughly a quarter of all homicides in this sample. More importantly, as Table 5–2 illustrates, in counties where violence was prevalent (defined as counties that reported at least twice the per county average [ten] of homicides), there were sharp disparities between homicides related to property-rights issues and homicides related to other disputes over land and debt. For example, in Nanhai county, Guangzhou, and Qujiang county, Shaozhou, property-rights disputes ending in homicide were negligible. In Chaoyang and Raoping counties, Chaozhou, however, the number of homicides related to property-rights issues accounted for slightly more than half the total. Jieyang county, Chaozhou, on the other hand, seems to have been more prone to homicide regardless of the cause. In fact, Chaozhou pre-

Table 5–2. *Counties with the Greatest Number of Homicides Related to Disputes over Land and Debt*

County	Property Rights	Debt and Others	Total
Jieyang	20	31	51
Dongguan	8	35	43
Yingde	9	24	33
Nanhai	1	32	33
Chaoyang	16	14	30
Guishan	4	24	28
Panyu	4	20	24
Xinhui	2	21	23
Boluo	9	14	23
Qujiang	1	21	22
Raoping	12	10	22
Haiyang	4	17	21
Maoming	2	18	20

fecture as well as Dongguan county, Guangzhou, which experienced a good deal of violence, were notorious as sources of semiprofessional fighters who were employed in lineage feuds. As late as the twentieth century, these areas also supplied a disproportional share of recruits for the Chinese Communist Party's army.[3] Local peculiarities aside, this table does demonstrate that the geographic pattern of homicides related to property rights did not simply mirror a general spatial pattern of homicide in Guangdong. In other words, the geographic pattern of violent disputes over property rights cannot be explained solely in terms of local conditions that were generally conducive to violence.

Geographic Distribution of Property-rights Disputes

In fact, the spatial pattern of homicides related to property rights displayed several interesting features that suggest connections to population density and commercialization. For example, a striking geographic feature of violent disputes over property rights was the predominance of disputes in eastern Guangdong and the relative

3 Frederic Wakeman, Jr., 1966, p. 23.

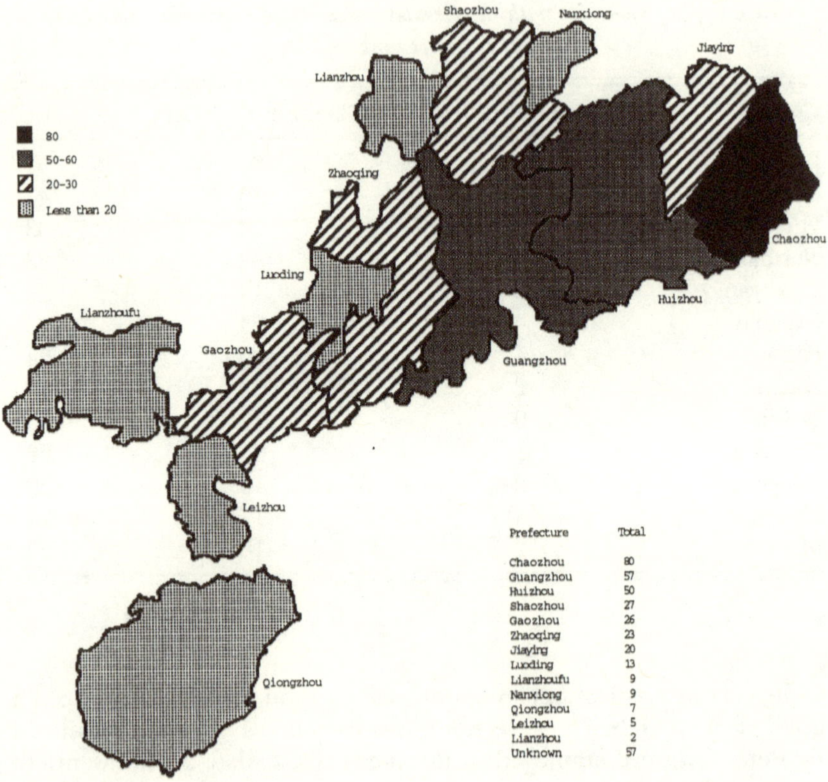

Map 5–1 Geographic Distribution of Homicides Related to Property Rights by Prefecture

peacefulness of western Guangdong (see Map 5–1).[4] On the one hand, this pattern suggests a link between overcrowding and violence. As early as the Yongzheng reign (1723–35), provincial officials had expressed concern about overpopulation in the eastern Guangdong, particularly Chaozhou and Jiaying prefectures, and actively encouraged migration to the western prefectures of Lianzhoufu and Leizhou (see Chapter 2). On the other hand, without population data to estimate the per capita homicide rate, the mere fact that the eastern prefectures were more populous would have meant that there were more opportunities for all types of homicides. The lack of county and prefectural-level population

4 Includes disputes from archival and published sources.

data makes it difficult to judge the relative importance of homicides related to property rights in different prefectures without a per capita measure. Given this limitation of the data, we must resort to a comparison between homicides related to property rights and homicides related to other disputes over land and debt in order to judge their relative importance. Here again the comparison is useful. For example, Guangzhou, the most populous prefecture in Guangdong, had the greatest number of homicides, but homicides related to property rights comprised the smallest percentage of the total number of homicides for any prefecture in this sample. Conversely, according to provincial officials, Jiaying and Chaozhou prefectures, which reportedly were seriously overcrowded, had the highest percentage of homicides related to property rights. The relationship between overpopulation and property-rights disputes is not entirely consistent, however. Contemporary observers also characterized Huizhou prefecture as overcrowded; but in this sample, Huizhou had a relatively lower percentage of homicides related to property-rights disputes. (Interestingly, in a separate sample used to compare Guangdong, Shandong, and Sichuan provinces in Chapter 6, Huizhou prefecture had the highest percentage of homicides related to disputes over property rights.) Nevertheless, it would seem that population pressure, which undoubtedly helped to drive up the value of land, also was an important factor shaping the geographic distribution of disputes. Not only was population greater in the eastern prefectures, recent research has shown that Chaozhou and Jiaying prefectures also had the highest average rice prices during the eighteenth century.[5] Assuming that overcrowding coupled with higher prices for rice and therefore higher prices for land would provide powerful inducement to define and enforce property rights, it is not surprising that both prefectures had a higher percentage of homicides related to land and debts (see Table 5–3).

While economic and demographic conditions may have increased the likelihood of homicides related to disputes over property rights in eastern Guangdong, this imbalance also suggests that there may have been some peculiar ecological, historical, and economic factors that predisposed this region toward violence. As stated, some areas of Chaozhou prefecture were notorious breeding grounds for professional fighters who were frequently employed in lineage-based violence. In fact, collective violence had been a hallmark of eastern Guangdong as early as the Ming dynasty. A study of collective violence in China during the Ming

5 Robert B. Marks, 1991, p. 100.

Table 5–3. *Homicides Related to Disputes over Property Rights as a Percentage of All Disputes over Land and Debts by Prefecture*[a]

Prefecture[b]	Total	Property Rights	Other Land and Debts	Percentage
Chaozhou	170	65	105	38%
Jiaying	35	13	22	37%
Luodingzhou	33	10	23	30%
Shaozhou	82	24	58	29%
Zhaoqing	78	18	60	23%
Gaozhou	72	16	56	22%
Huizhou	137	29	108	21%
Guangzhou	234	44	190	19%

[a]This table includes only those documents that I directly sampled at roughly five-year intervals and only from the category of land and debt cases in Routine Memorial Collection.
[b]Prefectures with less than thirty total homicides have been omitted.

revealed that the greatest number of incidents occurred in eastern Guangdong, which included the area that was Chaozhou during the Qing dynasty.[6] A local history of Chaozhou compiled during the Shunzhi reign (1644–61) also noted that the majority of tenants were "violent and crafty" and "despised and looked down on property owners."[7] Apparently, a violent tradition had existed in the Chaozhou region for some time.

In terms of disputes over property rights, the strength of lineage organization, the history of coastal resettlement, and the ecology of Chaozhou prefecture probably contributed to the likelihood of violent disputes. As Table 5–4 indicates, almost all the large-scale disputes, which bore familiar signs of lineage feuding, occurred in either Jieyang or Chaoyang counties. Similarly, environmental factors also may have contributed to the high concentration of water-rights disputes in Jieyang and Chaoyang counties. Reports on natural disasters in Guangdong during the Qianlong reign indicated that the eastern areas of the

6 James Tong, *Disorder under Heaven: Collective Violence in the Ming Dynasty (1368–1644)* (Stanford: Stanford University Press, 1991).
7 KYQ, p. 124.

Table 5-4. *Disputes Resembling Lineage Feuding*[a]

County	Year	Major Issue	Participants
Sanshui[b]	QL 9	Water rights	19
Chaoyang[c]	QL 60	Boundary	24
Jieyang[d]	QL 30	Water rights	27
Jieyang[e]	QL 56	Water rights	31

[a]It should be noted that in each of these cases the investigating magistrate clearly stated that these were not incidents of organized violence, *xiedou.*
[b]XKTB 0445, QL 10.5.23.
[c]XKTB 4061, QL 60.3.14.
[d]XKTB 1748, QL 30.11.28.
[e]XKTB 3781, QL 56.1.1.

province were more susceptible to the vagaries of nature.[8] Lastly, during the Kangxi reign, the coastal resettlement policy that was designed to deny resources to anti-Qing partisans based in Taiwan, affected Chaozhou and Huizhou prefectures more severely than other regions.[9] Under this policy, residents were forced to move ten miles or more inland. After the policy was rescinded in the late seventeenth century, competing claims to abandoned lands created much confusion and were a noted source of conflict. In conclusion, environmental features as well as a history of violent behavior may also explain the higher incidence of homicide in Chaozhou prefecture.

Market Structure of Guangdong Province

Finally, with regard to the spatial distribution of homicides related to property-rights disputes, a comparison of the least violent and the most violent counties suggests a connection between the marketing structure

8 While I have not made a systematic study of natural disasters in Guangdong, reports on crop damage due to floods, drought, and typhoons were sometimes encountered in Routine Memorials to the Ministry of Revenue reporting on harvests. Based on reports made in 1741, 1742, 1745, 1746, and 1764, the eastern prefectures of Huizhou, Jiaying, and Chaozhou often bore the brunt of flooding and typhoons.

9 Hsieh Kuo-ching, pp. 590–2, "Removal of Coastal Population in Early Tsing Period," *Chinese Social and Political Science Review* (1932) 15: 559–96.

of the province and the variable impact of commercialization. According to G. William Skinner's model of economic macroregions, most of Guangdong fell into a single macroregion. Except for the eastern prefectures of Chaozhou and Jiaying, most of the province of Guangdong falls within the Lingnan macroregion, which also includes most of the province of Guangxi directly to the west of Guangdong.[10] The economic core of this macroregion was the provincial capital, Guangzhou, in the fertile and economically advanced Pearl River Delta. Estimates place the population of Guangzhou and its surrounding area between 750,000 and 1.5 million in the mid-eighteenth century.[11] Chaozhou and Jiaying prefectures fall into the more fissiparous Southeast Coast macroregion, which extended northward and included most of Fujian province and parts of southern Zhejiang province. The capital of Chaozhou prefecture had an estimated population of 250,000 to 500,000 in the mid-eighteenth century. The existence of two distinct regional centers was also apparent in viewing United States Army survey maps prepared during the Second World War, which revealed two regions with high population densities centered in the Pearl River Delta and Chaozhou prefecture, respectively. As Skinner's model implies, there were no convenient lines of communication either overland or via waterways between these regions, but the two areas were hardly isolated from each other. Coastal shipping was highly developed and readily linked eastern Guangdong with other parts of the province. According to Fan I-Chun, interport trade in Guangdong "was at least as prosperous as the commerce of many other regions more actively involved in interregional trade."[12] It should also be noted that despite the natural barriers that separated this region from the rest of Guangdong province, central government and provincial-level officials observed the political and administrative boundaries of the province when formulating economic policies. This was readily apparent in official efforts to encourage land reclamation and to alleviate overcrowding in eastern Guangdong during the eighteenth century. Official policy envisioned overpopulation as a provincial problem and promoted migration from eastern prefectures, including Jiaying and Chaozhou, to western prefectures. On the other hand, research on the structure of Guangdong's rice market tends to confirm the Skinner model. Statistical tests indicate that Chaozhou and Jiaying prefectures were not as closely integrated into the

10 See G. William Skinner, "Regional Urbanization in Nineteenth Century China," pp. 212–49 in *The City in Late Imperial China*, G. W. Skinner, ed. (Stanford: Stanford University Press, 1976).

11 Marks and Chen, p. 144.

12 Fan, 1992, p. 249.

Guangdong grain market.[13] Although the Pearl River Delta core was the hub of an entire macroregion and the Chaozhou core area was only a regional center with a smaller hinterland, hereafter, when discussing geographic patterns I shall refer to these regions as the Pearl River Delta core and the Chaozhou core areas.

Despite its rugged terrain, Guangdong province was densely settled, with over ninety county-level reporting units (see Map 5–2). Three major rivers, the East, North, and West rivers, and their tributaries drained the central area of Guangdong before converging in the Pearl River Delta. Together with the Han River in eastern Guangdong, these three rivers divided the mostly mountainous areas of the province into a series of fertile valleys. The North River and its tributaries flowed southward from Baochang and Shixing counties, Nanxiong, in the northeast corner of the province through Yingde and Lechang counties, Shaozhou, and Qingyuan county, Guangzhou, to Nanhai and Panyu counties, Guangzhou, where it joined the Pearl River (see Map 5–2). All of these counties were designated commercial centers (*zhong*) under the four-character system used to rank administrative districts during the Qing dynasty.[14] The West River, an important artery for grain supply, originated in Guangxi Province and flowed across Gaoyao and Deqingzhou counties, Zhaoqing, and Sanshui county, Guangzhou, on its way to the Pearl River Delta. Each of these counties, along with Xinxing and Yangchun counties, Zhaoqing, were also designated as commercial centers. The East River entered Huizhou prefecture from the northeast and passed through the commercial centers of Guishan, Heyuan, and Longchuan counties, Huizhou, before reaching the Pearl River Delta. Mountains separated Jiaying and Chaozhou prefectures from the rest of the province and the Han River and its tributaries, which

13 See Robert B. Marks, 1991.

14 During the Qing dynasty, four characters, *fan, zhong, nan,* and *pi*, which, respectively, designated a heavy work load; commercial importance; high crime rate; and difficulty in collecting taxes, were used to rank administrative posts. See G. William Skinner, pp. 314–17, "Cities and the Hierarchy of Local Systems," pp. 275–351 in *The City in Late Imperial China*, G. W. Skinner, ed. (Stanford: Stanford University Press, 1976), and Gilbert Rozman, p. 155, *Urban Networks in Ch'ing China and Tokugawa Japan* (Princeton: Princeton University Press, 1973). Skinner acknowledges the ambiguities of the system but asserts that the character *zhong* was probably an accurate indication of a commercial center. In the absence of any clear explanation of the standards used to apply these designations, Rozman has interpreted the characters as "rough indications of differences between areas." In Guangdong, Panyu, and Nanhai in Guangzhou prefecture; Haiyang in Chaozhou prefecture; and Gaoyao in Zhaoqing, were all "four character" posts. All Guangdong counties that contained the character *zhong* in their ranking were located along major rivers.

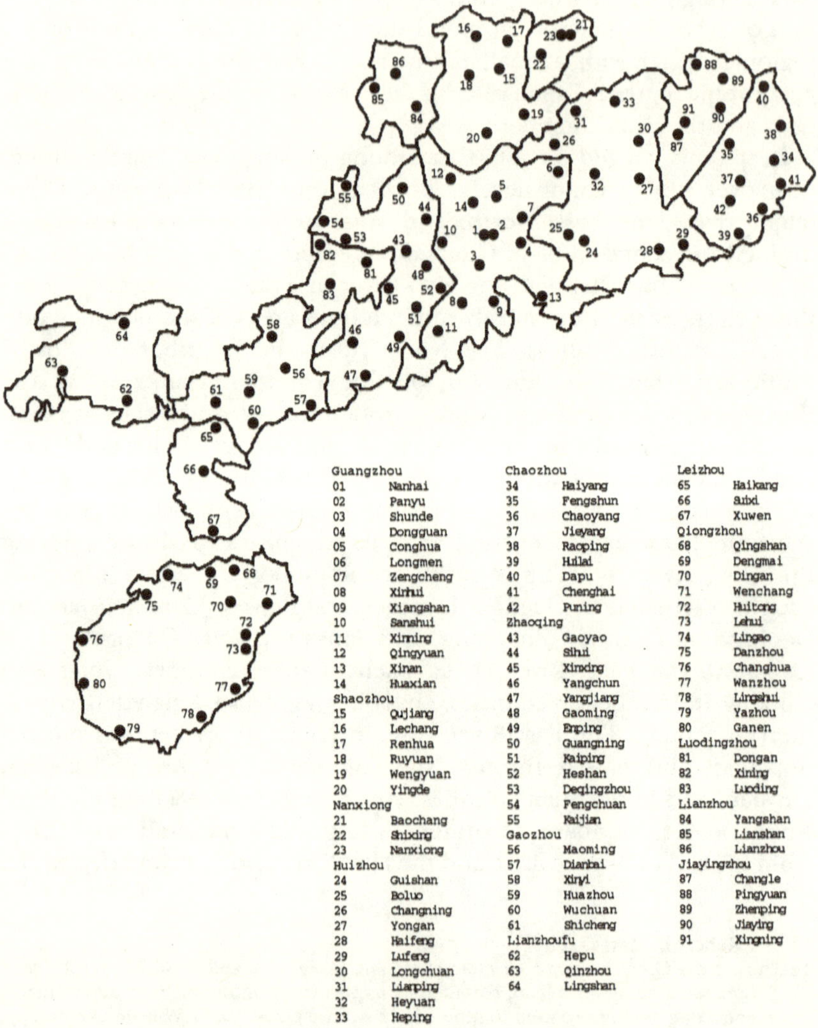

Map 5–2 Guangdong Province Reporting Units

drained this area, linked the commercial centers of Haiyang county, Chaozhou, with Changle county and Jiaying (see Map 5–3). This brief sketch of the marketing structure and distribution of commercial centers cannot capture the full complexity of the evolving commercial networks in eighteenth-century Guangdong, but it serves as a useful framework for an examination of the spatial distribution of least violent

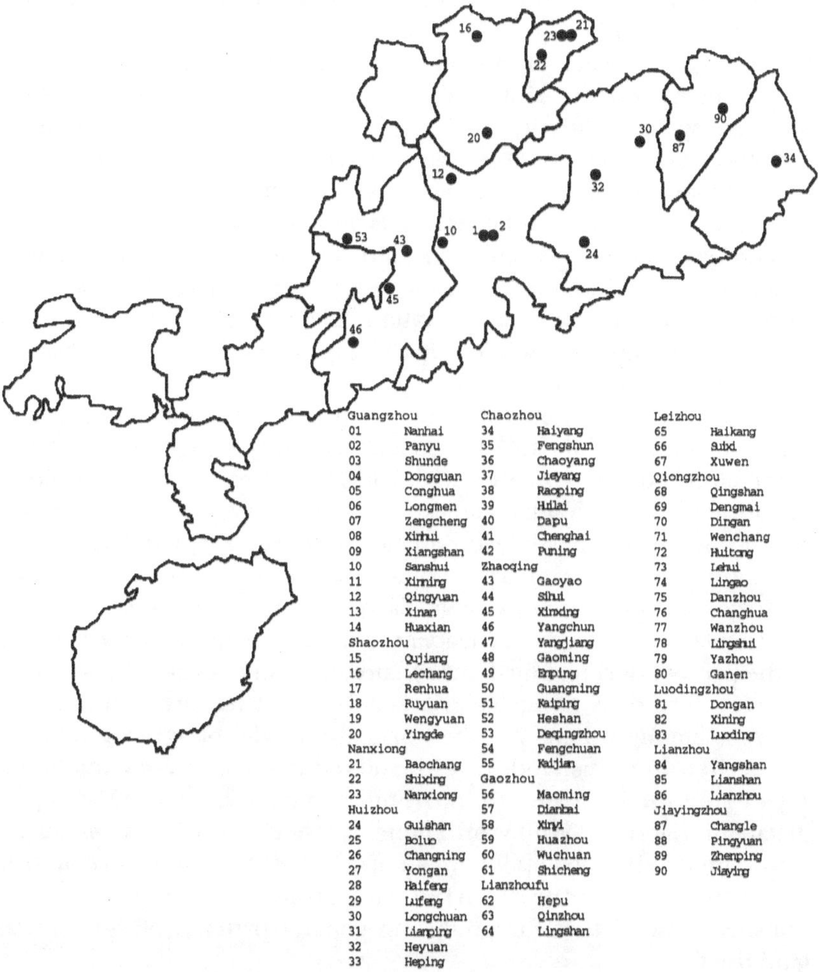

Map 5–3 Guangdong Province Commercial Centers

and most violent counties. Understanding the marketing framework is particularly useful when we consider the connection between market structures and patterns of agricultural land use.

Patterns of Agricultural Land Use

The significance of location and transportation costs for all types of economic activities has been widely recognized and studied. The same principles have also been useful in understanding the impact of markets on the spatial patterns of agricultural land use. In agriculture, according to Edgar Dunn, "attempts to minimize distance inputs in the assembling of production factors and in the marketing of agricultural produce imparts a spatial regularity that is particularly significant."[15] In fact, location and transportation costs are important determinants of both land use and land values. The more valuable the land, the greater the "location rent" – a measure of the relative economic advantage of one parcel of land over another – it will command. The key variables determining location rent are distance from market; price per unit of output; and costs of production and transportation.[16] Theoretically, sustained shifts in any of these variables will lead to a change in land values and an alteration in the pattern of land use.

The German economist Johann Heinrich von Thunen developed the first model to illustrate the spatial regularity of agriculture in the nineteenth century.[17] Briefly stated, Von Thunen envisioned a town that was located on a circular and isotropic plain and isolated from the outside world. All possible production factors, except transportation costs, were held constant. The resulting pattern of agricultural land use took the form of concentric rings. Each successive ring was occupied by a particular staple product, cheaper to transport than the staple product of the preceding ring. Von Thunen later went on to examine such complicating factors as navigable rivers, differential fertility, and multiple markets, among others, but the normative model of agricultural land use derived from his model, which showed that land values and intensity of land use increase with proximity to markets, recurred with predictable variations.[18] While von Thunen's model has obvious limitations (most notably, it oversimplifies relationships between town and country) and assumes competitive markets and profit-maximizing farmers, it remains a useful tool for predicting general patterns of agricultural land use.[19]

15 Edgar S. Dunn, Jr., p. 2, *The Location of Agricultural Production* (Gainesville: University of Florida Press, 1967).

16 See Dunn, p. 13. Mathematically, location rent is expressed as $R = E\ (p - a) - Efk$. R = location rent; E = the output per unit of land; k = the distance to market; p = market price per unit of output; a = production cost per unit of land (including labor); f = transport rate per unit of distance per unit of output.

17 See Peter Hall, p. 8, *Von Thunen's Isolated State* (London: Pergamon Press, 1966). Von Thunen originally published his work *The Isolated State* in 1826.

18 Anthony R. de Souza and J. Brady Foust, pp. 179–83, *World Space-Economy* (Columbus, OH: Charles E. Merrill Publishing Co., 1979).

19 Ibid., pp. 186–90. De Souza and Foust demonstrate how United States agriculture reflects the general principles of von Thunen's model.

How useful is this model for understanding the spatial pattern of social conflict in eighteenth-century Guangdong? Guangdong province was not isolated from the outside world nor did it resemble an isotropic plain. As noted, the province was very mountainous and possessed an extensive river system that reduced the relative costs of transportation and skewed the patterns of land use. But, as G. William Skinner's application of central place theory has demonstrated, the location of urban areas in Chinese macroregions dictated a discrete marketing pattern that also imparted a discrete pattern of agricultural land use. Intensive forms of agriculture with higher yields per unit afforded a higher location rent and occupied the most valuable land situated closer to commercial centers. The conversion of rice paddies to the mulberry embankment and fish pond system of farming in the Pearl River Delta core in response to the foreign demand for silk was a dramatic example of this principle during the late seventeenth and early eighteenth centuries. Conversely, more-extensive forms of agriculture usually were located farther away from the market where lower location rents compensate for higher transportation costs.

Given these expectations about patterns of agricultural land use, it would be reasonable to expect that the effects of rising land values and rice prices would have had a disproportionately larger impact at the boundaries between successive zones of intensity of cultivation. The intermediary zone between the core and periphery where location rent would be most sensitive to changes in price per unit of output, and production and transportation costs would have been especially sensitive. Conversely, only an increase of great magnitude in the price per unit of output would have created the economic incentives to alter the pattern of land use in both the core, where location rent was highest and transportation cost to market was lowest, and the periphery, which had the lowest location rent and highest transportation cost. Since incentives to alter or redefine property rights were sensitive to changes in the relative value of land, which would be more stable in the core and periphery, we would expect less potential for violence in these regions. Ignoring other factors that may have contributed to the likelihood of violence, we would therefore expect less violence related to property-rights disputes in both the core and extreme periphery of the province.

Land Values and Violent Disputes

While we lack detailed historical data on land use and land values in Guangdong, it seems reasonable to assume that they were sensitive to changes in prices of agricultural goods. As previously discussed in

Chapter 2, the long-term trend of rice prices for the eighteenth century was upward. Rice prices in Guangdong increased in a linear trend from 1731 until 1758. After a sharp decline from 1759 to 1761, prices were more stable, rising slowly until the late 1770s, when they declined slightly. Logically, the rise in the price per unit of output for rice, and presumably other agricultural products, during the first twenty-three years of the Qianlong reign would have had an effect on land values and patterns of land use. The conversion of rice paddies to the mulberry embankment and fish pond system of agriculture in response to foreign demand for silk during the late seventeenth and early eighteenth centuries was a dramatic example of the impact of commercialization on Guangdong. Changes in the pattern of land use and rising land values would also induce demand for change in property rights and economic institutions.

Homicide reports contain anecdotal evidence of land prices increasing in Huizhou and Guangzhou prefectures in the 1750s. Three incidents from Shunde county, Guangzhou between 1752–53 (these homicides did not involve property-rights issues) provide vivid examples of how rising prices for rice and land could induce unusual behavior. For instance, the He clan went as far as hiring workers to exhume ancestral graves in order to sell the land that the graves had occupied. Given the normal respect and reverence accorded ancestral graves, this was a truly drastic action. When the local magistrate discovered what had happened, he sentenced the worker who had exhumed the graves to be strangled and severely punished the members of the He family who hired him.[20] While we have no explanation for the He family's motivation, the fact that the incident occurred when rice prices were nearing their eighteenth-century peak undoubtedly was not a coincidence. This incident also reveals the extent to which economic interests could sometimes override the most fundamental ethical beliefs.

In another case, the economic motivations were more explicit. In 1752, the Li clan of Shunde met and decided to sell 11 *mu* of clan-owned land set aside to fund ceremonies to honor ancestors (*changtian*). Perhaps to mitigate the stigma associated with selling such land, the leader of the clan specifically stated that the reason for selling the land was that rice prices had been "steadily increasing" (*mijia jianchang*), and the ostensible purpose of the sale was to acquire cash to purchase rice for poor members of the clan.[21] Interestingly, proceeds from the sale were dispersed to the poor, but a dispute over the payment of commissions arose among clan members who had served as middlemen and

20 XKTB 0966, QL 18.10.2. 21 XKTB 0875, QL 17.3.7.

had brokered the sale. Clearly, there was more than altruism at work in this case. In a third case, the clan leaders had decided to sell off some land in 1753 because rice prices were high.[22] It is obvious from reading these cases that there clearly was a social stigma attached to selling clan land, but the economic incentives to sell were apparently too powerful to ignore. Indeed, the exhumation of ancestral graves and the sale of land set aside to fund sacrifices to the ancestors further demonstrate the power of economic incentives to override the cherished ideological imperative of respect for one's ancestors.

A cursory examination of the most violent and least violent counties, while hardly conclusive, does support the hypothesis that core and periphery areas, which were presumably less sensitive to changes in the relative value of land, would have experienced comparatively less violence. The least violent counties, those that reported one or no homicides related to property-rights disputes, were located either in the remote periphery or near the economic core of the province (see Map 5–4).[23] At the extreme periphery, we find that in remote Qiongzhou prefecture all but one county had one or no homicides related to disputes over property rights. In the economic core area, centered on the provincial capital of Guangzhou, Panyu and Nanhai counties, which together comprise the heart of the Pearl River Delta core area, there were only six homicides[24] compared to fifty-two homicides related to other land and debt disputes. In Chaozhou prefecture, the overall number of homicides was much greater than in any other prefecture, but the designated commercial center of the prefecture, Haiyang county, had only four homicides related to disputes over property rights, despite the fact that it was among the most violent counties for all types of disputes, with twenty-one total homicides (see Table 5–5).

The relatively low number of disputes in major commercial centers of the core areas was consistent with the assumption agricultural land in the vicinity of major commercial centers would be the most valuable and least susceptible to the fluctuations in price per unit of output, cost of transportation, or other determinants of location rent. Given that land values were consistently high in the vicinity of major commercial centers, and that there had always been greater incentive to define and enforce property rights, we would expect that there was also the least potential for violent conflict over property rights in these counties. Using only those reports that I directly sampled from archival sources, we find that,

22 XKTB 0855, QL 17.7.20.
23 Includes disputes from all archival and published sources.
24 Includes disputes from all archival and published sources.

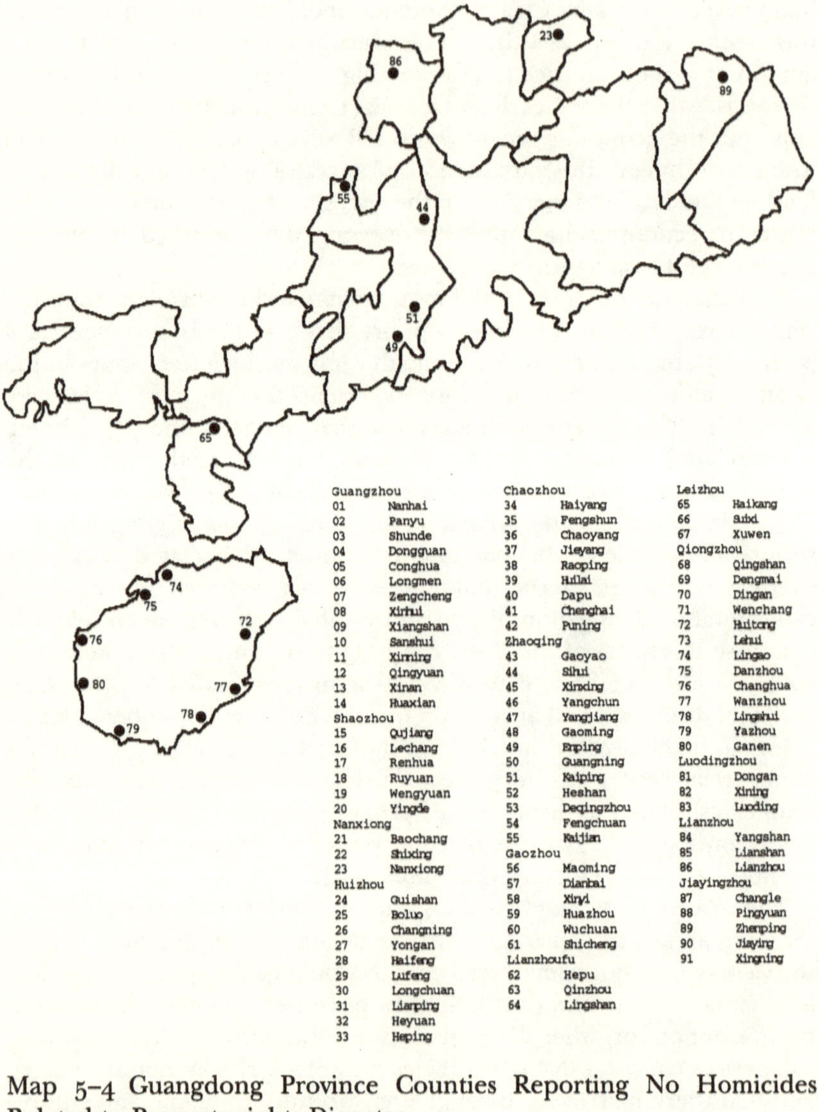

Map 5–4 Guangdong Province Counties Reporting No Homicides Related to Property-rights Disputes

Table 5–5. *Homicides Related to Land and Debts in Counties Designated as Commercial Centers*

County	Property Rights	Debt and Others	Total
Nanhai	1	32	33
Yingde	9	20	29
Guishan	4	24	28
Panyu	4	20	24
Haiyang	4	17	21
Heyuan	4	13	17
Yangchun	3	13	16
Shixing	3	11	14
Qingyuan	4	9	13
Baochang	5	7	12
Changle	7	3	10
Gaoyao	2	8	10
Jiaying	2	6	8
Longchuan	1	6	7
Sanshui	1	6	7
Deqingzhou	2	5	7
Lechang	1	3	4
Xinxing	1	2	3
Nanxiong	0	1	1

with the exceptions of Changle and Yingde, counties designated as commercial centers had an average or below-average number of homicides related to property rights and that homicides related to property rights were significantly outnumbered by homicides related to other disputes over land or debts (see Table 5–5).

Explaining the geographic pattern of the most violent counties presents greater difficulties. The most violent counties in the immediate vicinity of the Pearl River Delta core area formed an arch from Qingyuan in the north through Zengcheng and Dongguan in the east to Xinning in the south (see Map 5–5).[25] Elsewhere in the Pearl River Delta core area, other counties that displayed high levels of violence were all acces-

25 Includes disputes from all archival and published sources.

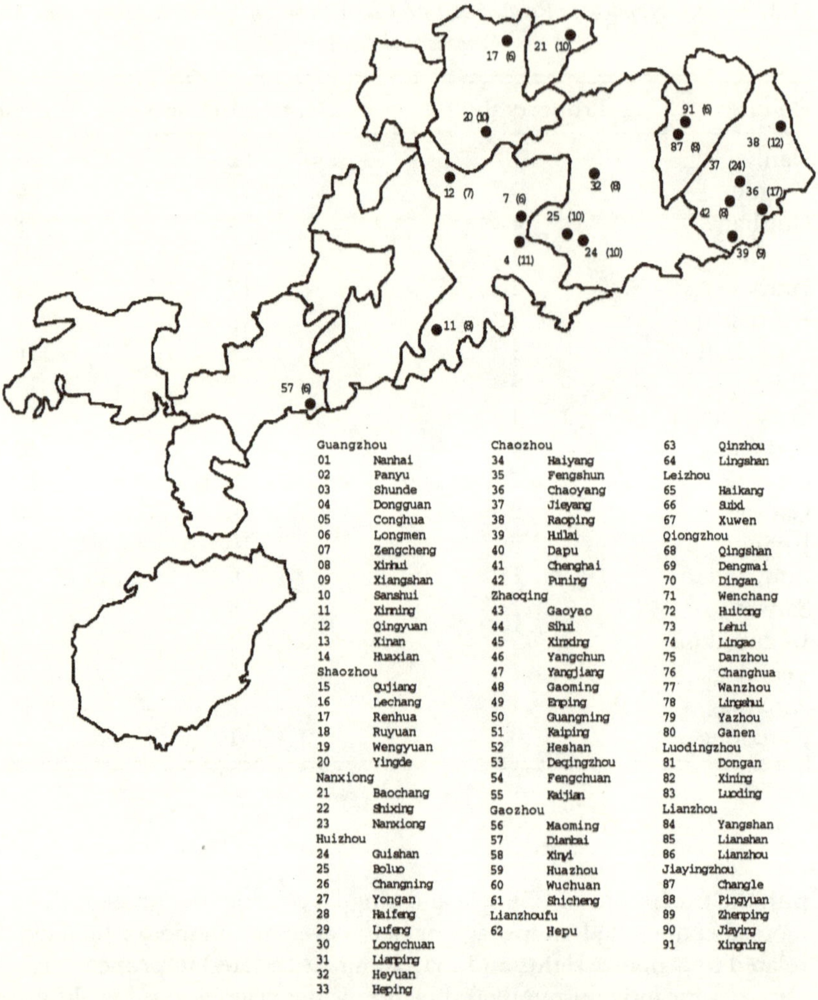

Map 5–5 Guangdong Province Counties Reporting Six or More Homicides Related to Property-rights Disputes (Number of Cases)

sible via inland waterways and coastal shipping, and four were important prefectural commercial centers: Yingde county, Shaozhou; Guishan and Heyuan counties, Huizhou; and Baochang county, Nanxiong. All these counties were located approximately in the intermediary zone between the core and the periphery. In the Chaozhou core area, the important commercial centers of Jiaying and Changle counties were among the most violent counties. Once again, the high level of violence in Chaozhou prefecture cannot be explained solely in terms of economic factors. It may have been the case that in the broader scheme of the macroregion commercial centers in intermediate zones were more sensitive to economic change despite their dominant positions in the local economy.

To summarize briefly, the sharp disparities between the number of homicides related to property rights and homicides related to debt and other land disputes in various counties suggests that economic factors affected the geographic distribution of homicides related to property rights. Returning to the underlying assumption of this study, that economic change provides incentives to alter or redefine property rights and thereby creates the potential for disputes over property rights, using a simple model of spatial patterns of agricultural land, I have attempted to identify areas that would be less sensitive to shifts in the relative value of land. This explanation seemed to hold well for the Pearl River Delta core area, but not as well for the Chaozhou core area. To explain the high concentration of disputes in the Chaozhou core area, it was necessary to examine local conditions more carefully. One possible explanation, which was consistent with the emphasis on volatility in the value of land, was that overpopulation in the Chaozhou core area was so severe that it had an extensive impact on land values throughout the region. Admittedly, noneconomic factors affected the pattern of violence over property rights, but the economic evidence seems sufficient to argue that the spatial pattern of disputes was also related to the variable impact of economic change.

Temporal Distribution of Disputes over Property Rights

Delineating long-term secular changes in economic history poses relatively fewer difficulties than describing and explaining the transitional periods between one stage of economic development and the next. Since the advent of settled agriculture over ten thousand years ago, the long-term historical trend has been toward more-intensive use of agricultural land, requiring more-complex and exclusive property rights in land. Ester Boserup, who has taken the period of fallow as the focus of her study of agricultural growth and change, has identified sustained population growth as a key variable that determined a society's agricultural system. As population grows and becomes more concentrated, agriculture also becomes more intensive. According to Boserup, each ascending agricultural system also produces a more complex social framework.[26] While the long-run effects of sustained population growth "might be to raise output per man hour in agriculture," in the short term the transitional period often can cause social tensions, rural depopulation, and reductions in food productivity.[27] Guangdong conforms to this pattern of intensification of agriculture. As noted earlier, population growth in Guangdong during the eighteenth century produced an increasingly more intensive form of agriculture. Harvest reports for the province reveal that by 1738 every county in Guangdong practiced double cropping; and by 1795 two-thirds of the counties practiced triple cropping. Furthermore, as the analysis of violent disputes has illustrated, the process of economic change also disrupted the existing property-rights structure and engendered a substantial amount of social conflict. Nevertheless, as we shall see, over time the number of violent disputes eventually declined.

Ideally, any attempt to determine change over time in the number of homicides would take into account population growth. Unfortunately, the data necessary to measure the rate of population growth are not available. In order to get a reasonably accurate reading of change over time in homicides related to property-rights disputes, I have compared homicides related to property rights to homicides related to debts and other disputes over land (see Table 5–6). It is important to remember that taken together these homicides were only a portion of all homicides reported in the sampled years. (Based on data for 1765, homicides related to land and debts accounted for only 42% of all capital offenses.) Table 5–6 supplies a year-by-year comparison between homicides related to property-rights disputes and a combination of all other homicides related to debts and other disputes over land.

Given the limitations that the sources have imposed, the comparison of homicides related to property-rights disputes versus other types of homicides allows us to see the relative importance of homicides related to property rights and is the only reasonable method available to gauge historical change. All these documents were obtained from the same archival collection, which was subject to the same selection biases and maintained in the same physical environment from the eighteenth to the twentieth century. If the eighteenth-century reporting, the subsequent storage of the documents, or the modern-day cataloging had introduced any biases into the collection, these biases would be consis-

26 Ester Boserup, Chapter 8, *The Conditions of Agricultural Growth* (New York: Aldine Publishing, 1965).
27 Ibid., p. 118.

Table 5–6. *Homicides Related to Land and Debts for Sampled Years*

Year	Total	Property Rights in Land	Debts and Others	Property Rights As % of Total
1736	31	9	22	29%
1737	54	14	40	26%
1740	41	16	25	39%
1745	49	19	30	39%
1750	52	22	30	42%
1755	52	18	34	35%
1760	65	18	47	28%
1765	83	25	58	30%
1771	67	13	54	19%
1775	91	22	69	24%
1780	99	17	82	17%
1785[a]	72	21	51	26%
1791	95	17	78	18%
1795	107	20	87	19%

[a]Due to extensive losses in the routine memorial collection for the years 1775–1785, I have combined cases from 1785 and 1786 to obtain these numbers.

tent for the entire collection. Figure 5–1 reveals an unambiguous temporal pattern. The absolute number of homicides related to property rights was fairly stable, while homicides related to debts and other land disputes rose steadily after 1755.[28] Over time, disputes over property rights as a cause of homicides declined as a proportion of all homicides related to land and debts. Furthermore, considering that population roughly doubled during the Qianlong reign, the apparent stability over time in the absolute number of homicides related to property-rights disputes actually represented a decline in the per capita rate.

Although the temporal pattern of homicides related to disputes over property rights was less ambiguous than the geographic pattern, we are once again forced to rely on some broad assumptions in order to deduce

28 I believe that the sharp drop in debt and other land disputes in 1785 was probably due to the severe losses of documents for that year. See Appendix for details.

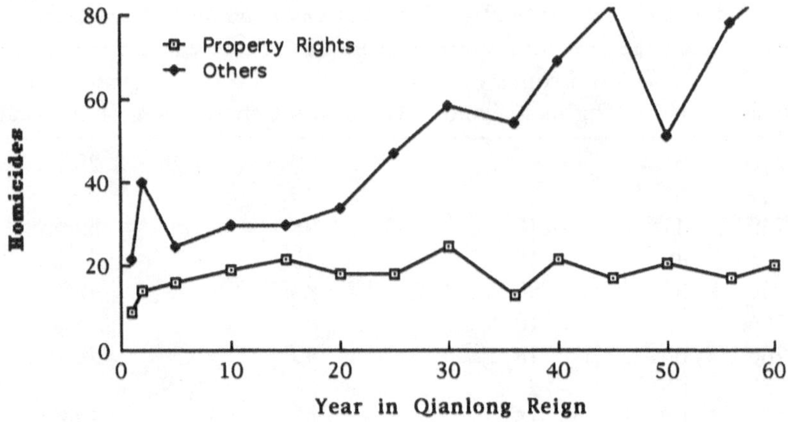

Figure 5–1 Homicides Related to Land and Debt Disputes in Guangdong

an explanation for this pattern. Based on the fact that in homicides related to property-rights disputes over two-thirds of the individuals who initiated violence were the eventual victims and that the overwhelming majority of killers were sentenced to execution, I assume that the use of lethal violence was neither a preferred nor effective method of settling property-rights disputes. Economically, I also assume that after adjustments to population growth and commercialization took place, the demand for new property rights was gradually satisfied. All things being equal, we would logically expect to see a declining number of homicides related to property rights over time as individuals acted to alleviate or eliminate sources of conflict and to develop more-peaceful methods of dispute resolution.

As the analysis of the long-term trends in development of economic institutions has shown, innovation in the structure and enforcement of property rights was protracted and primarily the product of the everyday struggles of common people. When an issue, such as redemption or rent default, chronically disrupted social order, high-level government officials acted. For example, as noted in Chapter 4, the government implemented legislation in the area of conditional sales, but these measures lagged behind grassroots innovations and largely served to ratify practices established at the village level. Such legislation assisted local magistrates in adjudicating disputes, but customary law remained the foundation of economic transactions. Another example of private innovation was the growing use of intermediaries or guarantors to facilitate sales and transfers of ownership in the expanding land market.[29] As research by Chen and Myers has demonstrated, the practice of using guarantors or intermediaries was not limited to land sales and was a common feature in many other types of contractual agreements.[30] In this case, private institutional arrangements based on custom compensated for the lack of official efforts to meet the demand for new economic institutions and the limited capability of local courts to enforce legal decisions during a period of economic change. Because homicide was a serious crime and a threat to social order, we would also expect that the state would take an active interest in mitigating the causes of violent disputes; but when it came to direct intervention at the local level, it appears that official intervention was, as Perdue has noted for Hunan, often limited to invoking "ideals of cooperation for mutual benefit."[31] Finally, the decline in violence was related to commercialization in another way. By all accounts, the economic development of the eighteenth century led to greater prosperity. Greater prosperity meant that tenants had the wherewithal to pay cash rent deposits. As noted in Chapter 4, the increase in use of cash deposits coincided with a decline in violent disputes over rent defaults. Similarly, as land became an actively traded commodity, personal ties to land, which had been the basis for claims that triggered violent disputes over redemptions of conditional sales, were weakened. Thus, the decline in violent disputes was, in many ways, linked to the transition to a more commercialized economy.

The disputes described in this study represent the microlevel struggles of individuals to protect or improve their personal lots in the face of macrolevel economic changes. Attempting to demonstrate a link between violent disputes and economic change has posed several problems. Contemporary reports of economic and social conditions leave no doubt that population and prices were on the rise, but the precise rate of change or local fluctuations for either variable is unknown and impossible to estimate. Despite the lack of data, however, it was possible to draw some reasonable connections between violent disputes and economic change. Using economic theories of patterns of agricultural land use, it was possible to make a plausible conjecture regarding what areas would be most sensitive to market forces and compare it to the pattern of violent disputes. Geographically, it seems plausible that there was a

29 ZYG, p. 5. According to the editors of ZYG, the widespread use of middlemen in land sale was a phenomenon of the Qing dynasty. For documentary evidence, see Yang Guozhen, 1984.

30 See Chen and Myers, 1976, pp. 1–32. 31 Perdue, p. 163.

connection between the location of violent disputes and what can reasonably be assumed to have been the variable impact of economic change. Temporally, the decline in violent disputes was unmistakable. Given the harsh penalties and the ultimate futility of lethal violence as a means of resolving disputes, the decline in homicides is not surprising. Tensions in rural society undoubtedly remained, but there was a clear indication that over the course of the eighteenth century the likelihood of disputes and potential for violence declined. As customary law was refined, the state belatedly responded with legislation to clarify property rights and rural inhabitants came to accept the new economic order. It remains to be seen if these patterns hold true for other areas of China.

6

Violence North, West, and South: Property-rights Disputes in Shandong, Sichuan, and Guangdong

The previous chapter examined the temporal and geographic pattern of violent disputes in Guangdong province and their relationship to economic change. How widespread were violent disputes over property rights in the rest of China? With over 56,000 extant reports of homicides related to disputes over land and debts for all of China during the Qianlong reign, it is clear that violent disputes over property rights were not an isolated phenomenon, but, as we shall see, there was significant regional variation. The sheer volume of documents available rules out a "national" study. Instead, I have drawn a second sample of homicide reports for Guangdong, Shandong, and Sichuan. The second sample also shifts the temporal focus to two time periods: 1750–53 and 1779–80. For Guangdong province, there is some overlap between the new sample and the original sample; however 63% of the cases in the second sample (ninety-five disputes) were not part of the original sample. During both periods, grain prices in Guangdong were at or near record highs for the Qianlong reign, with the 1750–53 sample covering the first sharp, upward spike in grain prices during the Qianlong reign, when grain prices were most volatile. During the second period, 1779–80, the market for grain in Guangdong was more integrated. In this sample, as in the large sample discussed earlier, there was a relative decline in the number of homicides related to property-rights disputes in the later part of the Qianlong reign. This approach allows us to compare two distinct economic cycles during the Qianlong reign and to examine the cumulative effects of population growth and commercialization on economic institutions. Finally, the years examined in this sample are ones for which losses to the archival sources seem to have been minimal (see Appendix).

Economic Conditions in Sichuan and Shandong

Expanding the geographic scope of this study to Sichuan and Shandong provides two valuable points of comparison to the original study of Guangdong. While Shandong and Sichuan were subject to similar social and economic pressures as Guangdong, the timing and intensity of these pressures varied regionally and was reflected in the temporal distribution of disputes. The peculiar histories, existing structure of property rights, and peculiar geographic characteristics of each province clearly shaped the impact of social and economic pressures in each province. For the most part, all three provinces fell within separate "macro regions" as defined by G. William Skinner.[1] With the exception of the mountainous western third of the province, all of Sichuan falls within the Upper Yangzi macroregion. The core of the Upper Yangzi macroregion was the agriculturally rich Chengdu basin, a region that experienced severe depopulation during the Ming-Qing interregnum. From the late Ming dynasty (1368–1644) through the early Qing, Sichuan suffered greatly from the ravages of one of the largest peasant uprisings during the late Ming dynasty, the invasion of the Manchus, and the rebellion of Wu Sangui in 1680. In the late seventeenth century, land-hungry peasants from south central and southeastern China, driven by hardships in their home regions and drawn by the availability of land, began moving to Sichuan in great numbers.

Government policy during the early Qing further fueled the spontaneous resettlement of Sichuan. In an effort to aid the recovery of this once prosperous region, the Qing government offered a variety of incentives, including tax breaks, certificates of permanent ownership to new settlers, and promotions for local officials who restored land tax rolls to encourage the economic revival of Sichuan.[2] These measures

1 See G. William Skinner, "Marketing and Social Structure in Rural China," *Journal of Asian Studies* (1964–5) 24: 3–44, 195–228, 363–400.

2 See Liu Yuan, "'Huguang tian Sichuan' yu Sichuan liumin wenti" ("Huguang fills up Sichuan" and the problem of Sichuan's floating population), *Qingshi yanjiu* (1994) 1: 39–44.

were similar to those that the central government had undertaken throughout China during the late seventeenth and early eighteenth centuries in an effort to ameliorate the damage inflicted on the Chinese economy during the Ming-Qing transition, except that they lasted much longer in Sichuan. The effects in Sichuan were expeditious and salubrious.

Migrants brought abandoned fields under cultivation, introduced new handicraft industries and crops from their former homes, expanded commerce with their native provinces, and opened mines. Settlers from Guangdong and Fujian brought terracing techniques that facilitated the cultivation of hillsides.[3] By 1692, the Governor of Sichuan reported that population and land taxes of the province had surpassed Ming levels.[4] By the Qianlong reign Sichuan was still recovering in some areas, but it had already begun to produce the surplus grain that entered interregional trade.[5] The Chengdu plateau, which benefited from double cropping and a superior irrigation network, was a particularly productive area and the economic core of the province.[6]

The influx of migrants continued throughout the eighteenth century despite the curtailment of government support in 1722. Evidence gleaned from homicide reports, which note the official county of residence of perpetrators and victims, reveals that migrants from Hubei, Hunan, Gansu, Guangdong, Guangxi, Guizhou, Shaanxi, and Yunnan were involved in homicides that took place in Sichuan throughout the Qianlong reign (see Table 6–1). In fact, roughly one-fifth of all homicides related to disputes over land and debts in Sichuan involved migrants from other provinces, with Hunanese settlers outnumbering all others. By contrast, in Shandong and Guangdong there were only a handful of homicides involving migrants, and these migrants were usually from nearby counties within the same province. Finally, it is important to note that southern Sichuan was also the frontier of Han Chinese civilization. Han migration into the southwest also triggered ethnic tensions between Han Chinese and indigenous peoples. As the area of Han settlement encroached on the homeland of native peoples, one result was violence between Han and Miao, and Han and Yi.

As Sichuan "filled up" in the eighteenth century, new settlers faced

3 Liu Zhenggang, p. 72.
4 Liu Yuan, pp. 40–1.
5 Fang Xing, 1996b, p. 38.
6 Guo Songyi, 1994, p. 14.

Table 6–1. *County and Province of Origin of Sichuan Migrants*

Hunan	**Jiangxi**	**Guangxi**
Baling	Changning	Xingan
Dongan	Dehua	
Guiyangzhou	Huichang	**Hubei**
Hengshan	Longnan	Huangan
Hengyang	Nanchang	Huanggang
Huitong	Nanzheng	Jiangling
Jingzhou	Shicheng	Lizhou
Leiyang	Taihe	Macheng
Linxiang	Xin'gan	Songzi
Longyang	Xinfeng	Wuchang
Mayang		Wugangzhou
Nanwei	**Guizhou**	Xingguozhou
Shaoyang	Anhua	
Wuling	Cunyi	**Shaanxi**
Xiangxiang	Huangping	Baocheng
Xinhua	Maotan	Goucheng
Xupu	Pingyuefu	Heyang
Yiyang	Renhuai	Juqiang
Zhijiang	Xiuwen	Qishan
		Sanyuan
Guangdong	**Gansu**	Yongshou
Changle	Jiezhou	
Jieyang	Minzhou	**Yunnan**
Lianping	Ningzhou	Yongshan
Ruanyuan		Zhenxiongzhou
Xingning		

diminishing prospects. Early settlers in Sichuan were able to claim 30 *mu* of paddy land or 50 *mu* of dry land, while government grants provided seed, draught animals, tools, and food. Perhaps because of the abundance of land during the early eighteenth century, Sichuan had many "self-made" commoner landlords.[7] Similarly, lower rents and

7 Li Wenzhi, 1991, p. 18.

taxes in Sichuan left more capital in the hands of peasant households.[8] Even after government support ended and quality arable land was increasingly in short supply, migrants continued to arrive. Partly driven by natural disasters in their home areas, settlers who arrived during the Qianlong reign were lucky to end up as tenants, while the less fortunate became vagrants. By 1768, officials in Sichuan proposed a ban on new migration. The Qianlong emperor rejected this strategy and instead called for a rigorous monitoring of new settlers and a crackdown on the burgeoning "floating population" who, many officials seemed to believe, were often engaged in illegal activities.[9] As a consequence of the ongoing migration into Sichuan during the eighteenth century, the province had a frontier atmosphere where individual property rights were not as deeply rooted as those in Guangdong and Shandong, and many households did not have ancestral ties and historical claims to their land. Economically, the continued influx of new migrants drove down the value of labor relative to land and heightened competition among Sichuan peasants. In this way, the balance of economic power in eighteenth-century rural Sichuan, like Guangdong, tilted in favor of landowners.

Agriculturally, Shandong province had less in common with both Guangdong and Sichuan. Shandong was part of the North China macroregion that included the North China plain, the birthplace of Chinese civilization and the political center of the empire. It was an area of tremendous strategic importance that was heavily garrisoned during the Qing. Both eastern and western Shandong had easy access to waterborne transportation and consequently were more commercialized.[10] The Grand Canal crossed western Shandong, and counties along this route sold their wheat to traders from Jiangsu. The city of Linqing was an import center of trade on the Grand Canal since the late Ming. The eastern Shandong peninsula was readily accessible by sea routes, and during the Qianlong reign it accounted for two-thirds of the soybean oil and bean cake shipped to Jiangnan.[11] Many of the ports along the northern coast of Shandong were active in interregional trade in the Zhili Gulf. By comparison, in mostly mountainous central Shandong, transportation was difficult and commerce was less developed.

Physically and institutionally, Shandong possessed a distinctly different agricultural system than Guangdong or Sichuan. Shandong was

8 Fang Xing, 1996b, p. 43. 9 Liu Yuan, p. 44.

10 Xu Tan, p. 81, "Ming Qing shiqi Shandong di liangshi liu tong" (The circulation of grain in Shandong during the Ming and Qing), *Lishi dangan* (1995) 1: 81–9.

11 Ibid., p. 85.

largely a dry-farming region and the important crops were wheat, sorghum, millet, soybeans, and cotton. Farms were larger on average, but yields were lower in Shandong. Lower productivity and higher tax burdens led many landlords in North China to rely on hired laborers and to supervise farming more closely. According to one historian, managerial landlords in Shandong were also more productive due to greater investment.[12] Employment was more tenuous in Shandong. Landlords hired managers who had much greater power over tenants and laborers than landlords in Sichuan and Guangdong to supervise large estates in Shandong. Evidence from homicide reports reveals that these managers readily dismissed tenants and laborers for poor performance and that the managers could be fired at the whim of the landowner. Northern tenants also had less freedom and independence. Many lived in their landlords' home and relied on their landlords for draft animals, plows, and seeds.[13]

Given its strategic location, Shandong had suffered greatly during the Ming-Qing transition. Located in the north, Shandong experienced social upheaval and economic dislocation earlier than other regions of China. According to one account from the late Ming, every family lost members and "only one or two *mu* of land out of every ten was planted."[14] Consequently, Shandong was an early target for government measures to relieve economic distress. In order to restore its tax base, the new Qing government took immediate steps to encourage resettlement of lands that had been abandoned during the fighting. Beginning in the Shunzhi reign (1644–61), tax rebates were offered and settlers were given title to land when the original owners failed to reclaim their property. Although Manchu bannermen occupied large tracts of land in northern Shandong, there were no disputes involving Manchu bannermen in this sample. In fact, violent disputes over property rights of any sort were relatively rare in Shandong during the Qianlong reign, and those disputes that did occur often involved individuals on the lower rungs of the society. As the qualitative analysis of disputes will reveal, individuals involved in property-rights disputes in Shandong were often poor and tenants were in a much weaker economic position vis-à-vis landlords and estate managers.

12 Li Sanmou, p. 34, "Qingdai beifang nongdi liyong di tedian (Special characteristics of agricultural land use in northern China during the Qing dynasty), *Zhongguo shehui jingji shi yanjiu* (1988) 3: 31–4.

13 Yang Guozhen, 1988, p. 54.

14 Xing Long, p. 51.

Violence in Shandong and Sichuan

Another reason for choosing Shandong and Sichuan as counterpoints to Guangdong was the apparent difference in overall level of homicides related to disputes over land and debt. Based on extant homicide reports in the category of land and debt, Sichuan was consistently among the most violent provinces, while Shandong was among the least violent (see Table 6–2). Needless to say, there are formidable obstacles to constructing an index of violent behavior in eighteenth-century China. A more meaningful comparison would require detailed demographic data to compute a per capita rate. Based on a crude estimate using data on executions for capital crimes, Sichuan Province had the highest rate of capital crime while Shandong Province was at the lower end of the scale and Guangdong fell in the middle range (see Table 6–3). While admittedly crude, this estimate is consistent with data on extant homicide reports related to disputes over land and debt. More importantly, the temporal and geographic pattern of violent disputes over property rights for Sichuan and Shandong demonstrates remarkable similarities with the patterns for Guangdong.

Temporal and Geographic Patterns in Shandong and Sichuan

Not surprisingly, given the distinctive social and economic features of Shandong and Sichuan, these two provinces exhibited significant differences, but also important similarities, with the temporal and geographic pattern of violent disputes in Guangdong. Shandong stands out as a relatively peaceful region. Homicide was not only less common in Shandong, it was also less concentrated geographically. Only 19 of 107 county-level units in Shandong reported homicides related to disputes over property rights, and only one county, Caoxian in Caozhou, with four homicides, reported more than two homicides for the six years considered in this sample. This compares to Guangdong, where sixty-one of ninety-one county-level units reported homicides related to disputes over property rights and twenty-six counties reported more than two homicides over the same period. In Sichuan, homicides related to property-rights disputes were more dispersed than Shandong but less so than Guangdong. In Sichuan, seventy-two of one hundred forty-four county-level units reported violence, but only seventeen county-level units reported more than one homicide for the six years examined.

In terms of the spatial pattern of disputes, Shandong (see Table 6–4) and Sichuan (see Table 6–5) were similar to Guangdong (see

Table 6–2. *Number of Extant Reports of Homicides Related to Disputes over Land or Debts by Province and Year*

Year	1736	1740	1745	1750	1755	1760	1765	1771	1775	1780	1791	1795	Total
Sichuan	30	54	59	80	75	81	185	196	275	181	187	268	1,671
Shanxi	27	61	30	56	70	75	132	120	142	118	116	151	1,098
Fujian	27	56	59	44	71	72	120	65	114	70	87	78	863
Guangdong	31	41	49	52		65	83	67		99	95	107	832
Zhili	32	67	45	22	68	43	84	82	83	76	102	91	795
Hubei	20	21	31	37	31	38	116	96	123	71	98	91	773
Jiangxi	30	66	51	47	59	41	86	77	76	60	84	85	762
Henan	14	31	31	38	28	60	68	66	96	89	89	86	696
Shaanxi	18	6	21	28	22	19	63	76	90	54	111	137	645
Jiangsu	33	28	24	37	31	38	65	74	65	50	77	83	605
Anhui	10	37	37	48	46	47	53	68	68	38	68	77	597
Hunan	15	49	52	39	52	40	48	59	66	40	63	67	590
Zhejiang	19	25	24	24	39	27	64	74	51	51	52	66	516
Shandong	33	31	28	41	17	33	42	31	65	48	56	55	480
Guizhou	2	18	22	30	30	25	64	60	41	29	32	39	392
Yunnan	5	5	6	10	10	40	20	52	31	45	45	49	318
Guangxi	12	24	21	15	10	18	11	22	38	12	24	50	257
Gansu	10	12	10	15	8	14	19	14	14	20	23	25	184

Table 6–3. *Estimated Rate of Executions for All Capital Crimes per 100,000 Population in 1789 by Province*[a]

	Population (100,000)	Excecutions	Excecution Ratc
Sichuan	**85**	**323**	**3.80**
Shaanxi	84	223	2.65
Yunnan	34	86	2.53
Shanxi	132	315	2.38
Guizhou	51	77	1.51
Guangdong	**160**	**224**	**1.40**
Fujian	120	165	1.38
Guangxi	63	60	0.95
Henan	210	198	0.94
Hubei	190	175	0.92
Hunan	161	147	0.91
Jiangxi	191	143	0.75
Jiangsu	314	231	0.74
Shandong	**225**	**158**	**0.70**
Zhejiang	217	130	0.60
Anhui	289	145	0.50
Gansu	151	44	0.29

[a]For population figures see Ho Ping-ti, 1959, p. 281. Zhili has been excluded because Ho's data does not include population for Beijing. Execution figures for 1789 were taken from James Lee, Appendix A, "Homicide et Peine de Capitale en Chine a la fin de L'empire: Analyse Statistique Preliminaire des Données," *Etudes Chinois* (Spring–Autumn 1991) 10.1–2.

Table 6–4. *Homicides Related to Property Rights as a Percentage of All Homicides over Land and Debt for Shandong Province*

Prefecture	Property Rights	Debt and Others	Percentage Property Rights
Wuding	3	9	33%
Jinan	4	13	31%
Yizhou	5	21	24%
Caozhou	4	17	24%
Laizhou	5	24	21%
Yanzhou	2	14	14%
Dengzhou	1	13	8%
Qingzhou	1	29	3%

Table 6–5. *Homicides Related to Property Rights as a Percentage of All Homicides over Land and Debts for Sichuan Province*

Prefecture	Property Rights	Debt and Others	Percentage Property Rights
Shunqing	14	17	45%
Chongqing	23	60	28%
Yuzhou	9	28	24%
Tongchuan	9	30	23%
Suiding	5	17	23%
Jiading	5	18	22%
Baoding	5	33	13%
Chengdu	9	94	9%

Table 6–6. *Homicides Related to Property Rights as a Percentage of All Homicides over Land and Debts for Guangdong Province*

Prefecture	Property Rights	Debt and Others	Percentage Property Rights
Huizhou	34	34	50%
Chaozhou	23	36	39%
Gaozhou	13	22	37%
Luodingzhou	8	15	35%
Shaozhou	10	24	29%
Zhaoqing	11	42	21%
Guangzhou	22	96	19%

Table 6–6) in one important respect: The prefectures that reported the most homicides associated with land and debt disputes overall also had the lowest percentage of homicides related to property-rights issues, indicating that homicides related to property-rights disputes did not merely mirror a general pattern of violence in the province. In all three provinces, the spatial pattern of homicides related to disputes over property rights differed significantly from the pattern of homicides related to debt and other land disputes. Furthermore, in every province the pre-

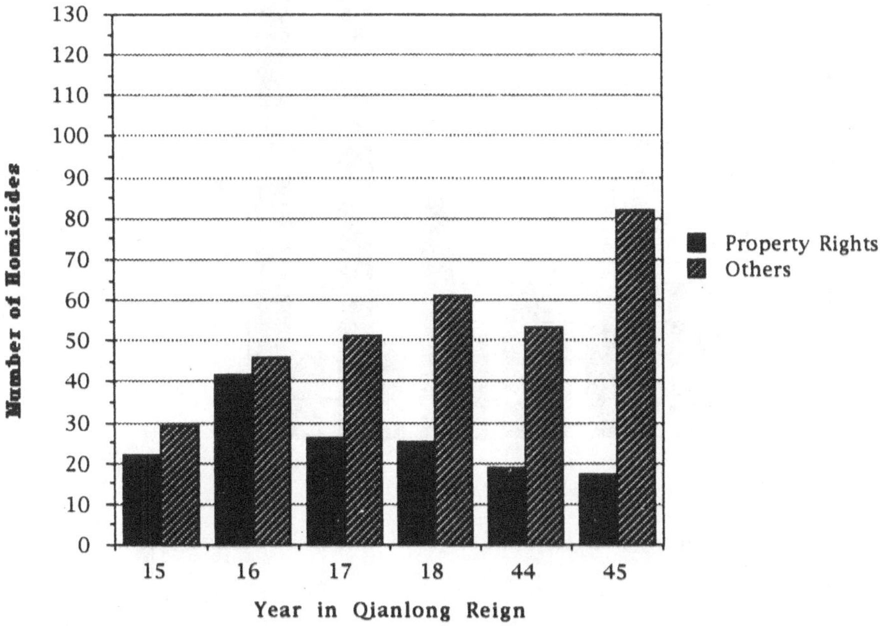

Figure 6–1 Homicides Related to Land and Debt Disputes in Guangdong

fecture with the least number of homicides related to property rights was also in the core economic area of the province.

Turning to the distribution of disputes over time (see Figures 6–1, 6–2, 6–3 and Table 6–7), with the exception of relatively quiescent Shandong, which had too few cases to warrant a meaningful comparison, the graphs indicate that the temporal pattern of disputes in Sichuan and Guangdong mirrored the pattern exhibited in the in-depth study of Guangdong. Comparing earlier and later years in the Qianlong reign, the absolute number of homicides related to disputes over property increased only slightly in Sichuan, but sharply declined as a percentage of all homicides related to land or debt (see Table 6–7). The significance of property-rights issues as a cause of homicides in Guangdong, on the other hand, declined more sharply in both relative and absolute terms. The patterns in Guangdong and Sichuan were also consistent with the evidence from the in-depth examination of Guangdong, which indicated that violent disputes over property rights declined after a new balance of economic power between land and labor was achieved and new economic institutions were accepted more widely. To the extent that

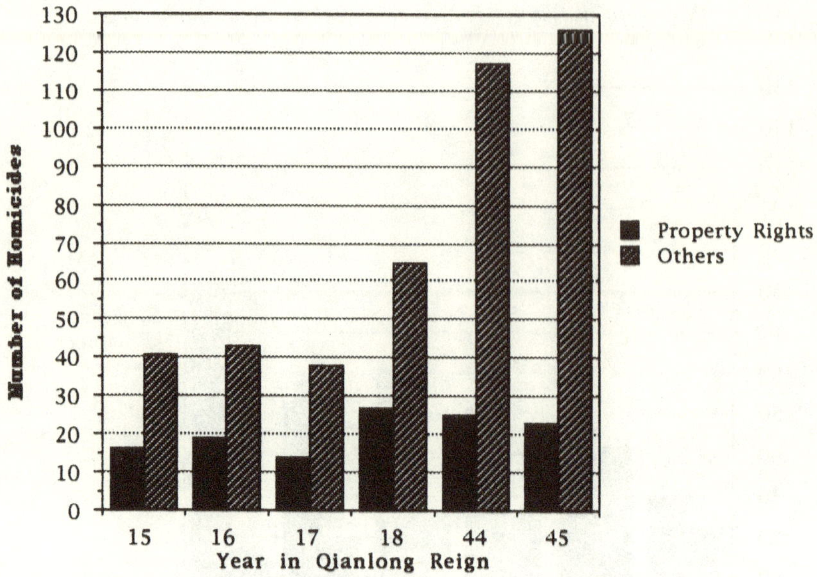

Figure 6–2 Homicides Related to Land and Debt Disputes in Sichuan

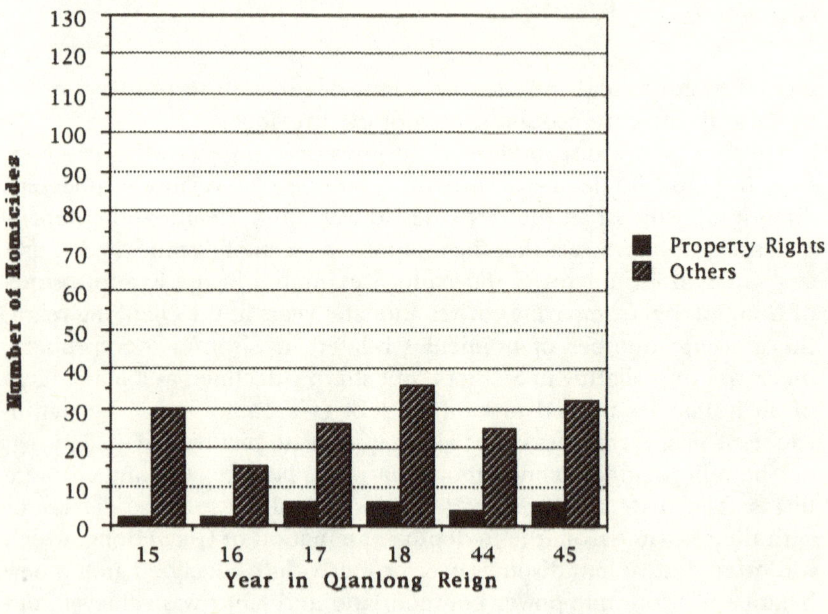

Figure 6–3 Homicides Related to Land and Debt Disputes in Shandong

Table 6–7. *Homicides Related to Disputes over Land and Debts by Province and Reign Year*

	Shandong		Sichuan		Guangdong	
Year	Property Rights	Others	Property Rights	Others	Property Rights	Others
QL 15	2	30	16	41	22	32
QL 16	2	16	19	44	41	47
QL 17	5	27	15	39	26	52
QL 18	6	36	27	66	25	64
QL 44	4	25	25	121	19	53
QL 45	6	35	23	129	17	84
Total	25	169	125	440	150	332

demographic pressure and commercialization explain the temporal patterns of violence, the similarities between Guangdong and Sichuan suggest that both provinces were undergoing similar cycles of economic change. What about Shandong?

One possible explanation for the relative lack of violent disputes over property rights in Shandong would be that the impact of demographic pressure and commercialization had been felt in Shandong prior to the Qianlong reign. Several factors would favor this interpretation. Shandong accounted for 14% of the population of China in 1749, compared to 4% for Guangdong and 1% for Sichuan; but by 1851, Shandong had only 8% while Sichuan had jumped to 10% and Guangdong had reached 7%.[15] These figures indicate that Shandong began the Qianlong reign with a large base population. The figures also suggest that Sichuan and Guangdong had greater potential for demographic expansion. The Qing conquerors also consolidated control over Shandong much earlier and implemented measures aimed at relieving the devastation of the dynastic transition and restoring the rural economy earlier than Sichuan and Guangdong. Under this scenario, Shandong probably experienced the effects of demographic pressure sooner and reached the threshold necessary to trigger disputes over property rights earlier than Guangdong and Sichuan.

15 See Gao Wangling, "Ming Qing shiqi di Zhongguo renkou" (Chinese population during the Ming-Qing period), *Qingshi yanjiu* (1994) 3: 27–32. I have rounded Gao figures.

As noted, qualitative evidence from homicide reports also indicates that Shandong landlords exercised greater control over their land, and the tenants or laborers who worked it. This would suggest that a shift in relative value of land and labor that tilted the balance of economic power in favor of landowners was well under way in Shandong at an earlier date. Similarly, according to Fan I-Chun, the Grand Canal that crosses western Shandong was the major artery of interregional change during the Ming dynasty. It was not until later in the Qing that interregional trade included the middle and upper Yangzi, and coastal trade, which included Guangdong, developed more fully.[16] Thus, the impact of commercialization also would have been felt earlier in Shandong.

It is also important to recall that violence was only one response to the economic changes that transformed China during the eighteenth century. Another response was migration, and Shandong was not far from one of the few areas with a surplus of high-quality land, Manchuria. Although the Qing court prohibited Han Chinese migration into Manchuria, there was an influx of migrants from Shandong, Henan, and Hebei in the early eighteenth century.[17] Shandong farmers were also moving into Mongolia, in this case with the support of the Qing Court.[18] Migrants from Shandong and throughout the Yellow River Basin were moving into Inner Mongolia and Manchuria in unprecedented numbers during the Qianlong reign. One imperial order noted that more than 100,000 Shandong farmers had moved to Inner Mongolia.[19] It may have been the case that Shandong peasants more readily "voted with their feet" when faced with the demands of population growth. While a range of variables might explain the lower incidence of violence in Shandong – to the extent that violent disputes over property rights abated as rural inhabitants adapted to population pressure and increased commercialization, and newly designed economic institutions gained acceptability – it may have been the case that landlords, tenants, and peasants in Shandong had adjusted to commercialization and population growth sooner than their counterparts in Sichuan and Guangdong.

Major Issues

Turning to specific issues that caused violent disputes, regional variation among the three provinces was pronounced. As Table 6–8 indicates, the relative importance of major issues varied significantly among the three

16 See Fan, Chapters 4 and 5.
17 Ye Xianen, 1991, p. 39. 18 Jiang Taixin and Duan Xueyu, p. 60.
19 See Dai Yi, pp 1–8.

Table 6–8. *Major Issues by Province*

Major Issue	Guangdong	Sichuan	Shandong	Total
Rent/Rent defaults	31	9	3	43
Evictions	17	10	2	29
Redemption/Sales	36	48	8	92
Boundary	29	49	10	88
Water	37	9	2	48
Total	150	125	25	300

provinces. The prevalence of rent defaults and water-rights disputes in Guangdong was undoubtedly related to the overwhelming predominance of paddy rice farming, and the higher rates of tenancy and need for irrigation associated with that type of agriculture. Rent defaults were not as serious a problem in Shandong or Sichuan, which may simply reflect lower rates of tenancy. Many of the disputes over evictions in Guangdong arose when a new owner took possession of land, and evictions in Sichuan were similar in most respects. Shandong eviction disputes were few, but a qualitative examination of these disputes reveals the weakened economic position of Shandong tenants. Disputes over redemptions of conditional sales were numerous in each province and also expose many nuances in the practice, not only among the three provinces, but among different counties within each province.

Because each dispute has its idiosyncrasies, only a detailed analysis of individual disputes can do justice to the richness of the sources and the complicated nature of these disputes. An in-depth analysis of individual cases demonstrates both striking similarities and telling contrasts. Despite variations in the timing of demographic pressure and commercialization and differences in agricultural practices from province to province, there were similar changes in the content and focus of disputes over time. While paying careful attention to the idiosyncrasies of each case, for heuristic purposes I will employ the categories of disputes developed for Guangdong and examine disputes by individual issues.

Water-rights Disputes (47 Cases)

Not surprisingly, the tenor and content of water-rights disputes did not vary much by region. As noted in the discussion of Guangdong, most water-rights disputes occurred when someone drained water from a neighboring field, released excess water into a neighboring field, or obstructed or diverted the usual flow of water within an existing irrigation system. Typically, individuals reacted immediately after detecting a disruption in the normal flow or customary allocation of water and retaliated swiftly and decisively. Given the complexity of some irrigation systems, and the involvement of lineage or village associations in their management, it is no surprise to find that the largest disputes in all three provinces were over water.

Although Shandong only had two disputes over water, the largest dispute in the sample, involving twenty-eight participants, took place in Jinxiang county, Jining where residents from the villages of Tianjiahai and Niuguantun, fought for control of water. The majority of the disputants from Tianjiahai were surnamed Tian, and most of those from Niuguantun were surnamed Guo or Gao. After a heavy rain, which lasted for two days, the Niuguantun residents dammed the river to save water for irrigation. By damming the river, the Niuguantun residents caused flooding of homes and fields in upstream Tianjiahai. Apparently, the Niuguantun residents were aware of the flooding and anticipated trouble. The village assigned about a dozen individuals to guard the point where the channel was dammed. Many of them were armed, and at least one individual had a bird gun. Two days after the rain had begun, on QL 15.6.17 (1750), residents of Tianjiahai arrived with hoes and picks to destroy the dam. In the melee that followed, Gao Wu from Niuguantun was injured and later died of his wounds. From Tianjiahai, Tian Zhusan died of stab wounds and Tian Shirui was shot to death.[20]

The other water dispute from Shandong deserves mention because it involved private mediation. Zhao Fengjue of Yixian county, Yizhou, dammed his irrigation channel, causing water to back up and flood Zhao Gengqi's field and damage his crop of beans. The Zhaos were distant relations in the same clan, and Zhao Jikui, the head of the clan (*zuzhang*), intervened to negotiate the matter. He persuaded Zhao Fengjue to remove the obstruction, and the problem appeared settled. Two weeks later, Zhao Fengjue taunted Zhao Fengqi as he was returning from a day's work in the field. According to Zhao Fengqi, who was already angry because he had not been compensated for the damage to his soybeans, the taunting pushed him over the top and he lashed out at Zhao Fengjue with his pickax. A struggle ensued, and Zhao Fengqi fatally wounded Zhao Fengjue by landing a blow at the base of his ear with the blade of his pickax.[21]

With only nine cases, water was a relatively minor cause of disputes

20 XKTB 0773, QL 16.1.1. 21 XKTB 3252, QL 45.9.26.

in Sichuan. Like Shandong and Guangdong, however, the largest dispute in Sichuan was over water. It involved eighteen participants and occurred in Hongya county, Jiading, where the Lis and the Songs accessed the same irrigation system.[22] Water disputes in Sichuan, like those elsewhere, generally erupted suddenly. For example, in Mianzhu county, Mianzhou, Liu Chenglong, Dai Zhi, Dai Rong, and Duan Hongshu carried their hoes to the irrigation ditch to water their fields. Farmers on both sides of the ditch used it on an alternating basis. When Liu and company arrived, they discovered that Jiang Wanhong had opened a breach in the ditch and was diverting water to his field in violation of an agreement to alternate use.

Jiang's brother, Jiang Wantao, apologized and Liu promptly repaired the ditch. Liu and company were ready to leave and continue their work without saying a word. Unfortunately, Jiang Wanhong loudly complained that his brother should not have apologized. Dai Rong was angered by this comment and opened a hole in the embankment of Jiang's field. Jiang was irate, with a pole in hand, he charged toward Dai and the others. Everyone fled except Liu Chenglong, who presumed he could deter Jiang with his hoe. Jiang was undaunted, so Liu took a swing at him. Apparently, Liu struck Jiang with some force since he broke his leg. As was the practice, Liu was responsible for nursing Jiang back to health. Despite Liu's efforts, Jiang died two weeks later, and Liu was subsequently tried and convicted of manslaughter.[23]

Turning to Guangdong, water-rights disputes in this sample contain interesting evidence of the fragmentation of land holdings. The fragmenting of land holdings meant that farmers in Guangdong were forced to cooperate because water sometimes had to flow through one field to reach another. Two cases from Nanhai and Panyu, the core of Guangzhou's economic core, are illustrative. Luo Lingzhang could not irrigate his field without the water crossing Luo Yadi's field (same surname, no family ties). The customary practice, which Luo Lingzhang asserted, was to allow water to flow across fields. The two parties quarreled when Luo Yadi refused to allow the water to pass through his field because he feared it would wash away his manure. After Luo Yadi punched him, Luo Lingzhang returned home.

Two days later, Luo Lingzhang armed with a spear went to "discuss" the matter with Luo Yadi. Along the way, he met his cousin, Luo Wansi. Carrying a sickle on his way to cut grass, Luo Wansi joined him. Together on the road to Luo Yadi's, Lingzhang and Wansi encountered Luo Yanran, the local constable (*dibao*) and uncle of Luo Yadi. Foreseeing

22 XKTB 0707, QL 15.6.8. 23 XKTB 0778, QL 16.5.15.

trouble, Luo Yanran attempted to stop them, but Lingzhang attacked and wounded him in the ribs. At that moment, a passerby, Luo Yuebin, sought to intervene and Wansi cut him with his sickle and struck him with a rock. Finally, Luo Yadi arrived on the scene armed with a spear. In the ensuing battle, Yadi fatally wounded Luo Lingzhang in the belly. In concluding the homicide investigation, the county magistrate affirmed local custom and upheld Lingzhang's right to demand access to water across a neighbor's field.[24]

In a similar case in the neighboring county of Panyu one year later, the county magistrate made a slightly different ruling. In this case, Luo Xixing refused to allow water to pass over his land because he had just fertilized it. Chen Lijun protested, and they began to argue. Chen threw the first punch, but Luo quickly got the better of him. Calling out for help, Chen fled. His wife, Ms. Cen, heard him and rushed to the scene. She began cursing Luo, who responded in kind. Ms. Cen grabbed Luo by the testicles and would not let go. Luo was in serious pain and beat her about the head and shoulders. Finally, Ms. Cen lost her grip, fell to the ground, and injured herself on some rocks. She died shortly afterwards. Interestingly, the magistrate in this case upheld the right of access to water, but not during times when fertilizer was being applied.[25]

In both cases, the magistrates clearly noted that the right to access water across another person's property was contingent on there being no other route. This raises another question. In a triple-crop rice region like the Pearl River Delta, how could one farm land that did not have direct access to water? My surmise is that with land values rising and sales more common, farmers were undoubtedly tempted to sell some if not all their land. (Both these disputes occurred between 1750–51, a period when rice prices were on a sharp upswing.) The resulting fragmentation of land holdings could have isolated some parcels from access to water. It seems reasonable to assume that landowners would share a common interest in creating new rules or that customs would be created to ensure access to water. The right to allow water to pass through neighboring fields seems a natural corollary to the commoditization of land and fragmentation of holdings that took place in the eighteenth century.

Boundary Disputes (88 Cases)

As in Guangdong, the most frequent causes of boundary disputes in Shandong and Sichuan included the reduction of the area occupied

24 XKTB 0804, QL 16.9.15. 25 XKTB 0836, QL 17.7.26.

by boundary markers (e.g., trees, raised footpaths, embankments, or other structures that delineated boundaries) in order to maximize the amount of land under cultivation; overplanting boundaries or harvesting produce from adjacent fields; flooding that eradicated existing boundary markers; disagreements over the boundaries of newly reclaimed land; and encroachment or violation of land reserved for graves. Many boundary disputes resulted from seemingly trivial matters. For example, in Shandong Wu Yucan of Wenshang county, Yanzhou, accidentally cut down two trees on Yang Songpan's neighboring field. In the subsequent affray, Yang knifed Wu's elder brother, Wu Yupan.[26] Two disputes in Shandong could be traced to floods, six were simple cases of encroachment similar to the case described previously, and only two cases involved marginal lands. The remaining case is telling for what it reveals about agriculture in Shandong. Jiang Hansan, Fan Wuyuan, Li Jing, and Wang Yin were all tenants on Chen Gengwu's land. Han Deshui owned land that bordered on the land that Jiang Hansan tilled. On the afternoon of QL 44.7.24 (1779), Jiang caught Han Deshui's brother, Han Sishui, harvesting some soybeans from his field. They argued and fought to a standstill until Han Deshui arrived. The Hans swore at Jiang and chased him away. The next day, Jiang organized his fellow tenants, Fan, Li, and Wang, to retaliate against the Hans. Armed with bamboo staves to defend themselves, Jiang and company set out to attack the Hans. Arriving at the gate of Han Sishui's home, Jiang began cursing Han Deshui. Han Sishui, Han Deshui, and Han Liang, a nephew, emerged from the house bearing metal spears and sickles, causing Jiang and his supporters to flee. Han Deshui struck Fan Wuyuan from behind with a spear. Fan turned and stabbed Han with his bamboo stave. Han was hurt, but he continued to pursue Fan, who stabbed him again in the neck. Han died soon after.[27]

What makes this case interesting is the fact that Jiang Hansan was from Guancheng county, Fan Wuyuan was from Dingtao county, and Li Jing was from Puzhou county. Only Wang Ying was from Caoxian county, where the dispute occurred. This was quite different from Guangdong, where tenants and landlords were almost always from the same county and many tenants, as former owners of the land they rented, had deep personal and customary ties to the land that they tilled. The absence of personal ties to the land that they worked along with the fact that Shandong landlords often supplied the necessary capital, such as seeds and tools, may explain why tenants were treated the same as hired laborers in Shandong. This proletarianization of agricultural

26 XKTB 0878, QL 17.9.29. 27 XKTB 3252, QL 45.9.26.

labor in Shandong had some interesting implications for relationships between tenant and landlord, as well as among tenants. As we will see in other cases discussed in the following paragraphs, Shandong tenants were frequently judged solely on their performance and could be dismissed for laziness. Interestingly, the alacrity with which Jiang's fellow tenants came to his aid also suggests a degree of class solidarity not found in Sichuan or Guangdong.

Petty disagreements over boundaries can also be found in Sichuan and Guangdong. In Dongguan county, Guangzhou, while measuring the boundaries of a plot of land his brother had recently purchased, Chen Shuzhou broke four branches off Ye Shengru's jasmine tree. Chen and Ye argued until Chen lost his temper and punched Ye. Ye fled but returned shortly with two clansmen (*zuren*) to settle the score with Chen. Chen was beaten to death in the struggle that followed.[28] Similar disputes occurred in Sichuan between family members. In Mianzhou, the capital of Mianzhou prefecture, Liu Chaolong stabbed to death his elder brother, Liu Chaoxing, after Chaoxing encroached on his land. Apparently, the land had been divided between the two brothers and there was no fixed boundary. The presiding magistrate ordered the family to erect a stone boundary marker to avoid future disputes and, in an example of Confucian justice, sentenced Liu Chaolong to "lingering death" (*lingchi chusi*) for killing his elder brother.[29]

Compared to Shandong, however, Sichuan and Guangdong boundary disputes were more likely to concern reclamation of waste land, hill land, encroachment on graves, and other marginal lands. In Sichuan, twenty-one of forty-nine boundary disputes were fought over reclaimed land or encroachment on graves. For Guangdong, it was more than half, nineteen of twenty-nine disputes. One would expect that there would be more boundary disputes in Sichuan, where there was a continual influx of land-hungry migrants from neighboring provinces during the Qianlong reign. Still, better than half of Sichuan boundary disputes were common cases of encroachment. Reflecting the growing shortage of arable land, many disputes that involved reclaimed land usually took place on hillsides. Several of these occurred in the more populous prefectures of Chengdu and Chongqing, which were resettled earliest and were thus more likely to experience shortages of arable land earliest.

The abruptness with which many boundary disputes gave way to violence is understandable given the heightened competition for land. However, not all boundary disputes arose suddenly, and there were

28 XKTB 0776, QL 16.5.14. 29 XKTB 3116, QL 44.4.22.

peaceful alternatives to settling disputes. For example, in Changshou county, Chongqing, Sichuan, the Pengs and the Dengs looked to the assistance of their neighbors to solve an altercation over the boundaries of their fields. The fields had already been planted by QL 17.5 (1752), when it was discovered that the boundaries were incorrect. Deng Qing and Peng Kaoshang, the owners of the two fields, called on their neighbors to decide the disputes (*ping zhu gong yi*). Apparently, the holdings were fragmented, and it was agreed that the Pengs and Dengs would exchange two parcels to make their respective fields contiguous. It was agreed that each side would harvest the land that they had already planted and the exchange of land would take place prior to the start of the next planting.

Yang Guogui, the tenant and maternal grandson of Deng Qing, and his nephew Deng Zhuwu began harvesting the land on QL 17.7.18 (1752). Deng Zhuwu mistakenly harvested some of Peng Kaoshang's corn. Before he could remove the corn, Peng saw him and took the corn himself. Two days later, Peng returned to the field and intentionally harvested grain on Deng Qing's plot. Yang called out to him to drop the grain, but Peng replied: "If your family can carelessly harvest my corn, can't I do the same?" At that, Peng began to curse Yang, who soon lost his temper. Yang only struck Peng once in the head with his carrying pole, unfortunately the blow was fatal. Among other things, this case indicates the limits of community intervention to devise solutions and mitigate violence. This is an important point that will be dealt with in depth in the following chapter.

In Guangdong, more than half of all the boundary disputes in this sample were over encroachment on burial grounds or reclaimed wasteland. Four disputes began when farmers encroached on the burial ground of their neighbors. Another fifteen disputes entailed reclaimed land. In Deqingzhou, Zhaoqing, He Juexu and his brother He Juehai reclaimed some riparian land (*shakan*) and planted it with taro in QL 16.2 (1751). Before the taro had ripened, He Jueao, a clansman of the fifth degree of mourning (*sima*), noticed that their claim encroached on land that he was in the process of reclaiming. He Jueao set out stakes to delineate the boundaries of the land, a legal requirement for reclaiming alluvial land. Upon discovering this, the He brothers tore up the stakes. On QL 16.3.10 (1751), the date of the Qingming festival that year, He Juehai and He Jueao passed the land in question on their way home from mourning ceremonies at their ancestral graves. He Jueao accused He Juehai of occupying his land. They started to argue, and He Jueao struck He Juehai with his carrying pole. Seeing his brother in danger, He Juexu came to his aid. He Juexu wrestled the pole away from

He Jueao and struck him across his left side. Another clansman arrived and broke up the fight, but He Jueao died twelve days later. The magistrate who tried the homicide also ruled that the land did not amount to much and that, in order to avoid future disputes, neither side should be allowed to reclaim it.[30]

A dispute from Dongguan county, Guangzhou, indicates that the drive to bring more land under cultivation also threatened common lands. Liao and the Tans lived in the same village. Outside the village was some wasteland that both sides used to graze oxen. On QL 14.7.24 (1749), Liao Meishu and Liao Tianpei hired Liao Yarun and Liao Yaluo to reclaim the land and plant it. Tan Yuxian saw them and suspected that the Liaos were encroaching on Tan land. Tan enlisted clansmen Tan Desheng, Tan Fengtian, Tan Degui, and Tan Yawu to attack the Liaos. The Tans were armed with bamboo spears and sickles. Liao Yaluo and Liao Yarun were outnumbered and unarmed. In the assault that followed, the Tans brutally bludgeoned Yaluo and Yarun to death. In a typically conservative ruling, the magistrate in this case ordered that the Tans and Liaos should honor the original boundaries and only use the land to graze oxen.[31]

Rent Defaults and Other Disputes over Rent (43 Cases)

Rent defaults were not as serious a problem in Shandong and Sichuan in contrast with Guangdong. In Shandong, there were only three rent disputes; Sichuan only witnessed nine cases; and Guangdong had thirty-two disputes. Numbers aside, these cases reveal important differences among tenants in different provinces. Guangdong tenants often displayed a greater degree of economic independence from their landlords. As noted earlier, in many cases tenants in Guangdong had formerly owned the land they tilled and had become tenants after selling their land to the landlord. In Shandong, on the other hand, tenants resembled hired laborers. Farms were generally larger in north China and productivity was lower, requiring closer supervision, with landlords supplying seed, tools, and draft animals.[32] As noted, landlords were frequently absentee owners, and they hired overseers (*guanzhuang*) who served at the landlord's pleasure and were easily fired if they failed to produce. For example, in Tancheng county, Yizhou, the landlord Wu Yue replaced Wu Zhiyu with Xu Ling in 1750. The tenants on Wu Yue's land divided the crop equally, and landlord and tenant supplied the seed

30 XKTB 0818, QL 17.3.10. 31 XKTB 0789, QL 16.1.28.
32 Li Sanmou, 1988, pp. 33–4.

in alternate years. Despite being fired, Wu Zhiyu, the erstwhile overseer, later killed Ma Yonggong, a tenant and his wife's cousin, in an altercation over rent Ma had been unable to pay in the past.[33]

The weak economic position of Shandong tenants can be seen in a rent dispute that occurred in Haiyang county, Dengzhou. The tenant Sun Jineng leased 70 *mu*, not a particularly large parcel of land, in Shandong from Liang Yuzhuo in QL 11.7 (1746). According to the report, Sun was poor and had a hard time making a living. Liang loaned Sun 3 *shi* of grain. Sun was expected to repay Liang the following spring. Sun planted half the field in winter wheat. The following spring, Liang Yuzhuo wanted Sun to repay 8 *shi* of the loan because the price of grain was high; but because Sun was poor, he was often away, hiring out his labor, and could not be found. On QL 12.5.15 (1747), the wheat was ripe and Liang ordered Sun to prepare the threshing ground. Sun replied that he could not because he had to work in order to eat. Liang rebuked him and left.

Later that day, Liang went to the field himself and began harvesting the wheat that Sun had planted. Sun was returning home when he saw Liang in the field. Sun went to stop him, and the two were soon embroiled in a violent altercation. Liang attacked with a sickle, and Sun fled. As Liang chased Sun through a ditch, Sun picked up a rock and hit Liang directly in the heart. Liang collapsed, but he continued cursing vehemently. Unable to control his anger, Sun took his own sickle from his back and hacked Liang several times. Four days later, Liang died.[34]

Sichuan rent defaults were infrequent compared to Guangdong, but the position of tenants was somewhat better than in Shandong. Migrants were still arriving in Sichuan in search of land during the eighteenth century, and it may have been the case that economic conditions, at least in the first half of the Qianlong reign, were still favorable for tenants. Seven of the nine disputes over rent occurred in later years of the survey, 1779 and 1780, by which time Sichuan's population had recovered, the economic balance of power had shifted in favor of landowners, and the Qing government had rescinded its policy of encouraging migration. Government policy notwithstanding, migrants continued to arrive in Sichuan, despite the fact that Sichuan was no longer a "land of opportunity." As noted, early migrants during the Kangxi reign (1662–1722) could expect title to 30 or 50 *mu* of land, as well as government support in the way of seeds, food, and draft animals. Later migrants were more likely to be unemployed or work as

33 XKTB 0837, QL 17.1.24. 34 XKTB 0738, QL 15.9.5.

tenants.[35] By the latter part of the Qianlong reign, land-hungry migrants were competing for land with locals. For example, in Santai county, Tongchuan, Yang Chun leased land from the Tongchuan Academy (*shuyuan*). In 1778 Yang defaulted on his rent, owing 3,200 copper cash (*wen*). On QL 44.1.6 (1779), Yang relinquished the land and Wei Yuanfang assumed the tenancy. (Wei had migrated to Sichuan from Longchuan county in Guangdong.) Wei was at work on the land turning the soil on QL 44.3.29 (1779) when Yang spotted him. Because he had already planted sorghum, Yang called on his two sons, Yang Xianfu and Yang Xianlu, to stop Wei. Wei refused to stop hoeing, and Yang ordered Yang Xianlu to seize his hoe. Eventually, Yang Chun, a man of sixty, joined the fray and tried to wrest the hoe from Wei. In the course of the struggle, Yang was struck in the head, fell down, and bruised his ribs and leg. Three days later, Yang Chun died.

For the most part, the rent defaults and disputes over rent for Guangdong in this sample are consistent with the findings of the earlier sample.[36] One case from Haiyang county, Chaozhou, in 1751 deserves mention for what it reveals about lineage control of land. The Xie brothers, Xie Zhuixian, Xie Wuxian, and Xie Qianxian, leased 6 *mu* of lineage-owned land (*jitian*) in 1743. The rent was 7 *shi* per year. In 1749 the Xie brothers defaulted on their rent. Because of the default, their "clan uncle"[37] (*zushu*), Xie Chengtao, along with other members of his lineage, Xie Chengxian and Xie Xiaoqu, met in QL 14.6 (1749) and decided to invite Ceng Liangxiang to lease the land. On QL 14.9.30 (1749), the late rice was ripe, and Ceng summoned Xie Chengtao to the field to divide the harvest. Perhaps anticipating the trouble to come, Xie Chengtao also brought along his nephew, Xie Jiexian, to help. When the former tenants, the Xie brothers, heard what was happening, they went to the scene and demanded money for the expenses and work they had done preparing the field. Xie Chengtao refused, and he and Xie Wuxian got into a heated argument that soon turned violent. A prolonged affray ended with Xie Chengtao dead at the hands of Xie Xuxian. Among other things, this case reveals how economic considerations could outweigh kinship or lineage ties. Apparently, the Xie Chengtao and other

35 Liu Yuan, p. 41.

36 In fact, only one-third of the cases are new. As noted previously, the compilers of the published documents had a penchant for selecting examples of class conflict. Many of the cases included in the three published sets were rent defaults or other disputes over rent.

37 The Xie brothers were actually distant relatives with no mourning (*wufu*) obligations to Xie Chengtao.

lineage leaders had no qualms about evicting their delinquent clansmen in favor of Ceng Liangxiang, though in the end the lineage did meet and decide to forgive the Xie brothers' debt.

Evictions (31 Cases)

Evictions for reasons other than rent defaults provide numerous examples of the declining economic power of tenants throughout China and the increasing commercialization of land. As we have seen, many of the disputes over evictions in Guangdong arose when a new owner took possession of land. In some cases, the seller did not inform the buyer of agreements with existing tenants. In extreme cases, the seller never even informed the buyer that he had a tenant. Another common source of disputes was the failure of the owner to return the tenant's rent deposits. Evictions in Sichuan were similar in many respects. Shandong had only two eviction disputes, but these disputes reveal once again the diminished economic position of Shandong tenants.

In a case briefly discussed in Chapter 1, Wang Chen of Wenshang county, in Shandong province, leased 24 *mu* from Guo Jingyuan. Guo Jingyuan, who had served as a clerk in Beijing, lived some distance from the field, so he entrusted Cheng Zhao with the management of the land. On the morning of QL 14.4.29 (1749), it rained, and Wang Chen decided it was a good time to plant soybeans. He asked Cheng for the seeds. At this point, events took a tragic turn. Cheng not only refused to give him the seeds, he also accused Wang of being lazy and demanded that he return the land. In his subsequent testimony, Cheng claimed that Wang had done a poor job of planting the sorghum and millet. Wang had not hoed the ground or pulled up the weeds. Cheng feared that the landlord, Guo Jingyuan, would criticize him for Wang's poor work. Cheng told Wang Chen that he had done a poor job and that he would not allow him to till the field.

Wang Chen suggested that they wait until after autumn harvest. Unfortunately, Cheng not only rejected his request but also accused him of dishonesty. Cheng later claimed that he was only trying to frighten Wang in order to motivate him to work harder and did not really mean to evict Wang. Wang, however, took this threat quite seriously and desperately replied: "If you demand that I return this land now, is it not the same as killing my family?" At that, Wang lowered his head and attempted to butt Cheng. Cheng punched him in the left temple. Wang tried a second time to butt him. Cheng side-stepped him, and Wang fell to the ground, injuring his left ear and the left side of his head. Wang died of his wounds two days later.[38]

Most local officials only briefly addressed property-rights issues at the end of their reports after they had thoroughly dealt with the criminal matters. Usually, these comments did not exceed a sentence or two. Indirectly, however, magistrates often provided intriguing insights into property-rights issues in the body of their reports. The landlord, Guo Jingyuan, felt compelled to explain that he did not manage his field personally because he lived some distance away. Similarly, he carefully noted that he did not have a contract (*wenqi*) with Cheng and that Cheng was "emphatically not" (*bingbu*) a bonded servant (*nupu*). Keeping in mind that local officials carefully crafted every word of a homicide report, it is also significant to note that the magistrate included Wang's desperate plea to keep the land. Both the statement from the landlord and his tenant's entreaty indicate the growing gulf between tenant and landlord in eighteenth-century Shandong. Similarly, in the other eviction that occurred in Caoxian county, Caozhou, the landlord, Zhang Qiyun, evicted his tenant, Wang Facai, for laziness. In this case, the tenant asked a neighbor to plead with Zhang on his behalf. When Zhang would not relent, a drunken Wang went to Zhang's home and attacked him. Zhang killed Wang in self-defense.[39]

While Shandong tenants were evicted for laziness, evictions in Sichuan and Guangdong were usually not so simple. Lawsuits preceded three of ten evictions in Sichuan, though winning a judgment did not prevent violence. For example, Ding Youshang successfully defended his property rights at the yamen but lost his life afterwards when the dispute turned violent.[40] Indications that tenants' bargaining power was deteriorating can also be found in Sichuan evictions. As competition for land sharpened, landlords extracted cash rent deposits from tenants. For example, Yang Xihe and his son Yang Ruwei leased land from a temple through a monk named Zhenglin. The rent was 40 *shi* of grain per year. They paid a further 30 ounces of silver as a deposit and spent another 30 ounces of silver to repair a house on the property. According to the written contract, the entire 60 ounces of silver should have been returned when the Yangs relinquished the field. In QL 17.3 (1752), the master of the temple (*shizu*), Chi Xian, decided to raise the rent. When the Yangs refused to pay more, Chi Xian evicted them and leased the land to Deng Yuanchen.

On QL 17.3.18 (1752), Deng Yuanchen and his brother found Yang

38 XKTB 0714, QL 15.4.17. 39 XKTB 3209, QL 45.9.22.
40 XKTB 0723, QL 15.1.22.

Ruwei watering the field. The Dengs confronted Yang, who responded with a stream of curses. The Dengs replied in kind, and a fistfight broke out, ending in the death of Yang Ruwei. Once again, the magistrate who investigated the homicide ruled that it was wrong to raise the rent for profit. He punished the monk, Zheng Lin, because he did not possess a license (*dudie*) to be a monk, and, more importantly, he punished Chi Xian for privately profiting from temple land.[41] Zheng Lin was flogged and defrocked, and Chi Xian was fined.

A further indication that over time tenants faced sharper competition for land comes from another case in Luzhou prefecture, Sichuan. In QL 42.7 (1777), Dan Erming enlisted the aid of a middleman, Fang Yucai, to arrange a lease of Fang Shaorao's land. They decided on the rent and wrote a contract. For providing his services, Dan paid Fang Yucai 440 copper cash in "liquor money" (*jiushui qian*). Later, for reasons unstated in the document, Fang Shaorao decided to lease the land to someone named He instead. Dan Erming wanted his liquor money back from Fang Yucai, but Fang only had 200 *wen* left. Pleading poverty, Fang asked for a delay. For over a year, Dan had dunned Fang repeatedly. Finally on QL 44.5.19 (1779), Dan was on his way to the market to have his cleaver repaired. He saw Fang Yucai returning from the market carrying a basket of rice. Dan tried to seize the basket of rice in lieu of the money he was owed. They argued, and Dan hacked Fang in the back of the neck with his cleaver and dragged him by the queue into a rice paddy. Dan then proceeded to hack Fang repeatedly in the head, neck, and throat. Technically, this was not an eviction because Dan Erming never took possession of the land, but the case illustrates the declining economic power of tenants in Sichuan. Prior to 1779, there were no examples of tenants paying money to middlemen to acquire leases. Finally, although he was not implicated in the violence, the landlord, Fang Shaorao, was also flogged for reneging on his lease to Dan Erming and thereby creating a situation that led to the loss of life.[42]

As for the Guangdong cases in this sample, frequently it was a change in ownership or the owner's demand to cultivate the land himself that precipitated a dispute. A case from Maoming county, Gaozhou, represents a variation on this scenario. Wei Yidai leased his land to Mo Chaocai in 1747. Alongside the field were two plots of wasteland. Mo and Wei agreed that Mo would reclaim the land, and after ten years Mo would pay rent on the land to Wei.

Wei's maternal cousin Tan Xingyuan's "mouth watered" (*chuixian*) for the reclaimed land, and he plotted to "steal" it. Tan ordered Wei Yidai to

41 XKTB 0971, QL 18.7.28. 42 XKTB 3279, QL 45.2.28.

take the land back and lease it to him. On QL 16.6.1 (1751), Mo Chacai and his son Mo Jindu were at the field planting. Carrying a hoe, Wei arrived at the field and demanded that they return the portion of the land that they had reclaimed. The Mos refused, an argument erupted, and they soon came to blows. When it ended, Mo Jindu lay dead from the blows of Wei's hoe. Wei was sentenced to death, and Tan Xingyuan was flogged for creating the situation by plotting to seize reclaimed land. The magistrate stated that Mo could keep the land and that "bullies (*haoqiang*) should not be permitted forcibly to occupy land."[43] Here we have another instance of a magistrate supporting the small farmer, attempting to protect him from the machinations of his landlord.

Finally, one other case deserves mention because both the tenant and landlord were women. In QL 41.11 (1776), Zhuo Yada's aunt, Ms. Li, paid 19,000 copper cash to lease land from Huang Zheng's daughter, Ms. Huang. Huang Zheng wrote up the lease contract for them. Later, Ms. Huang had no land to till, so she evicted Ms. Li from the land but did not return her deposit. Ms. Li dunned Ms. Huang several times to no avail. On QL 44.1.2 (1779), Ms. Li asked her husband's brother, Zhuo Kaiqi, to demand restitution. Zhuo went to Huang's home and took her water buffalo instead of the cash. Two days later, Huang Zhang and his cousin, Cheng Weizhong, went to demand the return of the water buffalo. Zhuo was away, but his wife was home, and she criticized Huang's daughter for not returning the cash. Huang then argued with Ms. Wu, who took up a knife and tried to stab Huang. Ms. Wu missed her mark and hit Chen Weizhong instead. In retaliation, Chen clouted Ms. Wu on the head with his tobacco pouch. At this point, Zhuo Yada, seeing his mother injured, came forward and pummeled Chen, knocking him to the ground. The fight ended there, but Chen was already fatally wounded and died a short while later.

From the standpoint of property rights, this was a typical eviction dispute. The fact that the transaction took place between two women was exceptional, however. While there were cases of widows leasing land, Ms. Huang was unmarried and presumably younger. Furthermore, her father was alive, yet she herself leased the land. It was also unusual for a woman to rent land. Unfortunately, we have no information about what Ms. Li did with the land. Interestingly, the fact that both landlord and tenant were women made little difference in how the dispute began or how it ended. Ms. Huang, who did not return the deposit; her father, Huang Zheng, who wrote the contract; and Zhuo Kaiqi, who snatched the Huang's water buffalo, were all punished for "doing what they

43 XKTB 0852, QL 17.7.20.

should not do." As was the case for women, Ms. Huang was spared a flogging and received a fine instead.[44]

Redemptions and Land Sales (93 Cases)

Disputes over the specific practice of redemption of conditional sales of land accounts for sixty-four disputes, a little more than two-thirds of the disputes in this category. As noted earlier, *dian* and *dang* have also been translated as mortgage, pawn, and pledge, as well as conditional sale. The difference between the two practices is not always apparent, and in one case the term *diandang* was used as a compound.[45] In some instances, the *dian* was indistinguishable from the *dang*, which is often translated as *pawn*, but clearly they were different practices. In one case, a plot of land in Sichuan was both *dian* and *dang* at the same time. The terminology was similar, but the practice varied subtly from county to county and overtime, making it difficult to distinguish the two practices. At the risk of overgeneralizing based on the cases I have read, land that was *dang* was usually security for a loan, while land that was *dian* was often a prelude to an outright sale of the land, and the person who paid the *dian* would often take control of the land. *Dang* seems to have been more popular in Sichuan, while *dian* was the more frequent practice in Guangdong, though both could be found in either province. In either case, however, the *dang* or *dian* could be redeemed. I have chosen to designate this particular issue "redemption disputes" since the disputes usually centered on the conditions under which the original owner of a plot of land could regain control of the land. In addition to redemptions, this category also includes twenty-nine other disputes over land sales. Land sales were normally accompanied by a written contract. Over time, contracts became more specific with regard to the right to redeem.

Tensions over changing concepts of land, from patrimony to commodity, is readily apparent in the struggles over redemptions.[46] As land was increasingly bought and sold, the practice of redemption underwent adjustments. Whereas it was common practice in the early part of the Qianlong reign to view land that had been owned for generations, usually referred to as *zuye*, as something apart from land that had previously exchanged hands in the market, in the later years of the Qianlong reign landowners could no longer take the right of redemption for

44 XKTB 3183, QL 44.10.11. 45 XKTB 3131, QL 44.6.6.

46 See Thomas Buoye, "From Patrimony to Commodity: Changing Concepts of Land and Social Conflict in Guangdong Province during the Qianlong Reign (1736–95)," *Late Imperial China* (December 1993) 14.2: 19–46.

granted. Over time, customary rights were under pressure as purchasers of land began to demand contracts that clearly stipulated the terms of the sale. Similarly, purchasers of land sought to curtail the practice of former owners demanding supplemental payments to compensate for the increased value of land over time. As noted, the problems caused by conditional sales were so sufficiently widespread and troublesome during the Qianlong reign that the central government twice amended the Qing law code to clarify the issue. Still, as the cases from Shandong and Sichuan demonstrate, not all regions of the country had similar experiences.

Disputes over redemptions and land sales in Shandong were mostly over small plots of marginal land. Unlike Sichuan and Guangdong, where land sales were largely indicative of a vibrant, commercialized economy, desperation and economic hardship drove many land sales in Shandong. In three of the eight cases, the land was sold to raise money to pay for a funeral. The Wang family of Putai county, Wuding, had 8 *mu* of land and a six-room dilapidated house that was inherited property. In 1768, the Wang brothers, Wang Sheng and Wang Chao, split the land and rooms evenly and set up separate households. Wang Chao died that year without an heir. Wang Chao's wife, Ms. Zhao, sold her 4 *mu* of land to Wang Qiyou for 24,000 copper cash and used the money to pay for her husband's funeral. Ms. Zhao kept the three rooms because no one wanted to buy them.

Upon seeing his sister-in-law penniless, Wang Sheng invited her to live with his family. On QL 40.7.9 (1775), Ms. Zhao secretly borrowed 6,000 copper cash from Wang Dan, using 2 *mu* of Wang Sheng's land as security. She returned to her family's home, where she made several items of clothing before returning to Wang Sheng's home. Since she had no money to repay the loan, Wang Sheng used his own cash to redeem the land in QL 41.1 (1776). In QL 43.5 (1778), Ms. Zhao complained that she had "nothing to wear and little to eat." She asked Wang Sheng to sell her three rooms so that she could return to her family's home permanently. Wang Sheng replied that the current harvest had not been as good as in past years, the bad times were temporary, and besides no one wanted to buy the three rooms. Wang Sheng urged her to stay. Ms. Zhao was dissatisfied and often argued with Wang Sheng.

On the evening of QL 43.5.8 (1778), Wang Qisui, Wang Sheng's son, was in the garden behind their home building an awning. He heard his father and Ms. Zhao arguing. Because the two were always bickering, Wang Qishui did nothing at first. Meanwhile, the bickering became more vociferous, and Ms. Zhao attacked Wang Sheng. Wang Qishui heard his father yelling loudly and quickly went to see what was wrong. Arriving on the scene, he found his aunt lying on the ground with his father standing over her straddling her body. Ms. Zhao had a firm grip on his testicles and would not let go. According to Wang Qishui, his father's face had already turned white. Overcome by concern for his father, Wang Qishui took up an iron pick and bashed Ms. Zhao on the left knee and right knee. Ms. Zhao finally released Wang Sheng, and a local constable, Wang Guangxian, arrived. Surprisingly, Ms. Zhao died from her injuries that evening. Wang Qishui was sentenced to imminent (*lijue*) beheading for killing his aunt. Wang Sheng was found guilty of being an accessory; but since he was over seventy, he only received a fine.[47]

In another case, in Pingduzhou county, Laizhou, Li Zhaoqi had purchased 2 *mu* of land from his "clan elder brother" (*zuxiong*), Li Songlin, in 1738. This was an outright sale. When Li Zhaoqi died, his nephew, Li Yong, mortgaged (*dang*) Li Zhaoqi's land to pay for his funeral. Li Zhaoqi had a son who had left the area long ago and had not been heard from since. Li Yong continued to till the land and pay rent. Later, Li Yong decided to leave the land and go into business (*waichu yingsheng*), so he sold the land to Zhu Keguan for 5 ounces of silver. The deed only contained one condition: If Li Zhaoqi's long-lost son should ever return, he would have the right to redeem the land. No other person had the right to redeem it. These words were written into the deed.

Some time later, Li Songlin wanted to buy the land because it was near his ancestral graves. Li asked Zhu Keguan many times to redeem the land, but Zhu refused, citing the clause in the deed. When Zhu Keguan died, Li went to his son, Zhu Decai, and requested to redeem the land. Once again, in accordance with the deed, Zhu Decai refused to redeem the sale with anyone except Li Zhaoqi's son. On the morning of QL 43.6.25 (1778), on the pretext that the Zhus had encroached on his ancestral graves, Li Songlin went to the field and harvested Zhu's millet precipitating a bloody confrontation that cost Li his life.[48]

In a third case, from Bingzhou county, Wuding, two brothers fought with their stepmother over the sale of land that was meant to pay for their father's funeral.[49] In the remaining cases from Shandong, we can find stepbrothers from Lanshan county, Yizhou, who mortgaged a tiny plot of land on which they grew radishes. Both brothers spent long periods away from home, hiring out in other areas. Another case involved the sale of 2 *mu* of swampland. The remaining cases entailed

47 XKTB 3138, QL 44.2.7. 48 XKTB 3138, QL 44.1.24.
49 XKTB 3145, QL 44.3.4.

fraudulent sales. Suffice it to say that disputes over land sales in Shandong took place mainly at the bottom rungs of the economic ladder and usually involved smaller parcels of marginal land.

In Sichuan, the sources of disputes varied from the attempts of family members to preempt sales, fraudulent sales, failure to pay in full, demands for supplement payments, disagreement with owners of neighboring fields, and rights to crops on land at the time of the sale. In China, kin and neighbors customarily had first claim to land transactions, and interference by family and neighbors was one important source of disputes in Sichuan. In Fuzhou county, Chongqing, when Yang Ban wanted to sell his land to Yan Shirong for 130 ounces of silver in QL 14.3 (1749), Yang Shirong also paid each of Yang Ban's brothers, Yang Xian and Yang Chun, 9 ounces of silver to sign the contract (*hua zi qian*). Yang Chun received an additional ounce of silver for drawing up the contract. Later, Yang Xian, who stated that he was poor and had no food, wanted Yang Shirong to pay him 1 ounce of silver so that things would be "equal" between him and Yang Chun, who had received the additional ounce for drawing up the contract. When Yang Shirong refused, Yang Xian threatened to demand a redemption. Later, Yan Xian stole crops from the field, but Yang Shirong ignored him and did not report the incident. Perhaps emboldened by Yang Shirong's capitulation, Yang Xian deceived several of his neighbors into helping him harvest Yang Shirong's entire field. Yang Shirong went to the head of the *baojia*, Chen Kuishi, for assistance, and on the way to the field Zhang Quande joined them. When they arrived at the field, a fight broke out between Zhang Quande and Yang Xian. Yang beat him over the head with a pole and killed him.[50]

A very similar case occurred in Nanchong county, Shunqing, where the Li brothers, Li Shen, Li Chuan, Li Wei, and Li Ren, owned inherited land. In QL 13.10 (1748), Li Shen and his younger brother, Li Ren, pawned (*dang*) five plots of inherited land to Zheng Qishun for 8 ounces of silver. In the contract it was clearly written that the land could be redeemed at any time (*buju yuanjin yin dao tian hui*). In QL 14.12 (1749), a third brother, Li Wei, sold outright a portion of his inherited land for 147 ounces of silver to Zheng Qishun. Zheng also paid 10 ounces of "signing money" to Li Ren and Li Shen. According to Li Ren, despite the fact that they received signing money, he thought that he and his brother would still be able to lease the land. When he discovered this was not the case, he wanted to redeem the sale. Zheng Qishun believed that it was an irrevocable sale and refused.

50 XKTB 0721, QL 15.12.15.

When Li Shen saw the ripe corn in the field at the autumn harvest, his anger for Zheng returned. On QL 15.7.18 (1750), Li Shen was armed with a bird gun. He called on his brother Li Ren, and together they left to harvest the field. Zheng Quoru, the son of Zheng Qishun, found out, and he called on his brother, Zheng Longru, and his uncle, Zheng Qiwei, together with the middlemen in the land sale, Xiong Shengfu and Liu Maoxiang, to accompany him to stop the Lis. Fearing that the Zheng and company were coming to beat them, Li Shen fired the gun, ostensibly to frighten them, but he peppered Zheng Guoru's upper body with buckshot. Zheng Guoru died the next day.[51]

As these cases reveal, the practice of paying relatives signing money to sever their claims to property had become a widely accepted custom. Buyers of land appear to have accepted the practice, though they balked at efforts to use the custom to extract additional payments. How did this custom fare over time? In Tongjiang county, Baoding, Li Peixue sold his land and house to his brother, Li Peiqing. According to the report, the land was sold outright (*guanye*). Five years later, Li Peiqing mortgaged (*dang*) the land to Luo Shaoli. When Li Gui, Li Peixue's grandson, discovered the transaction, he immediately confronted Li Peiqing. Li Gui demanded payment of signing money because the land had been mortgaged without informing the original owner (*yuan yezhu*). Li Peiqing not only refused to pay, he also cursed Li Gui. Just as the confrontation verged on violence, a passerby stopped and broke it up.

When Li Gui was returning home, it was already dark. Li Gui was angry over Li Peiqing's refusal to pay signing money. At that moment, he spotted Lin Nuzi; his younger brother, Li Sigui's, child bride of thirteen, who lived with Li Gui; his younger brother; and grandfather. She was stealing turnips from Li Peiqing's field. Li cursed at her and told her to go home, but she refused. In a ghastly turn of events, Li Gui, still angry over the confrontation with Li Peiqing, grabbed her and stabbed her in the head with his knife. Realizing she was seriously wounded and no one was around, he stabbed her repeatedly until she was dead. Li Sigui had heard her cries and came running. Under duress, Li Sigui, who was only fourteen, helped his brother move the body to Li Peiqing's doorstep. Li Sigui reported the grisly killing the next day, and Li Gui was sentenced to be beheaded.[52]

Comparing these cases from the standpoint of property rights, it would appear that in the space of thirty years, with population increasing and land values rising, the traditional notion of land as patrimony

51 XKTB 0785, QL 16.5.13. 52 XKTB 3237, QL 45.5.6.

was being undermined. Similarly, on QL 17.4.8 (1752), Liu Tingxiang of Neijiang county, Zizhou, enlisted Zhang Maofeng as a middleman to sell his land to Yang Taizhen. They assembled the owners of neighboring fields to mark off the boundaries of the land. Zhang Shengyuan wanted to exercise his right to "bind buy" (*xiangmai*) a portion of Liu's land that bordered on his home. An argument began, but the neighbors quickly quelled it. The measurement of the land continued until another neighbor, Wang Yuanda, suspected that Liu had surreptitiously occupied some of his land. Wang refused to allow the survey to continue until the original deed was examined. Once again, the neighbors subdued the disputants, and everyone broke for lunch at Liu's home. While they were eating at Liu's home, Wang again demanded to see his deed. This time, peace could not be restored; and in the ensuing brawl, Wang Yuanda killed Zhang Maofeng, would-be middleman in the land sale.

Three of the four cases where neighbors objected to a sale occurred in 1750 or 1752. Also, six of nine disputes where kin interfered in a sale occurred between 1750 and 1753. Only three cases occurred in 1779 or 1780. In addition to the case in Tongjiang county described earlier, a dispute in Jianzhou county, Longan, arose after Xiong Nenghong mortgaged his land to his brother Xiong Nengdi in 1754. Afterwards Xiong Nenghong moved to another county. In 1779 Xiong Nenghong's son returned to Jianzhou and forcibly attempted to take back the land that his cousin, Xiong Damei, now controlled.[53] In the other dispute, which occurred in Dingyuan county, Chongqing, in 1778, Wei Deli was poor and wanted to sell his land. His sister-in-law, Ms. Wang, wanted to buy the land, but she did not offer enough money. Ms. Wang later attacked Wei after he sold the land to someone outside the family.[54]

Rising land values also prompted the original owners or their descendants to demand supplemental payments to compensate for the increased value of their land. While it is not entirely clear in every case, in Sichuan it often appears that those who demanded supplemental payments were desperate and caught in a downward economic spiral. Zhang Weizhong of Xichong county, Shunqing, sold his land and house to his cousin, Zhang Weijing. Afterwards, Zhang Weizhong died and son Zhang Can left home to find some land to rent. In QL 43.11 (1778), Zhang Can returned. He had no land, so Zhang Weijing gave him a room to live in temporarily. On QL 44.1.8 (1779), Zhang Can returned home drunk and demanded supplemental payments for his father's

53 XKTB 3182, QL 44.5.9. 54 XKTB 3180, QL 44.9.8.

land. Zhang Weijing rebuked him for attempting to cheat him this way. In the fight that followed, Zhang Lian, the son of Zhang Weijing, mortally wounded Zhang Can when he hit him over the head with a piece of firewood.[55]

Usually, those who demanded supplemental payments based their claims on the increased value of the land over time. Chen Zishan's demand for supplemental payments, however, was unique and revealing. In QL 42.12 (1777), Chen Bangjian purchased Chen Tingfu's land. Originally, this land belonged to Chen Zishan, who had sold it to Cheng Tingfu the previous year. (Chen Zishan and Chen Bangjian were distant relatives of the same clan.) In the field was a ditch that Chen Tingfu filled in and planted. On QL 43.5.16 (1778), Cheng Bangjian was plowing the field. Chen Zishan arrived, and, as the original owner of the land, he demanded supplemental payment because, with the ditch filled in, the land was now larger. Chen Zishan was not making a polite request. He seized the blade of Chen Bangjian's plow and went home. Several days later, a violent dispute ended with the death of Chen Zishan's son, Chen Xiang. Not only did Chen Zishan lose his son, the magistrate also ruled that the land in question was entirely the property of Chen Bangjian.[56]

Most of the cases in this sample of Guangdong, twenty-six of thirty-five, entailed redemptions of conditional sales. Fraudulent sales accounted for ten disputes, demands to redeem sales caused eleven disputes, and appeals for supplemental payments triggered seven disputes. As in Sichuan, the impression one garners from these disputes is of a vibrant market in land that was muddled by uncertainty over property rights. As noted, the motivation for selling land is usually not mentioned. However, many individuals who sold land in Guangdong used the proceeds to engage in trade or business. Redemptions and disputes over sales in Guangdong have already been discussed, but several cases in this sample are worthy of note.

Demands to redeem irrevocable sales was a frequent source of trouble in Guangdong. For example, in 1729 Lai Yongsai of Guishan county, Huizhou, sold his land through a middleman, Ceng Shiguang, to the brothers Peng Guozhen and Peng Guoquan for 39.5 ounces of silver. In 1732, Lai also received an additional 1,300 copper cash to sign an addendum to the original deed that stated the sale could never be redeemed. In QL 16.1 (1751), twenty-two years after the initial sale of the land, because he had no land and the price of land had risen, Lai went to the middleman, Ceng Shiguang, and asked to request a redemp-

55 XKTB 3189, QL 44.6.13. 56 XKTB 3181, QL 44.5.2.

tion. Reminding him of the terms of the sale, Ceng informed him that it was impossible.

On QL 17.3.2 (1752), Lai and his son, Lai Sucong, took a plow to the field. According to Lai, his purpose was to let the Pengs know that he wanted to redeem the land. The Peng brothers arrived with Ceng Shiguang, and the cursing soon began. Peng Guozhen threw a punch at Lai Yongsai. A man of sixty-three, Lai fled, fearing a fight. Lai Sucong went to his father's aid and beat Peng Guozhen to death with the wooden handle of his plow. The investigating magistrate showed no sympathy for the Lais. Lai Sucong was sentenced to be strangled, and his father, Lai Yongsai, was ordered flogged for creating the situation by seizing land that had been irrevocably sold (*juemai*). Citing the deed, the magistrate went further and stated that no one named Lai was permitted to demand a redemption of the land.[57]

This case illustrates the weight of written agreements and the critical role of the middleman in land sales. In another case from Lianping county, Huizhou, Xie Fuhong in QL 8.2 (1743) irrevocably sold 2 *mu* of land through a middleman, Xie Xichuang, to his uncle once removed (*xiaogongfu*), Xie Xilian, for 50,000 copper cash. Xie Xilian had tilled the land and paid taxes on it for seven years by the time Xie Xichuang died in QL 15.2 (1750). Taking advantage of the fact that the middleman had died, Xie Fuzhong falsely claimed that the sale was conditional (*dianmai*) and wanted to redeem the sale from Xie Xilian. Xie Xilian refused.

On QL 15.3.7 (1750), Xie Xilian and his sons, Xie Shenghui, Xie Shengchuan, and Xie Shengjie, were leading a cow to the field to begin plowing. When Xie Fuhong heard, he and his sons, Xie Shaohui and Xie Shaocan, along with a nephew, Xie Shaoqiu, went to stop them. It was not long before both sides were brawling. It proved to be a costly struggle for Xie Xilian as Xie Shaohui killed two of his sons, Xie Shenghui and Xie Shengchuan. Because Xie Shaohui had killed senior members of his own clan, he was sentenced to beheading pending final sentencing at the autumn assizes. His father, Xie Fuhong, was stripped of his *jiansheng* degree, flogged, and sentenced to one-and-a-half years of penal servitude for his part in the melee. Xie Fuhong's nephew, Xie Shaoqiu, was flogged and sentenced to one year of penal servitude. The magistrate ruled that the land was irrevocably sold and was the property of Xie Xilian.[58]

This case reveals the importance of both the personal role of the middleman as well as the written contract. It was the death of the middle-

57 XKTB 0866, QL 17.12.14. 58 XKTB 0795, QL 16.12.15.

man that emboldened Xie Fuhong to demand an illegal redemption, but ultimately the county magistrate relied on the written contract to decide the property-rights dispute. A similar case occurred in Yangchun county, Zhaoqing. In 1728, Wu Dingyong sold 1 *mu* to Lu Shuixi, maternal cousin, for 12 ounces of silver. The deed clearly stated the land could never be redeemed (*yong bu shoushu*).

Twenty-four years later, in 1752, Lu Shuixi died, and his brothers tilled the land. On QL 17.3.4 (1752), Wu Dingyong went to the field, where Lu Shuifeng, Lu Shuixi's younger brother, and his mother, Ms. Wu, were hoeing, and demanded to redeem the land. Lu Shuifeng refused. The two began quarreling, a scuffle broke out, and Ms. Wu was injured. Lu Shuifeng and Ms. Wu reported the incident to the county magistrate, who ordered an arrest and investigation. By the time Ms. Wu recovered from her wounds, the magistrate was away on official business and the investigation had not begun. With the dispute still unresolved on QL 17.6.14 (1752), Wu Dingyong and his wife, Ms. Zhang, attempted to steal the standing grain in the field, precipitating another violent confrontation between the Wus and Lus. The magistrate who investigated the homicide also decided that the land had been irrevocably sold and could not be redeemed.[59]

The balance between personal ties and legal documents was also apparent in cases of fraud. In Dingan county, Qiongzhou, Wu Fengcai, a tenant on Ms. Mo Yang's land, had secretly sold portions of her land to Shen Meiyu, a *jiansheng* degree holder, who leased the land to Ma Tulong. Wu did not fear detection because Ms. Mo Yang's husband had died and her children were young. The fraud came to light when Ms. Mo Yang sold the land to Chen Dagao. Chen thought he was buying 17.3 *mu* for which he paid 120 ounces of silver, but he quickly realized that the amount of rent paid was insufficient given the stated size of the field. After investigating the rent records that Mo Yang's husband had kept, Chen confirmed his suspicion. On QL 43.9.28 (1778), Chen hired three laborers to harvest the field. The results were predictable: Chen and his hired laborers faced off against Ma Tulong, his brother Ma Minren, and the "landlord" Shen Meiyu. The fighting ended after Chen Dagao picked up a rock and struck a fatal blow to Ma Tulong's head. Wu Fengcai was not present, but he was flogged for illegally mortgaging 4.3 *mu* under the Yongzheng law that punished crafty tenants who cheat their landlords.

As in the previous sample for Guangdong, demands for supplemental payments could lead to violence. These demands were frequently

59 XKTB 928, QL 18.5.12.

made despite written contracts that clearly stated irrevocable and final sales. For the most part, it was poor, down-on-their-luck former owners who made demands for supplements. In an extreme case, Hu Zihua, the aged uncle of Hu Yunjie, volunteered to take poison in order to extort a supplemental payment from Zhu Yuncai. Hu Yunjie had sold his land through intermediaries to Zhu several years earlier. In the contract, it was plainly stated that the sale was irrevocable and that no future supplements would be paid. Tragically, Hu Zihua died in vain. The plot was easily uncovered and, with regard to property-rights issues, the magistrate upheld the contract to the letter.[60]

A more typical case occurred in Fengshun county, Chaozhou, where Ms. Liu and her aunt (father's younger brother's wife), Ms. Hong, both widows, sold 1.2 *mu* of land to Wu Shixue, a *jiansheng* degree holder, for 14 ounces of silver in 1744. The contract clearly stated that the sale was irrevocable. Wu Shixue was a distant (no mourning obligation) clan relative of Ms. Liu. In 1745, Ms. Liu asked for a supplemental payment. According to his testimony, Wu Shixue ignored the terms of the contract and, taking pity on her because she was a widow, gave Ms. Liu an additional 6 ounces of silver. In 1751, Ms. Liu requested another supplemental payment; however, Wu refused this time. Two days later, Ms. Liu saw Wu Shixue in the market and repeated her demand for more money. This time, they quarreled and Ms. Liu tore Wu's clothing. The following day, the two met again beside a stream outside the village. Ms. Liu cursed and attacked Wu Shixue, who punched her several times. As the struggle continued, they both fell into the stream. At that moment, Wu's wife and a neighbor helped them out, but Ms. Liu could not walk on her own. Wu took her to his home to treat her. She died that evening. Wu Shixue offered bribes to Ms. Liu's son-in-law and the local authority (*liancong*) to say that she had drowned, but the cover-up failed.[61] Interestingly, despite Wu Shixue's crimes, manslaughter and bribery, the investigating magistrate held to the letter of the contract regarding the land sale and stated unequivocally that the land belonged to Wu.[62]

As in Shandong and Sichuan, disputes within families could be com-

60 XKTB 0819, QL 17.10.21.

61 In the sample of 385 cases for Guangdong, there were 14 failed cover-ups. Attempted cover-ups usually occurred when the circumstances of the killing provided a pretext, such as when Ms. Liu fell in the river it provided a pretext to say she had drowned. For more on such cases, see Thomas Buoye, p. 243, "Economic Change and Rural Violence: Homicides Related to Disputes over Property Rights in Guangdong during the Eighteenth Century," *Peasant Studies* (Summer 1990) 17.4: 233–59.

62 XKTB 0858, QL 17.11.10.

plicated. In Qujiang county, Shaozhou, Xiao Xikuan and his wife, Ms. Qiu, were old and childless. They adopted Xiao Shusheng as their heir. When Xiao Xikuan died, Xiao Shusheng wanted to sell the land, the income from which was set aside to provide for Ms. Qiu to pay for the funeral. Ms. Qiu objected. On QL 15.1.22 (1750), Ms. Qiu asked her brother, Qiu Rupiao, to intercede. Meanwhile, Xiao Shusheng invited clansman Xiao Dianwei, a *shengyuan* degree holder, Xiao Hongkuan, and Xiao Cai to urge Ms. Qiu to reconsider. As soon as Qiu Rupiao arrived, he immediately began chastising Xiao Shusheng. He also grabbed Xiao Dianwei and accused him of cheating the Xiao family. A fight ensued and, outnumbered four to one, Qiu Rupiao was fatally beaten.

The investigating magistrate determined that Xiao Hongkuan had administered the fatal blow. Xiao Shusheng was flogged for trying to force his adoptive mother to sell her land and creating the circumstances that led to the death of her brother. Xiao Dianwei did not take part in the fighting, but he was punished for not criticizing Xiao Shusheng's effort to sell his adoptive mother's land and, on the contrary, urging Ms. Qiu to sell the land. Furthermore, when the fighting began, Xiao Dianwei did not attempt to stop it. According to the law, which treated educated persons who broke the law the same as commoners, Xiao was flogged and stripped of his degree without the possibility of having it restored. With regard to the land, it should remain in Ms. Qiu's possession, Xiao Shusheng was disinherited, and Ms. Qiu was permitted to find a new heir.[63]

Another case in Luoding county, Luoding, provides an interesting variation in disputes based on claims of land as patrimony. In 1740, Deng Yitian mortgaged (*dian*) 4.3 *mu* of corporate land set aside to pay for ancestor worship to Deng Diran for 3.5 ounces of silver. (The Dengs were distant relatives in the same clan.) In QL 15.4 (1750), Deng Diran needed cash quickly. He borrowed 13.2 ounces of silver from Deng Yitian. As security, he allowed Deng Yitian to till 1.8 *mu* of the 4.3 *mu* he had mortgaged. They verbally agreed that Deng Diran could redeem the land at any time. On the evening of QL 16.5.22 (1751),[64] Deng Diran and Deng Yitian met. Deng Diran wanted to redeem the land. Deng Yitian refused on the grounds that it was his family's inherited property (*jiazuye*). Deng Yitian shoved Deng Diran, and a fistfight began that ended when Deng Diran mortally wounded Deng Yitian. The investigating magistrate ruled that the land was indeed Deng Yitian's family's land and, skirting the issue of the verbal agreement over the later loan,

63 XKTB 0779, QL 16.5.30. 64 It was the fifth intercalary month.

that the amount of the loan should be deducted from the mortgage price at the time of redemption. Once again, the local magistrate ruled in accord with local custom, recognizing Deng Yitian's long-standing tie to the land in question.

Broadening the study of violent disputes over property rights to include Shandong and Sichuan reveals striking similarities as well as important regional variations. The similarities reflect the common characteristics of China's agrarian economy, the widely shared customs that governed the use of land, and the corresponding impact of commercialization and population growth in all three provinces. The variance reflects unique natural endowments and, more importantly, points to the importance of the diachronic effects of commercialization and population pressure. The economic forces that induced demand for change in property rights struck each province at different times. Given that homicides related to property rights was a transitional phenomenon, it makes sense that provinces experiencing economic change at different times would also exhibit different patterns of violence. Finally, the most remarkable consistency across all three provinces was the work of the district magistrate. Almost invariably, local magistrates upheld local custom and the shared moral values on which the rural economy was based. At a time when the economic and social institutions were in flux, local magistrates regularly supported principles of fairness and deftly balanced competing economic interests. Time and again, magistrates strictly punished individuals whose cupidity, unbridled self-interest, or underhandedness contributed to the outbreak of violence. Given the pivotal role of the local magistrate in the resolution of disputes and enforcement of property rights, it behooves us to examine their performance in detail. As I will argue, this will also help us to understand why individuals resorted to violence.

7
"You Will Be Rich but Not Benevolent": Changing Concepts of Legitimacy and Violent Disputes

In the preceding chapters, we have examined the economic conditions that created the potential for conflict, the issues that caused violent disputes, and the temporal and geographic patterns of disputes. A more nettlesome question remains: Why did individuals resort to violence? Homicidal violence was not a preferred method of resolving property disputes, nor was it very effective. The futility of violence is readily manifest when we consider that two-thirds of the parties who initiated violence ended up as homicide victims. Given the risks entailed in taking violent action, it seems reasonable to assume that the parties to a dispute would have availed themselves of more peaceful methods of conflict resolution, if such a remedy was available; yet in 630 homicides (combining both samples used in this study), we find that only 14% of disputants (86 cases) took their cases to court. Disputes that ended in lethal violence despite efforts at official adjudication attest to the depth of the social tensions in the eighteenth century. These disputes also offer insights into why many people resorted to violence. Focusing on disputes that were preceded by lawsuits discloses the process of adjudicating property-rights disputes and reveals the limits of state power, even when fairly and competently exercised, to enforce property rights. This focus also highlights the competing visions of social justice and economic self-interest in rural society, which were at the heart of many violent disputes.

Table 7–1. *Duration of Disputes by Issue for All Homicides Related to Property-Rights Disputes*[a]

	1 day	1–30 days	30 days–1 year	Over 1 year	Total
Rent default	32	40	55	8	135
Eviction	14	27	24	9	74
Redemption	37	40	46	11	134
Boundary	82	18	24	16	140
Water	112	29	4	2	147
Total	277	154	153	46	630

[a]The duration of a dispute is measured from the date the dispute is first mentioned in the document until the day the homicide was committed. Unfortunately, not every document mentions the date on which the dispute first arose. In sixty-two cases, it was apparent that a dispute was ongoing, but no specific start date was mentioned. I have included these cases under the heading "1–30 days."

Before considering the issue of official adjudication further, it is important to remember that homicide reports primarily addressed criminal matters. It is possible that a lawsuit preceded a homicide but was not mentioned in the homicide report. If that were the case, official adjudication might have been even more widespread though ultimately ineffectual. On the other hand, the figure of 14% might be accurate and could indicate that official adjudication did prevent many violent disputes. A third possibility also exists: Disputants may have desired official adjudication, but access to it was difficult or costly. (These are important issue that I will return to in the following text.) The source materials do not allow us to rule out any of these possibilities. What the sources do reveal, however, is that even efficient and judicious displays of official adjudication did not necessarily forestall violence.

Given the limitations of the source materials, it is difficult to determine exactly why individuals eschewed official intervention, but the urgency of some disputes may have been one reason. As Table 7–1 indicates, in many cases there was no time to seek official intervention. Many disputes, particularly those arising from water or boundary disputes, exploded violently in less than a day without any apparent warning or opportunity to file a complaint. But given an opportunity, for example when a dispute had dragged on for months, resorting to

Table 7–2. *Duration of Disputes by Issue for Homicides Preceded by Official Intervention*[a]

	1 day	1–30 days	30 days–1 year	Over 1 year	Total
Rent default	0	7	7	3	17
Eviction	1	0	7	3	11
Redemption	3	6	12	4	25
Boundary	0	3	10	12	25
Water	2	3	1	0	6
Total	6	19	37	22	84

[a]In eight cases, it was apparent that a dispute was ongoing, but no specific date was mentioned. I have included these cases under the heading "1–30 days."

official adjudication was more likely. Only about one-third of all disputes ending in homicide lasted for more than thirty days (see Table 7–1), but in two-thirds of all violent disputes preceded by official mediation, the disagreement that led to violence had existed for over thirty days (see Table 7–2). It would seem that given the chance many disputants were not necessarily adverse to taking their complaint to the local yamen, yet many did not.

Other factors, such as the cost of filing a complaint, the ease of access to the local magistrate, confidence in the reliability of official adjudication, and the ability of the local magistrate to enforce decisions may have been important considerations that deterred some from going to court. Recent scholarship on civil law, however, reveals that "civil cases constituted a significant proportion of the local courts' caseloads" during the Qing and that "local courts regularly and consistently upheld property and contractual rights."[1] According to Philip Huang, "official representations" of the Qing legal system exaggerated the evils of "litigation sticks" and "yamen worms," who were frequently denounced as barriers to the efficient administration of justice.[2] Huang has also found that the cost of civil litigation in the Qing "though high from the point of view of the small peasant was not entirely prohibitive."[3]

1 Philip C. C. Huang, pp. 49, 108, *Civil Justice in China: Representation and Practice in the Qing* (Stanford: Stanford University Press, 1996).
2 Ibid., p. 186. 3 Ibid., p. 184.

Homicide reports were concerned with criminal law and cannot shed light on all issues surrounding the adjudication of civil cases. However, what these reports do reveal is quite interesting. As the following cases indicate, magistrates generally performed efficiently and fairly, respecting both law and custom. Magistrates were usually competent and sometimes innovative in their decisions. It was clearly in their interest to defuse potentially violent disputes for the sake of social stability as well as their own careers. As these cases reveal, in most cases violence did not reflect a failure of official adjudication.

Getting the Case Heard

Why did disputes preceded by official adjudication end in violence? In thirteen cases, the answer was simple: Violence erupted before the court had rendered a decision. Complaints filed in county courts did not necessarily receive prompt attention. In three cases, Xingning county, Guangdong, in 1751[4]; Sihui county, Guangdong, in 1752[5]; and again in Xingning county, Guangdong, in 1752,[6] action was postponed because it was the busy agricultural season. In another seven disputes, no explanation was available, but the cases were still pending when violence broke out. For example, with land prices rising in Changshou county, Sichuan, Huang Yuxian sued Zhu Xialing to redeem land that his grandfather had sold in 1713, despite the fact that Huang's father had received a supplemental payment and had signed a contract stating that the land had been sold outright. The magistrate agreed to hear the case, but the dispute turned violent when Huang, his son, and a cousin, armed with spears, tried to harvest the field before the case was heard. In this instance, the consequences were excruciatingly tragic. The victim, Zhu Xialing's neighbor, Li Jingan, died after being speared in the testicles.[7]

Delays often occurred for legitimate reasons. In boundary disputes, magistrates usually ordered surveys that took time to complete. Two boundary disputes were awaiting an official land survey when a killing took place. Magistrates were sometimes ill or away on official business. For example, in 1780 families in Gaomi county, Shandong, who had endowed a local temple with land, sued because the monks were frequently drunk, sold trees felled on temple lands, and illegally mortgaged temple lands.[8] Unfortunately, violence erupted because the magistrate was unable to hear the case due to illness.

4 XKTB 0794, QL 16.12.15. 5 XKTB 0856, QL 17.9.15. 6 XKTB 0837, QL 17.1.21.
7 XKTB 0902, QL 18.3.13. 8 XKTB 3197, QL 45.4.28.

Even the best efforts to resolve disputes peacefully sometimes went awry. Perhaps most unfortunate, because it involved efforts at both formal and informal mediation, was the case of Ceng Guixing of Huilai county, Guangdong. After Ceng had defaulted on the rent, his landlord, Wen Rongmu, evicted him and sued him for back rent. Fearing the outcome of the lawsuit and hoping to avoid further trouble, Ceng invited Wen to his home for a meal and some drink. Ceng offered Wen 1,000 copper cash to forget the arrears and drop the suit, but Wen wanted more. In fact, he even demanded interest on the outstanding debt. The distraught Ceng scoured his neighborhood, trying to borrow more money. Failing to find any lenders, he returned home. Humiliated and upset, Ceng accused Wen of being greedy for demanding interest on the back rent. Wen cursed Ceng and struck him. Enraged, Ceng fatally stabbed Wen with a knife.[9] This case is interesting because it was the only rent default in which a landlord demanded interest on the arrears. Apparently, this was unusual because the magistrate who tried the homicide commented that the demand for interest was unjustified.

Magistrates at Work

When magistrates did hear cases, they usually rendered clear-cut decisions even when asked to sort out some rather convoluted cases. For example, a dispute in Jiangan county, Sichuan, arose from a particularly messy land sale. The original landowners were the Wu brothers, Wu Tianquan and Wu Zhiquan. At first, the Wu brothers accepted a partial payment of 177 ounces of silver on the total price of 440 ounces from Wang Xingjian. Wang then leased the land to Zuo Longfu and his brother, both of whom had migrated to Sichuan from Hunan. Before Wang Xingjian could make good on the balance due, the Wu brothers sold the land again to Dong Zijun for 660 ounces of silver. Since the Wu brothers had not yet refunded his initial payment, Wang Xingjian sued and the magistrate ordered the Wu brothers to refund Wang's money. A violent confrontation resulted when Wang, having yet to receive his money, went ahead and ordered his tenants to harvest the field. Concluding the homicide investigation, the magistrate reiterated his earlier ruling that the land now belonged to Dong Zijun and that the Wu brothers must compensate Wang.[10] A less convoluted case involving a double sale occurred in Santai county, Sichuan. Zhang Xianxu had sold a plot of land to Zhang Shiji. Later, when Zhang Xianxu died, Zhang Shilu induced his widow to sell the land to him. Zhang Shiji, who had

9 ZYG, pp. 652–4. 10 XKTB 0756, QL 16.4.1.

already planted the field, promptly sued, and the magistrate ruled that the land could not be sold until after the harvest.[11] Despite what seemed to be a clear-cut ruling, the dispute ended violently when Zhang Shilu attempted to harvest the field in defiance of the magistrate's decision.

Documentation was extremely important in civil suits, and any official documentation strengthened legal rights in court.[12] When faced with a dispute over a sale or mortgage, a magistrate's first response was usually to examine the sale contract or land deed. In six cases, the magistrate easily settled competing claims after examining the documentation of the sale. Why was violence not averted? When Chen Shibao of Longchuan county, Guangdong, sued to redeem land his grandfather had mortgaged, the magistrate upheld his claim but asked him to wait until after the upcoming harvest.[13] Frustrated, Chen went to the field and attempted to destroy the crop. When Zhang Guanyou of Jieyang county, Guangdong, wanted to redeem his right to till a plot of land, Zhang Hongshan refused. Zhang Guanyou sued, and the magistrate decided that Zhang Guanyou could till the land and pay rent after he repaid Zhang Hongshan. Violence ensued because Zhang Guanyou did not have the money to redeem the land.[14] In similar cases in Gaoyao[15] and Shicheng[16] counties, Guangdong, and Fuzhou[17] county, Sichuan, magistrates settled claims quickly and efficiently, allowing individuals to redeem land. However, when claimants did not have sufficient resources to redeem the land, they resorted to violence.

By comparison, boundary disputes were straightforward and the remedy was obvious. Regardless of what gave rise to a boundary dispute, all a magistrate needed to do was examine land deeds and order a survey. This is precisely what most magistrates did. In four cases where floods or the diversion of an irrigation channel led to disputes, surveys were immediately ordered. For example, in Caoxian county, Shandong, floods inundated land owned by the Shaos and the Fans. Both families had purchased their land from Cheng Yan. The Shaos owned 600 *mu*, and the Fans owned 1,200 *mu*. As the waters receded, both sides wanted to till whatever land was available. The Shaos sued when the Fans refused to share the harvest on the partially recovered land. Before the case was heard, the Shaos, because the weather was right, attempted to sow the field, triggering a violent confrontation.[18] Similar disputes arose in

11 XKTB 0913, QL 18.7.3. 12 See Yang Guozhen, 1988, p. 74.
13 XKTB 0163, QL 5.6.27. 14 XKTB 0847, QL 17.4.18.
15 XKTB 0769, QL 16.9.11. 16 XKTB 0776, QL 16.1.29.
17 XKTB 0743, QL 15.12.19. 18 XKTB 0866, QL 17.12.16.

Juzhou county, Shandong,[19] and Maoming county, Guangdong.[20] The diversion of an irrigation channel in Shicheng county, Guangdong,[21] also generated a dispute. In each case, the magistrate ordered the land surveyed and divided according to the original boundaries; nevertheless, all four disputes ended in homicide. In each of these cases, the property-rights issues were clear-cut, though the resolution was not.

Magistrates were efficient at handling incidents of encroachments that did not present complicated property-rights issues. Attempts to steal a furrow or two from a neighbor were readily uncovered and dealt with in Kaixian;[22] Xuyongting (twice),[23] Jianwei,[24] Pingshan,[25] Xiushan,[26] and Huayang[27] counties in Sichuan; and in Haikang county in Guangdong. Violation of graves, another indication of the lengths to which peasants were driven to expand the area under cultivation, in Renshou[28] and Zizhou[29] counties, Sichuan, and Changning[30] county, Guangdong, were also readily decided at the county court, but violence was not averted.

Another source of boundary disputes was land reclamation. With population growing steadily throughout the eighteenth century and land values rising, marginal land was increasingly being brought under cultivation. Erstwhile wasteland had become so valuable that some farmers were willing to risk their lives fighting over it. Such was the case in Deqingzhou,[31] Jieyang,[32] Huaxian,[33] and Huazhou[34] counties, Guangdong; Dingyuan[35] and Pingwu[36] counties, Sichuan; and Daba[37] county, Shandong. Boundary disputes over reclaimed land could be more complicated because the land had not previously been registered for taxation and not recorded on the land deeds of the disputants. Nevertheless, magistrates ably handled these disputes by examining deeds and ordering surveys to sort out competing claims. The dispute in Daba was notable because it involved an elaborate fraud that hinged on forged documents. A former legal secretary who was studying to take his civil service examination, Niu Sitian, was enlisted to produce a land reclamation certificate on blank forms that Niu had stolen during his tenure at the local yamen. Despite the deceit of the wayward Niu, the entire fraud unraveled under official scrutiny.

19 XKTB 0879, QL 17.11.10. 20 XKTB 3725, QL 56.9.19.
21 XKTB 0719, QL 15.5.20. 22 XKTB 0749, QL 15.3.22.
23 XKTB 0759, QL 16.5.15 and XKTB 0895, QL 18.12.17.
24 XKTB 0878, QL 17.9.25. 25 XKTB 0930, QL 18.5.2.
26 XKTB 0761, QL 16.11.16. 27 XKTB 0826, QL 17.7.12.
28 XKTB 0936, QL 18.6.9. 29 XKTB 0841, QL 17.3.16. 30 XKTB 0206, QL 5.7.4.
31 XKTB 1068, QL 20.6.13. 32 XKTB 0156, QL 5.2.9. 33 XKTB 0780, QL 16.5.4.
34 XKTB 0923, QL 18.5.17. 35 XKTB 0826, QL 17.7.14.
36 XKTB 0836, QL 18.7.30. 37 XKTB 0903, QL 18.4.11.

The division of land within a family or clan could sometimes present knotty problems, such as cases in Juzhou[38] county, Shandong, and Ruyuan[39] county, Guangdong, and required some discretion on the part of the magistrate. The Qing courts frequently left such disputes to "kin-group mediation."[40] (These disputes were included under the heading of boundary disputes though they actually involved the division of family or clan holdings.) For example, Xie Gongfu was the adopted son of Ms. Xie. The old lady had instructed Xie Gongfu to provide his daughter (Ms. Xie's granddaughter) with land as a dowry. Sadly, Ms. Xie died before the marriage. Xie dispatched his daughter to her husband's home but did not give her the land. Instead, he leased this land to Ka Shi, who planted cotton. To no avail, Wang Qing, the father of the groom, demanded the land. Finally, Wang Qing sued, and the magistrate ordered Xie Gongfu to transfer 8 *mu* of land to Wang's son. Because it was fall, the magistrate fixed a date one month hence to survey the land. Before the survey could be conducted, Wang made what turned out to be a fatal mistake. He attempted to pick cotton from the land that he assumed would be his, precipitating a struggle with Ka Shi during which Wang lost his life. In the other case, two branches of the Hou lineage rotated management of land set aside to support ancestor veneration. Hou Qiwen wanted to divide the land evenly between the branches, but Hou Ximei refused, apparently because his branch had more members. Both sides filed complaints, and the case went all the way to the prefectural court, which upheld the county magistrate's decision not to allow the division. Afterwards, Hou Ximei criticized a member of Hou Qiwen's branch for initiating the lawsuit. The argument soon got out of hand. It ended when Hou Ximei struck him in the head with a rock and killed him.

Some magistrates rendered decisions cautiously, while others were more innovative. In water-rights cases, like other disputes, official decisions sometimes simply served to clarify and define, not enforce property rights. For example, two villages in Lufeng county, Guangdong, had brought their dispute to the county magistrate, who ordered a survey of the irrigation systems in the area. According to the magistrate, the purpose was to delineate the systems clearly to prevent confusion and disputes.[41] Similarly, when the Huangs sued the Pengs in Heping county, Guangdong, the magistrate ruled against the Pengs, who wanted to plant trees that would have obstructed the irrigation channel used by the Huangs, and ordered the parties to settle the case according to the

38 XKTB 0908, QL 18.4.29. 39 XKTB 1806, QL 30.11.5. 40 Huang, 1996, p. 28.
41 XKTB 0969, QL 18 (month and date unknown).

boundaries of their property. If the passive approach did not forestall violence, the active and innovative approach was not necessarily more effective. In four other water-rights cases, magistrates sometimes took direct steps to alleviate the source of the dispute. For instance, in Jieyang county, Guangdong, a shortage of rain created serious difficulties for the Yangs, whose land lay downstream from the Xies. The Yangs sued because water was not reaching their land. The magistrate ruled that they could open a new irrigation channel so that water would reach their fields. In Xinan county, Guangdong, the Chens sued the Mais after they dammed the irrigation channel to create a fish pond. The magistrate in this case ordered the Mais to dismantle the dam.[42] In each of these cases, the magistrates proactively attempted to rectify the disputes; nevertheless, violence ensued.

Dealing with Fraud

Magistrates frequently had to deal with fraudulent claims. Four eviction disputes arose from fraudulent claims. One such case occurred in Heyuan county, Guangdong. Liu Hongchang had been the tenant on a plot of land that four Ye brothers – Ye Benhui, Ye Benlun, Ye Benkun, and Ye Bensong – had purchased in 1737 as a hereditary estate that would be used to defray the cost of ancestor veneration (*changye*). The land was comprised of sixty-two parcels that totaled 6.25 *mu*. Originally, this land had belonged to Liu Rirong, Liu Hongchang's nephew, who previously had sold the land to Ye Mengsong, a clansman (*zuren*) of the Ye brothers. Liu Hongchang leased the land from Ye Mengsong after the sale. After the Ye brothers purchased the land, Liu was no longer willing to till it. The Ye brothers returned his silver deposit and leased the land to another tenant.

Unbeknown to the Ye brothers, the land they had purchased was larger than the amount stated in the deed. The original owner had reclaimed additional land but had not reported it. Liu Hongchang fraudulently claimed that the additional land was his. Ye Benhui then filed a complaint with the county magistrate. The magistrate inspected the deed but did not survey the land. Based on this evidence, the magistrate punished Liu for "falsely occupying" (*yingzhan*) Ye's land and officially evicted Liu. Ye was now free to find a new tenant.

Apparently, the magistrate's decision did not sit well with Liu. When Ye Benhui died fifteen years later, Liu and his son Liu Yuanshi, a minor degree holder (*jiansheng*), fabricated a phony deed to the land. Subse-

42 XKTB 0003, QL 1.9.12.

quently, Ye Benlun filed another complaint with the county magistrate, requesting that the land be surveyed. The magistrate authorized the survey; but when the Lius heard that the field was being measured they tried to obstruct the survey. The result was a violent confrontation between the Lius and the Yes that ended in the death of Liu Hongchang's son Liu Rikan.[43]

In the aftermath of the homicide, Liu Hongchang and his son were blamed for creating the situation that led to the loss of life and were punished under the law of "doing what one should not do." As for the land, the survey revealed an additional 5.168 *mu* that had not been registered for taxation. This land was officially confiscated, and the magistrate ordered the Ye brothers to pay the back taxes on this land for the previous sixteen years.

In another case of fraud, a distant clan member was evicted after he attempted to occupy a widow's land in Xuyongting, Sichuan.[44] When a landlord in Luzhou county, Sichuan, wanted to evict so he could till the land, the tenant who had leased the land for several decades falsely claimed he owned it.[45] In Yibian county, Sichuan, Wang Zhixuang fraudulently included land owned by the Ding family in the sale of his land to Li Junpo.[46] In the former case, the Dings had previously sued Wang when he had attempted to seize their land. Unaware of the situation, the new owner, Li Junpo, attempted to evict the Dings. In all of these cases, the magistrates had no difficulty exposing the frauds, but violence erupted when the perpetrators of the frauds defied the officials' decisions.

Redemption disputes often hinged on contracts that had been concluded years if not decades earlier. The parties to these disputes often had no firsthand knowledge of the original terms of exchange. The uncertainty surrounding redemption claims led to misunderstandings, and provided opportunities for the deceit and fraudulent claims that fueled seven disputes. For example, Wen Shiqin of Jieyang county, Guangdong, declared that his mother had told him that the land his grandfather had previously sold had in fact only been "entrusted" to the care of a distant clansman, Wen Shijin. Actually, Wen Shijin had purchased the land outright from the previous owner, Lin Zhenxu, who had purchased it outright from Wen's grandfather. Acting on this mistaken assumption, Wen's mother sued and lost. Later, Wen Shiqin filed a new complaint to regain control of the land.[47] A subsequent "discussion" of

43 XKTB 0893, QL 18.11.26. 44 XKTB 0771, QL 16.4.25.
45 XKTB 0737, QL 15.5.26. 46 XKTB 0723, QL 15.1.22.
47 XKTB 0043, QL 2.2.28.

the case between the two parties became heated and proved fatal for Wen Mingrong, son of the rightful landowner.

In comparable cases of fraud, a widow in Guishan county, Guangdong, falsely claimed that a fishpond that her husband had sold as part of a larger transaction, in fact had not been part of the sale. The magistrate examined the contract (*qi*), denied her assertion, and punished her for bringing a false claim.[48] In Maoming county, Guangdong, Jiang Gaosong conditionally sold (*dian*) 7.67 *mu* to his clansman for 50,000 copper cash with a three-year buyback. Jiang continued to till the land and pay rent. After his mother's death, Jiang Gaosong conditionally sold 1.2 *mu* of the same land to Li Liangao for 11,000 copper cash. At this point, Jiang's clansman demanded repayment of his 50,000 copper cash. Next, Jiang conditionally sold all the land to Huang Jierong, paid off his clansman, and continued to till the land and pay rent to both Lin and Huang. The deceit went undetected for several years until Huang made a supplemental payment, obtaining the land outright. Assuming the land was his, Huang then leased the land to a new tenant. Ignorant of Jiang's machinations, both Lin and Huang ended up in court. The magistrate had no trouble untangling Jiang's contrivances and ruled that the land had become Huang's property after he made the second payment to Jiang Gaosong and that Jiang should return Lin's 11,000 copper cash.[49]

In another altercation from Jieyang county, Guangdong, Huang Zhenchuang wanted to redeem land that his father had conditionally sold (*dang*) to Yang Mingwen. Yang made the bogus claim that the land had been sold outright. In an effort to deceive the court, Yang enlisted a relative of Huang's to lie and state that he had been the middleman in the sale. When the magistrate found that Huang indeed had the right to redeem, the case was officially resolved, but violence was not averted. Sometime after the case was heard, Huang's mother publicly criticized the phony middleman, sparking a deadly brawl.[50]

In four other cases, individuals sought to redeem their land after it had been illegally sold by a relative or clansman. In a Guangdong case (county unknown) in 1745, Yang Youfu sued to redeem land that his uncle had illegally sold.[51] In Fuzhou county, Sichuan, Zhang Wenxiang "privately" sold corporate clan land (*gonggong*) to Luo Qitian for 390,000 copper cash. Other members of the Zhang clan immediately sued and won the right to redeem the land.[52] In Dongan county, Guangdong, members of the Liu clan successfully redeemed land that

48 XKTB 0168, QL 5.1.25. 49 ZYG, pp. 216–19. 50 XKTB 0761, QL 16.11.26.
51 SS 1579, QL 10.12.15. 52 XKTB 3257, QL 45.4.27.

had been sold sometime during the Kangxi reign (1662–1722), only to have one clan member who held the deed to the land "privately" sell it again.[53] When members of the Liu clan sued, the magistrate ruled that they could redeem the sale and rotate management of the land. A more intricate case occurred in Guanxian county, Sichuan, where the Zhou brothers, Zhou Guohua, Zhou Fenghua, and Zhou Fengrong, were in debt to a rice merchant. After the merchant sued, the magistrate ordered the Zhous to sell their land to cover the debts. The magistrate entrusted the local headman (*lizhang*), He Long, to supervise the matter. Undaunted by their financial woes, the Zhous found a new lender, Cai Yu. After getting further into debt with Cai, the Zhous arranged to have two middlemen mortgage the land to Cai Yu. Apparently, neither the middlemen nor Cai were aware that the land was encumbered. When he heard of the sale, He Long sent Xiao Guiren to ask Cai Yu to bring in the mortgage contract for inspection. Tragically, this led to an argument that ended when Cai struck Xiao with a rock and killed him.[54] Once again, the best efforts of the local magistrate went for naught.

Magistrate as Innovator

While most magistrates carefully followed the code and respected local customs when deciding lawsuits, others were innovative. Magistrates normally based their judgments on the terms of the agreement between the two parties, but in five redemption disputes magistrates exercised some discretion and went beyond the bounds of the original agreements, ordering cash compensation in the course of settling the dispute. For example, when Liang Fushen's mother died, he sold his land to Liao Jun for 40 ounces (*liang*) of silver. Later, in 1753, Liang received a supplemental payment of 20 ounces of silver. The contract accompanying this payment specified a six-year limit on redemption, after which the sale would be considered final. After six years, Liang did not have the cash to redeem. Fourteen years after the supplemental payment in 1767, Liang had the cash but Liao refused to redeem the land, citing the agreement of 1753. Liang then sued. The magistrate inspected the contract and ordered that Liao could retain possession of the land permanently if he paid an additional 16 ounces of silver, which presumably reflected the increased value of the land during the ensuing fourteen years. Liang refused to accept the payment. He later organized his nephew, brothers, and cousins, a total of seven men, to steal the grain standing in the field. Liao reported the theft to the magistrate, but that did not deter

53 XKTB 0706, QL 15.9.4. 54 XKTB 3171, QL 44.7.14.

Liang. Liang defiantly returned to steal more of the grain, triggering a bloody battle that ended with the death of Liao's son.[55]

In Chongqing prefecture, Sichuan, Zheng Zifa mortgaged his land to Wang Weixian, who then tilled the land. Zheng also owed 12,000 copper cash to Jiang Shiyuan but was unable to repay him. Zheng agreed to sell the land outright and repay the debt, but Jiang was impatient. Fearing that Zheng may have already sold the land, Jiang planted buckwheat on it. Wang Weixian was angry and sued. Legally, Jiang had no right to plant the field, but the magistrate attempted to fashion a solution amenable to all. He ordered Wang to compensate Jiang for the buckwheat that had been planted, and he allowed Wang to continue to till the land. The murderous encounter occurred when Jiang's son refused to accept payment of the compensation from Wang's son.[56]

A redemption case from Xingning county, Guangdong, concerned a dispute over compensation for improvements made to land and centered exclusively on the amount of compensation for these improvements. Lai Jiankang had purchased two plots of land from Chen Fubai for 15.6 ounces (*liang*) of silver in 1765. The terms of the sale clearly stated that the land could be redeemed in nine years, and that at the time of the redemption the original seller would provide compensation for the costs of improvements and the addition of any adjacent wasteland. Lai subsequently enclosed the existing field and brought an additional 1 *mu* of land under cultivation.

Nine years later, Chen Fubai was living in Guangxi, where he had "business" (*shengli*). Chen's younger brother, Chen Kuibai, had the original sale document and sought to redeem the land from Lai Jiankang's son, Lai Tianshou. (Lai Jiankang had died sometime during the previous nine years.) Lai Tianshou accepted the original amount and demanded compensation for his investment and expenses (*gongben*). Chen Kubai offered 2 ounces of silver (*liang*). Lai Tianshou rejected the offer and refused to return the land.

At an impasse, Chen Kubai then sued Lai Tianshou at the local yamen. After examining the evidence, the magistrate, Jiang Longchang, urged both sides to cooperate. Jiang estimated that the improvements to the land were worth 25 Mexican silver dollars (considerably more than Chen had offered). The magistrate ruled that Chen should pay this amount and that the land should be given to him. Apparently, though the document is not entirely clear, the land reverted to Chen's control, but Lai did not go to the prefecture seat to receive his payment. (It seems that Chen had deposited the money with the magistrate.)

55 ZYG, pp. 479–82. 56 XKTB 3273, QL 45.12.4.

At this point, the mothers of the disputants became involved. Lai Tianshou's mother, Ms. Li, often complained that her son had no land and that he refused to go to the prefectural capital to receive the compensation he had been awarded. Matters came to a head on QL 40.2.4 (1775), when Chen Kuibai and his mother, Ms. He, went to till the field. Ms. Li enlisted her younger bother, Li Yuncai, and her second son, Lai Asi, to stop them. Initially, a fight broke out between the two women, but the men soon joined them. While the fighting was in progress, Lai Tianshou arrived and joined the fray. Lai beat Chen repeatedly with a pole until he collapsed to the ground. Lai Tianshou and his relatives fled, and Ms. He helped her son home.

Interestingly, the violence did not end here. The following day, both sides reported the details to the local authorities. Lai Tianshou was jailed, and the Lai family was ordered to care for Chen Kuibai, whose injuries included a broken leg. The spiteful and cantankerous Ms. Li, who now found that the family not only had lost its land but that her son also was in jail, put a torch to a house and shed that belonged to Ms. He, the mother of Chen Kuibai. Eventually, Chen Kuibai died of his wounds and Lai Tianshou was sentenced to death. Ms. Li was fined for destroying Ms. He's home and shed. Despite all the violence and bitterness, the magistrate repeated his original finding regarding the settlement of the land without further comment.[57]

Enforcement

Magistrates were not infallible. In an eviction dispute, which was highly unusual because both the killer and victim were female, the presiding magistrate was criticized for "carelessly investigating" and "recklessly" rendering a judgment.[58] However, the overwhelming majority of the cases discussed demonstrate that magistrates were generally competent, fair, efficient, and, when need be, innovative. Still, despite their best efforts, violence was not averted. This may explain why some disputants shunned the courts. What good was a competent, efficient, and innovative magistrate if he could not enforce his decision? Clearly, magistrates were not powerless to act when their decisions were openly challenged. Magistrates could command the infamous yamen runners or local constables to enforce the law, and they did so in several disputes. Recent research has shown, the misdeeds of the much maligned yamen employees have been somewhat exaggerated.[59] While this was likely true, their

57 XKTB 2796, QL 40.11.5. 58 SS 1566, QL 10.8.21.

59 Bradly W. Reed, "Money and Justice: Clerks, Runners, and the Magistrate's Court in Late Imperial Sichuan," *Modern China* (July 1995) 21.3: 345–82.

notoriety was not simply a product of scapegoating. Unfortunately, as the following cases reveal, the actions of yamen underlings sometimes made matters worse.

Homicide reports supply scant evidence of official intervention. For example, in twenty-five redemption disputes, only once did a magistrate directly intervene to enforce a ruling. In Guishan county, Guangdong, Ceng Yaba and Zhong Yingyu sued and countersued over the right to redeem a plot of land that Ceng Yaba's father had sold about two decades earlier. The magistrate ruled in favor of Zhong, but Ceng, who was a tenant on the land, refused to accept the verdict. Zhong subsequently sued again, and a yamen runner (*chai*) and the local constable (*dibao*) were sent to arrest Ceng Yaba. The runner took Ceng into custody; but instead of taking Ceng directly to the county yamen, they took him to Zhong's home. Fearing the worst, Ceng's stepbrother attempted to rescue him and killed the runner in the ensuing scuffle.[60]

In two other disputes, yamen runners were dispatched to arrest recalcitrant tenants who defied eviction. In a case that occurred in Qinzhou county, Guangdong, a yamen runner and the militia head (*liangzhang*) were sent to detain Liang Rencheng. Instead of arresting Liang, they took his neighbor into custody while they searched for Liang. The homicide resulted when the tenant's wife accused the neighbor of helping the runners arrest her husband. The runner himself was punished for taking innocent people into custody.[61] The second dispute occurred in Deqingzhou, Guangdong, where Deng Xuesheng and his clansmen refused to give up their land when a new owner, Fan Huanhui, tried to evict them. Eventually, Fan went to the local yamen to seek help. The magistrate assigned two runners to assist in harvesting the field. The dispute reached a violent denouement when the two runners, Fan's nephew, his tenant, and three hired laborers went to seize the crop in the field.[62] Despite being out numbered, Deng Xuesheng with the assistance of several female members of the Deng family drove Fan and company off in the initial confrontation. Once again, enforcement was problematic.

In two rent defaults, runners were sent to assist in collecting arrears. In Guangning county, Guangdong, He Yanye defaulted for several years and owed a total of 45.3 *shi* of grain. The landlord, Su Peixing, an absentee landlord from a neighboring county, sued, and the magistrate ordered runners and a local constable to harvest the current crop. Su realized that the grain would be insufficient to cover the arrears, so he

60 QDB, pp. 556–8. 61 XKTB 0068, QL 2.6.6. 62 XKTB 3515, QL 50.2.14.

decided to harvest the grain on an adjacent field that He Yanye also tilled. Taking matters into his own hands, Su – along with his son, two brothers, and three hired laborers – attempted to seize the crop. Tragically, He Yanye's granddaughter was killed in the brawl that followed.[63] In this case, Su Peixing had requested runners from the yamen, probably because he was an absentee landlord from a neighboring county. The runners who assisted him were not involved in any illegal actions, but neither did they intervene to halt the illegal seizure of He Yanye's crop.

Direct official intervention did not forestall a tragic ending in Zengchang county, Guangdong, either. When Ms. Lu enlisted official aid in collecting back rent from Lu Zaochun, a warrant was issued for Lu's arrest. Because the runner, Xu Sheng, was ill, he entrusted the warrant to Liu Yajing, a "white" or "unofficial" runner (*baiyi*). Liu Yajing hired a worker, Liu Yafu, to accompany him, and together they attempted to extort payment in silver from Lu. After extracting a gift of 600 copper cash, the extortionists demanded 3 Mexican silver dollars to settle the debt. Lu had no cash, so he pleaded for three more days to raise the money. Eager to get the cash, Liu Yajing and Li Yafu returned the next day. Unable to pay and facing the threat of being taken to jail in chains, Lu offered to pawn some clothing to raise the money. Overwhelmed by his dilemma, Lu ostensibly entered his house to get the clothing, but instead he hanged himself. The magistrate who investigated the homicide sentenced Liu Yajing for causing Lu's suicide, and the runner, Xu Sheng, was punished for creating the situation that led to a death.[64]

In the incidents described in the preceding paragraphs, official efforts to enforce decisions not only failed to avert conflict, but in some cases actually sparked violence. Peculation by a yamen underling exacerbated a case that spanned two years and involved two homicides. Li Along's grandfather had sold his land to Li Azhuan's grandfather in 1657. Subsequently, he received two supplemental payments that customarily turned a conditional sale into an outright sale. Li Along's father, Li Xingzheng, continued to till the land and pay rent, however. In 1743, Li Xing wanted to redeem the sale, but Li Duo, a minor degree holder (*jiansheng*) and the uncle of Li Azhuan, refused. In an attempt to forestall the redemption, Li Duo altered the original contract, increasing the original sale price of the land. Li Xinzheng sued. The magistrate discovered the fraud and decided that the land could be redeemed at the original price. Li Xinzheng paid the price to the magistrate, who stored

63 ZYG, pp. 628–31. 64 XKTB 3268, QL 45.4.21.

the money in the county vault. Li Duo was unhappy with the decision and appealed to the prefectural magistrate, who correctly overturned the ruling because two supplemental payments had been made.

To make matters more complicated, Li Xinzheng owed rent to Li Duo, who wanted to evict him. Li Xinzheng could not pay because a yamen underling had embezzled the money he had entrusted with the county magistrate to redeem the land! At harvest time, Li Duo sent his son, Li Afu, and nephew, Li Azhuan, to seize the grain in the field. A bloody confrontation at the field resulted in the death of Li Xinzheng's son, Li Along. The magistrate who investigated the killing sentenced Li Azhuan to death for the killing and forgave the arrears. He also stripped Li Duo of his degree and had him flogged for creating a situation that resulted in a homicide. Li Xinzheng was also flogged for attempting to redeem the land after two supplemental payments had been made. Li Duo was permitted to lease the land to a new tenant. Unfortunately, the tragedy did not end here. Two years later, Li Asheng, brother of the homicide victim, was on a ferry with Li Duo. Li Duo brought up the matter of the rent arrears again. Enraged by Li Duo's audacity, Li Asheng pulled a knife and stabbed Li Duo to death. As the foregoing cases reveal, a bumbling, corrupt, or malicious staff could easily undermine a capable magistrate, providing one more reason to eschew official mediation. Given the outcome of these cases, one can easily understand why parties to a land dispute might avoid the courts.

Open Defiance

Underpaid, understaffed, and overworked magistrates had troubles in the best of times. To make matters worse, there is also evidence that some litigants openly and blatantly defied official adjudication. Violence arose when the losers refused to abide by official judgments. For example, in Qinzhou county, Guangdong, after her husband died Ms. Li sued to have lineage-owned land used to plant tea, which had previously alternated management between two branches, divided equally and managed individually. Shi Lin, head of the other branch of the lineage, opposed her. The magistrate ruled in Ms. Li's favor, and she leased her half of the land to Huang Zhenggao. When Huang attempted to harvested his crop, Shi Lin dispatched an armed band to stop him. In the second dispute, Liang Fenyuan tried to evict his tenants, Liang Wenbao and Liang Jinbi, after their five-year lease had expired. The magistrate ruled in Liang Fenyuan's favor, but his former tenants did not accept the ruling. The following spring, they tore up the seedlings planted on the land in an effort to intimidate their former landlord. Not long afterwards, Liang Fenyuan lost his life in a violent confrontation with the former tenants.[65]

When landlords sued for arrears, magistrates invariably ruled in their favor and allowed them to seek new tenants. In four such cases, tenants resorted to violence to intimidate the landlord after losing in court. For example, in Fengchuan county, Guangdong, Dong Shiji leased 25.8 *mu* of land to Dong Xianyao. In 1769, Dong Xianyao did not pay his rent. When Dong Shiji dunned him, Dong Xianyao falsely claimed that the land was his inherited property (*zuye*). Dong Shiji sued, and the magistrate ruled that he could find a new tenant. Displeased with the ruling, Dong Xianyao and his brother later tried to steal the new tenant's crop, leading to the violent altercation in which Dong Xianyao lost his life.[66] The magistrate who investigated the homicide reaffirmed Dong Shiji's right to lease his land but forgave the arrears that Dong Xianyao owed since he had lost his life, a common practice in rent disputes when a defaulting tenant was killed.

A similar dispute occurred in Changle county, Guangdong. Over the course of several years, Zhuo Shuxin owed 64 *shi* of rent to his landlord, Guo Mao. When Guo sued, the magistrate ordered Zhuo to pay 24 *shi* immediately, with the balance due in three installments over the next three years. Despite the fact that he had received several years to repay the debt, not a common practice, Zhuo was angry. Several days later, Zhuo attacked Guo outside the gate of his home. In the ensuing clash, Guo killed Zhuo in self-defense.[67] In another dispute, in Longmen county, Guangdong, Huang Zuowen purchased land that Wen Wencong had rented from the former owner. When Wen refused to pay rent or return the land, Huang sued and won a judgment. The following spring, Wen's son, Wen Guanqing, and wife, Ms. Yu, attacked Huang when he attempted to till the land. In the ensuing melee, Huang killed Wen's wife.[68] Finally, in a slightly different case, over the course of several years Huang Wuru of Yongan county, Guangdong, owed 141 *shi* to Chen Dawen. Chen Dawen eventually sued. Huang Wuru offered to give up the land if Chen Dawen would forgive the arrears. Chen Dawen agreed to the settlement. The following spring, Huang Wuru blocked Chen's son when he arrived to plow the field. A fight broke out, and Chen Dawen accidentally killed Huang's father.[69]

In four other disputes, tenants who were in arrears sued to retain their right to till. In most of these cases, the tenant lost. For example, in Puning county, Guangdong, delinquent tenants, Weng Tianshi and Fu

65 XKTB 2822, QL 40.3.8. 66 XKTB 2405, QL 36.7.29. 67 XKTB 3131, QL 44.6.9.
68 XKTB 0201, QL 5.10.5. 69 XKTB 0883, QL 18.6.10.

Awai, sued their landlord when he leased his land to Xu Jinshi. After losing their case, they demanded that Xu compensate them for improvements they had made to the land. Xu's refusal cost him his life when the impasse took a violent turn.[70] In Guangning county, Guangdong, a defaulting tenant sued his landlord for the right to till because he had already planted the field before it was leased to a third party. The tenant lost the case and later his wife when she tried to stop the new tenant from harvesting the field several months later.[71] In a third case, in Huilai county, Guangdong, You Tinglie sublet the field he had rented to Wen Bixing. When Wen Bixing defaulted, the landlord dunned You Tinglie. You Tinglie feared future troubles, so he decided to till the field himself the following year. Wen Bixing sued, spuriously asserting that he had leased the land directly. The magistrate rejected Wen's claim, but Wen Bixing did not let the matter drop. Wen dispatched his "clan uncle" (*zushu*), Wen Huangzhen, and two other clansmen to destroy the seedlings that You Tinglie had planted. Unfortunately for Wen Huangzhen, in the resulting fray a cousin of You's arrived armed with a fowling piece, joined the fray and shot Wen dead.[72]

In the cases just discussed, the landlords won their complaints, but violence erupted when tenants refused to abide by the decision of the yamen. Sometimes landlords who had won their suits resorted to violence because they did not trust their tenants to respect the ruling of the court. For example, Ou Cuijie, a minor degree holder (*jiansheng*), mortgaged a 4.2 *mu* plot of land and a 2.5 *mu* plot of land to Xia Yunqing in 1750 and 1753, respectively. Ou continued to till the land and pay rent to Xia. In 1755, Xia demanded that Ou redeem the mortgage because he was in arrears in his rent. Ou pled poverty, and Xia sued. The magistrate determined that Ou should redeem both plots and also pay his outstanding rent. Since Ou was in financial straits, it was decided that he should redeem the 2.5 *mu* field immediately, pay his arrears, and redeem the 4.2 *mu* field after the winter harvest. When it came time to harvest, Xia did not trust Ou, so he and four of his relatives attempted to seize the crop. Ou Cuijie's nephew, Ou Shilin, was killed defending the field.[73]

In Xingning county, Guangdong, Ceng Renshen, a minor degree holder (*jiansheng*), won a judgment against his tenants, the Cai brothers, Cai Yanxian and Cai Yanshi. Interestingly, the local constable (*dibao*) allowed the Cai brothers to continue tilling the land on the condition that they pay the arrears after the winter harvest. Afterwards, the mother

70 XKTB 0020, QL 1.3.29. 71 XKTB 1081, QL 20.11.22.
72 QDB, pp. 644–6. 73 ZYG, pp. 241–3.

of the Cai brothers sold an adjoining piece of land, which Ceng Renshen erroneously thought was his. Fearing he had been cheated, Ceng Renshen, a relative, and a hired laborer went to take control of the land, instigating a violent confrontation that ended in death for Cai Yanxian. The magistrate investigating the homicide punished Ceng Renshen for creating the situation that led to the loss of life.[74]

In another dispute, Ou Xiaoyao sued in 1736 and won a judgment against his delinquent tenant, Wen Mingyong. When the landlord's brother Ou Xiaoyu tried to collect the arrears at the spring harvest in 1737, Wen Mingyong demanded a receipt stating that the payment was for the current year's rent. In the altercation that followed, Ou accidentally killed Wen's daughter. In concluding the homicide investigation, the magistrate allowed Ou to lease his land to a new tenant and ordered Wen to pay the back rent. Wen was also flogged under the "recalcitrant tenant" law.[75]

Finally, one case deserves mention because it seesawed through the courts for over a decade. Although boundary disputes ordinarily were fairly straightforward matters, such disputes occasionally produced protracted legal battles. Jiang Mingxi was from Dazhu county, Sichuan. Jiang's grandfather, Jiang Dengyi, owned land in the hills that bordered on Zhang Gui's land. In 1736, Jiang Dengyi fought with Zhang Gui over the boundary. Jiang brought a lawsuit before the county magistrate, Lin Liangchuan, who found that the land in question belonged to Zhang Gui. In 1743, Jiang Mingting's uncle, Jiang Wenshan, sued again. The magistrate at that time, Hu Tianen, overturned the earlier decision. Magistrate Hu ruled that the previous survey was incorrect and that the land did belong to Jiang Wenshan.

Despite the ruling, Zhang Gui continued to contest the boundary for several years. Finally, in 1749, a third county magistrate, Wang Xun, personally surveyed the land and found that it was indeed Zhang's property. Because the Jiangs had already managed the land for many years, he ruled that the Jiangs could keep the land if they paid Zhang the fair market value of the land. Zhang agreed to sell it for 40 ounces (*liang*) of silver. At that time, Jiang Wenshan, his son, Jiang Mingxi, and Jiang Mingting agreed to pay the sum to Zhang.

The results of this lawsuit were reported to the prefecture, but the dispute did not end there. It soon became apparent that the Jiangs were only feigning compliance. Jiang Mingting resubmitted the case to a higher court that ruled that the land belonged to the Jiangs and the Jiangs did not need to compensate Zhang Gui.

74 ZYG, pp. 347–50. 75 QDB, pp. 25–6.

Zhang Gui was not willing to accept this decision. On QL 17.7.12 (1752), Zhang and his younger brother went to the disputed land and cut down the artemisia that the Jiangs had planted. The Zhangs also chased the Jiangs' tenant, Li Hongyuan, from his home near the land. When Li cursed the Zhangs, Zhang Gui attacked him with a pole and chased him off the land. Calling out for help, Li fled.

When Jiang Mingting heard Li's cry for help, he and his brother Jiang Mingde took up weapons and went to stop the Zhangs. Fearing that Zhang Gui had organized a gang, Jiang Mingxi brought a musket. He fired the gun, purportedly to "frighten" the Zhangs. Zhang Zhenglong fled, but Zhang Gui held his ground. Zhang Gui, wielding a pole, and Jiang Mingde, armed with a spear, fought. Zhang got the better of Jiang, knocking him unconscious with a blow to the back of the head. At that moment, Jiang Mingting emerged from the woods with a spear. Seeing his brother passed out on the ground, Jiang Mingting was "suddenly overwhelmed with murderous intent." Raising his spear, he gored Zhang at the base of the throat, killing him instantly.

Vainly hoping to avoid punishment, Jiang attempted to cover up his crime. He cut his own forehead with his spear to make it appear that he had been wounded. He also ordered Li Hongyuan to set fire to his home. Jiang then went into town and reported that the Jiangs had merely defended themselves against Zhang Gui's violent rampage. The local magistrate was not fooled for an instant. For the crime of intentional homicide, Jiang Mingting was sentenced to be beheaded and was imprisoned, awaiting review of his sentence at the autumn assizes. Both Jiang Mingde and Jiang Mingxi were flogged for their participation in the violence. Li Hongyuan was also flogged for not attempting to stop the violence and for burning down his own home. As for the land, the magistrate ruled that the boundary should be marked according to the original decision, and Jiang Mingxi was ordered to pay the Zhangs for the land. Provincial-level officials also ordered an investigation into the conduct of every official involved in the dispute over the previous seventeen years.[76]

Limits of Official Intervention

The homicide cases discussed in the preceding paragraphs afford important insights into the role of the county magistrate in adjudicating property-rights disputes. Magistrates were usually fair and thorough in

76 XKTB 0855, QL 17.7.20. Unfortunately, the details of the subsequent investigation into the official misconduct were not part of the homicide report.

their investigations. They examined contracts, tax records, and deeds; adeptly exposed frauds; surveyed boundaries; weighed competing claims judiciously; and sometimes used coercion to ensure compliance with their rulings. As Mark Allee has found in his study of nineteenth-century Taiwan, when necessary, magistrates were versatile, drawing not only on the provisions of the Qing law code to support their rulings but also on custom and culture to bolster the legitimacy of their decisions.[77] Based on his extensive study of Ming and Qing contracts, Yang Guozhen argued that magistrates respected customary law and when settling cases magistrates followed custom and contract to render decisions not "empty regulations."[78] If magistrates were generally versatile, fair, and competent in rendering decisions, why did so many property-rights disputes end in violence? The answer would seem to be enforcement. Once a magistrate had rendered a decision, he had scant resources at his disposal to ensure its enforcement. This in part explains the impunity with which some disputants defied official verdicts.

The problem of enforcement was related in part to the Qing law of avoidance. Every magistrate was an outsider in his jurisdiction and was dependent on an entrenched local staff for enforcement. As the cases discussed illustrate, the corrupt behavior or incompetence of yamen underlings sometimes undermined the work of the county magistrate and contributed to the outbreak of violence. In the redemption case of Ceng Yaba, who refused to vacate the land after losing his right to till, the runner was punished for taking Ceng to the local constable's home, where the homicide occurred, rather than the magistrate's yamen. In the rent default case of Lu Zaochun, the runner who was assigned to arrest Lu gave the warrant to an "unofficial" runner who attempted to extort money from Lu, eventually causing him to commit suicide. In the eviction of Liang Rencheng, runners dispatched to detain him instead took his neighbor into custody, precipitating a violent dispute between the neighbor and Liang's wife. If these cases are any indication, there was a better than fifty-fifty chance that calling out the runners would cause violence. With only a dubious source of coercive power available to back up his decisions, the best hope that a magistrate had for resolving a dispute was to fashion a ruling that members of the local community would accept as fair and legitimate.

77 Mark Anton Allee, "Code, Culture, and Custom: Foundations of Civil Case Verdicts in a Nineteenth-Century County Court," pp. 122–41 in *Civil Law in Qing and Republican China*, K. Bernhardt and P. Huang, eds. (Stanford: Stanford University Press, 1994).

78 Yang Guozhen, 1984, p. 117.

In fact, in two cases magistrates directly enlisted the local community to sustain their decisions. For example, in the aftermath of a homicide resulting from a dispute over a land sale in Anyue county, Sichuan,[79] the magistrate ordered both sides in the dispute to "rely on the community" (*pingzhong*) to delineate the boundaries of the land and afterwards the magistrate would issue a deed. In the case of the boundary dispute between Zhang Dali and Shuai Tingqing in Jianwei county, Sichuan, the magistrate instructed them to call together their neighbors to clarify the boundaries and then sign an agreement.[80] Philip Huang has referred to this combination of informal mediation and official intervention as the "third realm" of Qing justice.[81] But this type of solution was not possible in all disputes, and it also presented another danger to the magistrate's authority. If a magistrate relied too heavily on the direct involvement of the community, he risked abdicating his authority to local elites. Furthermore, settling disputes in the "third realm" did not solve the problem of enforcement. As this study reveals, a significant number of disputes were settled in a "fourth realm" of homicidal violence.

The success of the county magistrate often depended on his own ability to adjudicate disputes as evenhandedly as possible so that both sides would view him as fair. To the extent that the economic changes of the eighteenth century eroded the moral consensus of local society, however, this had become an increasingly difficult task. With limited resources and their standing as outsiders in the communities, due to the Qing rule of avoidance, the county magistrate's job was difficult even in ordinary times. Melissa Macauley's study of litigation brokers (*songgun* or *songshi*) in southeast coastal China from 1723–1820 has found that there was "more litigation in Fujian and throughout China than the Qing judicial administration could resolve satisfactorily."[82] Macauley attributes the "complexities of land tenure and property rights and not litigation broker incitation" for the increasing numbers of lawsuits in the region.[83] Litigation brokers proliferated in part because the Qing state declined to expand government services to meet the needs of a growing population. Philip Huang's study of civil suits in three counties for the eighteenth and nineteenth centuries also notes the failure of the Qing legal system to adjust to changing times. According to Huang, the legal

79 XKTB 0702, QL 15.10.29. 80 XKTB 0878, QL 17.9.25.

81 See Philip C. C. Huang, 1996, Chapter 5.

82 Melissa Macauley, p. 118, "Civil and Uncivil Disputes in Southeast Coastal China, 1723–1820," pp. 85–121 in *Civil Law in Qing and Republican China*, K. Bernhardt and P. Huang, eds. (Stanford: Stanford University Press, 1994).

83 Ibid.

system had been designed for a "relatively simple peasant society" in which the court could easily intimidate litigants. The legal system was ill equipped to deal with "the products of a commercialized and increasingly differentiated society." Huang concluded that "change in the composition of litigants, more than the evil actions of litigation mongers . . . or simple population growth was what accounted for the increased burdens on the courts."[84] Huang is undoubtedly correct; but as the eighteenth-century evidence of peasants blatantly defying official rulings demonstrates, in many cases the Qing legal system was having trouble intimidating even "simple peasants."

Whatever the structural weaknesses of the Qing legal system, what made matters worse in the eighteenth century were the social tensions engendered by economic change. As Philip Kuhn has noted, at the macroeconomic level the eighteenth century was a prosperous era, but the very economic changes that brought prosperity could be quite threatening to the ordinary peasant household. "From the standpoint of an eighteenth-century Chinese commoner, commercial growth may have meant, not the prospect of riches or security, but a scant margin of survival in a competitive and crowded society."[85] Similarly, the pressure to alter property rights in land could be quite menacing. Recall the words, quoted in Chapter 1, of Wang Chen, who faced eviction in Shandong in 1750. "If you demand that I return this land now is not the same as killing my family?" Cash rent deposits may have provided more security and economic freedom for some tenants, but the initial investment might be beyond the wherewithal of others. What was rational economically – for example, the commoditization of land and the attendant revision of the laws on conditional sales – appeared downright immoral and unjust to some. Some individuals resorted to violence precisely because they realized that the courts would likely support a property-rights regime detrimental to their individual interests. In this way, the spurt of violence that accompanied economic change in the eighteenth century was in part a desperate expression of moral outrage. For some, it did not matter how well a magistrate adjudicated a case; if the decision offended their sense of social justice and threatened their livelihood, they might resort to violence.

Making matters worse for the county magistrate was evidence contained in homicide reports that suggests the shared ethical norms of rural society, which arguably were more important to the maintenance

84 Philip C. C. Huang, 1996, p. 139.

85 Philip Kuhn, p. 36, *Soulstealers: The Chinese Sorcery Scare of 1768* (Cambridge, MA: Harvard University Press, 1990).

of social order than the legal code, were under pressure during the eighteenth century.[86] Those who, through no fault of their own, lost out during the shifting economic conditions of the eighteenth century understandably felt angered and indignant. Expressions of moral outrage came from rural inhabitants who found that changes in economic institutions threatened their livelihoods. Tenants who were forced off their land after successive defaults, landowners who were denied the opportunity to redeem sales of land, and peasants who were evicted from land they had tilled for many years sometimes angrily complained that their land or property rights had been "stolen." Many decisions, although legally sound, rankled and embittered the losers, who saw them as unjust. After losing two lawsuits over reclaimed land to Yang Fu, Zhou Wenxu bitterly complained that Yang would not give him "one inch of land." How could Zhou respect a ruling that, although legal, seemed so harsh?

Moral outrage was not limited to indigent peasants either. In a case that never reached court, moral outrage, not economic self-interest, motivated Chen Jingwei, a scholar and tutor. Chen became infuriated after witnessing Li Weizhen, the son-in-law of the landlord who employed Chen, abusing a delinquent tenant. Chen berated Li, saying: "If you insist on having the full rent, you will be rich but not benevolent" (*Ni bi ding yao zu, shi wei fu bu ren le*). Insulted and angered, landlord Li turned on Chen, who lost his life in the ensuing scuffle.[87] This incident illustrates both the emotionally charged atmosphere of the eighteenth century as well as the strength of ideological and ethical concerns.

Not surprisingly, county magistrates were the most consistent supporters of established ethical norms. The weakness of their position in terms of enforcing property rights left them no choice. When addressing the proximate causes of violent disputes, county magistrates consistently voiced support for principles of cooperation and reciprocity, the ideological props of the traditional peasant society. For example, in a rent default case not preceded by a lawsuit, Li Huang, the magistrate of Qinzhou county, Guangdong, rebuked and punished Xu Songxin, the landlord and a minor military degree holder (*wusheng*), because Xu pressed his tenants to pay their full rent, despite the fact that the harvest

86 See Mi Chu Wiens, 1980. Wiens identifies the erosion of "moralistic codes" that had "governed the behavior of rural social groups" as an important element of the social changes that occurred from the sixteenth to eighteenth century. See also Zhang Renshan, "Lun Qingchao zhongqi yi hou shehui shenghuo di fan lifa qushi" (A discussion of the tendency to oppose decorum in social life after the mid-Qing), *Zhongguo shi yanjiu* (1992) 2: 117–24.

87 ZYG, pp. 766–8.

was only 70% of normal. Although one of the tenants, Mo Guoqing, was sentenced to death for killing a hired laborer whom Xu sent to dun him, Xu was also punished for creating a dangerous situation by demanding his full rent during a poor harvest.[88] Another example was Zhao Youyan, the magistrate of Xingning county, Guangdong. When Sheng Zheng, a landlord and Buddhist monk, accepted a competing tenant's offer to pay more rent than Sheng's long-standing tenant, a violent confrontation between the competing tenants ensued. Although Sheng was not present at the time of the homicide, Magistrate Zhao held Sheng responsible and had him defrocked and flogged. Zhao felt that Sheng was at fault because he had leased his land to a new tenant solely to obtain a higher rent.[89] As the foregoing examples demonstrate, local magistrates reacted strongly when ethical standards were threatened.

In conclusion, an examination of homicides related to property-rights disputes that were preceded by official intervention reveals that on the whole magistrates were normally competent, thorough, and fair when adjudicating disputes. The fact that these disputes nonetheless ended in violence is not an indication of a failure on the part of the magistrates. The motive forces behind social conflict and economic change were the related phenomena of population growth, more intensive use of land, and the uncertainties of an expanding commercial economy. As the value of land relative to labor increased and the opportunities of a growing market beckoned, the incentive to redefine property rights became intense. This shift in economic power rippled through the Chinese economy, and the Qing state reacted to it, primarily to maintain social order. Magistrates had to be flexible in their decision making, relying on the legal code as well as custom and culture to craft acceptable solutions. The perception of fairness was critical given the limited resources available to enforce compliance. Unfortunately for the eighteenth-century county magistrate, the economic changes that had generated property-rights disputes also undermined the shared ethical norms of rural communities. Under these circumstances, no matter how skillful the magistrate, violence was difficult to avoid, and disputants were less likely to seek mediation if the parties to a dispute viewed changes in economic institutions as unjust. Until economic institutions were adjusted to reflect changing realities and until these economic institutions were widely accepted as fair, violent disputes, some of which ended in homicide, were inevitable.

88 XKTB 0714, QL 15.2.28. 89 QDB, pp. 186–7.

8
Conclusion

Understanding violent disputes over property rights in land in the broader context of the economic developments of the eighteenth century has been the primary task of this book. At first glance, the task does not seem difficult. Violent disputes were a widespread problem, and this book presents only a sampling of the voluminous evidence of the most violent disputes, those ending in homicide. As these homicide reports made their way up the bureaucratic ladder to Beijing, the problem of violent disputes over land was apparent and troubling to provincial and central-government officials, as noted in their reports to their superiors. There also is overwhelming and unmistakable evidence of the unprecedented demographic boom and economic development during the eighteenth century. The historical record demonstrates that the Chinese economy was increasingly commercialized and that peasant households were active participants in the market, with all the attendant benefits and risks that this entailed. Official reports also reveal that the economic changes that were taking place in the eighteenth century were abundantly clear to Qing officials.[1] Government concern about overcrowding was evident in the formulation of land reclamation and taxation policies that also addressed the potential social costs of economic and demographic expansion, such as increased lawsuits and feuding over land and landless peasants being driven into banditry.

While many of these concerns and proposed remedies had deep roots in Chinese economic thought, it is also clear that some eighteenth-century officials were seriously reconsidering the fundamental eco-

1 See Helen Dunstan, *Conflicting Counsels to Confuse the Age* (Ann Arbor: University of Michigan, Center for Chinese Studies, 1996). Dunstan translated a variety of official documents that reveal the opinions of Qing officials and the Qianlong emperor regarding problems of political economy in the eighteenth century.

nomic role of the state. Recent research by Helen Dunstan has identified the "sprouts of liberalism" in the debate among high-level officials over the role of government in the economy during the Qianlong reign (1736–95). Dunstan judiciously presents documentation of this debate to show that "in the early Qianlong period economically liberal thought was articulated and had a certain influence."[2] It is interesting to note that the development of a more complex and sophisticated commercial economy prompted some Qing officials to advocate policies usually associated with the rise of capitalism in the West. Similarly, Robert Marks's work on the environment and economy of South China reveals that the transformation of agriculture and the ecological impact of this transformation were on a scale normally associated with the "rise of capitalism" in the West.[3] This is not to say that the economic developments of the eighteenth century represented some form of incipient capitalism. It is simply to point out the magnitude and import of the economic developments of the eighteenth century.

Equally important, from the point of view of this study, were official reports that explicitly linked economic change and social conflict. During the early decades of the eighteenth century, provincial-level officials specifically decried a perceived increase in violence related to rent defaults, redemption disputes, and boundary disputes, which, they asserted, arose from the prevailing economic conditions. Other contemporary observers noted that greater competition for land and an increased "obstinacy" on the part of the peasantry contributed to rising tensions between tenants and landlords. As noted, a clear indication of the growing national concern with the problem of rent defaults came in 1727, when the Yongzheng emperor (1723–35) revised the Qing law code so that for the first time in Chinese history the failure to pay rent became a crime, which was punishable by eighty blows with heavy bamboo. Similarly, during the Qianlong reign (1736–95), further revisions to the Qing law code in 1740 and 1756 concerning the redemption of conditional sales of land and in 1750 concerning the standardization of official documentation of land sales, which was undertaken in part to avoid lawsuits and social conflict, indicated an empire-wide concern with disputes over property rights.

Eighteenth-century observations on economic change and social conflict were consistent with the general assumption of my research that demand for changes in economic institutions and property rights in land had increased the potential for violent disputes. Based on this assumption, this book has presented a qualitative analysis of violent dis-

2 Dunstan, 1996, p. 329. 3 Marks, 1997, pp. 338–40.

putes over property rights to explain changes over time in the major issues, participants, official dispositions, and geographic and temporal patterns of violent disputes in order to demonstrate their historical significance. Another goal of my research has been to understand Chinese history from a perspective that embodies insights from studies of economic and social development that do not privilege the history of the West. In the past, the predominance of theories of social and economic development that, either critically or unquestioningly, placed models of Western development, which take the Industrial Revolution and the rise of the nation state as defining criteria of modern development, at the heart of their explanations has been detrimental to the study of modern Chinese history in the West as well as China.[4] On the other hand, arguments that rely on cultural differences as an explanation for the divergent paths of development in Western and Eastern societies offer limited insights into our basic understanding of economic development. Simply stated, regardless of how a particular culture is structured, the fulfillment of material needs is a basic motivation of human effort and all human beings have essential needs for shelter, clothing, nourishment, and personal safety. This is not to say that cultural traits will not influence the manner in which individuals pursue their economic goals or that all human behavior is primarily motivated by material considerations. In fact, ideology, broadly construed, will influence human behavior and cultural differences are relevant to understanding economic behavior. Culture will affect tastes but is not likely to prevent effort driven by want. Thus, meaningful comparisons can be made between different societies and can contribute to the formulation of more general, cross-cultural theories of social and economic development.[5]

In constructing this study of economic change and social conflict in China, I have been inspired by the work of historians and social scientists who have been both historically minded and universalist in their approaches – for example, Eric Jones, whose work reframed world economic history in terms of intensive and extensive economic growth rather than force it into a Western-centric framework of capitalist development or industrialization. According to Jones, the values and customary institutions of Asia were "brakes and filters that gave local col-

4 Li Bozhong's work on Jiangnan provides an excellent example of the misunderstandings of this type of approach. See Li Bozhong, Chapter 9.

5 See Wong, 1997, pp. 1–2. For example, R. Bin Wong's comparative study of China and Europe seeks to "dislodge European state making and capitalism from their privileged position as universalizing themes" by identifying both the similarities and differences to develop "strategies of comparison that do not privilege European categories of analysis and dynamics of historical change."

oration to change,"[6] not final blockages to intensive economic growth. Another example is Charles Tilly, who has demonstrated how the resulting political, economic, and social structures of Western states were forged in the heat of centuries of international competition. Abandoning a strategy that marked earlier research into state making, Tilly examined the many forms of states that coexisted from 900–1990 and the diverse processes of political development in the West rather than presuming the superiority of the nation state and working backward in time from its "successful" establishment. This approach uses the study of European history to develop concepts that have broad applicability to our understanding of the development of political institutions. Rooted in the history of European political development, Tilly's study illustrates the dynamics of international competition in the eventual emergence of the nation state as a dominant political form in the West and also how the establishment of nation states in the West influenced the development of political institutions elsewhere.[7] Finally, incorporating political and economic institutions into a dynamic model of economic change, Douglass North's study of structure and change in economic history has taken economics beyond the bounds of Western-centric neoclassical analysis without abandoning its most valuable insights. In designing a far-reaching theory of structure and change in economic history, North has demonstrated the importance of property rights and has also successfully explained how the supposedly "irrational" behavior of precapitalist societies was actually a rational response to imperfect markets and high transaction costs. Although the research of North, Tilly, and Jones has addressed a variety of different issues, the importance of the ongoing competition over the control of resources between political entities, and between rulers and ruled, was an essential and common component in their works. In the process of reconsidering accepted explanations of Western development, these scholars have consciously formulated more-general theories of development that can accommodate a variety of historical experiences without imposing Western criteria of "success or failure."

Once the Western-centric framework is abandoned, differences between China and the West can be informative. A crucial difference between the historical experience of China and Europe was the economic role of the state. Freed from the political and economic burdens that international competition and warfare imposed on their European counterparts, Chinese rulers placed relatively lighter demands on the

6 Eric L. Jones, p. 106.
7 See Charles Tilly, *Coercion, Capital, and European States* (New York: Basil Blackwell, 1990).

resources of their subjects. Consequently, local communities retained a greater measure of autonomy, and the need for Chinese rulers to engage in the complex "bargaining" process with their subjects, which, according to Tilly, shaped the political and social institutions of the West, was less urgent. From the perspective of North's model of economic change, the absence of powerful internal or external competitors meant there was little political or economic incentive for Chinese rulers to intervene more actively to promote "modern" economic growth for the sake of enhancing the state power; therefore, institutional innovation and the elaboration of the property-rights structure largely remained in the realm of custom. As the example of eighteenth-century China shows, although the Chinese state reacted to economic change when social order was threatened, compared to Western Europe China's rulers did less to promote economic development. Instead, they pursued policies to support and maintain the agrarian economy, such as promoting land reclamation, facilitating migration, and creating an empire-wide system of granaries to stabilize grain prices. In most cases, government intervention in the economy was undertaken to ensure domestic order, not to stimulate economic development. The development of economic institutions, including the definition and enforcement of property rights, was largely left in the hands of individuals or voluntary organizations.[8] Without the overarching support of the state, with its comparative advantage in violence and power to tax constituents, the struggle over the creation of new economic institutions was more protracted in China, which in part explains the many small-scale property-rights disputes, such as those described in this study.

I do not mean to imply that when the rulers of a state support and promote economic change from above, such change will necessarily be less disruptive to the social order. From Europe to Asia, there are also numerous historical examples of "rent-seeking states which have stifled economic growth."[9] I am simply pointing out the consequences and limitations of grassroots economic change. Creating new economic institutions is inherently disruptive because it invariably alters the existing allocation of resources. The extent to which the existing economic order is changed and the relative balance of economic power is upset will

8 For a variety of examples that also include property rights in land, see Fu-mei Chen and Ramon Myers. Chen and Myers do not cover a very important large-scale example of the importance of voluntary organizations in China's economic organization, merchant associations (*huiguan*). These associations formed the basis of important regional and national commercial networks.

9 See Jones.

largely determine the social consequences of economic change. One thing is certain, however: When a shift in the relative value of the factors of production does occur, there will be an incentive to alter the existing economic organization, and efforts to change it will carry the potential for conflict. When these changes are protracted and occur in an ad hoc fashion, risk and uncertainty will be greater and the potential for small-scale conflict will also be greater.

From the standpoint of modern Chinese history, another goal of this book has been to evaluate two distinct approaches to the study of economic and social history. On the one hand, economic historians have applied straightforward, neoclassical approaches to explaining economic change in Chinese history. On the other hand, the moral economy model has inspired social historians who have juxtaposed the moral economy of traditional peasant society with the breakdown of social order and economic distress of peasant society in the nineteenth and twentieth centuries to explain rural revolution in modern China. From the point of view of someone who is interested in the link between economic change and social conflict, neoclassical economics provides a sound basis for understanding the general direction of long-term economic change in China. As Douglass North has pointed out, neoclassical analysis demonstrates that wealth maximizing occurs despite the existence of uncertainty because "competition in the face of ubiquitous scarcity dictates that the most efficient institution, policy, or individual action will survive."[10] Here, North was echoing the seminal work of Armen Alchain, who offered an "evolutionary" model of economic change.[11] Alchain proposed an approach to economic behavior that embodied "the principles of biological evolution and natural selection by interpreting the economic system as an adoptive mechanism that chooses among exploratory actions generated by the adaptive pursuit of 'success' or 'profits.' " According to Alchain, "like the biologist, the economist predicts the effects of environmental changes on the surviving class of living organisms."[12] The question remains as to what constitutes the economic environment. I agree with Douglass North that political and economic institutions and ideology must be included.

10 North, 1981, p. 7. As applied to a form of economic organization, North defines an efficient economic organization as one in which maximizing behavior on the part of participants will produce increases in output.

11 See Armen Alchain, "Uncertainty, Evolution and Economic Theory," *Journal of Political Economy* (1950) 58: 211–21. In this vastly influential article, Alchain modified economic analysis to incorporate "incomplete information and uncertain foresight."

12 Ibid., p. 221.

In the case of China, employing neoclassical principles to explain long-term secular change is valuable because it highlights the institutional changes that occurred in China's system of land tenure over the course of two thousand years. Various forms of land tenure survived over the centuries, but more economically efficient, though not necessarily the most efficient, forms of land tenure eventually predominated and supplanted less efficient forms.[13] Without taking anything away from neoclassical contributions to our understanding of Chinese economic history, however, it is still true that these arguments ignore the social costs of the transformation of the agricultural economy during the eighteenth century. When economic historians refer to the spread of contractual arrangements between tenants and landlords as a sign of a long-term trend toward the "triumph of market forces," they are identifying an important historical development of the late imperial economy of China, but we should not overlook the social conflict that attended this "victory." Herein lies the greatest shortcoming of neoclassical analysis. It offers no means to explain the behavior of those who, in their own rational self-interest, resist economic change. Replacing the concept of land as patrimony with the concept of land as commodity, for example, was essential to the triumph of market forces, but curtailing the right to redeem was particularly harmful to peasants with smaller holdings, who quite naturally fought against this change.

At first glance, the moral economy argument appears to offer a needed corrective to neoclassical analysis of economic change in preindustrial society. Discussing colonial Africa, Polanyi stated that the "catastrophe of the native community is a direct result of the rapid and violent disruption of the basic institutions of the victim."[14] According to Polanyi, institutions were destroyed when "the market economy" was "foisted upon an entirely differently organized community." Qualitative evidence for eighteenth-century China also points to the disruption of basic economic institutions, but the market economy that generated these disruptions was not foisted on China. Change came from within Chinese society, but this did not prevent economic self-interest from colliding with ethical norms. For example, we see that lineage members were willing to exhume ancestral graves in order to sell land or to evict clansmen to obtain higher rents from outsiders. Time and again, magistrates defended the ideological foundation of the rural economy and punished individuals for "doing what should not be done." But the tide of change could not be stemmed. Indigenously generated market forces

13 Here, I follow North's definition on economic efficiency. See Note 6.
14 Polanyi, p. 159.

were creating impersonal economic institutions that upset social harmony.

This book does not directly challenge the major thrust of the moral economy argument. Clearly, the destruction of existing social and economic institutions attended the development of capitalism in the West and elsewhere with the spread of Western influence; but whether we study the rise of capitalism or the prehistoric transition from hunting and gathering to settled agriculture, we should expect to see changes in political and economic institutions and ideology that were equally monumental and destructive to the existing social order as those encountered during the rise of industrial societies in the nineteenth and twentieth centuries. The association between the destruction of "traditional" peasant society and the rise of capitalism in the West has sometimes warped perceptions of non-Western societies. Perhaps because the social sciences developed contemporaneously with the rise of capitalism and the establishment of nation states, these events have come to dominate contemporary understandings of economic change and social conflict in both earlier historical periods of Western history and in non-Western societies. Consequently – and this point is particularly relevant to studies of China and other non-Western societies – if economic change does not lead to industrialization or modern economic growth, it somehow seems less significant.

Turning to specific applications of moral economy arguments to China, ascribing a leading role to the incorporation of the village into a broader world economy during the nineteenth and twentieth centuries obscures the fact that market forces and economic competition were at work in rural society at least as early as the eighteenth century. This statement should not be misconstrued as an attempt to downplay the subsequent acceleration of economic change and social conflict in the Chinese economy that proceeded apace with the active intervention of the militant commercial powers of the West in the nineteenth and twentieth centuries. The point is merely that any large-scale economic change, not necessarily the rise of capitalism or an industrial revolution, can have serious social consequences and can undermine economic institutions as well as the ideological foundations of rural society. So saying, the evidence of violent disputes over property rights provides a counterbalance to the sometimes overidealized and static picture of peasant society prior to the nineteenth century that moral economy proponents depict.

An analysis of violent disputes related to property rights based on the class and kinship of disputants highlights the complexity of conflict in eighteenth-century China. For example, one might assume that kinship bonds would mitigate the potential for violence. Undoubtedly, kinship bonds were an important source of unity, but in one-third of all violent disputes examined in this book the disputants were members of the same household or lineage. Turning to class, a comparison of disputes along class lines reveals that violence among competing peasants far outweighed interclass violence.[15] Using data from the comparative sample for Guangdong, Shandong, and Sichuan, which excludes published documents that were heavily biased toward interclass disputes, we find that intraclass violence accounted for 73 percent of the 150 disputes in Guangdong, 90 percent of the 125 disputes in Sichuan, and 88 percent of the 25 disputes in Shandong. Perhaps most distressing in a society that valued family and kinship, lineage leaders often turned their backs on poorer lineage members. Furthermore, evidence in homicide reports repeatedly suggests that the ethical norms of Chinese peasant society were under pressure in the eighteenth century. Expressions of moral outrage came from those who had been harmed by the changes in economic institutions. As noted, tenants who were forced off their land after successive defaults and peasants who were denied the opportunity to redeem sales of land sometimes angrily complained that their property or rights had been "stolen." Not surprisingly, county magistrates were the most consistent supporters of ethical norms. With limited resources with which to enforce their legal decisions, county magistrates voiced support for principles of cooperation, reciprocity, and fairness as the ideological props of rural society, when attempting to resolve property-rights disputes and when addressing the proximate causes of violent disputes. But the effort of officials to reassert these ethical norms and the outrage of those who resisted the economic change of eighteenth century was a rearguard battle. Over the course of the eighteenth century, the inexorable pressure of population growth and the lure of the market gradually altered the face of the rural economy and undermined existing economic institutions and principles of cooperation and reciprocity.

Historically, the incorporation of significant portions of China's economy into a global market economy was an important watershed that carried far-reaching social and political consequences, but these events should not be allowed to overshadow the deeper currents of Chinese history. Pre–Opium War Chinese rural society cannot be treated as a hermetic vessel awaiting rupture from the militant commercial powers of the West. The Chinese economy had already begun to outgrow the

15 Interclass violence is defined as violence between tenants and landlords. Intraclass violence is defined as violence between individual peasant cultivators.

highly personalized forms of economic exchange that generally characterize "pre-capitalist" societies in the eighteenth century. Commercialization of agriculture, extensive foreign trade, and unprecedented population growth were well under way in China prior to the nineteenth century. Furthermore, as evidence from violent disputes indicates, these economic developments had already begun to affect the economic organization and ideological foundations of peasant society, in ways similar to those that moral economy proponents have ascribed to capitalism in the West. Once we begin to view the eighteenth century as part of a longer continuum of economic and social change rather than a pristine counterpoint to a later period of social turmoil and political strife, violent disputes over property rights appear more significant.

A careful examination of the variety of disputes reveals a complicated and dynamic picture of Chinese peasant society adjusting to economic change in the eighteenth century. At the same time, the overall decline in homicides related to disputes over property rights relative to all homicides related to disputes over land and debts also indicates the resiliency and ingenuity of rural society and the strength of the traditional polity. But the decline in personalized, communal, and small-scale violence during the later half of the eighteenth century and the establishment of new economic institutions simply should not be viewed as a Durkheimian reintegration of a rapidly changing society.[16] The social conflict and economic change of the eighteenth century had significantly altered rural society.

By the late eighteenth century, we begin to see the emergence of large-scale collective violence for the first time since the seventeenth century; however, this violence took an entirely different form. This topic is beyond the scope of this book, but two developments are worth mentioning. First is the appearance of named brotherhoods and secret societies during the latter half of the eighteenth century. David Ownby describes these institutions as "informal, popular institutions created by marginalized men seeking mutual protection in a dangerous and competitive society."[17] Ownby emphasizes that despite its later reputation for collective violence and rebellion, the original appeal of one of the largest brotherhoods, the Tiandihui, was "the promise that the Tiandihui could provide supernatural protection from natural and human dangers."[18] Another important development of the late eighteenth

16 Indeed, it is questionable how well Emile Durkheim's theories apply to Western history. See Charles Tilly, Chapter 4, *As Sociology Meets History* (New York: Academic Press, 1981).

17 David Ownby, p. 2, *Brotherhoods and Secret Societies in Early Mid-Qing China* (Stanford: Stanford University Press, 1996). 18 Ibid., p. 26.

century was the establishment of gentry-led militia forces that Philip Kuhn examined in his seminal work on the militarization of Chinese society.[19] These militia were a critical adjunct to imperial military force in the suppression of large-scale rebellion, but they were initially a response to the limited ability of the state to maintain order in rural society. The appearance of local militias and sworn brotherhoods indicate that individuals from both the elite and popular ends of the social spectrum of rural society were actively engaged in creating new institutions outside the control of government to protect their local interests. Given what the record of violence-related to property-rights disputes reveals about the erosion of shared ethical norms and the problem of effectively and efficiently enforcing rulings in civil disputes, the appearance of militias and sworn brotherhoods in the eighteenth century comes as no surprise. These institutions would play important roles in the political and social upheavals of the nineteenth century, mobilizing people and resources both for and against the Qing dynasty. As C. K. Yang's research on collective violence has revealed, China faced greater and, ultimately, more destructive social upheaval during the latter half of the Qing. [20]

Ultimately, the reader will decide the degree to which I have convincingly drawn a link between violent disputes and economic change, but here it is worth remembering that the fundamental problem at the heart of economics is scarcity. As long as scarcity has existed, some level of economic competition has always been a part of human experience. As Armen Alchain and Harold Demsetz in their discussion of property rights have noted, "it is more useful . . . to view a social system as relying on techniques, rules, or customs to resolve conflicts that arise in the use of scarce resources."[21] Given pervasive scarcity, social conflict is inevitable, but the manner in which conflict will be resolved can take many forms, from peaceful mediation to war. Given the limited capacity of local government officials to enforce official adjudication and the erosion of ethical norms in the increasingly complex commercialized economy of eighteenth-century rural China, many conflicts tragically ended in homicide.

19 Philip A. Kuhn.

20 See C. K. Yang, "Some Preliminary Patterns of Mass Action in Nineteenth-century China," in *Conflict and Control in Late Imperial China,* F. Wakeman, Jr. and C. Grant, eds. (Berkeley: University of California Press, 1975).

21 Armen Alchain and Harold Demsetz, p. 16, "The Property Right Paradigm," *Journal of Economic History* (1973) 33.1: 16–27.

Appendix
Homicide Reports: Routine Memorials to the Ministry of Justice

Routine memorials were used in the Ming and Qing dynasties to communicate public matters to the Grand Secretariat, which forwarded the memorials with recommendations for action to the emperor for his consideration.[1] The Ministry of Justice used routine memorials to report on a variety of matters, including homicides.[2] The staff of the Number One Historical Archives has categorized these memorials by subject: autumn and spring assizes, homicides, robbery, official corruption, prisons, arrests and seizures, and others. Within the category of homicides, there are four subcategories: blows and affrays, land and debt, marriage and illicit sex, and other. This study utilizes only homicide cases that were related to land and debt (*tudi zhaiwu*) disputes.

Routine memorials reporting homicide originated at the county (*xian*) level and flowed upward through the bureaucracy. The entire process from the arrest until the case reached Beijing could take up to six months, though some cases moved through the system more quickly.[3]

1 Dan Shikui, "Qingdai tiben zhidu kaolue" (Brief examination of the Qing period routine memorial system), in Zhu Jinfu, ed., *Ming Qing dangan lunwen xuanbian* (Selected essays on Ming Qing documents), (Beijing: Dangan Chubanshe, 1985).

2 See Number One Historical Archives of China, *Zhongguo di lishi danganguan guanzang dangan gaishu* (Introduction to documents contained in the Number One Historical Archives of China), (Beijing: Dangan Chubanshe, 1985).

3 Officials could be penalized if there was any delay in processing a case. Most cases appear to have moved through the system smoothly. Each memorial included a detailed accounting of the progress of the cases through the judicial system. Unfortunately, this detail was contained in the final few pages of the document, a portion of the memorial frequently damaged. There seems to have been more delays during the final ten years of the Qianlong reign, 1785–95. Perhaps this declining efficiency was an indication of the onset of dynastic decline.

Each case was reviewed at the prefectural and provincial level. Thus, a complete document was very repetitive, containing reports from each administrative level, county, prefecture, province, and the Three Judicial Offices in Beijing. The county-level (*xian*) report was the most extensive, and usually included a formal complaint, depositions of the accused and eyewitnesses, a coroner's report, and the county magistrate's summary of the case and suggested punishments. Prefectural-level reports ordinarily repeated the summaries of the county-level report without additional comment. Provincial officials and the Three Judicial Offices, however, reviewed cases critically, evaluated the performance of the county magistrates, and addressed questions of sentencing.[4]

Land and Debt Cases

The organization of documents in the Number One Historical Archives began in 1952. According to materials on cataloging published by the Number One Historical Archives, the category of land and debt includes all disputes over land and debts, broadly defined, that ended in criminal homicide. Included in this category are disputes over sales of houses and land, conditional sales of land (*dianmai*), rental of land or houses, forcible occupation of land, forced sales, forced rental of peasant land or houses, landlords killing laborers, peasants killing landlords, private transfers of deeds, and fights over irrigation and boundaries. Disputes over debts included cash loans, debts for items sold on credit, unpaid wages, and gambling debts. The categories are quite broad and also could include loans of other items, such as a pot or farm implement, and disputes arising from alleged violations of principles of geomancy and accidental destruction of crops by animals. It seems that modern-day catalogers included any homicide, even those only tangentially related to land, in this category. For purposes of this study, I have selected only cases related to five specific property-rights issues: rent defaults, evictions, redemptions, water rights, and boundary disputes.

Losses in the Collection

Although it seems certain that contemporary catalogers were quite inclusive in their efforts, it is also apparent that over the years many doc-

4 Ch'u T'ung-tsu, p. 117, *Local Government in China Under the Ch'ing* (Stanford: Stanford University Press, 1969).

uments were lost or destroyed. During the late nineteenth century, the storage and preservation of documents had already become problematic. In 1899, Li Hongzhang proposed the destruction of all old, moldy copies of routine memorials contained in the Grand Secretariat Archives. This proposal was accepted, however all copies, regardless of their condition, were destroyed, except those for the Guangxu reign (1875–1908). The late Qing period was also marked by numerous wars and foreign invasions, which took their toll on the archives. Most notably, the looting and destruction of government offices, which occurred in 1900 during the Eight Nation Joint Expedition's occupation of Beijing in response to the Boxer Uprising, caused considerable damage to government archives.[5] Further losses occurred during the tumultuous years of the Republican Era (1912–49). Perhaps the most devastating loss was the "8,000 Hemp Sack Affair." In 1909, a large group of documents, which included routine memorials, were put into 8,000 hemp sacks and removed from the Grand Secretariat Archives while it was under repair. After the fall of the Qing dynasty in 1911, these documents became part of the new government's History Museum. In 1921, the History Museum had financial problems and sold an unknown portion of the 8,000 hemp sacks of documents as scrap paper to the Tongmao Paper Store in Beijing.[6]

The exact amount of routine memorials that were lost over the years cannot be determined, but undoubtedly the losses were significant for particular years. These losses are reflected in the figures listed in Table A–1 that were obtained from the Number One Historical Archives' catalog for Ministry of Justice routine memorials related to land and debt in the Qianlong period. Obviously, these figures do not represent the actual number of criminal homicides reported. For example, staff members at the Number One Historical Archives acknowledged that the sharp decline for the period 1783–5 was due to serious losses in the collection. Another problem occasionally encountered was duplicate documents for the same case. The provincial governor-general's report and the report of the Three Judicial Offices, which included all lower-level reports including the governor general's, could receive the imperial endorsement, and in some cases both reports have been included in the routine memorial collection. For Guangdong province, this "duplication" of documents ranged from 0 to 10 percent of the total number of extant documents for selected years in the Qianlong reign.

One method that I employed to check for losses in the routine memo-

5 Number One Historical Archives of China, p. 9. 6 Ibid., pp. 4–8.

Table A–1. *Total Holdings of the Ministry of Justice Routine Memorials for Homicides Related to Land and Debts in the Qianlong Period*

1736	423	1766	1,141
1737	763	1767	1,456
1738	233	1768	1,317
1739	308	1769	1,599
1740	600	1770	579
1741	362	1771	1,428
1742	473	1772	1,270
1743	488	1773	1,381
1744	781	1774	1,577
1745	**637**	1775	1,582
1746	784	1776	1,540
1747	664	1777	963
1748	661	1778	1,252
1749	442	1779	1,134
1750	708	1780	1,201
1751	698	1781	1,100
1752	825	1782	1,067
1753	981	1783	621
1754	792	1784	434
1755	758	1785	**499**
1756	1,437	1786	743
1757	891	1787	476
1758	1,141	1788	857
1759	967	1789	526
1760	776	1790	579
1761	854	1791	1,333
1762	1,452	1792	1,459
1763	1,355	1793	1,682
1764	287	1794	1,458
1765	**1,394**	1795	1,661

rial collection was a comparison with the Grand Secretariat's registry (*shishu*) for all Ministry of Justice routine memorials. These registries were separately maintained and generally in better physical condition than the routine memorials. Unfortunately, these registries only contain extremely brief, usually one-page, summaries of the routine memorial.[7] For these reasons, only the years 1745, 1765, and 1785 were examined (figures for extant memorials are in bold in Table A–1) for Guangdong province. These years were selected because they cover a broad time span and seem to represent varying degrees of potential losses. This cross-referencing yielded an additional fifteen cases for 1745, a year that appears to have had moderate losses, only seven cases for 1765, a year for which few documents appear to have been lost, and twenty-seven cases for 1785, a year for which the loss of documents was obviously substantial. This would suggest that the sharp fluctuations in number of documents for given years is probably due to losses in the collection rather than actual changes in homicide rates. Finally, the list of total executions for all capital offenses in years in the Qianlong reign for which we have data (see Table A–2) does not indicate extreme fluctuations in capital crimes that would support the proposition that criminal homicide rates were more stable than the listing for extant routine memorials would seem to indicate.

Clearly, there is no foolproof method to determine the extent of the losses in the collection. I assume that the sharp fluctuations in the number of cases reflected in the catalog of routine memorials is due to losses of documents rather than changes in actual homicide rates. In cross-checking the routine memorial collection against the Grand Secretariat's registry, it was apparent that the losses in the routine memorial collection tend to cluster in particular months. Since routine memorials were collected and organized according to the date they were written, this would suggest that when losses occurred it was entire bundles of documents that were lost. Thus, the losses in the collection

7 As stated previously, the Grand Secretariat maintained a registry of all routine memorials. The registries are quite voluminous and time-consuming to use since they are bound volumes of unindexed documents. The registries were organized according to the originating ministry. Documents were entered in the registry after they received the imperial endorsement. The registry and the routine memorial collection are not a perfect match. Routine memorials are catalogued according to the year in which they were written, but registries list documents according to the date that they received the imperial endorsement. A document written and forwarded by a provincial governor could take one to two months to be processed. If the document was written during the last two months of a given year, it would likely appear in the following year's registry. Use of documents taken from the registries will be discussed further.

Table A–2. *Executions for All Capital Offenses for Selected Years during the Qianlong Reign*[a]

	Total for China	Guangdong
1755	2,280	160
1760	2,589	255
1762	2,694	230
1765	2,863	221
1770	3,151	229
1771	2,913	225
1777	2,941	226
1789	3,299	224
1790	3,307	263

[a]Figures for 1755, 1760, 1765, 1770, and 1790 are from Neige qiushen huangce (Grand Secretariat autumn assizes yellow registers, 1755: 5541; 1760: 4095; 1765: 5550; 1770: 4098; 1790: 5566). Figures for 1762, 1771, 1777, and 1789 were taken from James Z. Lee, Appendix A, "Nouvelles, Données sur la Criminalité et la Peine de Mort en Chine a la fin de L'empire" (Etudes Chinois, 1990.)

were unrelated to the content of the memorials, and it is unlikely that these losses would introduce any systematic biases in the types of cases that have been preserved.

Sample Size

My original study covered 385 homicides related to disputes over land in Guangdong province for the Qianlong period. Of these cases, seventy-seven were obtained solely from three published sources, *Kang, Yong, Qian shiqi cheng xiang renmin fankang douzheng ziliao* (Materials on urban and rural peoples struggles in the Kangxi, Yongzheng, and Qianlong periods), Qing History Research Center of People's University, ed. (Beijing: Zhonghua Shuju, 1979), hereafter KYQ; and *Qingdai dizu boxiao xingtai* (Forms of rent exploitation in the Qing period),

Number One Historical Archives of China and Institute of Historical Research of the Chinese Academy of Social Sciences, eds. (Beijing: Zhonghua Shuju, 1982), hereafter QDB; and *Qingdai tudi zhanyou guanxi yu diannong kangzu douzheng* (Qing dynasty landownership relations and tenant rent resistance struggles), Number One Historical Archives of China and Institute of Historical Research of the Chinese Academy of Social Sciences, eds. (Beijing: Zhonghua Shuju, 1988), hereafter ZYG. These works were the result of collaborative efforts by teams of Chinese researchers and contain routine memorials that have been extensively edited, ranging in length from several paragraphs to a few pages. None of the published works provided detailed information on the criteria used for selection of cases. The documents in KYQ were chosen to illustrate rent resistance only. In the cases of QDB and ZYG, there was a greater effort to illustrate the complexities of land tenure. Nevertheless, issues such as boundary and water rights, the most frequent cause of violent disputes, were virtually ignored. One suspects that the major selection criteria may have been the amount of detail regarding land tenure and evidence of class conflict. As Table A–3 indicates, the compilers of these published collections did not seem concerned with getting a precise temporal distribution.

In order to obtain a more systematic sample, I visited the Number One Historical Archives and collected the remaining 308 documents. Of these 308 cases, 251 were culled at roughly five-year intervals from the routine memorial collection that contains the entire documents or whatever portion of the documents that has survived. For the routine memorial collection, I used cases for the years 1736, 1737, 1740, 1745, 1750, 1755, 1760, 1765, 1771, 1775, 1780, 1785,[8] 1791, and 1795. The remaining fifty-seven cases were found in the Grand Secretariat registry (*shishu*) of routine memorials for the Ministry of Justice. Only the documents from the routine memorial collection were used to analyze quantitative change over time in Guangdong. The cases obtained from the published sources and the Grand Secretariat registry were used to study qualitative changes in major issues over time. During a subsequent trip to the Number One Historical Archives, I collected my comparative sample for Guangdong, Shandong, and Sichuan for two time series, 1750–3 and 1779–80. This sample was not supplemented with published or other archival sources.

8 1785 includes cases from 1785 and 1786. This was necessary because losses in the routine memorial collection were very severe for the later years of the Qianlong reign.

Table A–3. *Published Ministry of Justice Routine Memorials for Homicides Related to Land and Debts in the Qianlong Reign by Year*

Year	Total	Published	Year	Total	Published
1736	423	10	1766	1,141	27
1737	763	11	1767	1,456	19
1738	233	9	1768	1,317	9
1739	308	7	1769	1,599	11
1740	600	9	1770	579	12
1741	362	4	1771	1,428	18
1742	473	6	1772	1,270	18
1743	488	7	1773	1,381	12
1744	781	15	1774	1,577	12
1745	637	9	1775	1,582	10
1746	784	6	1776	1,540	16
1747	664	11	1777	963	4
1748	661	21	1778	1,252	9
1749	442	13	1779	1,134	11
1750	708	11	1780	1,201	7
1751	698	9	1781	1,100	12
1752	825	15	1782	1,067	9
1753	981	17	1783	621	11
1754	792	18	1784	434	3
1755	758	9	1785	499	6
1756	1,437	27	1786	743	9
1757	891	13	1787	476	4
1758	1,141	17	1788	857	5
1759	967	10	1789	526	2
1760	776	6	1790	579	3
1761	854	2	1791	1,333	11
1762	1,452	24	1792	1,459	14
1763	1,355	12	1793	1,682	12
1764	287	1	1794	1,458	14
1765	1,394	12	1795	1,661	15

Problems in Using Crime Reports

Researchers who use crime reports are quick to point out that crime statistics can never reflect the extent of criminal behavior in a society.[9] Furthermore, fluctuations in crime statistics may not necessarily reflect actual changes in social behavior. Long-term analysis of crime statistics must account for the advent of modern police forces and changes in judicial procedures that frequently explain variance in crime statistics over time. Another study has found that demographic change can lead to an increase in the "favorite" crimes of those groups that change their relative size most rapidly. Citing examples for the United States in the 1950s and 1960s, when there was a rapid period of urbanization, there was also an increase in property crimes that are more common in cities.[10] Other research has checked the reliability of official crime statistics through victimization surveys. One such study has found that the more serious the crime in terms of threat to person, violation of personal space, and injury or cost, the more likely the crime will be reported.[11]

Studies of changes in violent crimes rates in Western countries during the nineteen and twentieth centuries either rely upon methods impossible to duplicate, such as victimization surveys, or introduce factors that were irrelevant for eighteenth-century China. More significantly, procedures for reporting homicides were consistent throughout the eighteenth century, and modern police forces were not established in China until the twentieth century. China's population grew steadily throughout the eighteenth century, but this did not produce any significant changes in the ratio of urban to rural population that can sometimes distort crime rates. One aspect of Chinese law that might have influenced the historical reporting of homicides was the provision that if the victim of an assault did not die within twenty days, or within fifty days when bones were broken, the incident was not considered a homicide. Improvements in medical treatment might explain a decline in the criminal homicide rate, but there is no evidence that any advances were made in the treatment of trauma during the Qianlong period. Thus, it would

9 V. A. C. Gatrell and T. B. Hadden, pp. 361–2, "Criminal Statistics and Their Interpretation," pp. 336–96 in *Nineteenth Century Society: Essays in the Use of Quantitative Methods for the Study of Social Data*, E. A. Wrigley, ed. (Cambridge, UK: Cambridge University Press, 1972).

10 Theodore N. Ferdinand, "Demographic Shifts and Criminality: An Inquiry," *British Journal of Criminology* (1970) 10: 169–75.

11 Wesley G. Skogan, "Citizen Reporting of Crime: Some National Panel Data," *Criminology* (1976) 13: 535–49.

seem safe to assume that any decline in the number of homicides related to property rights reported during the Qianlong period probably reflected an actual decline in such violence.

Reporting Homicides

Homicide was considered a serious crime in China. There were nineteen homicide statutes that distinguished among manslaughter, intentional murder, and premeditated murder and carefully delineated punishments on the basis of the relative status of the victim and perpetrator and the manner in which the homicide occurred. Strict administrative rules and guidelines for the investigation and trial of homicides also existed, and magistrates faced heavy penalties if they failed to dispose of cases in a timely manner. Magistrates were required personally to conduct an inquest at the scene of a killing or at the place where a corpse was found. Failure to conduct a prompt inquest was punishable by demotion of one grade and transfer to another post. If negligence led to a change in the condition of the corpse, the magistrate could be sentenced to sixty strokes.[12]

After an inquest was completed, the magistrate was responsible for identifying and apprehending the perpetrator. If the perpetrator was not apprehended within six months, the magistrate would be penalized, and the penalties increased the longer the perpetrator remained at large.[13] After a criminal was apprehended, the law required that the case be tried and completed by the local magistrate as well as his superiors in four to six months, depending on the seriousness of the crime.[14] In practice, it appears that deadlines could be extended in the case of homicides. In the course of reading over 600 cases for this study, it was not uncommon to find that delays occurred because the criminal was injured in the course of the violent dispute and unable to stand trial immediately.

Additional insights into the problems associated with the investigation and trial of homicides can be ascertained from Qing dynasty sources. During the nineteenth century, numerous compilations of criminal cases were published to provide guidance to local magistrates. These compilations contained leading cases (*chengan*) that illustrated common problems or provided precedents for difficult cases. These works are interesting because they reveal the problems that local magistrates faced when adjudicating criminal cases. In one such compilation, under the heading of homicides, two cases in which criminals were not immedi-

12 Ch'u, 1969, p. 119. 13 Ibid., p. 121. 14 Ibid., pp. 121–2.

ately apprehended were referenced. In the first case, the criminal had buried the body but later revealed the location to the victim's family. In the second case, the criminal, whose name was unknown to the local residents, left the scene of the killing before the victim had died. In both cases, the criminals were eventually apprehended and convicted.[15] In a similar work, a major concern of the homicide section was determination of pardons. Several cases involving manslaughter, rape in which the victim later committed suicide, and murder were pardoned because the criminals were either only sons of elderly parents or had widowed mothers.[16] Interestingly, while these compilations of leading cases covered a wide variety of issues, the problem of unsolved homicides was not discussed in either source, and it appears that it was not considered a serious problem.

In the case of homicides arising from land disputes, where the participants were usually fellow villagers and the violence usually occurred in broad daylight, it was rare for a killer to escape justice. If a magistrate failed to apprehend a killer before his term of office expired, however, the incoming magistrate assumed responsibility for the case. Apparently, unsolved homicide cases could remain open for years. For example, a homicide involving a debt took place in Deqing county, Zhaoqing prefecture, in 1794. The killer fled to Guangxi Province and later to Guizhou province, remaining at large for over five years. Eventually, he returned to Deqing county, where he was apprehended, tried, and sentenced to death.[17]

Reporting Biases and Cover-ups

Were there systematic biases in the reporting of homicides in the eighteenth century? Local elites, degree holders, former officials, and leaders of powerful lineages enjoyed special legal privileges, such as exemption from corporal punishment, and certainly were in a better position to influence the decisions of local magistrates in civil cases.[18] But while local notables may have some advantages in settling civil disputes, criminal cases were probably more difficult to "fix." Private mediation was common in rural China; but when a dispute ended in

15 Xiao Shu and Zhu Shu, eds., pp. 4–7 quan 1, *Yuedong chengan chubian* (Guangdong leading cases, 1st ed.), 1887.

16 Xu Lian and Xiong Shu, eds., quan 32, *Xingbu bizhao jiajian chengan* (Ministry of Justice rulings, sentencings, and leading cases), 1834.

17 XKTB 4097, QL 60.12.6.

18 Frederic Wakeman, Jr., 1970, pp. 13–14.

homicide, arbitration was much less likely and the case was "seldom settled out of court."[19]

There was some evidence of attempted cover-ups occurring at the sub-bureaucratic level of administration. In fourteen cases out of a total of 385 examined in my original study of Guangdong, there was either evidence of attempts to settle homicide cases privately or to conceal them before they reached the attention of the county magistrate. Such cases usually involved payments to the victim's family; bribes to sub-bureaucratic officials, such as a local constable and coroners or *baojia* heads; and bribery or intimidation of third-party witnesses, since failure to report any crime, let alone homicide, was considered a crime itself. Generally, these private settlements or attempted cover-ups took place under one or all of the following conditions: The perpetrator was a member of a wealthier family that could afford the payments to the victim's family and bribes to the sub-bureaucratic officials, the circumstances of the death were such that a cover-up was possible, or there were no third-party witnesses to the homicide.

Covering up homicide was always complicated, and bribery in homicide cases could be quite expensive. In one case, the killer paid bribes of 30 Mexican silver dollars (*fanyuan*) to the legal secretary and 10 Mexican silver dollars to the coroner to have the complaint suppressed and the corpse altered. The original magistrate was deceived by this ruse, but his successor reopened the case at the behest of a relative of the victim. Ironically, the killer qualified for a pardon as an only son of aged parents, but this was denied because of the bribery and attempted cover-up.[20] In another case, the peculiar circumstances in which the victim died – he was struck, fell into a pond, and drowned – provided an opportunity for deception. The killer and his uncle enlisted a clansman to offer a bribe of 70 Mexican silver dollars to the victim's brother and 2 ounces of silver to the local constable to report that the victim had been drunk and accidentally fell into the pond.[21] The memorial did not provide details, but apparently the succeeding magistrate uncovered the scheme and punished the killer and everyone involved in the cover-up. Again the attempt was costly and ultimately fruitless. In still another case, the father of the victim, a *shengyuan* degree holder, participated in an attempted cover-up that failed to deceive the local magistrate. For his crime, the father was stripped of his degree and flogged.[22] Apparently,

19 Hsiao Kung-chuan, 1967, p. 292.
20 XKTB 2784, QL 40.11.12. 21 XKTB 2768, QL 40.1.22.
22 XKTB 0046, QL 2.12.2.

one way to overcome the degree-holder's exemption from corporal punishment was to strip him of his degree.

The impression one gains after reading many cases is that cover-ups were desperate and risky acts. It seems that cover-ups were more likely to occur at the sub-bureaucratic level before the magistrate was aware of the homicide. Once a case reached the attention of the county magistrate, there was a clear incentive for him to expose any private settlements, since he was allowed to confiscate all bribes for his personal use. Even if the magistrate was deceived initially, irate relatives of the victim could raise complaints with newly arrived magistrates or with higher-level officials. Similarly, a new, more conscientious magistrate might expose the plot. Since magistrates were limited to three-year terms in a given locale and many served less than three years, this risk was also considerable. Despite the great risk involved, however, it is not surprising that cover-ups were attempted, given that the usual sentence for homicide was death.

Evidence of preferential treatment being accorded to the wealthy and powerful does exist, but it was within the bounds of the law. There were twenty-seven cases in which killers were pardoned or had their sentences reduced. Eighteen of these cases occurred in 1736 or 1755, when the Qianlong emperor issued a blanket pardon for all crimes. (A total of eleven blanket pardons, which were applied indiscriminately to all criminals throughout the empire, were granted during the Qianlong reign.)[23] In four other cases the victim died sometime after the assault, and the magistrate reduced the sentences because the wounds received in the affray were not the direct cause of death. In the remaining five cases, the pardons or sentence reductions were discretionary. In four of these cases the local magistrate recommended a pardon because the killer was the only son of parents over the age of seventy.[24] In the fifth case the death occurred while the killer was defending his father from attack. In all five cases the killers were landlords or members of landlord households. It would seem that the wealthy and powerful were more likely to benefit from loopholes in the law, but these benefits were within the bounds of accepted legal practice and theoretically available to anyone.

It could also be argued that local magistrates would underreport homicides because it would reflect badly on their tenure. But the homi-

23 Brian E. McKnight, p. 98, *The Quality of Mercy* (Honolulu: University of Hawaii Press, 1981).

24 The practice of commuting death sentences for criminals who were the only support of aged parents was known as *liuyang*. See Ch'u T'ung-tsu, p. 45, *Law and Society in Traditional China* (Paris: Mouton, 1965).

cide rate was never a criterion for evaluating or punishing local officials. Failure to investigate homicide cases in a timely manner, on the other hand, could result in a fine and reduction in rank. The only possible exception may have been certain types of violence, such as organized violence and feuding. Organized violence was quite a different matter than manslaughter. It would seem from the reports of these types of cases and the comments that magistrates made in other cases involving five or more individuals that magistrates were very sensitive to incidents that might indicate there was a capacity to mobilize for violent purposes in their jurisdiction. On the surface, these cases, which frequently arose from disputes over control of water rights, resembled the type of lineage feuding that occurred more frequently in the nineteenth century. In these cases, county magistrates usually downplayed or attempted to explain away the obvious evidence of advanced planning and organization. Although several such cases were reported, it does not seem unreasonable to argue that there may have been some slippage in the reporting of similar cases.[25]

Reliability of Reporting

Experts generally agree that among all crimes committed, homicide reports most closely reflect real changes in social behavior. Homicide is usually committed by a person known to the victim and ordinarily attracts close official attention, "making slippage in reporting less likely than for other violent crimes."[26] Underreporting of homicides related to land would be even less likely because participants were usually residents of the same locale or had a long-standing contractual agreement. Research on criminal procedure indicates that the handling of criminal matters was more conscientious and that magistrates "nearly always" accepted criminal complaints. In fact, under the Qing law code, officials investigated serious crime, including homicide, whether or not a complaint was lodged.[27] Criminal homicide was not uncommon in rural Guangdong, and the right to appeal for defendant and plaintiff alike

25 According to Harry Lamely, "no matter how corrupt the authorities" the government eventually would take action when faced with cases of "sustained" lineage-based fighting that caused serious crimes. See Harry Lamely, p. 47, "Lineage Feuding in Southern Fujian and Eastern Guangdong under Qing Rule," in *Violence in China*, J. N. Lipman and S. Harrell, eds. (Albany: State University of New York Press, 1990).

26 Ted Robert Gurr, 1981.

27 Derek Bodde and Clarence Morris, p. 118.

was readily exercised during the eighteenth century.[28] The homicide rate of a county was never a criterion for evaluating or punishing officials, but failure to investigate homicide cases in a timely manner did result in fines and reductions in rank.

Undoubtedly, some homicides probably still escaped detection, but the preponderance of evidence suggests to me that criminal homicide per se was not likely to go unreported during the Qianlong period. There were ample laws related to homicide in the Qing legal code; detailed administrative regulations and sanctions that governed the investigation and trial of homicides; guidebooks designed to aid magistrates in criminal matters that openly discussed the problems of investigating and trying homicide cases; and a reasonably plausible homicide rate (see Chapter 6). Although local magistrates might have underreported some homicide cases involving larger-scale organized violence and, under certain circumstances, attempted bribery and cover-ups may have kept other cases from coming to light, experience in the course of reading and coding hundreds of homicide cases for this study leads me to believe that there was little slippage in homicide reporting in the Qianlong reign. Furthermore, there is no evidence to indicate that the factors that may have caused slippages in reporting changed significantly during the Qianlong reign. Given the evidence presented here, it would seem that every magistrate was bound to encounter criminal homicide sometime in his career; and when he did, he investigated and reported it.

How accurately do homicides reflect the overall level of violence and conflict related to property-rights disputes? While it is true that this study is limited to only the most egregious acts of violence, it is also safe to assume that a decline in the number of homicides related to property-rights disputes would be a fair indicator of an overall decline in violent behavior related to property-rights disputes. (Of course, this is emphatically not the same as saying that nonviolent disputes over property rights also declined. In fact, studies suggest that the number of civil suits continued to increase into the nineteenth century.)[29] The detailed administrative regulations for investigating and reviewing homicides has bequeathed to historians a large and valuable body of primary source materials systematically compiled over time and across administrative boundaries.

28 Jonathan K. Ocko, p. 292, "I'll Take It All the Way to Beijing: Capital Appeals in the Qing," *Journal of Asian Studies* (1988) 47.2: 291–315.

29 See Zelin, 1986, and Melissa Macauley, "The Civil Reprobate: Pettifoggers, Property, and Litigation in Late Imperial China, 1723–1850," unpublished Ph.D. diss. University of California at Berkeley, 1993.

Table A–4. *Guangdong Province (480 Disputes)*

Rent Default and Other Disputes over Rent (123 Disputes)

	Routine Memorials (77 Cases)		
	Source	Reference #	Date
1.	XKTB	0020	QL 01.03.29
2.	XKTB	0029	QL 01.10.15
3.	XKTB	0157	QL 05.03.11
4.	XKTB	0190	QL 05.05.14
5.	XKTB	0207	QL 05.07.03
6.	XKTB	0204	QL 05.07.04
7.	XKTB	0201	QL 05.10.06
8.	XKTB	0476	QL 10.03.22
9.	XKTB	0446	QL 10.12.19
10.	XKTB	0714	QL 15.02.28
11.	XKTB	0742	QL 15.06.09
12.	XKTB	0750	QL 15.07.07
13.	XKTB	0759	QL 16.05.13
14.	XKTB	0772	QL 16.05.16
15.	XKTB	0799	QL 16.05.25
16.	XKTB	0765	QL 16.06.29
17.	XKTB	0765	QL 16.07.15
18.	XKTB	0803	QL 16.12.15
19.	XKTB	0832	QL 17.07.07
20.	XKTB	0878	QL 17.09.15
21.	XKTB	0968	QL 18.04.22
22.	XKTB	0942	QL 18.05.02
23.	XKTB	0923	QL 18.05.02
24.	XKTB	0933	QL 18.05.22
25.	XKTB	0883	QL 18.06.10
26.	XKTB	0891	QL 18.07.20
27.	XKTB	0932	QL 18.07.26
28.	XKTB	0943	QL 18.07.26
29.	XKTB	0982	QL 18.10.22
30.	XKTB	0893	QL 18.11.26
31.	XKTB	0963	QL 18.11.29
32.	XKTB	0973	QL 18.12.21
33.	XKTB	1073	QL 20.09.21
34.	XKTB	1076	QL 20.10.04
35.	XKTB	1081	QL 20.11.22

(cont.)

	Routine Memorials (77 Cases)		
	Source	Reference #	Date
36.	XKTB	1088	QL 20.12.07
37.	XKTB	1085	QL 20.12.15
38.	XKTB	1416	QL 25.04.15
39.	XKTB	1402	QL 25.11.11
40.	XKTB	1429	QL 25.12.15
41.	XKTB	1789	QL 30.02.04
42.	XKTB	1840	QL 30.02.27
43.	XKTB	1744	QL 30.03.03
44.	XKTB	1741	QL 30.04.04
45.	XKTB	1829	QL 30.05.24
46.	XKTB	1788	QL 30.06.09
47.	XKTB	2381	QL 36.04.23
48.	XKTB	2393	QL 36.07.06
49.	XKTB	2405	QL 36.07.29
50.	XKTB	2356	QL 36.12.02
51.	XKTB	2321	QL 36.12.04
52.	XKTB	2348	QL 36.12.06
53.	XKTB	2395	QL 36.12.21
54.	XKTB	2743	QL 40.02.02
55.	XKTB	2841	QL 40.04.17
56.	XKTB	2767	QL 40.09.03
57.	XKTB	2810	QL 40.10.26
58.	XKTB	3126	QL 44.02.25
59.	XKTB	3115	QL 44.05.18
60.	XKTB	3131	QL 44.06.09
61.	XKTB	3209	QL 45.03.16
62.	XKTB	3271	QL 45.04.12
63.	XKTB	3268	QL 45.04.21
64.	XKTB	3280	QL 45.10.03
65.	XKTB	3255	QL 45.11.12
66.	XKTB	3540	QL 50.05.12
67.	XKTB	3519	QL 50.05.28
68.	XKTB	3540	QL 51.05.12
69.	XKTB	3793	QL 56.02.14
70.	XKTB	3735	QL 56.03.04
71.	XKTB	3743	QL 56.05.16
72.	XKTB	3756	QL 56.07.23
73.	XKTB	3749	QL 56.07.28
74.	XKTB	3745	QL 56.09.28
75.	XKTB	4140	QL 60.03.17

	Routine Memorials (77 Cases)		
	Source	Reference #	Date
76.	XKTB	4076	QL 60.06.09
77.	XKTB	4108	QL 60.08.26

	Ministry of Justice Registry (8 Cases)		
	Source	Reference #	Date
78.	SS	1571, 11.10, vol. 1	QL 10.09.15
79.	SS	1579, 12.10, vol. 3	QL 10.10.25
80.	SS	3579, 6.50, vol. 1	QL 50.03.16
81.	SS	3582, 6.50, vol. 2	QL 50.04.15
82.	SS	3587, 7.50, vol. 2	QL 50.05.27
83.	SS	3609, 11.50 vol. 3	QL 50.09.19
84.	SS	3604, 10.50 vol. 4	QL 50.10.20
85.	SS	3618, 12.50 vol. 6	QL 50.11.05

	Published Memorials (38 Cases)		
	Source	Page Numbers	Date
86.	KYQ	127–8	QL 02.04.07
87.	QDB	19–20	QL 02.06.27
88.	QDB	20–1	QL 02.09.28
89.	QDB	25–6	QL 03.05.14
90.	ZYG	652–4	QL 04.08.22
91.	KYQ	129	QL 04.12.16
92.	QDB	503–6	QL 09.06.02
93.	QDB	506–8	QL 10.12.21
94.	ZYG	347–50	QL 11.11.26
95.	QDB	61–3	QL 16.10.28
96.	KYQ	139	QL 19.04.15
97.	KYQ	139–140	QL 19.04.24
98.	KYQ	140–2	QL 19.08.06
99.	QDB	99–101	QL 20.03.17
100.	ZYG	719–21	QL 21.05.15
101.	ZYG	241–3	QL 21.09.16
102.	QDB	631–2	QL 21.12.17
103.	QDB	405–8	QL 23.03.02
104.	ZYG	610–12	QL 24.05.14
105.	ZYG	766–8	QL 24.05.18
106.	ZYG	740–1	QL 24.06.17
107.	QDB	317–20	QL 24.11.06
108.	QDB	115–17	QL 24.11.06

(cont.)

	Published Memorials (38 Cases)		
	Source	Page Numbers	Date
109.	KYQ	142–3	QL 26.03.11
110.	QDB	637–9	QL 27.03.17
111.	QDB	415–17	QL 27.04.30
112.	QDB	644–6	QL 30.03.23
113.	ZYG	626–7	QL 34.05.22
114.	ZYG	628–31	QL 34.07.04
115.	QDB	432–5	QL 34.11.03
116.	ZYG	631–2	QL 35.11.08
117.	ZYG	728–30	QL 37.07.09
118.	KYQ	143–4	QL 37.08.08
119.	QDB	580–2	QL 37.10.28
120.	QDB	682–3	QL 41.09.08
121.	QDB	203–4	QL 49.03.18
122.	QDB	473–4	QL 52.08.07
123.	QDB	235–6	QL 58.12.20

Evictions (59 Disputes)

	Routine Memorials (45 Cases)		
	Source	Reference #	Date
124.	XKTB	0002	QL 01.04.26
125.	XKTB	0006	QL 01.07.13
126.	XKTB	0049	QL 02.05.20
127.	XKTB	0068	QL 02.06.06
128.	XKTB	0094	QL 02.10.07
129.	XKTB	0475	QL 10.02.19
130.	XKTB	0464	QL 10.03.07
131.	XKTB	0450	QL 10.03.23
132.	XKTB	0471	QL 10.06.25
133.	XKTB	0464	QL 10.09.15
134.	XKTB	0422	QL 10.10.22
135.	XKTB	0730	QL 15.05.07
136.	XKTB	0777	QL 16.06.17
137.	XKTB	0765	QL 16.07.16
138.	XKTB	0755	QL 16.09.15
139.	XKTB	0776	QL 16.11.29
140.	XKTB	0755	QL 16.12.15
141.	XKTB	0837	QL 17.01.29
142.	XKTB	0852	QL 17.04.29
143.	XKTB	0853	QL 17.07.20
144.	XKTB	0865	QL 17.12.07

	Routine Memorials (45 Cases)		
	Source	Reference #	Date
145.	XKTB	0902	QL 18.03.13
146.	XKTB	0915	QL 18.08.18
147.	XKTB	0981	QL 18.10.05
148.	XKTB	0893	QL 18.11.26
149.	XKTB	1046	QL 20.03.26
150.	XKTB	1081	QL 20.11.27
151.	XKTB	1419	QL 25.02.25
152.	XKTB	1410	QL 25.06.05
153.	XKTB	1450	QL 25.07.05
154.	XKTB	1840	QL 30.02.14
155.	XKTB	1747	QL 30.11.12
156.	XKTB	2300	QL 36.06.26
157.	XKTB	2382	QL 36.10.09
158.	XKTB	2822	QL 40.03.08
159.	XKTB	3183	QL 44.10.11
160.	XKTB	3250	QL 45.05.04
161.	XKTB	3201	QL 45.05.10
162.	XKTB	3252	QL 45.12.05
163.	XKTB	3515	QL 50.02.14
164.	XKTB	3564	QL 51.05.05
165.	XKTB	3567	QL 51.11.24
166.	XKTB	3560	QL 51.12.20
167.	XKTB	4114	QL 60.02.06
168.	XKTB	4084	QL 60.02.22

	Ministry of Justice Registry (4 Cases)		
	Source	Reference #	Date
169.	SS	1566, 10.10 vol. 1	QL 10.08.21
170.	SS	1575, 12.10 vol. 1	QL 10.10.19
171.	SS	2581, 5.30, vol. 1	QL 30.03.26
172.	SS	3600, 9.50, vol. 6	QL 50.08.02

	Published Memorials (10 Cases)		
	Source	Page Numbers	Date
173.	KYQ	126–7	QL 01.03.27
174.	KYQ	128	QL 02.04.07
175.	QDB	26–8	QL 04.09.11
176.	QDB	364–6	QL 12.05.26
177.	QDB	514–15	QL 13.10.24

(cont.)

	Published Memorials (10 Cases)		
	Source	Page Numbers	Date
178.	QDB	374–5	QL 13.11.18
179.	QDB	648–9	QL 31.11.16
180.	KYQ	143	QL 37.06.14
181.	QDB	186–7	QL 44.08.05
182.	QDB	227–8	QL 58.02.27

Redemptions and Disputes over Sales (81 Disputes)

	Routine Memorials (61 Cases)		
	Source	Reference #	Date
183.	XKTB	0029	QL 01.10.25
184.	XKTB	0043	QL 02.02.28
185.	XKTB	0168	QL 05.01.25
186.	XKTB	0163	QL 05.06.27
187.	XKTB	0475	QL 10.01.09
188.	XKTB	0423	QL 10.06.03
189.	XKTB	0733	QL 15.02.14
190.	XKTB	0706	QL 15.09.04
191.	XKTB	0706	QL 15.09.04
192.	XKTB	0714	QL 15.09.14
193.	XKTB	0776	QL 16.01.29
194.	XKTB	0765	QL 16.05.13
195.	XKTB	0779	QL 16.05.30
196.	XKTB	0769	QL 16.09.11
197.	XKTB	0755	QL 16.10.11
198.	XKTB	0761	QL 16.11.26
199.	XKTB	0762	QL 16.11.29
200.	XKTB	0797	QL 16.12.07
201.	XKTB	0794	QL 16.12.15
202.	XKTB	0795	QL 16.12.15
203.	XKTB	0837	QL 17.01.21
204.	XKTB	0859	QL 17.04.10
205.	XKTB	0847	QL 17.04.18
206.	XKTB	0856	QL 17.09.15
207.	XKTB	0819	QL 17.10.21
208.	XKTB	0858	QL 17.11.10
209.	XKTB	0831	QL 17.12.07
210.	XKTB	0866	QL 17.12.14
211.	XKTB	0865	QL 17.12.16
212.	XKTB	0928	QL 18.05.12

	Routine Memorials (61 Cases)		
	Source	Reference #	Date
213.	XKTB	0965	QL 18.07.22
214.	XKTB	0943	QL 18.07.26
215.	XKTB	1049	QL 20.03.06
216.	XKTB	1055	QL 20.03.23
217.	XKTB	1071	QL 20.07.20
218.	XKTB	1089	QL 20.11.07
219.	XKTB	1823	QL 30.04.25
220.	XKTB	1782	QL 30.06.09
221.	XKTB	1791	QL 30.07.08
222.	XKTB	1747	QL 30.11.16
223.	XKTB	2768	QL 40.01.22
224.	XKTB	2773	QL 40.03.28
225.	XKTB	2732	QL 40.04.24
226.	XKTB	2796	QL 40.11.05
227.	XKTB	2757	QL 40.11.18
228.	XKTB	2816	QL 40.12.02
229.	XKTB	2731	QL 40.12.21
230.	XKTB	2740	QL 40.12.21
231.	XKTB	3190	QL 44.06.02
232.	XKTB	3189	QL 44.06.30
233.	XKTB	3117	QL 44.07.11
234.	XKTB	3184	QL 44.10.19
235.	XKTB	3185	QL 44.11.17
236.	XKTB	3269	QL 45.11.16
237.	XKTB	3564	QL 51.09.07
238.	XKTB	3792	QL 55.08.20
239.	XKTB	3796	QL 56.02.28
240.	XKTB	3737	QL 56.04.22
241.	XKTB	3785	QL 56.11.10
242.	XKTB	4137	QL 60.02.12
243.	XKTB	4100	QL 60.06.18

	Ministry of Justice Registry (9 Cases)		
	Source	Reference #	Date
244.	SS	1570, 10.10 vol. 5	QL 10.09.15
245.	SS	1573, 11.10, vol. 4	QL 10.09.28
246.	SS	1574, 11.10, vol. 3	QL 10.11.14
247.	SS	1579, 12.10, vol. 5	QL 10.12.15
248.	SS	2564, 30.02, vol. 3	QL 29.12.08

(cont.)

	Ministry of Justice Registry (9 Cases)		
	Source	Reference #	Date
249.	SS	2591, 08.30, vol. 1	QL 30.06.16
250.	SS	3580, 06.50, vol. 2	QL 50.06.04
251.	SS	3599, 09.50, vol. 6	QL 50.07.24
252.	SS	3600, 10.50, vol. 6	QL 50.09.05

	Published Memorials (11 Cases)		
	Source	Page Numbers	Date
253.	QDB	497–500	QL 07.05.08
254.	ZYG	216–19	QL 07.10.14
255.	QDB	607–8	QL 08.06.11
256.	QDB	614–15	QL 13.10.23
257.	ZYG	367–9	QL 14.02.01
258.	ZYG	371–3	QL 14.03.21
259.	QDB	555–6	QL 23.11.15
260.	QDB	556–8	QL 24.05.15
261.	QDB	140–2	QL 32.07.29
262.	QDB	573–5	QL 32.10.03
263.	ZYG	479–82	QL 33.04.14

Boundaries (81 Disputes)

	Routine Memorials (63 Cases)		
	Source	Reference #	Date
264.	XKTB	0020	QL 01.03.14
265.	XKTB	0007	QL 01.07.29
266.	XKTB	0075	QL 02.07.23
267.	XKTB	0073	QL 02.07.25
268.	XKTB	0104	QL 02.09.07
269.	XKTB	0156	QL 05.02.09
270.	XKTB	0206	QL 05.07.04
271.	XKTB	0194	QL 05.11.08
272.	XKTB	0476	QL 10.02.02
273.	XKTB	0736	QL 15.01.24
274.	XKTB	0726	QL 15.04.03
275.	XKTB	0729	QL 15.05.04
276.	XKTB	0698	QL 15.05.14
277.	XKTB	0719	QL 15.05.20
278.	XKTB	0711	QL 15.06.09
279.	XKTB	0698	QL 15.06.14
280.	XKTB	0705	QL 15.06.21

	Routine Memorials (63 Cases)		
	Source	Reference #	Date
281.	XKTB	0714	QL 15.09.04
282.	XKTB	0738	QL 15.09.28
283.	XKTB	0789	QL 16.01.28
284.	XKTB	0768	QL 16.02.22
285.	XKTB	0780	QL 16.05.04
286.	XKTB	0776	QL 16.05.14
287.	XKTB	0779	QL 16.05.30
288.	XKTB	0779	QL 16.05.30
289.	XKTB	0774	QL 16.07.11
290.	XKTB	0769	QL 16.09.11
291.	XKTB	0762	QL 16.11.10
292.	XKTB	0870	QL 17.01.01
293.	XKTB	0818	QL 17.03.10
294.	XKTB	0868	QL 17.12.10
295.	XKTB	0923	QL 18.05.17
296.	XKTB	0935	QL 18.10.15
297.	XKTB	1053	QL 20.03.10
298.	XKTB	1051	QL 20.03.23
299.	XKTB	1068	QL 20.06.13
300.	XKTB	1090	QL 20.12.15
301.	XKTB	1447	QL 25.04.15
302.	XKTB	1450	QL 25.07.07
303.	XKTB	1794	QL 30.02.22
304.	XKTB	1802	QL 30.02.28
305.	XKTB	1835	QL 30.07.25
306.	XKTB	1806	QL 30.10.04
307.	XKTB	1806	QL 30.11.05
308.	XKTB	2354	QL 36.05.06
309.	XKTB	2367	QL 36.07.05
310.	XKTB	2781	QL 40.10.12
311.	XKTB	2746	QL 40.11.13
312.	XKTB	2757	QL 40.11.18
313.	XKTB	3146	QL 44.11.25
314.	XKTB	3163	QL 44.12.14
315.	XKTB	3269	QL 45.05.23
316.	XKTB	3198	QL 45.07.09
317.	XKTB	3236	QL 45.07.11
318.	XKTB	3259	QL 45.10.18
319.	XKTB	3540	QL 51.01.01

(cont.)

	Source	Reference #	Date
		Routine Memorials (63 Cases)	
320.	XKTB	3558	QL 51.07.28
321.	XKTB	3775	QL 56.06.26
322.	XKTB	3725	QL 56.09.19
323.	XKTB	4061	QL 60.03.14
324.	XKTB	4099	QL 60.05.07
325.	XKTB	4106	QL 60.08.30
326.	XKTB	4106	QL 60.11.15

	Source	Reference #	Date
		Ministry of Justice Registry (15 Cases)	
327.	SS	1555, 07.10, vol. 2	QL 10.07.05
328.	SS	1571, 11.10, vol. 1	QL 10.10.28
329.	SS	1574, 11.10, vol. 3	QL 10.11.13
330.	SS	2589, 07.30, vol. 2	QL 30.06.16
331.	SS	2601, 11.30, vol. 2	QL 30.11.13
332.	SS	3557, 01.50, vol. 1	QL 50.01.27
333.	SS	3578, 05.50, vol. 4	QL 50.05.27
334.	SS	3580, 06.50, vol. 2	QL 50.06.02
335.	SS	3583, 06.50, vol. 5	QL 50.06.05
336.	SS	3600, 09.50, vol. 6	QL 50.08.02
337.	SS	3600, 09.50, vol. 5	QL 50.08.07
338.	SS	3601, 10.50, vol. 1	QL 50.08.17
339.	SS	3598, 09.50, vol. 4	QL 50.09.12
340.	SS	3613, 12.50, vol. 1	QL 50.12.02
341.	SS	3564, 03.50, vol. 2	QL 50.12.03

	Source	Page Numbers	Date
		Published Memorials (3 Cases)	
342.	QDB	751–2	QL 09.07.04
343.	QDB	56–8	QL 13.11.06
344.	QDB	625–8	QL 21.10.07

Water Rights (136 Disputes)

	Source	Reference #	Date
		Routine Memorials (114 Cases)	
345.	XKTB	0009	QL 01.08.05
346.	XKTB	0003	QL 01.09.12
347.	XKTB	0046	QL 02.02.12
348.	XKTB	0046	QL 02.02.12

	Routine Memorials (114 Cases)		
	Source	Reference #	Date
349.	XKTB	0061	QL 02.05.26
350.	XKTB	0075	QL 02.07.06
351.	XKTB	0066	QL 02.07.07
352.	XKTB	0047	QL 02.07.13
353.	XKTB	0083	QL 02.09.26
354.	XKTB	0165	QL 05.01.01
355.	XKTB	0158	QL 05.03.07
356.	XKTB	0157	QL 05.03.11
357.	XKTB	0213	QL 05.06.14
358.	XKTB	0199	QL 05.12.04
359.	XKTB	0197	QL 05.12.14
360.	XKTB	0477	QL 10.02.21
361.	XKTB	0434	QL 10.03.10
362.	XKTB	0434	QL 10.03.11
363.	XKTB	0445	QL 10.05.23
364.	XKTB	0474	QL 10.07.04
365.	XKTB	0421	QL 10.10.06
366.	XKTB	0421	QL 10.10.19
367.	XKTB	0460	QL 10.12.17
368.	XKTB	0717	QL 15.02.12
369.	XKTB	0749	QL 15.06.19
370.	XKTB	0744	QL 15.06.29
371.	XKTB	0739	QL 15.07.02
372.	XKTB	0808	QL 16.01.20
373.	XKTB	0789	QL 16.04.10
374.	XKTB	0775	QL 16.05.15
375.	XKTB	0798	QL 16.05.16
376.	XKTB	0806	QL 16.05.19
377.	XKTB	0792	QL 16.05.29
378.	XKTB	0775	QL 16.08.18
379.	XKTB	0804	QL 16.09.15
380.	XKTB	0803	QL 16.10.16
381.	XKTB	0777	QL 16.12.20
382.	XKTB	0818	QL 17.03.10
383.	XKTB	0824	QL 17.05.23
384.	XKTB	0862	QL 17.05.23
385.	XKTB	0824	QL 17.05.27
386.	XKTB	0831	QL 17.07.06
387.	XKTB	0836	QL 17.07.26

(cont.)

	Routine Memorials (114 Cases)		
	Source	Reference #	Date
388.	XKTB	0858	QL 17.09.16
389.	XKTB	0821	QL 17.10.14
390.	XKTB	0969	QL 18.01.01
391.	XKTB	0901	QL 18.05.12
392.	XKTB	0973	QL 18.11.29
393.	XKTB	0893	QL 18.12.03
394.	XKTB	1051	QL 20.03.15
395.	XKTB	1072	QL 20.07.23
396.	XKTB	1089	QL 20.12.07
397.	XKTB	1416	QL 25.02.04
398.	XKTB	1467	QL 25.03.09
399.	XKTB	1410	QL 25.03.09
400.	XKTB	1417	QL 25.05.12
401.	XKTB	1417	QL 25.05.12
402.	XKTB	1413	QL 25.05.17
403.	XKTB	1441	QL 25.09.25
404.	XKTB	1405	QL 25.11.07
405.	XKTB	1434	QL 25.12.07
406.	XKTB	1401	QL 25.12.16
407.	XKTB	1769	QL 30.02.08
408.	XKTB	1752	QL 30.02.23
409.	XKTB	1810	QL 30.02.28
410.	XKTB	1811	QL 30.03.22
411.	XKTB	1781	QL 30.03.24
412.	XKTB	1836	QL 30.07.22
413.	XKTB	1739	QL 30.09.28
414.	XKTB	1748	QL 30.11.28
415.	XKTB	2304	QL 36.03.12
416.	XKTB	2295	QL 36.07.09
417.	XKTB	2733	QL 40.01.01
418.	XKTB	2782	QL 40.05.28
419.	XKTB	2752	QL 40.07.08
420.	XKTB	2781	QL 40.09.28
421.	XKTB	2830	QL 40.10.20
422.	XKTB	2784	QL 40.11.12
423.	XKTB	3174	QL 44.02.23
424.	XKTB	3123	QL 44.04.23
425.	XKTB	3143	QL 44.06.07
426.	XKTB	3130	QL 44.06.09
427.	XKTB	3192	QL 44.07.07

	Routine Memorials (114 Cases)		
	Source	Reference #	Date
428.	XKTB	3157	QL 44.10.12
429.	XKTB	3261	QL 45.06.05
430.	XKTB	3269	QL 45.07.25
431.	XKTB	3249	QL 45.09.27
432.	XKTB	3223	QL 45.11.11
433.	XKTB	3206	QL 45.12.03
434.	XKTB	3522	QL 50.05.12
435.	XKTB	3513	QL 50.06.04
436.	XKTB	3518	QL 50.11.17
437.	XKTB	3516	QL 50.11.22
438.	XKTB	3556	QL 51.08.20
439.	XKTB	3556	QL 51.08.20
440.	XKTB	3567	QL 51.10.17
441.	XKTB	3567	QL 51.11.28
442.	XKTB	3566	QL 51.12.04
443.	XKTB	3536	QL 51.12.08
444.	XKTB	3514	QL 51.12.16
445.	XKTB	3739	QL 55.05.12
446.	XKTB	3739	QL 55.09.07
447.	XKTB	3781	QL 56.01.01
448.	XKTB	3737	QL 56.03.17
449.	XKTB	3764	QL 56.06.21
450.	XKTB	4141	QL 60.02.06
451.	XKTB	4130	QL 60.02.19
452.	XKTB	4065	QL 60.04.13
453.	XKTB	4116	QL 60.04.25
454.	XKTB	4078	QL 60.07.11
455.	XKTB	4108	QL 60.08.25
456.	XKTB	4136	QL 60.09.18
457.	XKTB	4113	QL 60.10.26
458.	XKTB	4070	QL 60.11.25

	Ministry of Justice Registry (21 Cases)		
	Source	Reference #	Date
459.	SS	1550, 06.10, vol. 1	QL 10.05.29
460.	SS	1551, 06.10, vol. 3	QL 10.06.13
461.	SS	1570, 10.10, vol. 5	QL 10.09.06
462.	SS	1572, 10.12, vol. 2	QL 10.09.28
463.	SS	2562, 02.30, vol. 1	QL 29.11.07

(cont.)

	Ministry of Justice Registry (21 Cases)		
	Source	Reference #	Date
464.	SS	2564, 02.30, vol. 3	QL 29.12.05
465.	SS	2572, 03.30, vol. 3	QL 30.03.03
466.	SS	2586, 06.30, vol. 3	QL 30.04.25
467.	SS	2591, 08.30, vol. 1	QL 30.06.16
468.	SS	2606, 12.30, vol. 4	QL 30.10.26
469.	SS	3563, 03.50, vol. 1	QL 50.03.04
470.	SS	3576, 05.50, vol. 2	QL 50.03.08
471.	SS	3576, 05.50, vol. 2	QL 50.05.06
472.	SS	3589, 07.50, vol. 4	QL 50.05.27
473.	SS	3581, 06.50, vol. 3	QL 50.06.05
474.	SS	3581, 06.50, vol. 3	QL 50.06.06
475.	SS	3592, 08.50, vol. 1	QL 50.06.13
476.	SS	3586, 07.50, vol. 1	QL 50.06.26
477.	SS	3587, 07.50, vol. 2	QL 50.07.07
478.	SS	3600, 09.50, vol. 6	QL 50.08.02
479.	SS	3602, 10.50, vol. 2	QL 50.08.17

	Published Memorials (1 Case)		
	Source	Page Numbers	Date
480.	QDB	749–51	QL 03.03.29

Sichuan Province (125 Disputes)

	Rent Default and Other Disputes over Rent (9 Cases)		
	Source	Reference #	Date
1.	XKTB	0788	QL 16.12.11
2.	XKTB	0946	QL 18.04.16
3.	XKTB	3144	QL 44.02.19
4.	XKTB	3132	QL 44.09.16
5.	XKTB	3202	QL 45.03.02
6.	XKTB	3196	QL 45.03.08
7.	XKTB	3217	QL 45.03.29
8.	XKTB	3199	QL 45.09.17
9.	XKTB	3206	QL 45.10.12

	Evictions (11 Cases)		
	Source	Reference #	Date
10.	XKTB	0723	QL 15.01.22
11.	XKTB	0737	QL 15.05.26

	Evictions (11 Cases)		
	Source	Reference #	Date
12.	XKTB	0771	QL 16.04.25
13.	XKTB	0800	QL 16.05.25
14.	XKTB	0868	QL 17.12.24
15.	XKTB	0971	QL 18.07.28
16.	XKTB	0967	QL 18.09.10
17.	XKTB	3158	QL 44.02.18
18.	XKTB	3161	QL 44.03.18
19.	XKTB	3186	QL 44.03.25
20.	XKTB	3279	QL 45.02.28

	Redemptions and Disputes over Sales (48 Cases)		
	Source	Reference #	Date
21.	XKTB	0704	QL 15.04.06
22.	XKTB	0733	QL 15.06.01
23.	XKTB	0723	QL 15.06.22
24.	XKTB	0721	QL 15.10.24
25.	XKTB	0702	QL 15.10.29
26.	XKTB	0746	QL 15.12.13
27.	XKTB	0743	QL 15.12.19
28.	XKTB	0721	QL 15.12.19
29.	XKTB	0756	QL 16.04.01
30.	XKTB	0785	QL 16.05.13
31.	XKTB	0761	QL 16.05.20
32.	XKTB	0845	QL 17.02.13
33.	XKTB	0827	QL 17.07.02
34.	XKTB	0826	QL 17.07.12
35.	XKTB	0835	QL 17.07.16
36.	XKTB	0879	QL 17.10.10
37.	XKTB	0897	QL 18.02.02
38.	XKTB	0902	QL 18.03.13
39.	XKTB	0888	QL 18.07.05
40.	XKTB	0925	QL 18.10.29
41.	XKTB	3123	QL 44.02.03
42.	XKTB	3121	QL 44.03.17
43.	XKTB	3156	QL 44.04.24
44.	XKTB	3181	QL 44.05.02
45.	XKTB	3182	QL 44.05.09
46.	XKTB	3134	QL 44.05.20

(cont.)

	Redemptions and Disputes over Sales (48 Cases)		
	Source	Reference #	Date
47.	XKTB	3131	QL 44.06.06
48.	XKTB	3189	QL 44.06.13
49.	XKTB	3137	QL 44.07.02
50.	XKTB	3192	QL 44.07.07
51.	XKTB	3171	QL 44.07.14
52.	XKTB	3171	QL 44.07.14
53.	XKTB	3139	QL 44.08.17
54.	XKTB	3180	QL 44.09.08
55.	XKTB	3157	QL 44.10.26
56.	XKTB	3223	QL 45.02.17
57.	XKTB	3223	QL 45.03.23
58.	XKTB	3240	QL 45.03.26
59.	XKTB	3236	QL 45.03.27
60.	XKTB	3271	QL 45.04.17
61.	XKTB	3257	QL 45.04.27
62.	XKTB	3237	QL 45.06.05
63.	XKTB	3245	QL 45.06.15
64.	XKTB	3237	QL 45.10.11
65.	XKTB	3237	QL 45.10.28
66.	XKTB	3277	QL 45.11.30
67.	XKTB	3277	QL 45.11.30
68.	XKTB	3273	QL 45.12.04

	Boundaries (49 Cases)		
	Source	Reference #	Date
69.	XKTB	0724	QL 15.03.02
70.	XKTB	0741	QL 15.03.22
71.	XKTB	0722	QL 15.11.26
72.	XKTB	0720	QL 15.12.19
73.	XKTB	0816	QL 16.04.10
74.	XKTB	0778	QL 16.05.02
75.	XKTB	0780	QL 16.05.08
76.	XKTB	0780	QL 16.05.15
77.	XKTB	0759	QL 16.05.15
78.	XKTB	0772	QL 16.05.29
79.	XKTB	0755	QL 16.07.29
80.	XKTB	0780	QL 16.08.26
81.	XKTB	0796	QL 16.11.06
82.	XKTB	0761	QL 16.11.14

	Boundaries (49 Cases)		
	Source	Reference #	Date
83.	XKTB	0794	QL 16.12.01
84.	XKTB	0841	QL 17.03.16
85.	XKTB	0828	QL 17.05.26
86.	XKTB	0826	QL 17.07.12
87.	XKTB	0826	QL 17.07.14
88.	XKTB	0855	QL 17.07.20
89.	XKTB	0836	QL 17.07.30
90.	XKTB	0878	QL 17.09.25
91.	XKTB	0878	QL 17.09.29
92.	XKTB	0908	QL 18.04.18
93.	XKTB	0942	QL 18.04.19
94.	XKTB	0930	QL 18.05.02
95.	XKTB	0890	QL 18.06.01
96.	XKTB	0936	QL 18.06.09
97.	XKTB	0945	QL 18.06.17
98.	XKTB	0913	QL 18.06.28
99.	XKTB	0905	QL 18.06.28
100.	XKTB	0913	QL 18.07.03
101.	XKTB	0914	QL 18.09.23
102.	XKTB	0919	QL 18.10.11
103.	XKTB	0941	QL 18.10.22
104.	XKTB	0973	QL 18.11.01
105.	XKTB	0921	QL 18.11.02
106.	XKTB	0912	QL 18.11.19
107.	XKTB	0893	QL 18.12.03
108.	XKTB	0895	QL 18.12.17
109.	XKTB	0971	QL 18.12.19
110.	XKTB	3145	QL 44.02.12
111.	XKTB	3117	QL 44.02.13
112.	XKTB	3161	QL 44.03.15
113.	XKTB	3116	QL 44.04.22
114.	XKTB	3209	QL 45.02.17
115.	XKTB	3212	QL 45.02.28
116.	XKTB	3219	QL 45.04.04
117.	XKTB	3251	QL 45.09.30

	Water Rights (8 Cases)		
	Source	Reference #	Date
118.	XKTB	0707	QL 15.06.08
119.	XKTB	0749	QL 15.09.14

(cont.)

	Water Rights (8 Cases)		
	Source	Reference #	Date
120.	XKTB	0780	QL 16.05.12
121.	XKTB	0778	QL 16.05.15
122.	XKTB	0822	QL 17.05.11
123.	XKTB	0886	QL 18.05.22
124.	XKTB	0892	QL 18.07.20
125.	XKTB	3186	QL 44.03.03

Shandong Province (25 Disputes)

	Rent Default and Other Disputes over Rent (3 Cases)		
	Source	Reference #	Date
1.	XKTB	0738	QL 15.09.05
2.	XKTB	0837	QL 17.01.24
3.	XKTB	0895	QL 18.12.20

	Evictions (2 Cases)		
	Source	Reference #	Date
4.	XKTB	0734	QL 15.04.17
5.	XKTB	3209	QL 45.09.22

	Redemptions and Disputes over Sales (8 Cases)		
	Source	Reference #	Date
6.	XKTB	0821	QL 17.10.15
7.	XKTB	0932	QL 18.08.22
8.	XKTB	3138	QL 44.01.24
9.	XKTB	0833	QL 17.07.09
10.	XKTB	0889	QL 18.05.06
11.	XKTB	3145	QL 44.03.04
12.	XKTB	3138	QL 44.02.07
13.	XKTB	3197	QL 45.04.28

	Boundaries (10 Cases)		
	Source	Reference #	Date
14.	XKTB	0799	QL 16.05.25
15.	XKTB	0866	QL 17.12.16
16.	XKTB	0879	QL 17.11.10
17.	XKTB	0903	QL 18.04.11
18.	XKTB	0908	QL 18.04.29

	Boundaries (10 Cases)		
	Source	Reference #	Date
19.	XKTB	0917	QL 18.11.18
20.	XKTB	3182	QL 44.04.29
21.	XKTB	3252	QL 45.09.26
22.	XKTB	3262	QL 45.06.22
23.	XKTB	3213	QL 45.02.27

	Water Rights (2 Cases)		
	Source	Reference #	Date
24.	XKTB	0773	QL 16.01.01
25.	XKTB	3252	QL 45.09.26

Bibliography

Primary Sources

Archival Sources

Huke Tiben, nongye lei (Routine Memorials to the Ministry of Revenue related to agriculture) (Abbreviation: HKTB).

Neige Qiushen huangce (Grand Secretariat autumn assizes, yellow registers).

Neige Xingke shishu (Grand Secretariat registry of Ministry of Justice documents) (Abbreviation: SS).

Xingke Tiben, tudi zhaiwu lei (Routine Memorials to the Ministry of Justice homicide reports related to disputes over land and debt) (Abbreviation: XKTB).

Zhupi Zuozhe, nongye lei (Memorials with vermilion endorsements related to agriculture) (Abbreviation: ZPZZ).

Published Sources

Kang, Yong, Qian shiqi cheng xiang renmin fankang douzheng ziliao (Materials on urban and rural peoples' struggles in the Kangxi, Yongzheng, and Qianlong periods), People's University, Qing History Research Center, ed. (Beijing: Zhonghua Shuju, 1979), (Abbreviation: KYQ).

Qingdai dizu boxiao xingtai (Forms of rent exploitation in the Qing period), Number One Historical Archives of China and Institute of Historical Research of the Chinese Academy of Social Sciences, eds. (Beijing: Zhonghua Shuju, 1982), (Abbreviation: QDB).

Qingdai tudi zhanyou guanxi yu diannong kangzu douzheng (Qing dynasty land ownership relations and tenant rent resistance struggles), Number One Historical Archives of China and Institute of Historical Research of the Chinese Academy of Social Sciences, eds. (Beijing: Zhonghua Shuju, 1988), (Abbreviation: ZYG).

Qingshi gao jiaozhu (Draft history of the Qing dynasty), 10 volumes, National Academy of History, ed. (Taipei: National Central Library, 1987).

Zhongguo di lishi danganguan guanzang dangan gaishu (Introduction to documents contained in the Number One Historical Archives of China), Number One Historical Archive of China. (Beijing: Dangan Chubanshe, 1985).

Secondary Sources

Alchain, Armen. 1950. "Uncertainty, Evolution and Economic Theory." *Journal of Political Economy* 58: 211–21.

Alchain, Armen, and Harold, Demsetz. 1973. "The Property Right Paradigm." *Journal of Economic History* 33.1: 16–27.

Allee, Mark Anton. 1987. "Law and Local Society in Late Imperial China: Tanshui Subprefecture and Hsin-chu County, Taiwan, 1840–1895." Unpublished Ph.D. diss., University of Pennsylvania.

1994a. *Law and Local Society in Late Imperial China: Northern Taiwan in the Nineteenth Century.* Stanford: Stanford University Press.

1994b. "Code, Culture, and Custom: Foundations of Civil Case Verdicts in a Nineteenth-Century Court." Pp. 122–41 in *Civil Law in Qing and Republican China,* K. Bernhardt and P. C. Huang, eds. Stanford: Stanford University Press.

Anderson, Terry L., and P. J. Hill. 1973. "The Evolution of Property Rights: A Study of the American West." *Journal of Law and Economics* (April) 18.1: 163–79.

Atwell, William. 1982. "International Bullion Flows and the Chinese Economy 1530–1650." *Past and Present* (May) 95: 68–90.

Beattie, J. M. 1974. "The Pattern of Crime in England, 1660–1800." *Past and Present* (February) 62: 47–95.

Berkowitz, Leonard. 1978. "Whatever Happened to the Frustration-Aggression Hypothesis?" *American Behavioral Scientist* (May/June) 21.5: 691–708.

Bianco, Lucien. 1975. "Peasants and Revolution: The Case of China." *The Journal of Peasant Studies* (April) 2.3: 331–5.

1983. "Peasant Movements." In *Cambridge History of China, Volume 13: Republican China, 1912–1949, Part 2.* J. K. Fairbank and A, Feuerwerker, eds. New York: Cambridge University Press.

Bodde, Derek, and Clarence Morris. 1967. *Law in Imperial China.* Cambridge, MA: Harvard University Press.

Bond, Michael H., and Wang Sung-Hsing. 1983. "China: Aggressive Behavior and the Problem of Maintaining Order and Harmony." Pp. 58–74 in *Aggression in Global Perspective,* A. P. Goldstein and M. H. Segall, eds. New York: Pergamon Press.

Boserup, Ester. 1965. *The Conditions of Agricultural Growth.* New York: Aldine Publishing.

Brandt, Loren. 1987. "Review of *The Peasant Economy and Social Change in North China,* by Philip C. C. Huang." *Economic Development and Cultural Change* (April) 35.3: 670–81.

Buoye, Thomas. 1990. "Economic Change and Rural Violence: Homicides Related to Disputes over Property Rights in Guangdong during the Eighteenth Century." *Peasant Studies* (Summer) 17.4: 233–59.

1991. "Violent Disputes over Property Rights in Guangdong during the Qianlong Reign (1736–1795)." Ph. D. diss., University of Michigan.

1993. "From Patrimony to Commodity: Changing Concepts of Land and Social Conflict in Guangdong Province during the Qianlong Reign (1736–95)." *Late Imperial China* (December) 14.2: 19–46.

1995. "Suddenly Murderous Intent Arose: Bureaucratization and Benevolence in Eighteenth-Century Qing Homicide Reports." *Late Imperial China* (December) 16.2: 95–130.

Buxbaum, David C. 1971. "Some Aspects of Civil Procedure and Practice at the Trial Level in Tanshui and Hsinchu from 1789 to 1895." *Journal of Asian Studies* (February) 30.2: 255–79.

Chang, Chung-li. 1955. *The Chinese Gentry: Studies on Their Role in Nineteenth Century Chinese Society.* Seattle: University of Washington Press.

Chang, Yu-chuan. 1917. "The Chinese Judiciary." *Chinese Social and Political Science Review* 2.4: 68–88.

Chao, Kang. 1981. "New Data on Land Ownership Patterns in Ming-Ch'ing China – A Research Note." *Journal of Asian Studies* (August) 40.4: 719–34.

1986. *Man and Land in Chinese History.* Stanford: Stanford University Press.

Chen, Chunsheng. 1984. "Qingdai Qianlong nianjian Guangdong di mi jia he miliang maoyi" (Rice prices and trade in Guangdong during the Qianlong years). Unpublished M.A. thesis, Zhongshan University, Department of History.

1992. *Shichang jizhi yu shehui bianqian: Shiba shiji Guangdong mi jia fenxi* (Market structure and social change: An analysis of eighteenth-century Guangdong rice prices). Guangzhou: Zhongshan Daxue Chubanshe.

Chen, Fu-mei, and Ramon Myers. 1976. "Customary Law and the Economic Growth of China during the Ch'ing Period." *Ch'ing Shih wen-ti* 3.5: 1–32.

Chen, Hua. 1987. "Qingdai Guangdong di liangshi wenti" (Guangdong's grain problem in the Qing era). *Qingshi yanjiu tongxun* 4: 19–28.

1995. "Lun shi ba shiji Zhongguo shehui jingji di quyu tedian" (Discussion of the regional characteristics of eighteenth-century Chinese society and economy). *Qingshi yanjiu* 1: 38–50.

Chen, Qihan. 1985. "Guangdong di tan ding ru di" (The commutation of the poll tax to land tax in Guangdong). Pp. 363–72 in *Ming Qing Guangdong shehui jingji xingtai yanjiu* (Research on the economic formation of society in Guangdong during the Ming and Qing), Guangdong History Institute, ed. Guangdong: People's Publishing House.

Ch'u, T'ung-tsu. 1965. *Law and Society in Traditional China.* Paris: Mouton.

1969. *Local Government in China Under the Ch'ing.* Stanford: Stanford University Press.

Chuan, Han-sheng and Richard Kraus. 1975. *Mid-Ch'ing Rice Markets and Trade: An Essay in Price History.* Cambridge, MA: Harvard University, East Asian Research Center.

Cloward, Richard A. 1969. "Illegitimate Means, Anomie, and Deviant Behavior." Pp. 312–31 in *Delinquency, Crime and Social Process,* D. R. Cressey and D. Ward, eds. New York: Harper and Row.

Coase, Ronald. 1988. *The Firm the Market and the Law.* Chicago: University of Chicago Press.

Cockburn, J. S. 1977. "The Nature and Incidence of Crime in England, 1559–1625: A Preliminary Survey." In *Crime in England 1550–1800*, J. S. Cockburn, ed. Princeton: Princeton University Press.

Cohen, Jerome. 1966. "Chinese Mediation on the Eve of Modernization." *California Law Review* 54: 1201–26.

Cohen, Lawrence E., and Marcus Felson. 1979. "Social Change and Crime Rate Trends: A Routine Activity Approach." *American Sociological Review* 44: 588–607.

Cohen, Paul D. 1984. *Discovering History in China*. New York: Columbia University Press.

Chuan, Han-sheng and Richard A. Kraus. 1975. *Mid-Ch'ing Rice Markets and Trade: An Essay in Price History*. Cambridge, MA: Harvard University, East Asian Research Center.

Dai, Yi. 1996. "Jindai Zhongguo renkou di zengzhang he qianxi" (Increase and migration of modern China's population). *Qing shi yanjiu* 1: 1–8.

Dan, Shikui. 1985. "Qingdai tiben zhidu kaolue" (Brief examination of the Qing period routine memorial system). Pp. 971–82 in *Ming Qing dangan lunwen xuanbian* (Selected essays on Ming Qing documents), Zhu Jinfu, ed. Beijing: Archives Publishing House.

Dardess, John. 1983. *Confucianism and Autocracy*. Berkeley: University of California Press.

Davis, Lance E., and Douglass C. North. 1971. *Institutional Change and American Economic Growth*. New York: Cambridge University Press.

Demsetz, Harold. 1967. "Toward a Theory of Property Rights." *American Economic Association Papers and Proceedings* LVIII: 347–59.

de Souza, Anthony R., and J. Brady Foust. 1979. *World Space-Economy*. Columbus, OH: Charles E. Merrill Publishing Co.

Dobb, Maurice. 1963. *Studies in the Development of Capitalism*. New York: International Publishers.

Dunn, Edgar S., Jr. 1967. *The Location of Agricultural Production*. Gainesville: University of Florida Press.

Dunstan, Helen. 1975. "The Late Ming Epidemics: A Preliminary Survey." *Ch'ing shih wen-t'i* 3.3: 1–59.

1996. *Conflicting Counsels to Confuse the Age*. Ann Arbor: University of Michigan, Center for Chinese Studies.

Eastman, Lloyd E. 1988. *Family, Fields, and Ancestors*. New York: Oxford University Press.

Elvin, Mark. 1973. *The Pattern of the Chinese Past*. Stanford: Stanford University Press.

1984. "Why China Failed to Create an Endogenous Industrial Capitalism: A Critique of Max Weber's Explanation." *Theory and Society* 13: 372–92.

Eng, Robert Y. 1986. "Institutional and Secondary Landlordism in the Pearl River Delta, 1600–1949." *Modern China* (January) 12.1: 3–37.

Escarra, Jean. 1936. *Chinese Law*. Translated from the French by Gertrude R. Browne, 1961. Seattle: University of Washington Press.

Fairbank, John K., Alexander Eckstein, and L. S. Yang. 1960. "Economic Change in Early Modern China: An Analytic Framework." *Economic Development and Cultural Change* (October) 9.1: 1–26.

Fan, I-Chun. 1992. "Long-Distance Trade and Market Integration in the Ming-Ch'ing Period, 1400–1850." Ph.D. diss., Stanford University.

Fan, Shuzhi. 1984. "Nongdian yazu guili di lishi kaocha" (Investigation of the history of agricultural tenants deposit practices). *Jingji shi* 5: 129–35.

Fang, Xing. 1983. "Qingdai qianqi dizhuzhi jingji di fazhan" (The development of the landlord economy in the early Qing period). *Zhongguoshi yanjiu* 2: 88–99.

1989. "Why the Sprouts of Capitalism Were Delayed in China." *Late Imperial China* (December) 10.2: 106–38.

1996a. "Qingdai Jiangnan nongmin di xiaofei" (Consumption of Jiangnan peasants in the Qing dynasty). *Zhongguo jingjishi yanjiu* 3: 91–8.

1996b. "Qingdai nongmin jingji kuoda zaishengchan di xingshi" (The form of "extended reproduction" in the Qing peasant economy). *Zhongguo jingjishi yanjiu* 1: 32–46.

Feeny, David. 1988a. "The Development of Property Rights in Land: A Comparative Study." In *Toward a Political Economy of Development,* R. H. Bates, ed. Berkeley: University of California Press.

1988b. "The Demand for and Supply of Institutional Arrangements." In *Rethinking Institutional Analysis and Development,* V. Ostrom, D. Feeny, and H. Picht, eds. San Francisco: International Center for Economic Growth.

1989. "The Decline of Property Rights in Man in Thailand, 1800–1913." *Journal of Economic History* (June) 49.2: 285–96.

Feng, Erkang. 1980. "Qingdai di yazuzhi yu zutian guanxi dijubu bianhua" (Rent deposits in the Qing period and changing tenancy relations). *Nankai Xuebao* 1: 61–7.

Ferdinand, Theodore N. 1970. "Demographic Shifts and Criminality: An Inquiry." *British Journal of Criminology* 10: 169–75.

Feuerwerker, Albert. 1968. "China's History in Marxian Dress." Pp. 14–44 in *History in Communist China,* Albert Feuerwerker, ed. Cambridge, MA: M.I.T. Press.

1976. *State and Society in Eighteenth-Century China.* Michigan Papers in Chinese Studies, No. 27. Ann Arbor: University of Michigan, Center for Chinese Studies.

1995. *Studies in the Economic History of Late Imperial China: Handicraft, Modern Industry, and the State.* Ann Arbor: University of Michigan, Center for Chinese Studies.

Finley, Moses I. 1985. *The Ancient Economy.* Berkeley: University of California Press.

Fogel, Joshua A. 1984. *Recent Japanese Studies of Modern Chinese History.* Armonk, NY: M. E. Sharpe.

1989. *Recent Japanese Studies of Modern Chinese History,* Vol. 2. Armonk, NY: M. E. Sharpe.

Foster, George M. 1960. "Interpersonal Relations in Peasant Society." *Human Organization* 19: 174–80.

Freedman, Maurice. 1980. *Lineage Organization in Southeastern China.* London: Athlone Press.

Fu, Tongqin. 1985. "Ming Qing shiqi di Guangdong shatian" (Bottom land [shatian] in Guangdong during the Ming and Qing periods). Pp. 65–74 in *Ming Qing Guangdong shehui jingji xingtai yanjiu* (Research on the economic formation of society in Guangdong during the Ming and Qing), Guangdong History Institute, ed. Guangdong: Renmin Chubanshe.

Fu, Yiling (I-ling). 1979. "Ming Qing shidai jieji guanxi di xin tansuo" (Exploration of class relations in the Ming and Qing periods). *Zhongguoshi yanjiu* 4: 65–74.

1981. "A New Assessment of the Rural Social Relationship in Late Ming and Early Qing China." *Chinese Studies in History* Fall–Winter: 1981–2.

Gao, Wangling. 1993a. "Ming Qing shiqi di gendi mianji" (The area of arable land during the Ming-Qing period). *Ming Qing shi* 1: 11–16.

1993b. "Chuantong moshi di tupo Qingdai Guangdong nongye de jueqi" (Breaking the traditional mold: The rise of Qing-era Guangdong's agriculture). *Qingshi yanjiu* 3: 105–13.

1994. "Ming Qing shiqi di Zhongguo renkou" (Chinese population during the Ming-Qing period). *Qingshi yanjiu* 3: 27–32.

Gatrell, V. A. C., and T. B. Hadden. 1972. "Criminal Statistics and Their Interpretation." Pp. 336–96 in *Nineteenth Century Society: Essays in the Use of Quantitative Methods for the Study of Social Data,* E. A. Wrigley, ed., Cambridge, UK: Cambridge University Press.

Given, James Buchanan. 1977. *Society and Homicide in Thirteenth Century England.* Stanford: Stanford University Press.

Grove, Linda, and Joseph Esherick. 1980. "From Feudalism to Capitalism: Japanese Scholarship on the Transformation of Chinese Rural Society." *Modern China* (October) 6.4: 397–438.

Gunderson, Gerald A. 1982. "Economic Behavior in the Ancient World." Pp. 235–56 in *Explorations in the New Economic History: Essays in Honor of Douglass C. North,* R. L. Ransom, R. Sutch, and G. M. Walton, eds. New York: Academic Press.

Guo, Chengkang. 1996. "Shiba shiji Zhongguo wujia wenti he zhengfu duice" (The problem of eighteenth-century Chinese price inflation and government countermeasures). *Qingshi yanjiu* 1: 8–19.

Guo, Songyi. 1980. "Qing chu fengjian guojia kenhuang zhengce fenxi" (An analysis of the state policy of land reclamation in the early Qing). Pp. 111–38 in *Qingshi luncong* (Symposium on Qing history) 2, Chinese Academy of Social Sciences, History Research Institute, ed. Beijing: Zhonghua Shuju.

1994. "Qingqianqi nanfang dao zuo qu di liangshi shengchan" (Grain production of Southern paddy rice areas in the early Qing). *Zhongguo jingjishi yanjiu* 1: 1–31.

Gurr, Ted Robert. 1979. "On the History of Violent Crime in Europe and America." Pp. 343–73 in *Violence in America: Historical and Comparative Perspectives,* 2d ed., H. D. Graham and T. R. Gurr, eds. Beverly Hills: Sage Publications.

1981. "Historical Trends in Violent Crime: A Critical Review of the Evidence." Pp. 295–353 in *Crime and Justice: An Annual Review of Research*, Vol. 3, M. Torny and N. Morris, eds. Chicago: University of Chicago Press.

Gurr, Ted Robert, Peter N. Grabosky, and Richard C. Hula. 1977. *The Politics of Crime and Conflict: A Comparative History of Four Cities.* Beverly Hills: Sage Publications.

Hall, Peter. 1966. *Von Thunen's Isolated State.* London: Pergamon Press.

Han, Hengyu. 1980. "Luelun Qingdai qianqi di dianpu zhi" (An observation on servile tenancy in the early Qing). Pp. 89–110 in *Qingshi luncong* (Symposium on Qing history) 2, Chinese Academy of Social Sciences, History Research Institute, ed. Beijing: Zhonghua shuju.

Hanawalt, Barbara A. 1979. *Crime and Conflict in English Communities, 1300–1348.* Cambridge, MA: Harvard University Press.

Harrell, Stevan. 1990. "Introduction," In *Violence in China*, J. N. Lipman and S. Harrell, eds. Albany: State University of New York Press.

Hartwell, Robert M. 1982. "Demographic, Political, and Social Transformations of China, 750–1550." *Harvard Journal of Asiatic Studies* 42.2: 365–442.

Hayashi, Kazuo. 1980. "Min-Shin jidai, Kanto no kyo to shi: Dentoeki ichiba no keitai to kino ni kan suru ichi kosatsu" (A survey of the structure and function of traditional markets: Fairs and market towns of Guangdong province during the Ming and Qing periods). *Shirin* 63: 69–105.

Henry, Andrew F., and James F. Short, Jr. 1977. *Suicide and Homicide.* New York: Arno Press.

Ho, Ping-ti. 1959. *Studies in the Population of China, 1368–1953.* Cambridge, MA: Harvard University Press.

Hsiao, Kung-chuan. 1967. *Rural China: Imperial China in the Nineteenth Century*, Seattle: University of Washington Press.

1979. *Compromise in Imperial China.* Occasional Papers of China, 6. Seattle: University of Washington, School of International Studies.

Hsieh, Kuo-ching. 1932. "Removal of Coastal Population in Early Tsing Period." *Chinese Social and Political Science Review* 15: 559–96.

Hsu, Daulin. 1970. "Crime and Cosmic Order." *Harvard Journal of Asiatic Studies* 30: 111–25.

Hu, Chunfan, Hua Yu, Huang Shiqing, and Wen Ji. 1984. "Shilun Qing qianqi di juanmian zhengze" (Preliminary discussion of tax remission policy in the early Qing). *Qingshi yanjiu ji*, Chinese People's University, 3: 150–65. Qing History Research Center, ed. Chengdu: Sichuan Renmin Chubanshe.

Huang, Philip C. C. 1985. *The Peasant Economy and Social Change in North China.* Stanford: Stanford University Press.

1990. *The Peasant Family and Rural Development in the Yangzi Delta, 1350–1988.* Stanford: Stanford University Press.

1996. *Civil Justice in China: Representation and Practice in the Qing.* Stanford: Stanford University Press.

Huang, Qichen, and Kong Gonglin. 1984. "Ming Qing Guangdong renkou yu tudi di biandong" (Changes in land and population in Guangdong during the Ming and Qing). Paper presented at the Second Conference on Guangdong Society and Economy in the Ming and Qing. Zhongshan University.

Hucker, Charles. 1978. *The Ming Dynasty.* Ann Arbor: University of Michigan, Center for Chinese Studies.

Jamieson, George, et al. 1888. "Tenure of Land in China and the Condition of the Rural Population." *Journal of the North China Branch of the Royal Asiatic Society* 23: 59–174.

Jiang, Taixin. 1980. "Qingdai qianqi yazuzhi di fazhan" (Development of the rent deposit system in the early Qing period). *Lishi yanjiu* 3: 133–49.

Jiang, Taixin, and Duan Xueyu. 1996. "Lun Qingdai qianqi tudi kentuo dui shehui jingji fazhan di yingxiang" (Discussion of the influence of land reclamation on socioeconomic development in the early Qing period). *Zhongguo jingjishi yanjiu* 1: 47–62.

Jones, Eric L. 1988. *Growth Recurring.* New York: Oxford University Press.

Jones, Susan Mann, and Philip A. Kuhn. 1978. "Dynastic Decline and the Roots of Rebellion." Pp. 107–62 in *The Cambridge History of China: Late Ch'ing, 1800–1911,* Vol. 10, Part 1, J. K. Fairbank, ed. Cambridge, UK: Cambridge University Press.

Kobayashi, Kazumi. 1984. "The Other Side of Rent and Tax Resistance Struggles: Ideology and the Road to Rebellion." Pp. 215–44 in *State and Society in China,* L. Grove and C. Daniels, eds. Tokyo: University of Tokyo Press.

Kuhn, Philip A. 1970. *Rebellion and Its Enemies in Late Imperial China.* Cambridge, MA: Harvard University Press.

1990. *Soulstealers: The Chinese Sorcery Scare of 1768.* Cambridge, MA: Harvard University Press.

Lamely, Harry. 1990. "Lineage Feuding in Southern Fujian and Eastern Guangdong under Qing Rule." In *Violence in China,* J. N. Lipman and S. Harrell, eds. Albany: State University of New York Press.

Lavely, William, and R. Bin Wong. 1998. "Revising the Malthusian Narrative: The Comparative Study of Population Dynamics in Late Imperial China." *Journal of Asian Studies* (August) 57.3: 714–48.

Lee, James. 1991. "Homicide et Peine de Capitale en Chine a la Fin de L'empire: Analyse Statistique Preliminaire des Données." *Etudes Chinois* (Spring–Autumn) 10.1–2: 113–34.

Li, Bozhong. 1998. *Agricultural Development in Jiangnan, 1620–1850.* New York: St. Martin's Press.

Li, Hua. 1983. "Qingchao qianqi Guangdong di shangye yu shangren" (Guangdong commerce and merchants in the early Qing dynasty). *Xueshu yanjiu* 2: 39–44.

Li, Jingzhi. 1985. "Qianlong nianjian you Taiguo jinkou dami shiliao xian" (Selected materials on the importation of rice from Thailand in the reign of Qing emperor Qianlong). *Lishi dangan* 3: 13–27.

Li, Pengnian. 1985. "Luelun Qianlong nianjian cong Xianluo yun mi jinkou" (A brief account of the importation of rice from Siam in the reign of the Qing emperor Qianlong). *Lishi dangan* 3: 83–90.

Li, Sanmou. 1988. "Qingdai beifang nongdi liyong di tedian" (Special characteristics of agricultural land use in northern China during the Qing dynasty). *Zhongguo shehui jingji shi yanjiu* 3: 31–4.

Li, Wenzhi. 1980. "Lun Zhongguo dizhu jingjizhi yu nongye zibenzhuyi mengya" (Discussion of China's landlord economy and the sprouts of agrarian capitalism). Unpublished conference paper presented to Sino-American Symposium on Chinese Social and Economic History from the Song to 1900 Beijing.

1989. Lun Qingdai Yapianzhan qian dijia he goumai nian" (Discussion of land prices and amortization in the Qing era prior to the Opium War). *Zhongguo shehui jingji shi yanjiu* 2: 1–12.

1991. "Cong dichuan xingshi di bianhua kan Ming Qing shidai dizhuzhi jingji di fazhan" (A look at the development of the Ming-Qing era landlord controlled economy, from changes in the form of land rights). *Zhongguo shehui jingji shi yanjiu* 1: 12–22.

Liew, Foon Ming. 1988. "Debates on the Birth of Capitalism in China During the Past Three Decades." *Ming Studies* (Fall) 26: 61–75.

Little, Daniel. 1990. *Understanding Peasant China.* New Haven: Yale University Press.

Liu, Kwang-Ching. 1981. "World View and Peasant Rebellion: Reflections on Post-Mao Historiography." *Journal of Asian Studies* 60.2: 295–326.

Liu, Yongcheng. 1979a. "Lun Zhongguo zibenzhuyi mengya di lishi qianti" (On the historical prerequisites of the Chinese sprouts of capitalism). *Zhongguo lishi yanjiu* 2: 33–46.

1979b. "Qingdai qianqi diannong kangzu douzheng di xin fanzhan" (The new development of tenant rent resistance struggles in the early Qing period). Pp. 54–77 in *Qingshi luncong* (Symposium on Qing history) 1, Chinese Academy of Social Sciences, History Research Institute, ed. Beijing: Zhonghua shuju.

1980. "Qingdai qianqi di nongye zudian guanxi" (Agricultural tenancy relations in the early Qing period). Pp. 56–88 in *Qingshi luncong* (Symposium on Qing history) 2, Chinese Academy of Social Sciences, History Research Institute, ed. Beijing: Zhonghua shuju.

Liu, Yuan. 1994. "'Huguang tian Sichuan' yu Sichuan liumin wenti" ("Huguang fills up Sichuan" and the problem of Sichuan's floating population). *Qingshi yanjiu* 1: 39–44.

Liu, Zhenggang. 1996. "Qingdai Sichuan Man Yue yimin de nongye shengchan" (The agricultural production of Fujian and Guangdong immigrants to Sichuan in the Qing). *Zhongguo jingjishi yanjiu* 4: 71–9.

Lung, C. F. 1935. "A Note on Hung Liang-chi, the Chinese Malthus" *Tien Hsia Monthly* (October) pp. 248–50.

Ma, Jianshi, and Yang Yutang, eds. 1992. *Daqing luli tongkao jiazhu* (Compendium of revisions to the Qing law code). Beijing: Zhongguo Zhengfa Daxue Chubanshe.

Macauley, Melissa. 1993. "The Civil Reprobate: Pettifoggers, Property, and Litigation in Late Imperial China, 1723–1850." Unpublished Ph.D. diss., University of California at Berkeley.

1994. "Civil and Uncivil Disputes in Southeast Coastal China, 1723–1820." Pp. 85–121 in *Civil Law in Qing and Republican China*, K. Bernhardt and P. Huang, eds. Stanford: Stanford University Press.

Marks, Robert B. 1984. *Rural Revolution in South China.* Madison: University of Wisconsin Press.

1991. "Rice Prices, Food Supply, and Market Structure in Eighteenth-Century China." *Late Imperial China* (December) 12.2: 64–116.

1997. *Tigers, Rice, Silk, and Silt.* New York: Cambridge University Press.

Marks, Robert B., and Chen Chunsheng. 1995. "Price Inflation and Its Social, Economic and Climatic Context in Guangdong, 1707–1800." *T'oung pao* 81.1: 109–52.

McAleavy, Henry. 1958. "*Dien* in China and Vietnam." *Journal of Asian Studies* (May) 17.3: 403–15.

McDermott, Joseph P. 1981. "Bondservants in the T'ai-hu Basin During the Late Ming: A Case of Mistaken Identities." *Journal of Asian Studies* (August) 40.4: 675–718.

McKnight, Brian E. 1981. *The Quality of Mercy.* Honolulu: University of Hawaii Press.

McKnight, Brian E., trans. 1981. *The Washing Away of Wrongs: Forensic Medicine in Thirteenth Century China.* Ann Arbor: University of Michigan, Center for Chinese Studies.

Metzger, Thomas A. 1973. *The Internal Organization of Ch'ing Bureaucracy.* Cambridge, MA: Harvard University Press.

1979. "On the Historical Roots of Economic Modernization in China: The Increasing Differentiation of the Economy from the Polity during Late Ming and Early Ch'ing Times." Pp. 3–14 in *Modern Chinese Economic History*, C. Hou and T. Yu, eds. Taipei: Academia Sinica, Institute of Economics.

Mokyr, Joel. 1985. "The Industrial Revolution and the New Economic History." In *The Economics of the Industrial Revolution*, J. Mokyr, ed. Lanham, MD: Rowman and Littlefield.

Morita, Akira. 1974. *Shindai suirishi kenkyu* (Research on irrigation in the Qing dynasty). Tokyo: Aki Shobo.

Muramatsu, Yuji. 1966. "A Documentary Study of Chinese Landlordism in Late Qing and Early Republican Kiangnan." *Bulletin of the School of Oriental and African Studies* 29.3: 566–99.

Myers, Ramon. 1974. "Transformation and Continuity in Chinese Economic and Social History." *Journal of Asian Studies* 33.2: 265–77.

1980. *The Chinese Economy: Past and Present.* Belmont, CA: Wadsworth Press.

1982. "Customary Law, Markets, and Resource Transactions in Later Imperial China." Pp. 273–98 in *Explorations in the New Economic History: Essays in Honor of Douglass C. North*, R. L. Ransom, R. Sutch, and G. M. Walton, eds. New York: Academic Press.

1986. "The Agrarian System." Pp. 230–69 in *The Cambridge History of China*, Vol. 13, J. K. Fairbank and A. Feuerwerker, eds. Cambridge, UK: Cambridge University Press.

1988. "Review Article: Land and Labor in China." *Economic Development and Cultural Change* (July) 36.4: 797–806.

1991. "How Did the Modern Chinese Economy Develop? A Review Article." *Journal of Asian Studies* (August) 50.3: 604–28.

Naquin, Susan, and Evelyn Rawski. 1987. *Chinese Society in the Eighteenth Century.* New Haven: Yale University Press.

Ng, Chin-keong. 1983. *Trade and Society: The Amoy Network on the China Coast 1683–1735.* Singapore: Singapore University Press.

North, Douglass. 1977. "Markets and Other Allocation Systems in History: The Challenge of Karl Polanyi." *Journal of European Economic History* (Fall) 2: 703–16.

1978. "Structure and Performance: The Task of Economic History." *Journal of Economic Literature* (September) 16: 963–78.

1981. *Structure and Change in Economic History.* New York: W. W. Norton.

1984. "Government and the Cost of Exchange in History." *Journal of Economic History* (June) 44.2: 255–64.

1987. "Institutions, Transaction Costs and Economic Growth." *Economic Inquiry* (July) 25.3: 419–28.

1990. *Institutions, Institutional Change and Economic Performance.* New York: Cambridge University Press.

North, Douglass, and Paul Thomas. 1973. *The Rise of the Western World.* Cambridge, UK: Cambridge University Press.

Ocko, Jonathan K. 1988. "I'll Take It All the Way to Beijing: Capital Appeals in the Qing." *Journal of Asian Studies* 47.2: 291–315.

Ownby, David. 1996. *Brotherhoods and Secret Societies in Early Mid-Qing China.* Stanford: Stanford University Press.

Oxnam, Robert B. 1975. *Ruling From Horseback: Manchu Politics in the Oboi Regency 1661–1669.* Chicago: University of Chicago Press.

Peng, Yuxin. 1990. *Qingdai tudi kaiken shi* (The history of land reclamation in the Qing era). Beijing: Nongye Chubanshe.

1992. *Qingdai tudi kaiken shi ziliao huibian* (Compilation of materials on the history of land reclamation in the Qing era). Wuhan: Wuhan Daxue Chubanshe.

Perdue, Peter. 1987. *Exhausting the Earth: State and Peasant in Hunan, 1500–1850.* Cambridge, MA: Harvard University, Council on East Asian Studies.

Perkins, Dwight. 1969. *Agricultural Development in China (1368–1968).* Chicago: Aldine Publishing Co.

Perry, Elizabeth. 1985. "Rural Violence in Socialist China." *China Quarterly* 103: 414–40.

Polanyi, Karl. 1957. *The Great Transformation.* Boston: Beacon Press.

Popkin, Samuel L. 1979. *The Rational Peasant: The Political Economy of Rural Society in Vietnam.* Berkeley: University of California Press.

Rawski, Evelyn S. 1972. *Agricultural Change and the Peasant Economy of South China.* Cambridge, MA: Harvard University Press.

1985. "Economic and Social Foundations of Late Imperial Culture." Pp. 3–33 in *Popular Culture in Late Imperial China,* D. Johnson, A. J. Nathan, and E. S. Rawski, eds. Berkeley: University of California Press.

Rawski, Thomas, and Lillian M. Li. 1992. *Chinese History in Economic Perspective.* Berkeley: University of California Press.

Reed, Bradly W. 1995. "Money and Justice: Clerks, Runners, and the Magistrate's Court in Late Imperial Sichuan." *Modern China* (July) 21.3: 345–82.

Rowe, William T. 1985. "Approaches to Modern Chinese Social History." In *Reliving the Past*, O. Zunz, ed. Chapel Hill: University of North Carolina Press.

Rozman, Gilbert. 1973. *Urban Networks in Ch'ing China and Tokugawa Japan*. Princeton: Princeton University Press.

Samaha, Joel. 1974. *Law and Order in Historical Perspective: The Case of Elizabethan Essex*. New York: Academic Press.

Schurmann, H. F. 1956. "Traditional Property Concepts in China." *Far Eastern Quarterly* 15.4: 507–16.

Scott, James C. 1976. *The Moral Economy of the Peasant: Rebellion and Subsistence in Southeast Asia*. New Haven: Yale University Press.

1989. "Everyday Forms of Resistance." Pp. 3–33 in *Everyday Forms of Peasant Resistance*, F. D. Colburn, ed. Armonk, NY: M.E. Sharpe.

Shanin, Teodor. 1987. "Introduction: Peasantry as a Concept." Pp. 1–11 in *Peasants and Peasant Societies*, T. Shanin, ed. New York: Basil Blackwell.

Skinner, G. William. 1964–5. "Marketing and Social Structure in Rural China." *Journal of Asian Studies* 24: 3–44, 195–228, 363–400.

1976a. "Regional Urbanization in Nineteenth Century China." Pp. 212–49 in *The City in Late Imperial China*, G. W. Skinner, ed. Stanford: Stanford University Press.

1976b. "Cities and the Hierarchy of Local Systems." Pp. 275–351 in *The City in Late Imperial China*, G. W. Skinner, ed. Stanford: Stanford University Press.

Skogan, Wesley G. 1975. "Measurement Problems in Official and Survey Crime Rates." *Journal of Criminal Justice* 3: 17–32.

1976. "Citizen Reporting of Crime: Some National Panel Data." *Criminology* 13: 535–49.

Song, Xiuyuan. 1985a. "Cong 'Qianlong xingke tiben' kan Qingdai yazu zhi" (A look at the Qing period deposit system from Qianlong Ministry of Justice routine memorials). Pp. 821–30 in *Ming Qing dangan lunwen xuanbian* (Selected essays on Ming Qing documents), Zhu Jinfu, ed. Beijing: Dangan Chubanshe.

1985b. "Qingdai qianqi dizu xingtai di fazhan bianhua" (The development and change in forms of rent in the early Qing period). Pp. 568–76 in *Ming Qing dangan lunwen xuanbian* (Selected essays on Ming Qing documents), Zhu Jinfu, ed. Beijing: Archives Publishing House.

Spence, Jonathan. 1978. *The Death of Woman Wang*. New York: Viking Press.

State Statistical Bureau of China. 1989. *China Social Statistics 1986*. New York: Praeger.

Stone, Lawrence. 1983. "Interpersonal Violence in English Society." *Past and Present* 101: 22–33.

Sutch, Richard. 1982. "Douglass North and the New Economic History." Pp. 13–38 in *Explorations in the New Economic History: Essays in Honor of Douglass C. North*, R. L. Ransom, R. Sutch, and G. M. Walton, eds. New York: Academic Press.

Tanaka, Masatoshi. 1984. "Popular Uprisings, Rent Resistance and Bondservant

Rebellions in the Late Ming." Pp. 165–214 in *State and Society in China,* Linda Grove and Christian Daniels, eds. Tokyo: University of Tokyo Press.

Tang, Sen, and Li Longqian. 1985. "Ming Qing Guangdong jingji zuowu di zhongzhi ji qi yiyi" (The cultivation of economic crops in Guangdong and its significance during the Ming and Qing). Pp. 1–21 in *Ming Qing Guangdong shehui jingji xingtai yanjiu* (Research on the economic formation of society in Guangdong during the Ming and Qing), Guangdong History Institute, ed. Guangdong: Renmin Chubanshe.

Taueber, Irene B., and Nai-chi Wang. 1960. "Population Reports in the Ch'ing Dynasty." *Journal of Asian Studies* 19.4: 403–17.

Thompson, E. P. 1971. "The Moral Economy of the English Crowd in the Eighteenth Century." *Past and Present* (February) 50: 76–136.

Tilly, Charles. 1976. "Rural Collective Action in Modern Europe." Pp. 9–40 in *Forging Nations: A Comparative View of Rural Ferment and Revolt,* J. Spielberg and S. Whiteford, eds. East Lansing: Michigan State University Press.

1978. *From Mobilization to Revolution.* Reading, MA: Addison-Wesley.

1981. *As Sociology Meets History.* New York: Academic Press.

1985. "Retrieving European Lives." In *Reliving the Past,* O. Zunz, ed. Chapel Hill: University of North Carolina Press.

1990. *Coercion, Capital, and European States.* New York: Basil Blackwell.

Tong, James. 1991. *Disorder Under Heaven: Collective Violence the Ming Dynasty (1368–1644).* Stanford: Stanford University Press.

Tsurumi, Naohiro. 1984. "Rural Control in the Ming Dynasty." Pp. 245–78 in *State and Society in China,* L. Grove and C. Daniels, eds. Tokyo: University of Tokyo Press.

Van der Sprenkel, Sybill. 1962. *Legal Institutions in Manchu China.* London: Athlone Press.

von Glahn, Richard. 1996. "Myth and Reality of China's Seventeenth-Century Monetary Crisis." *Journal of Economic History* (June) 56.2: 429–54.

Wakeman, Frederic, Jr. 1966. *Strangers at the Gate.* Berkeley: University of California Press.

1970. "High Ch'ing: 1683–1839." Pp. 1–28 in *Modern East Asia: Essays in Interpretation,* J. B. Crowley, ed. New York: Harcourt, Brace & World.

1975. "Introduction: The Evolution of Local Control in Late Imperial China." In *Conflict and Control in Late Imperial China,* F. Wakeman, Jr. and C. Grant, eds. Berkeley: University of California Press.

1977. "Rebellion and Revolution: Studies of Popular Movements in Chinese History." *Journal of Asian Studies* 36.2: 201–35.

Wang, Rongsheng. 1985. "Ming Qing zudian guanxi yu diannong kangzu douzheng" (Tenancy relations and tenant rent resistance struggles in the Ming and Qing). Pp. 53–70 in *Qingshi luncong* (Symposium on Qing history) 6, Chinese Academy of Social Sciences, History Research Institute, ed. Beijing: Zhonghua shuju.

Wang, Yeh-chien. 1972. "The Secular Trend of Prices during the Ch'ing Period (1644–1911)." *Journal of the Institute of Chinese Studies of the Chinese University of Hong Kong* (December) 5.2: 347–68.

1973. *Land Taxation in Imperial China, 1750–1911*. Cambridge, MA: Harvard University Press.

1992. "Secular Trends of Rice Prices in the Yangzi Delta, 1638–1935." Pp. 35–68 in *Chinese History in Economic Perspective*, T. Rawski and L. Li, eds. Berkeley: University of California Press.

Wei, Qingyuan, Wu Qiyan, and Lu Su. 1980. "Qing dai nubi zhidu" (The bond servant system of the Qing dynasty). Pp. 1–55 in *Qingshi luncong* (Symposium on Qing history) 2, Chinese Academy of Social Sciences, History Research Institute, ed. Beijing: Zhonghua shuju.

Wiens, Mi Chu. 1976. "The Origins of Modern Chinese Landlordism." Pp. 285–344 in *Festschrift in Honor of the Eightieth Birthday of Professor Shen Kang-pao*. Taipei: Lianjing shuju.

1980. "Lord and Peasant in China: The Sixteenth to the Eighteenth Centuries." *Modern China* (January) 6: 3–39.

Will, Pierre-Etienne, and R. Bin Wong. 1992. *Nourish the People: The State Civilian Granary System in China, 1650–1850*. Ann Arbor: University of Michigan, Center for Chinese Studies.

Wolfgang, Marvin E. 1958. *Patterns in Criminal Homicide*. Oxford: Oxford University Press.

1969. "Victim-Precipitated Criminal Homicide." Pp. 1029–42 in *Delinquency, Crime and Social Process*, D. R. Cressey and D. Ward, eds. New York: Harper and Row.

Wong, R. Bin. 1992. "Chinese Economic History and Development; A Note on the Myers-Huang Exchange." *Journal of Asian Studies* (August) 51.3: 600–11.

1997. *China Transformed*. Ithaca, NY: Cornell University Press.

Xiao, Shu, and Zhu Shu, eds. 1887. *Yuedong chengan chubian* (Guangdong leading cases, 1st ed.).

Xie, Guozhen. 1981. *Mingdai nongmin qiyi shiliao xuanbian* (Selected historical materials on peasant uprisings in the Ming dynasty). Fuzhou: Fujian Renmin Chubanshe.

Xing, Long. 1992. "Renkou yali yu Qing zhongye shehui maodun" (Population pressure and social contradictions in the mid-Qing). *Zhongguo shi yanjiu* 4: 51–8.

Xu, Ke, compiler. 1984. *Qing beilei chao* (Informal historical materials of the Qing), 13 volumes. Beijing: Zhonghua shuju. Reprint of late Qing compilation.

Xu, Lian, and Xiong Shu, eds. 1834. *Xingbu bizhao jiajian chengan* (Ministry of Justice rulings, sentencing, and leading cases).

Xu, Tan. 1995. "Ming Qing shiqi Shandong di liangshi liu tong" (The circulation of grain in Shandong during the Ming and Qing). *Lishi dangan* 1: 81–9.

1997. "Ming Qing shiqi nongcun jishi di fazhan" (Development of rural markets during the Ming and Qing). *Jingji shi* 5: 13–33.

Yang, C. K. 1975. "Some Preliminary Patterns of Mass Action in Nineteenth-century China." in *Conflict and Control in Late Imperial China*, F. Wakeman, Jr. and C. Grant, eds. Berkeley: University of California Press.

Yang, Guozhen. 1984. "Qingdai Zhejiang tian qi dian yi pie" (A glimpse at tenancy contracts in Zhejiang in the Qing period). *Jingji shi* 1: 101–18.

1988. *Ming Qing tudi qiyue wenshu yanjiu* (Research on Ming-Qing period land contracts). Beijing: Renmin Chubanshe.

Yang, Tai-shuenn. 1987. "Property Rights and Constitutional Order in Imperial China." Unpublished Ph.D. diss., Indiana University.

Ye, Xianen. 1984. "Ming Qing Zhujiang sanjiaozhou nongye shangyehua yu xu shi di fazhan" (The development of markets and agricultural commercialization in the Pearl River Delta during the Ming and Qing). *Lishi xue* 2: 73–90.

1991. "Luelun Yong Qian shiqi shehui jingji di jiegouxing bianqian ji qi lishi diwei" (A brief discussion of changes in the structure of the social economy of the Yongzheng and Qianlong periods and its historical position). *Zhongguo jingjishi yanjiu* 4: 33–45.

Ye, Xianen, and Tan Dihua. 1985. "Lun Zhujiang sanjiaozhou di zutian" (On clan land in the Pearl River Delta). Pp. 22–64 in *Ming Qing Guangdong shehui jingji xingtai yanjiu* (Research on the economic formation of society in Guangdong during the Ming and Qing), Guangdong History Institute, ed. Guangdong: Renmin Chubanshe.

Zagoria, Donald S. 1974. "Asian Tenancy Systems and Communist Mobilization of the Peasantry." In *Peasant Rebellions and Communist Revolution in Asia,* J. W. Lewis, ed. Stanford: Stanford University Press.

Zehr, Howard. 1976. *Crime and the Development of Modern Society: Patterns of Criminality in Nineteenth Century Germany and France.* Totowa, NJ: Rowan and Littlefield.

Zelin, Madeline. 1984. *The Magistrate's Tael.* Berkeley: University of California Press.

1986. "The Rights of Tenants in Mid-Qing Sichuan: A Study of Land-Related Lawsuits in the Baxian Archives." *Journal of Asian Studies* 49.3: 499–526.

1991. "The Structure of the Chinese Economy During the Qing Period: Some Thoughts on the 150th Anniversary of the Opium War." Pp. 31–67 in *Perspectives on Modern China: Four Anniversaries,* K. Lieberthal, J. Kallgren, R. MacFarguhar, and F. Wakeman, Jr., eds. Armonk, NY: M. E. Sharpe.

Zhang, Renshan. 1992. "Lun Qingchao zhongqi yi hou shehui shenghuo di fan lifa qushi" (A discussion of the tendency to oppose decorum in social life after the mid-Qing). *Zhongguo shi yanjiu* 2: 117–24.

Zhou, Linong. 1993. "Effects of Government Intervention on Population Growth in Imperial China." *Journal of Family History* 18.3: 213–30.

Zhou, Zuoshao. 1997. "Qingdai qianqi renkou wenti yanjiu lunlue" (Brief discussion of research on population question in the early Qing period). *Ming Qing shi* 2: 59–64.

Zillmann, D. 1979. *Hostility and Aggression.* Hillsdale, NJ: Erlbaum.

Index

For EU product safety concerns, contact us at Calle de José Abascal, 56–1°,
28003 Madrid, Spain or eugpsr@cambridge.org.

www.ingramcontent.com/pod-product-compliance
Lightning Source LLC
LaVergne TN
LVHW090313210926
848480LV00001B/231

* 9 7 8 0 5 2 1 0 2 7 8 1 6 *